THE PHILOSOPHY

OF SYMBOLIC FORMS

VOLUME ONE: LANGUAGE

BY ERNST CASSIRER

translated by Ralph Manheim

preface and introduction by Charles W. Hendel

NEW HAVEN & LONDON: YALE UNIVERSITY PRESS

Contents

Preface by Charles W. Hendel

It was thirty years ago that the first translation into English of any of the works of Ernst Cassirer appeared—*Substance and Function* (by William Curtis Swabey and Mary Collins Swabey, Chicago and London, Open Court Publishing Co., 1923). Nothing followed until nineteen years later, in 1944, when Cassirer himself wrote in English *An Essay on Man*. Since then scarcely a year has passed without the announcement of another work in translation.

This interest in Cassirer's writings was due at first to his own personality as he came to be known by many during his four years of residence in this country, teaching at Yale and Columbia universities. But it has mounted steadily since his death in 1945, and the chief reason may be that readers have discovered a new aspect of his philosophy.

For it was in truth much too limited a view of Cassirer that prevailed before his arrival in America. The book entitled *Substance and Function* contained two items, the major piece being a rendering of *Substanzbegriff und Funktionsbegriff* which Cassirer had written and published thirteen years earlier, the second a writing of more recent date, *Zur Einsteinschen Relativitätstheorie* (1921). At the time this volume came out there was an absorbing general interest in the Einstein theory and in the philosophical aspect of physical science. The consequence was hardly avoidable that the philosophy of Cassirer should appear to be solely a philosophy of science. Though the first piece did contain indications of a wider range of meaning they were practically unnoticed amid the contemporary scientific preoccupations of the readers.

It is a remarkable historic coincidence that the year of the publication of *Substance and Function* in America was also the date of *Philosophie der symbolischen Formen: Die Sprache,* in Germany (Berlin, Bruno Cassirer). A second volume followed in 1925 with the subtitle *Das mythische Denken.* After four years came the third part, on *Phänomenologie der Erkenntnis.* And all this remained largely unknown in this country except to those scholars who were studying German philosophy in the original texts or some others interested as specialists in the different subjects of language, myth, and the theory of knowledge. Thus when Cassirer came to America in 1941, as visiting professor to Yale University, he found himself welcomed everywhere in the guise of his earlier self, as it were, the philosopher of science. It is true, of course, that he was by that time recognized also as a remarkable historian of philosophy because of a great and invaluable work on the problem of knowledge, and his interpretations of Kant as well as of many other luminaries in the history of ideas and indeed of whole periods of intellectual history such as the Renaissance and the eighteenth century. Yet Cassirer was hardly regarded as a philosopher who had developed an original philosophy of his own.

Nevertheless the reason he was called to Yale University from his exile in Sweden was a recognition of the significance of the *Philosophie der symbolischen Formen*. It happened that the late Professor Wilbur M. Urban was about to retire from active service: he had been working in the philosophy of language and theory of value, and it was essential to maintain teaching and research in these fields of philosophy. However, in supplying its need in that quarter the university gained in Cassirer a versatile scholar who was superbly qualified for many enterprises. He conducted three different seminars jointly with other professors, seminars in the philosophy of history, in the philosophy of science, and in the theory of knowledge. It should be reported, too, that Cassirer accepted not only willingly but adventurously various other assignments of duty in the undergraduate as well as the graduate school, as when he undertook on short notice in an emergency to give the undergraduate course on the history of philosophy during a summer session when the university was on its wartime "accelerated program." Cassirer then sacrificed a summer which he had planned for writing—but it was part of his "Odyssey," as he said, that undertaking to teach American undergraduates. Thus he accommodated himself to the needs of the university rather than the university to him. More of his own philosophy might have been solicited had it not been for the necessities of the situation. Even in the case of that specialized seminar on the philosophy of language in which he was a master, the interest of the members of the course was in "semantics" and not in a comprehensive philosophy of language. Those semantic preoccupations in 1943 like those with the philosophy of science of 1923 precluded immediate appreciation of Cassirer in his true capacity as a significant philosopher of the contemporary world.

Suddenly in 1943 Cassirer decided to show himself in a new light by writing a book especially designed for the America that he had come to know and love, a book which, as he tells in the Preface, would be "symbolic" of his sojourn in this country. Thus he came to compose *An Essay on Man*, which was published by the Yale University Press in 1944.

Some have called this *Essay* a "summary" of "the philosophy of symbolic forms," but it cannot quite be regarded as that. For after he had finished in 1929 the third part of the *Symbolischen Formen* Cassirer had gone on to apply its philosophy to scientific subjects, as in his *Determinismus und Indeterminismus in der modernen Physik* (1936). There was also his *Zur Logik des Symbolbegriffs* (*Theoria*, Göteborg, Sweden, Vol. 4, 1938) and his recent *Zur Logik der Kulturwissenschaften* (Göteborg, 1942). Earlier he had written, too, the *Philosophie der Aufklärung* (1932) in which the whole of a period of modern culture had been delineated; and this work, incidentally, is perhaps the finest interpretation available of the eighteenth-century Enlightenment. Cassirer had also written significantly of many individual figures of modern culture: Descartes, Kepler, Galileo, Spinoza, Leibniz, Shaftesbury, Rousseau, Schiller, and always Kant, and of course Goethe, that kindred spirit who elicited the poetic imagination in Cassirer himself. Moreover, unknown to any but a few intimates, he had left behind him in Sweden the manuscript of a fourth volume of his *Erkenntnis-problem* series, this last one treating of philosophy, science, and history "from the death of Hegel to the present." In this writing he had treated the problem of knowledge in the nineteenth and twentieth centuries by taking it *in situ,* so to speak, as it emerges in each case within the several different disciplines of mathematics, physics, biology, and history. These varied tasks had occupied him after the publication of the volumes on symbolic forms. Hence his preface to *An Essay on Man* speaks of something new as well as giving a summary view of that original masterpiece itself.

The first impulse for the writing of this book came from my English and American friends who repeatedly and urgently asked me to publish an English translation of my *Philosophy of Symbolic Forms*. Although I should have liked very much to comply with their request, after the first tentative steps I found it impracticable and, under the present circumstances [1944], unjustifiable to reproduce the former book in its entirety. . . . [Moreover] from the point of view of the author it was scarcely possible or advisable to publish a work planned and written more than twenty-five years ago. Since that time the author has continued his study on the subject. He has learned many new facts and he has been confronted with new problems. For all these reasons I decided to make a fresh start and to write an entirely new book.

And then came an express caution not to take the *Essay* as a substitute for the original.

My critics should, however, be warned that what I could give here is more an explanation and illustration than a demonstration of my theory. For a closer discussion and analysis of the problems involved I must ask them to go back to the detailed description in my *Philosophy of Symbolic Forms.*

It is important to note how those "old problems" did appear to him later and what the "new" ones were and where Cassirer was tending in his further thinking about the matter. A clue to the new direction is to be found in what happened next. The ink was hardly dry on his last pages of manuscript when he started on another writing in English, and on a new subject. This was to be a book on the *Myth of the State.* There were good reasons why that publication would seem justifiable "under the present circumstances." The Western civilized world was still in crisis, before the final decision of battle in Europe. It might help the defenders of civilization to give them more of an idea of their hoped-for victory over the totalitarian power politics which had projected the world into war and whose power lay not simply in guns but in the minds and wills of those who were led into the catastrophe. It was commonly assumed that propaganda of recent contriving had produced the mentality in virtue of which the authorities could rule and wage war. But there was the deeper question of the philosopher—what was it that gave such propaganda its firm purchase on the minds of those who had succumbed? Propaganda only uses forces already at work—and the most potent was a "myth" of very long standing which had time and again threatened progress in the Western world and which political philosophy and statesmanship had managed again and again to overcome, thus preserving in Western society a civilizing leaven of reason and culture. To do battle for this in our time was the task of the peoples of America and the rest of Europe, and these nations should be made to understand both the history and the meaning of the "myth of the state." And of all persons qualified to treat of that myth Cassirer was supreme. He had studied the whole phenomenon of myth in the second part of the *Philosophy of Symbolic Forms* where he showed that myth is not evil as such, as if it were simply the diametrical opposite of rational knowledge, for it has a proper, indeed, inevitable function in life and society. The important thing is to know what manner of myth one lives by, and to realize its true value through knowledge of its works and its consequences for human life, especially in the relations between man and the state and between whole peoples.

While Cassirer was busy writing his new book, word of this enterprise was quietly passed on to an editor of *Fortune,* Mr. Richardson Wood, who saw the timely merit of it and proposed straightway an essay on the subject, which was very shortly published under the title "The Myth of the State" (*Fortune,* 29, No. 6, June, 1944). Before Cassirer could finish the final revision of the book he was suddenly stricken fatally in New York on April 13, 1945. The work was subsequently made ready for the press by the editor of the present volume, and *The Myth of the State* appeared in 1946, published by the Yale University Press.

The Myth of the State is important to the student of Cassirer because while it was a work of occasion it also affords a clue to the meaning of those statements in *An Essay on Man:* "The author has *continued his study on the subject,*" and "he has been confronted with *new* problems." Before one concludes any survey of Cassirer's philosophy he must consider what such a writing as this, and others subsequent to the last volume of the *Philosophy of Symbolic Forms,* may disclose about "new directions" and even about "new views" of old problems.

For the *Essay* plainly hinted that the possibilities of Cassirer's "theory" were not yet completely realized. One is tempted to surmise, for instance, that *The Myth of the State* might have had a sequel in another "entirely new book" or perhaps that the author would have recorded his "continued study" in a fourth part of the *Symbolic Forms.* For his system in that work was not a tightly closed one: it admitted of further studies and other "parts" similar to those treating of language, myth and religion, and science. Having already ventured to treat of man and the state, he might well have proceeded to study the symbolic forms of the ethical life of man in society. All this, of course, is sheer speculation. Nevertheless, the contents of the various writings subsequent to the three volumes of *Symbolic Forms* cannot be disregarded without the risk of missing the full meaning of the work. The references, explanations, illustrations, and applications in these later writings reflect light upon that masterwork. In order to interpret it aright one should make use of the latter-day pieces, a procedure which Cassirer would certainly have approved as a philosophical idealist, for it follows the classic maxim that one learns the truth of what *is* by what it is seen to be tending toward or its teleology.

The truth of the matter is that the *Philosophy of Symbolic Forms* is not completely self-explanatory. Cassirer knew and said this himself, and his actions in writing two entirely new pieces in 1943 and 1945, offering "explanation" and "illustration" and timely application, are further evidence that this was his own opinion. He, moreover, had become more conscious during his sojourn in America of the needs of "the reader." The subject, he confessed, was "difficult and abstract," and "when writing my *Philosophy of Symbolic Forms* I was so engrossed in the subject itself that I forgot or neglected" wise maxims about style and presentation. He said all these things notwithstanding the fact that his first volume on *Symbolic Forms* had opened with an "Introduction and Presentation of the Problem." In retrospect, in 1944, he saw that for the reader's sake it would be necessary to provide more guidance and interpretation.

But what about making the work itself, the *Philosophy of Symbolic Forms,* available? There seemed to be no immediate prospect after Cassirer's death of providing for a translation. Nevertheless, his pupils, friends, and admirers started a movement of interpretation through the publication of his other writings. Thus his associates at Columbia brought out the inaugural volume of a new series in the History of Ideas, a translation of two essays, *Kant and Rousseau* and *Goethe and the Kantian Philosophy,* done by James Gutmann, Paul Oskar Kristeller, and John Hermann Randall, Jr., and published under the title *Rousseau, Kant, Goethe* by Princeton University Press (1945). Then Susanne K. Langer made a translation of *Sprache und Mythos,* published in 1946 as *Language and Myth* by Harper and Brothers. This particular work offers an illuminating sidelight upon the development of the *Philosophy of Symbolic Forms,* inasmuch as it had been published in 1925, between the second part dealing with Myth and the third part on Science. Mrs. Langer's translation had been preceded, moreover, by her own book, *Philosophy in a New Key,* that presented a view of Cassirer's theory of form and symbol with great freshness and vivacity. In her preface to the translation Mrs. Langer paid an enthusiastic tribute to his "new philosophical insight." The interest in Cassirer was thus being directed toward the *Philosophy of Symbolic Forms,* and readers were being prepared for it.

Then, too, a memorial volume. *The Philosophy of Ernst Cassirer,* appeared in 1949. It had been in preparation before Cassirer's death as a volume in the Library of Living Philosophers under the editorship of Paul Arthur Schilpp, Evanston, Illinois. The contributors to that volume had been previously endorsed by Cassirer himself, as the scholars qualified to speak of and criticize his work. Those contributors wrote their parts as joint authors and not as collaborators, which thus makes all the more significant their unanimous agreement that "the philosophy of Cassirer" is essentially contained in the work on *Symbolic Forms*. Several of the essays are wholly or in large part devoted to the interpretation of this work —those by Carl H. Hamburg, I. K. Stephens, Felix Kaufmann, Dimitry Gawronsky, Robert S. Hartman, Folke Leander, M. F. Ashley Montagu, Susanne K. Langer. But it is even making invidious distinctions to cite a limited number without referring to the remainder of the authors. In one place or another everyone testifies to the value of the *Philosophy of Symbolic Forms* as original and important philosophy. But the tribute of Wilbur M. Urban is particularly noteworthy, for he was not related as a pupil to Cassirer and wrote as a philosopher of the same generation, being also a student of the philosophy of language and a recognized spokesman, as Cassirer himself was, of modern idealism.

Instead of the usual "Reply of the Author," the memorial volume contained a concluding piece, " 'Spirit' and 'Life' in Contemporary Philosophy," where Cassirer had taken his stand with respect to both the philosophy of "Spirit" and the philosophy of "Life." The original work had appeared in 1930, close upon the third volume of the *Symbolic Forms* in 1929, and it defines Cassirer's position in contemporary philosophy by reference to that work. The "explaining" of the *Symbolic Forms* had already begun in Germany, in the very year after publication.

This piece and the various essays collected in *The Philosophy of Ernst Cassirer* offer expert help toward understanding. For the reader who is confining himself to what is translated into English other side lights are obtainable through recent publications. The fourth volume of the *Problem of Knowledge,* translated by William H. Woglom and Charles W. Hendel, was published in 1950 by the Yale University Press. Written by Cassirer in 1940, eleven years after the third part of the *Symbolic Forms,* it approaches the theory "from a different angle" and shows it "in a new light." *The Philosophy of the Enlightenment* appeared in 1951, translated by Fritz C. A. Koeln and James P. Pettegrove and published by the Princeton University Press. The work had come out in Germany in 1932. Here the investigator of cultural forms shows his own genius of interpretation in dealing with a historical period where he exhibits the unity and the interrelationships of its natural science, psychology, epistemology, religion, history, state and society, aesthetics and art. Such a work brings to this "abstract and difficult subject" the concreteness and fullness of life of a work of art which, according to Cassirer's own view, is also a form of knowledge.

These versions of Cassirer besides his own two last writings have become available to English readers since his death and afford them various opportunities to come to know his philosophy. But it may be questioned whether this is enough for "the reader" about whom Cassirer had become concerned. Is it enough to refer him beyond the volume in which he is reading to a diverse collection of books and learned critical articles? Is the reader to be expected to glean from a set of very different pieces the needed explanation of this "abstract and difficult subject"? Surely Cassirer would have provided some foreword of his own "for the reader" of today.

Nobody can supply the introduction as Cassirer himself might have done, nor will any attempt be made in the following Introduction to "explain" the work. Nevertheless some help may be offered in the form of an interpretation which looks forward as well as backward, which not only dwells on those "rich sources of inspiration" of which he speaks himself (p. 71) but also construes the work of those years 1923-29 in the light of the ideas in the works which were published subsequently and which show the new direction of thought and the reflection upon old problems. A friend and student can sometimes do, moreover, what the modesty of the philosopher himself would never allow him to do; that is, to present a view of him as a historic figure and venture to say where he stands in the development of modern thought.

What follows in the Introduction, then, is an interpretation for that reader about whom Cassirer was so solicitous. The further warrant for so doing may be found in his own words in *An Essay on Man* (pp. 184-185): ". . . human works are vulnerable . . . They are subject to change and decay . . . in a mental sense. Even if their existence continues they are in constant danger of losing their meaning. Their reality is symbolic, not physical; and such reality never ceases to require interpretation and reinterpretation."

March 10, 1953

Introduction by Charles W. Hendel

"WHEN SPEAKING of Plato in his *Critique of Pure Reason,*" Cassirer wrote, quoting Kant himself, "it is by no means unusual upon comparing the thoughts which an author has expressed in regard to his subject . . . to find that we understand him better than he has understood himself. As he has not sufficiently determined his concept, he has sometimes spoken, or even thought, in opposition to his own intention." Then Cassirer goes on to speak for himself: "The history of philosophy shows us very clearly that the full determination of a concept is very rarely the work of that thinker who first introduced that concept. For a philosophical concept is generally speaking rather a problem than the solution of a problem—and the full significance of this problem cannot be understood so long as it is still in its first implicit state. It must become explicit in order to be comprehended in its true meaning and this transition from an implicit to an explicit state is the work of the future." [1]

What Cassirer said in endorsing and developing Kant's remarks apropos of Plato's thought we may say with pertinence of Cassirer himself, that a concept first implicit in earlier philosophy had a future when it became explicit in the philosophy of Ernst Cassirer. And the concept in question is that of "symbolic form."

The reader's first query is likely to be: what does the expression "symbolic form" mean? And another naturally follows—why is that concept so significant that the whole of a philosophy should be centered about it and named after it?

1. THE PHILOSOPHY OF FORM IN KANT

The recollection of Kant is ever-present in the pages of Cassirer's writing. Whenever he started for any goal he went back to the philosophy of Kant

1. Cassirer, *An Essay on Man*, p. 180. The reference to Kant is *Critique of Pure Reason* (2d ed., 1787), B 370. Trans. by Norman Kemp Smith (London, Macmillan, 1929), p. 310.

as a base from which to proceed. And it was specifically the Kantian conception of "form" that was basic for the whole of his thought. The concept apparently had proven suggestive of possibilities to him beyond those realized by Kant himself. And Cassirer made the concept "explicit" so that it could be "comprehended in its true meaning."

Even Kant himself in making that comment on Plato in the second edition of the *Critique of Pure Reason* may well have spoken from the wisdom of his own experience: an author often does not first grasp the full import of his own conceptions. The new preface Kant wrote for the second edition constituted a reinterpretation of his own work—and Cassirer, it should be noted, never fails to dwell on its significance. There Kant had sought to make more precise the nature of the revolutionary point of view of his Critical Philosophy. A radical change of outlook was required: philosophy in the form of the metaphysics of pure reason had fallen from grace in the eyes of intelligent men. On the other hand natural science enjoyed the very greatest credit and it elicited, too, the most impressive efforts of mind from the men of genius at that time, the age of Newton. Kant had studied the secret of that unquestioned scientific achievement. Science was not haunted by unnerving skepticism as metaphysics had been. It provided for its own correction without losing enterprise and cogency. It guarded against building hypotheses often mistakenly assumed to be facts. In this respect scientific knowledge was better off than even the empiricist philosophy which seemed so close to it but which was nonetheless quite as far away from the right method of knowledge as rationalism had been. Hume had truly seen what philosophy was coming to—"nothing but doubt, uncertainty and contradiction." [2] With youthful prescience, at the end of the first book of his *Treatise of Human Nature,* he had described himself as having ventured out to sea on a frail raft and being ever and again frightened by the unknown reefs and dangerous waters of the deep and fated to be tossed in that "suspense of judgment," the name for which is skepticism. How could a modern philosopher ever proceed with any more confidence than Hume, whether he take the way of pure reason or that of experience? Kant perceived the fundamental need of a fresh charting of the course beforehand by means of a new philosophical astronomy, something comparable with that of Copernicus in the physical world. It is the orientation and the proper method that must first be determined. Both the rationalistic and the empiricist philosophies had one assumption in com-

2. Hume, *Dialogues concerning Natural Religion,* Pt. I.

mon which resulted in both terminating in a skepticism from which nothing positive seemed forthcoming. They had assumed that in knowledge one could possess what is ultimately real, either in terms of sense information or in the form of rational thought. One reflection had apparently not occurred to the philosophers, or if it had, it had been forgotten as they became absorbed in their systems of thought, namely, that there are *limitations* in the nature of the case, for since man is involved in the knowing, his doing so has part in the resultant knowledge and so there can be no pure transcript of the truth in either sense or reason. We must study the knowing before we can claim a knowledge of something beyond it called ultimate reality. There is no doubt about the knowing—certainly it is itself a fact, but there is a question concerning the character of the relation between the knowing and the reality known. And the change of outlook Kant proposes is stated as a hypothesis: instead of assuming that our knowledge represents absolutely what is real, suppose we proceed with the idea in mind that whatever reality we do know is precisely such as "conforms to" our human ways of knowing. Philosophy may then be able to advance securely as science had already done.

It was to "the exact sciences," as Cassirer later designated them,[3] that Kant had looked for his examples of the value and the truth of this new view of knowledge. It had been very early realized by the ancient Greek geometers that knowledge is not what one *sees* in the geometrical figure, or even what he can trace out as contained in his pure concept of the figure; knowledge must be brought about through a construction of thought, made in accordance with a priori concepts which are not in the foreground for inspection but which nonetheless determine whatever is relevant to the matter at hand.[4] This remarkable aspect of knowledge, the role both of the a priori and of thought constructions, was not realized in natural science until modern times. Several physicists served as good examples of the right procedure, Galileo and Torricelli, for instance; and later Stahl, all of whom grasped the truth that reason only possesses insight into that which reason itself constructs according to its own plan, and hence that reason must take the lead with its own proposals, and then by means of experiment elicit from nature precise answers to them. It is only because reason has a priori principles—to answer Hume, for example—that the experienced "conjunc-

---

3. The title of Part I of the fourth volume of *Das Erkenntnisproblem*, *The Problem of Knowledge*.

4. A paraphrase of *Critique of Pure Reason*, B 12–13.

tion" of appearances can be taken as a rule for or law of these things. By virtue of the universal concept of cause and effect a priori man is able to order the material of his experience according to causal law and then to discover empirically the various particular laws of science. That is the first condition of knowledge, the a priori concept treated as a rule for the organization of the data. The second condition is the experimentation which tests the particular theory conceived in accordance with the ruling principles of thought. Experiment is not merely supplying more pieces of experience, for reason is involved in all genuine experiment and is necessary if one is to learn anything from it. And further when reason does receive the sought-for instruction from nature it is not at all in that too familiar role of a docile pupil who only repeats what the teacher says; reason acts rather as a judge possessing authority who can require a witness to answer to the point, and precisely to those questions, too, that are asked.[5]

Kant had mixed his metaphors liberally but they conveyed the sense well enough. Reason is two-handed, and the operation of knowing requires both hands. With one hand man constructs a theory of the order of things and events in nature according to an inner plan; with the other he frames the experiments in accordance with that preformed theory which will put nature through her course and subject the theory to the test. At this juncture nature looms large on the scene as being able either to dispose of the theoretical construction or to confirm it through the event. But in describing the relation of man to nature, even in that last phase where nature tells the answer, the image of man changes from that of a simple learner to that of a judge with authority. However, one should remember here the limits of authority according to Kant who was so strong in his faith in freedom—it is the function of a judge to render the decision which the evidence in court sustains and to abide by it, never to overrule it. When all these roles are played by man in his several parts and by nature, then man obtains genuine scientific knowledge. There is a time for him to propose theory and a time to await the disposition of nature. Every factor in the procedure has its distinctive function and place in the achievement of knowledge, both nature and man, and man's theory and man's experimentation and man's rational judgment exercised on the basis of the evidence of experience. Knowledge is the outcome of such complex rapports and processes. But there is a special emphasis upon the forwardness, or better, the responsibility of man in the whole affair. A faithful Kantian will always remember

5. *Critique*, B 13–14.

this, as Cassirer did, and it is not surprising that he later bethought himself of *An Essay on Man.*

Examples or illustrations are always used at some risk to the meaning, and Kant's references to the way of learning in science have had a misleading effect. There has been a common opinion that Kant is entitled to fame only for his fresh and original analysis of the nature of scientific method. Whatever else he has done may be of dubious value, but this, it is thought, may pass as his solid achievement which survives the uncertain fate of his bold adventure in the three *Critiques* as well as the large corpus of other writings. Since Kant's day the "scientific method in philosophy" has been so exalted that there is none other beside it. In consequence philosophical thinking tends to be assimilated to scientific thinking, and the adventure of philosophy has often come to be regarded as only a preliminary phase of science and the employment of the same method in fields the knowledge of whose material has not yet attained the definitive formulation of a strict science. Those who hold such views tend to read Kant as if the whole of the instruction proffered in the *Critique* were already contained in these illustrative passages in the preface to the work. It is easy to do this for other reasons: Kant greatly admired Newtonian physics and spoke of it as the perfect example of the knowledge of nature. Add to this his strongly negative criticism of metaphysics, and the case seems complete that Kant was in reality arguing for the reduction of philosophy to science. But Cassirer rejected vigorously such a view of Kant and rightly so. Science may properly be cited as the best example and yet not be considered to be in itself the ultimate ideal of knowledge. It is still only an "example"—a term Kant had repeatedly emphasized in the preface. But if so then other examples are conceivable. Kant also called the cases cited "analogies." [6] They indicated what ought to obtain analogously in philosophy. But it must be remembered that there is always more in the thing being introduced by analogy than is contained in the instance used for that introductory purpose. The analogies in this instance give the idea of an appropriate procedure for philosophy, one that might be as fruitful for progress in philosophy as the method of science had been in the knowledge of nature. But this implies that philosophy is itself a *distinctive* mode of knowledge and is not reducible to science.

And Kant was actually thinking in that preface of varying modes of knowledge. Mathematics, he says, has an ideal perfection for it is purely

6. Ibid., B 16.

a priori and absolutely certain; but it has no intrinsic connection with the appearances in time and space. Science bears a resemblance to mathematics in the functional priority of its principles and theories, but in addition these a priori elements are applied to experience and yield genuine knowledge of nature. This is the realm of the understanding. But the understanding, Kant emphasizes, draws upon "experience which is itself another mode of knowledge." [7] Furthermore, as itself a "mode of knowledge," experience depends upon understanding with its a priori elements. Thus *several* modes of knowledge are distinguished and at the same time they are related to each other. Experience, unintelligible without the understanding, is one extreme and pure mathematics with its apriority the other, and between them is science which is at once the knowledge of whatever appears in space and time and the matter of experience *and* knowledge in a mode that possesses the certainty of mathematics. There is here suggested a kind of progression in these contrasted modes of knowledge—experience, mathematics, science. What then of metaphysics, which is also enumerated in the sequence? Is it a relapse or break in the progress, when pure reason runs wild and is neither mathematical nor empirical? Well, whatever metaphysics may have been in the past, Kant clearly intends that any future metaphysic, as his title to the work intervening between the first and second editions of the *Critique, A Prolegomena to Every Future Metaphysic,* reveals, shall be a further advance beyond other modes of knowledge, even beyond natural science. He claims, in fact, in this very *Critique* that he has made a "successful attempt . . . at setting metaphysics on the secure path of genuine knowledge." [8]

However, the *Critique* is not itself a full-fledged "system of knowledge" or metaphysics but only the prior condition of a possible metaphysics. It is, Kant says, "a tractate on method," since the first step in advance is "to transform the previous procedure of metaphysics." [9]

The transformation is as momentous as a Copernican revolution, a wholly new orientation toward the problem of knowledge. It is the hypothesis that, instead of human knowledge being shaped to reality, it is our human judgment which determines whatever is to have the character of being reality for us. The roles are reversed—the judgment conditions reality.

7. Ibid., B 17.
8. Ibid., B 18–19.
9. Ibid., B 22–23.

The prime task of this new philosophy then is to study "the forms of judgment" through which we attain to a genuine and certain knowledge of objective reality. So the philosopher is only taking his *cue* from the method of knowledge in science. The actual procedure in philosophy will have to be distinct from that in science and relative to the subject matter. For a new subject matter has been discerned. All the "modes of knowledge," experience, science, and mathematics, apparently involve a priori factors. The problem is to discover them and determine precisely what they are. And the "speculative reason" has this "peculiarity" about it, that it can from its own resources delimit its own competence and spell out completely the various modes in which it determines whatever shall be objects of knowledge. For in respect of the principles of knowledge there is a distinct and self-consistent "unity in which every member is there for the sake of all the others and all for one just as in an organised body." [10] This organic corpus of principles, as it were, is the proper study of the Kantian metaphysics.

Since Kant had drawn his "analogies" and "examples" from physics, it is important to distinguish at once between the universal principles of any knowledge, principles which are metaphysical, and the special principles of a science, which are particular laws. What Kant has said about a priori elements is that they are not a lot of scattered and random factors but an organic unity. They are not arbitrary inventions or ad hoc assumptions. They are the conditions of all knowledge which has the true marks of universality and necessity. But knowledge is always particular and definite as well—it is the knowledge of what is actually given in sensuous intuition and experience. Here there is plenty of contingency. The discovery of any law of physics depends upon the data that pose the problem, and they cannot pose a problem except for a mind ready to perceive it and equipped by previous knowledge and experience to theorize concerning the matter at hand. The special theory of physics—that of Galileo or of Torricelli, whom Kant cited—does involve a particular genius who can discover what is not apparent to others or not yet accepted in the science to date. This is the empirical level of advancing knowledge. But all this play of scientific discovery takes place upon a foundation which is not variable or dependent upon special genius—the foundation of any knowledge whatsoever, that which enables us to envisage the eventual law as being universal and necessary and thus possessing the character of being objectively true. The critical

10. Ibid., B 23.

study of this foundation in reason is a new logic underlying all knowledge.

The a priori elements are "forms" of reason, using "reason" in the large sense indicated above. It is only by virtue of form that there can be universality and necessity in the knowledge of the things of the world in space and time, the matter of our experience. Form, then, is the distinctive subject matter of this new philosophy of knowledge.

But Kant anticipated a question coming from others who still cherished the ancient subjects of metaphysics—such as God, freedom, and immortality. Was he not confining philosophy unduly when he limited it to the a priori conditions of knowledge? Yet form is so central that the systematic analysis of it as it appears in the whole range of experience and action takes the philosopher over the entire universe of human interest and thought. In the preface Kant refers to the ethical realm and the realm of beauty and sublimity and that of religious and theological interest.[11] A comprehensive philosophy is foreshadowed, and besides this first critique, "the metaphysics of knowledge," there will be the second, "the metaphysics of ethics," and the third which is at once a metaphysics of nature and art and teleology. The first semblance of undue restriction disappears as the scope of this philosophy of form comes to be grasped.

It is Cassirer's language that we have been using in this interpretation of the preface to the second edition of the first *Critique.* Kant's own name for his philosophy was "critical" or "transcendental." The latter term is not to be thought of in connection with transcendence. This philosophy is not pretending to treat of transcendent things of a higher order, so to speak, than man's experience in this world. The name of the philosophy is derived from the new method, and the method is so strangely named because of the unobvious nature of the problem. Cassirer explains Kant as follows:

> His transcendental method has to assume "the fact of the sciences" as given, and seeks only to understand the possibility of this fact, its logical conditions and principles. But even so, Kant does not stand merely in a position of dependence on the factual stuff of knowledge, the material offered by the various sciences. Kant's basic conviction and presupposition consists rather of this, that there is a universal and essential *form* of knowledge, and that philosophy is called upon and qualified to discover this form and establish it with certainty. The critique of reason achieves this by reflective thought upon the function of knowl-

11. Ibid., B 32–33 ff.

edge instead of upon its content. It discovers this function in judgment, and to understand judgment in its universal structure and in its specification in different lines becomes one of the main problems of the critique.[12]

FORM AND FUNCTION

It is this functional aspect of form in Kant's philosophy that is relevant to our purpose. The Kantian position in general is of course quite familiar to readers of modern philosophy. Space and time are two "pure forms of sensuous intuition." Then there is a galaxy of twelve "pure forms of understanding," the prime instances of which are the two categories or relational concepts that relate things perceived in space and time in terms of cause and effect and of substance and attribute. Both classes of forms, the "sensible" and the "intelligible," are a priori, that is, they are not learned from experience in the course of time nor derived by inductively generalizing from particulars. In contradistinction to the forms all contents of knowledge are given through the contacts of experience—this is the material and it is assimilated and understood only by virtue of the a priori forms of both intuition and thought. Nothing ever enters our ken without conforming to their combined prescription. The forms are the universal and necessary conditions of the very first appearance of anything whatsoever to our human perception, and furthermore of its becoming progressively intelligible to our understanding. The forms are thus "constitutive" of our whole experience of the world.

Kant overstated his point in the phrase "the understanding *makes* nature." What he showed, however, was that nature is understood in accordance with such forms of the mind. Though nature-understood, is the only nature there is, yet not all of nature is understanding-made. The content or the appearances are independent, and it is only their intelligible order and form that derive from the constitution of man's mind. The overemphasis of Kant's statement seems due to a further thought about the creative role of man in connection with form. Later in his philosophy what is only a matter of "faith" in this first critique, viz., that man has freedom, is asserted as a justifiable postulate of reason. In the present passage where

12. *The Problem of Knowledge*, pp. 14–15.

Kant speaks of the making of nature by the understanding he may be anticipating that later assertion. The contention here is this, that the world is "constituted" in accordance with the forms of man's intuition and understanding. This constitutive function of the forms is the theme of Cassirer.

As conditions under which appearances in space and time become knowable, the forms seem to be underlying logical factors. They are "transcendental elements" which can only be grasped through an intellectual analysis by the philosopher and through his constructing a theory (for Kant emulates the scientist in his own procedure here) explaining how knowledge as we actually have it is possible. Everything involved in this proceeding is "transcendental," the analysis, the theoretical construction, the elements, and the forms among the elements. The term "transcendental" which is applied to all of these items marks the fact that none of them is directly or empirically identifiable. We do not find in our direct experience that we first receive sensations and then construe them by means of a priori concepts (also distinguishable as being there prior to our thinking in terms of them) and then fashion the result into knowledge. Even the content or material of knowledge *as an element* must be transcendental: it is only distinguishable as a moment or factor in the analysis of knowledge. Concretely we have appearances and experience, and in experience these elements and factors are already funded or, to use Kant's expression, they are "constitutive." This was a point that Cassirer watched carefully and he remarked critically of his master: "Even Kant seems, in the first chapters of the *Critique of Pure Reason,* to start from this presupposition ['that the first data of human experience are in an entirely chaotic state']. Experience, he says, is no doubt the first product of our understanding. But it is not a simple fact; it is a compound of two opposite factors, of matter and form. The material factor is given in our sense perceptions; the formal factor is represented by our scientific concepts . . ." [13] But the phrase "Even Kant seems to start" implies that Kant eventually knew better or at least that he was plainer about his meaning, which Cassirer made plainer still by treating these elements of form and matter in a functional and not in a substantive way. The discriminations of content and form are made only for the logic of knowledge.

Yet the choice of the term "constitutive" suggests a quasi-ontological meaning. For one must keep in mind the important difference in Kant's thought between logic-ordinary and his proposed transcendental logic. The former or older logic was purely formal whereas this logic functions in organic relation with the content of actual experience. Kant has argued both that there is a logical structure of all empirically given reality and that the logical forms are forms of the appearances or objects in the world. They are formal characters woven in, to use a Goethean metaphor, as ingredient of whatever is experienced and known. The world has determinate form in the very least experience of it, and such form is nothing that is merely externally superposed upon the material. For such a function of form in knowledge it is difficult to find a better descriptive term than the one Kant actually used, viz., "constitutive."

Another key phrase pregnant with meaning in the Kantian philosophy is "synthetic unity." It is everywhere discovered through the transcendental analysis. While form and matter are distinguished from each other as well as the forms of intuition and those of understanding, all of them must be conceived in combination and in their functional relations with each other in the formation of knowledge. They are all together involved in the constitution of experience which has the character of being a "synthetic unity." Now it is true that Kant tends to reserve the term "synthesis" for the work of judgment in knowledge, the field to which it was first relevant. The difficulty which Hume had exposed concerning the principle of cause and effect in reasoning had been the foremost logical problem of the *Critique*. How can "necessary connection" ever be grounded logically, in face of the obvious distinction between and possible separation of the idea of the cause and the idea of the effect in our actual experience? We presume that things are necessarily related without having any insight into the supposed necessity of their connection. The justification which Kant gives is that in the very possession of experience there is already synthesis, that is, a necessary relationship according to rule, and this is the basic logical warrant for all specific inferences to cause or effect. This "proof" is the burden of the *Analytic of Concepts*. However, the situation with respect to cause and effect is really typical of all cases of human judgment. And the proposed way of solving the difficulty in general is to show that there is always a "synthetic unity of a manifold" which is only to be grasped through transcendental analysis. There is one order or "one experience" as there is "one nature." An "original synthetic unity of apperception" is the ground of all knowledge whatsoever. But synthesis is so fundamental that it can no longer be thought of as applying only to concepts but is pertinent to all that is analyzed as having any part in knowledge. The union of form and content and the combination of forms of sense and forms of understanding with each other and with the content or material— all this is synthesis. And in order to take care of this complex synthesis Kant introduced another transcendental function, namely, the "productive imagination." It appears then that the task Kant had set himself was far from being fulfilled merely when he achieved a "deduction of the categories" and answered Hume. He still had to make intelligible that complex constituting of experience and knowledge in which sensuous intuition and logical concepts and matter are all synthesized in imagination. To this further task Kant turned in the *Analytic of Principles*.

The Schema's the Thing

At the outset of this further analysis there is a reminder that the "transcendental" logic differs significantly from ordinary logic. The latter abstracts the form from all content and is purely formal; the transcendental logic is a "logic of truth" which involves the application of a priori forms or rules of thought to sensuous content. How is this application to be conceived? How does it happen that the a priori concepts can be applied as "principles" to particular contents? But "happen" is the wrong term, for it implies that matters could be otherwise, or that there could be experience in which principles like cause and effect might be inapplicable. But no experience according to Kant's argument can ever show such a possibility of concepts and sensuous intuitions failing to meld. The question then is how we are to conceive the *via media* between concept and intuition in the actual construction of specific knowledge by the human understanding. Kant states his proposed solution as follows:

"It is clear that a third thing must be given which must stand in a relation of being of the same sort (*gleichartig*) with the category on the one hand and with the appearance on the other, and which makes possible the application of the former to the latter. The mediating representation must be pure (without anything empirical) and yet not simply *intellectual;* it must at the same time be *sensuous.* Such a thing is the *transcendental schema.*" [14]

14. *Critique*, A 137–138, B 176–177.

The schema is the uniting "representation," the synthetic "medium" in which the forms of understanding and the sensuous intuitions are assimilated so that they constitute experience. The schema comprises the category but contains more than a category can supply. In this respect we can say that the schema is something better than the category, for it is more adequate, making possible what neither logical form nor content could yield by themselves. The schema has something of both in its nature —it is a sensuous-intellectual form.

But the schema is not merely the medium through which the sensuous and the intellectual are brought into unity. The affair is more complex than that. We are not to forget that whatever is matter of sensuous apprehension always appears in the universal form of time. The schema must be a relation of the concepts of understanding with temporal appearances. Thus, for example, cause and effect is a concept relevant to the succession of *events* in the world and making definite the necessary connections of things that occur in time. As Kant himself explains:

The concept of understanding contains pure synthetic unity of the manifold in general. Time as the formal condition of the manifold of the inner sense,[15] and consequently the condition of the connection of representations, contains an *a priori* manifold in pure intuition. Now a transcendental time-determination is of the same sort as the category (which constitutes the unity of the same) insofar as it is universal and grounded on an *a priori* rule. But on the other hand it is also of the same sort with the appearance insofar as time is contained in every empirical representation of the manifold. So it follows that an application of the category to appearances is possible by means of the transcendental determination of time which, as the schema of the concept of understanding, effects the subsumption of the appearances under the category.[16]

"Thus," Kant says toward the close of the section on the Schematism of the "Categories," "the schemata of the pure concepts of the understanding are the true and sole conditions that make possible any relationship of the concepts to objects, and consequently the conditions of their having any meaning."[17] The schemata of pure concepts are both "schemata of sensi-

15. "Inner sense." This is a moot point the discussion of which must be by-passed here where we are concerned only with the general purport of the passage.
16. *Critique,* A 138–139, B 177–178.
17. Ibid., A 146–147, B 185–186.

bility" and "the first realization of the categories." In this fashion the schema is a more complete thing than either the category or the form of time or the sensuous content—it is all these together, in their synthesis. But as such it is no longer merely logical in character—it is "real," in the sense of phenomenal, of being a concrete constituent of the appearances. Kant says: "Hence it follows that the schema is actually only the phenomenon, or the sensuous concept of an object in agreement with the category."[18] The "only" in that passage excludes an identification with ultimate reality or things in themselves. But it is striking enough that the schema should be itself called the "phenomenon" as far as it is consonant with the form of understanding. For this means that the schema is no longer a hidden "transcendental" factor only conceivable in and through an analysis. It is a real phenomenal presence.

The schema's the thing that caught the imagination of Cassirer. He interpreted the whole subsequent post-Kantian philosophy in Germany by reference to it. And his own philosophy of symbolic form was a development of the possibilities of this new concept of form.

It is worth noting in detail how important Kant's notion of schema had been in Cassirer's own thinking. In *Kants Leben und Lehre* (1916) he regarded that notion as the focal point of the constructive thought leading from the *Critique of Pure Reason* to the *Critique of Judgment*, the latter being expressly described as the "outcome of the further development of the transcendental schematism."[19] Again the Introduction of the third volume of *Das Erkenntnisproblem* (1920) opens with a survey of the outstanding problems remaining to be solved by those who had mastered the total meaning of Kant's Critical Philosophy. Here the third work in the trilogy of critiques, the *Critique of Judgment*, was again spoken of as an "advance" upon "the abstract schematism" of the first *Critique*.[20] Furthermore, the variety of the attempts at a solution made by the post-Kantian philosophers, from Fichte to Hegel, is not to be understood as merely due to subjective idiosyncrasies of the different philosophers but to the rich suggestiveness of Kant's own development of the schema doctrine, a development toward greater concreteness. There were many problems brought into focus in the teaching of the third critique, concerning the thing in itself, the a priori and synthetic unity and the antithesis of form and matter, but these all revolved about a new conception of one of the oldest problems

18. Ibid., A 146–147, B 185–186.
19. Cassirer, *Kants Leben und Lehre*, esp. Chap. 6, pp. 291, 327–328, 336, 375–379.
20. *Das Erkenntnisproblem*, 3, 13, 15.

of philosophy, "the relation of universal and particular." All derived from the doctrine of schematism. And Cassirer closed his introductory remarks even with a play upon the word schema, saying that this very survey which he has just given itself offers "a schema that enables us to orient ourselves to the main lines of future speculation." [21]

But it is also an orientation for his own philosophy. The notion of schema that enabled him to interpret the achievements of others lighted the way to his own position and he was fond of using the term and in quite new contexts of his own choosing. The primary meaning is stated thus: "The schema is the unity of concept and intuition, the common achievement of both factors." [22] Then in the *Essay on Man* he speaks of "that other schema which we call space." [23] In the same *Essay* he treats of Art as a concrete manifestation of the union of intuitive and structural form, in other words, the schema.[24] This varied usage is to be traced even in the first volume on *Symbolic Forms* when he writes: "Thus the particular can be posited only on the basis of a universal schema which is merely filled with new concrete content as our experience of the 'thing' and its 'attributes' progresses." [25] Farther in this same book when dealing specifically with its subject of language he writes: "language possesses a schema," "a monogram of the pure imagination a priori." [26]

There is no doubt, then, that the imagination of Ernst Cassirer busied itself much with the concept of schema. Had he not been led by various other important considerations to the discovery of a more original theme and title for his work, he might well have presented his own philosophy as an extension of the doctrine of Schema, for it is clearly a stage in his thinking toward the concept of "symbolic form."

The Three Problems of the Critique of Judgment Involving the Theory of Form

It is necessary to examine more closely Cassirer's preoccupation with the *Critique of Judgment* in order to realize the important development of

21. Ibid., *3*, 16.
22. Ibid., *3*, 11.
23. *Essay*, p. 51.
24. Ibid., chap. on "Art," pp. 137–170 and esp. 167–169.
25. See below, p. 102.
26. See below, p. 200.

the philosophy of form in that work. He makes a great point of the fact that this third *Critique* brings to fulfillment the thought of the previous *Critiques*. This opinion confirms, of course, Kant's own view that he there reconciled the moral freedom of man with the universal lawfulness of nature. But some critics have belittled the motive and purpose of Kant's undertaking in this work when they suppose that he was merely animated by his love of system, and consequently they see here only a medley of really unrelated themes lumped together in an artificial unity of "architectonic," the whole lot somehow construed together by a reference to the transcendental imagination. But Cassirer wages war vigorously against this opinion. He has found in this *Critique* an important new inquiry that penetrated "to the uttermost depths, the very fundamentals of the Kantian structure of thought itself," and that showed besides a prevision of the "problems of profoundest significance in the cultural development of the eighteenth and nineteenth centuries." [27] The third *Critique* is no artificial synthesis, then, but the maturest work of a philosopher pursuing a logical and comprehensive inquiry which developed his own philosophy and at the same time interpreted a whole "epoch."

The great problems of the "epoch" which Cassirer selected for attention were three in number, the unity of empirical science, purpose in nature, and the nature of art. How these all belong together was the special concern of Cassirer the historian in his two writings, *Kants Leben und Lehre* and the third volume of *Das Erkenntnisproblem* which gives an opening survey of the state of the philosophical questions before the post-Kantian philosophy begins.

The Function of the Idea of System in the Organization of Scientific Knowledge

The first problem is a direct consequence of the *Analytic of Principles* in the *Critique of Pure Reason* which examines the employment of concepts in the actual construction of specific scientific knowledge. The forms of understanding have previously been deduced logically as necessary to the constitution of the experience from which man will derive all his knowl-

27. *Kants Leben*, pp. 291 and 375.

edge in detail of what actually happens in nature. But the further application of any of these logical concepts as a principle must always be made to what is really contingent material of sensuous intuition. And then one gains a determinate concept of an actual relationship of phenomena in space and time. An example is the concept of some definite causal law expressing a necessary connection between things in nature. The law of falling bodies, as a Galileo or Newton determines it, is also such an empirical concept in the sense that it cannot be analyzed out and deduced a priori solely from the concepts of matter and motion but depends likewise on what nature shows upon inquiry and experiment. Any knowledge so acquired is always a *piece* of knowledge, the conception of some particular determinate law. Here a new aspect of the nature of all our knowledge calls for examination: notwithstanding the step-by-step and piecemeal advance in scientific knowledge from law to law and truth to truth there is consistent progress and an integration of these laws and truths into a comprehensive knowledge of the structure of the world. How is that unity among the empirical laws possible? How are we to understand this fact about science itself that it progressively moves toward unification and systematic relationship? This is the occasion for a critique— for it is something to wonder at and it must be made intelligible through a further analysis and reflection. The older philosophy took a leap at this point without any consciousness of the seriousness of the problem. The system attained in knowledge was assumed without question to reflect the reality of a "system of nature" and many philosophers proceeded straightway to base a theistic inference to a cause of nature upon such an assumption of the perfection of system or order in reality. That procedure had been rightly questioned by the skeptics like Hume.[28] Let us stick, Kant said in effect, to the new point of view of our critique of reason and only say this much at the outset, that there is a unity and system *in our knowledge*. We do not really have a grasp of the system of nature as a whole so that we can proceed therefrom "to specify all the particular laws and individual cases" which actually constitute our material knowledge of science as "subsumptions" under a comprehensive universal concept.[29] Our logic does not yet reach that far. Here, however, is an arresting fact, that our science does proceed toward perfect system as toward a goal, *as if* the ultimate system were guaranteed from the first. What human reason

28. See Hume, *Dialogues concerning Natural Religion.*
29. *Kants Leben,* pp. 294, 312.

is "guided by" in this progress of its science of nature is something new
to the critical argument. It is the Idea, a guiding or "regulative" principle.
It is a rule implicit in the *seeking* of knowledge. It is a postulate of the
inquiring consciousness and its justification is to be found in the fact of
scientific progress toward unity and system.

This concept of the "regulative" Idea in the first *Critique* was destined
to have quite a history in the third *Critique*. It was when Kant was propos-
ing this meaning for the term "Idea" that he made the above-quoted remark about Plato, that he had introduced something into the history of
thought of whose significance even he had not the clearest appreciation or
even a consistent view. Kant believed that he himself was now giving the
concept "Idea" its true characterization as a guiding principle toward the
goal of empirical knowledge, a goal which is organic with the parts of truth
out of which it is necessarily constructed. This organic conception of the
contingent knowledge of empirical natural science is the first problem
which occasions the inquiries of the third *Critique*.

THE CONCEPT OF PURPOSIVE FORM IN THE KNOWLEDGE
OF NATURE

Independent of this theme is another problem which anyone who had
attended carefully to the state of knowledge in his day would not fail to
examine as another "fact." There is the case of what was then called "natural history," and in later times biological science. Here the inquiring mind
of man "ascribes to an existing thing a *purposive* character as being the expression of an inner form." [30] The older metaphysics had again uncritically
assumed at once the reality of purpose in nature. We must follow the rule
of the new Critical Philosophy and see instead that there is a problem here
—the problem, namely, "by what right do we ascribe purposiveness to
any phenomenon of nature? [31] Is the very *concept* of purpose a legitimate
one as a principle to be applied to nature?

There is a point of similarity between this problem and the previous
one: we are asking in the first case whether we have a right to construe the

30. Ibid., p. 303.
31. Ibid., pp. 303, 360. Cf. *Problem of Knowledge*, pp. 120, 124–125.

whole mechanism of the world as a system and, in the second case, whether we have the right to envisage a realm within Nature as everywhere governed by an additional principle of purpose. In both cases the critical philosophy refrains from attributing either the system or the purpose directly to Nature but recognizes that they are nevertheless essential and relevant to our knowledge. Hence the examination of both cases is a fundamental task for "the critique of knowledge."

But an advance is achieved in this critique of knowledge in the realm of natural history or biology. According to Cassirer, Kant in studying the "problem of organic purposive forms gains a new and richer concept of nature." [32] Though the problem is analogous with that of the system of empirical knowledge it also discloses something new and signally different. In physical science man proceeds with his research and discovery by constructing a whole out of parts, thanks to the regulative Idea of the whole; but in biological research the scientist *sees* in any *individual* organism the whole actually given and as already determinative of the several distinct parts.[33] The whole is present, in a sense, in the beginning and in the very appearances where we can identify parts. Here nature offers to the imagination of man what that imagination is seeking and what it demands for satisfaction. That remarkable suitability of the organic form in nature to the imagination of man is the thing to marvel at and explore further in this "transcendental" philosophy.

THE PURE CONCRETE FORM IN ART

In his discussion of this second problem of the *Critique of Judgment* Kant has already advanced beyond "the abstract schematism" of the earlier Critique.[34] But the treatment of the third problem, that of art, makes greater strides toward concreteness. For art is the "realm of pure forms." [35] "A work of art is an individual and distinct thing, something self-contained and possessing its own purpose within itself; yet there is at the same time represented in it a new 'whole,' a new total image of reality and of the

32. *Das Erkenntnisproblem, 3*, 15; see also *Kants Leben*, p. 361.
33. *Kants Leben*, pp. 362–363.
34. *Das Erkenntnisproblem, 3*, 14–15.
35. *Kants Leben*, p. 327. Cf. *Essay*, chap. on "Art," p. 148.

spiritual cosmos." [36] Once again it is the phenomenon of consciousness we
are to examine critically, the distinctive judgment. The aesthetic consciousness possesses a unique form of concrete fulfillment: while being completely engrossed with its own passing states it apprehends even in those
momentary conditions that which is of absolutely timeless signification." [37]
Here at last the imagination can be perfectly satisfied: art is the manifestation of pure, concrete form.

The whole discussion of these three problems resolves itself into the one
great question concerning form and its function. As Cassirer expresses it,
each one of these special problems has to do with "the formation of that
which is individual." [38] Or we may say alternatively, it is the problem of
the relation of form and the individual in all existence. Thus in the first
case each particular law of the physical world has its specific character only
within a total system of concepts of the special science to which it belongs,
and only by reference to that whole does it have its individual status as
a particular law of that science. Otherwise the so-called knowledge might
be only some chance apprehension of an actual regular connection of events
but it would not be understood because it would not be seen in relationship with all the other known connections. Thus if any individual law is
apprehended, the whole must be conceptually in mind. In the second case,
that of the knowledge of organisms, there is the phenomenon of "individual forms" and they are organic beings in which the whole is realized
as essentially determining the nature and function of the parts. Here the
individual forms seem more "natural" and are not attributed to any obvious artifice of the mind of the inquirer. There is, as Kant calls it, a "principle of formal purposiveness" involved in our understanding of individual
form in nature. But the most direct and immediate apprehension of individuality and form is in art, which is a concrete representation where the
phenomenon is experienced as the whole being determinant of the parts
and disclosing itself through them. Here form is both "pure" and "concrete." [39] Thus the drift of this entire argument, Cassirer claims, is toward
a new view of universal and particular as they are together involved in
the realization of individual form.[40]

36. *Kants Leben*, p. 328.
37. Ibid., p. 331.
38. Ibid., pp. 306, 327, 363.
39. Ibid., pp. 327–334. Cf. *Essay*, pp. 145–148.
40. *Das Erkenntnisproblem, 3*, 16.

In this sketch of the problems treated in the third *Critique* we have followed Cassirer's own interpretation, for our purpose is to see what he derived from that work for his own philosophy of symbolic form. It is also worth while, and indeed essential, to study Cassirer's views about the epochal significance of Kant's achievement, relating it to subsequent philosophy and to his own in particular.

2. THE EPOCHAL SIGNIFICANCE OF KANT'S WORK AND WHAT CASSIRER MADE OF THE DEVELOPING THEORY OF FORM

We shall pass in review the "advances" attributed by Cassirer to Kant and consider at the same time how Cassirer himself developed them in the whole context of modern thought and culture. This involves Cassirer's evaluation of Kant and showing some of the other "rich sources of inspiration" that entered into the making of his own philosophy. And it may reveal, too, the authentic originality of Cassirer's thought.

SYSTEM AND PHYSICAL NATURE

The development of the first of Kant's theses from the *Critique of Judgment* can be briefly dealt with. On this matter Cassirer had reached his own position long before writing his work on Kant, namely, in his book *Substanzbegriff und Funktionsbegriff* (1910). There he explored in detail that "steady progress of science" of which Kant had spoken. The "way of advance" is ever a "logical" one.[41] It is exemplified first in mathematics. Here Cassirer rejected the traditional doctrine that the formation of a mathematical concept is by way of abstracting a common element from a multiplicity of similar particulars. Instead, the process is that of setting up forms of order

---

41. *Substanzbegriff und Funktionsbegriff*, p. 96. See Swabey trans., *Substance and Function*, p. 73.

which serve as principles for distinguishing and relating the many different particulars. These forms function actually as rules by which the diverse particulars can be represented as a series of identifiable elements in lawful relation with each other.[42] Scientific research into Nature is a further extension of this process. What Kant had envisaged here was a "dynamic unity," the kind of unity necessary for phenomena in time which have to be given determinate order and relationship. The "dynamic" aspect of this unity means that seemingly ultimate laws of nature prove inadequate to account for the very facts discovered by their means so that "constants of a higher order" become necessary.[43] Thus science progresses toward its goal of unity by a regular development and transformation within itself. The key to the advance is the new forms that function in the ordering of the content already at hand. But at no time are these contents merely data given apart from form. The notion of such absolute "facts" as well as that of absolute fixed "laws" is due to a false abstraction whereby things are isolated artificially from the organic whole of which they are functioning parts.[44] For nothing has any place or value in knowledge independently of the constructive, functional forms through which experience is organized as a system.[45] Throughout we are operating within a whole where the connectedness of the elements as well as their reciprocal relations with each other is the first original fact. And every element has its objective reality precisely in so far as we grasp how it "weaves itself into a whole" [46]—incidentally a favorite metaphor taken from Goethe. Wholeness and system are then of the essence of scientific knowledge and of the reality which is known in it. And the forms function thus creatively in making possible both the continuing progress and the unity of science. Thus Cassirer followed out consistently the lead given by Kant and in turn gave fresh form and explicit demonstration to the "critical" thesis regarding knowledge and the system of Nature.[47]

---

42. Ibid., p. 196. Swabey, p. 148.

43. Ibid., p. 352. Swabey, p. 266.

44. Ibid., p. 377. Swabey, p. 284.

45. Ibid., p. 369. Swabey, pp. 277–278. See also *Kants Leben*, pp. 307–309, 311–313, 317–318, 328–329, 357–358; *Problem of Knowledge*, pp. 62–63, 109.

46. *Substanzbegriff und Funktionsbegriff*, p. 377. Cf. *Faust*, Pt. I, "Nacht": "Wie alles sich zum Ganzen webt" (line 447).

47. The argument of *Substanzbegriff* was restated in *Kants Leben*, pp. 306–313, and briefly in *Das Erkenntnisproblem*, 3, 12–14.

ORGANIC FORMS AND THE REALM OF LIFE

But Cassirer had to take a considerable time to develop his position on the second subject, where it is a question of determining both the value of the concept of purpose in biological science and the resultant general conception of nature in accordance with that science. In this case we would be well advised to follow Cassirer's own characteristic procedure and to sketch the background of modern thinking about purpose and organic existences.

"Rich Sources of Inspiration": Leibniz

For nearly a century prior to the appearance of the *Critique of Judgment* the theme of organic life had engaged the attention of philosophers and men of science. Perhaps it is not too extreme to say that Leibniz wrote the character of life into the very nature of ultimate reality. He was, however, not engaging simply in pure speculation for he was aware of the empirical discoveries made through the microscope and the work of Swammerdam and Leeuwenhoek which were widely publicized and discussed. But Leibniz' own specific contribution, according to Cassirer, is summed up in this, that "the concept of the *whole* has gained a different and deeper significance. For the universal whole which is to be grasped can no longer be reduced to a mere sum of its parts. The new whole is organic, not mechanical; its nature . . . is presupposed by its parts and constitutes the condition of the possibility of their nature and being." [48] The last phrase "constitutes the condition of the possibility of . . ." recalls the formula of the Kantian theory of knowledge and intimates that the "concept of the whole" is functioning according to Cassirer as "form," constituting the nature of the living world. Cassirer here attributes to Leibniz the leading idea for the newly emerging "philosophy of nature within which the rigid concept of form gradually breaks down." [49] The "foundation for a new philosophy of the organic was laid." [50]

48. *The Philosophy of the Enlightenment*, p. 31.
49. Ibid., p. 34.
50. Ibid., p. 84.

BUFFON, MAUPERTUIS, DIDEROT. From the year 1750 the idea of a new "interpretation of nature" caught hold of the imaginations and engaged the serious attention of some of the most important thinkers of the Enlightenment. Buffon, the author of the brilliantly written and comprehensive *Natural History* (1750–70), had begun a scientific career as a student of Newton's physics and translated the *Fluxions,* but he was interested particularly in the phenomena of life and when he proceeded to interpret and organize the data of natural history he realized the insufficiency of the "mechanical" conception of nature. One should not use unguardedly the inductive rule of reasoning so well described by Newton in the third part of his *Principia* ("Rules for Reasoning in Natural Philosophy"), that of judging the whole by those parts of which we have had experience, for, Buffon said, "on observing closely one perceives that its [nature's] course is not absolutely uniform; one recognizes that it admits of sensible variations . . . mutations of matter and form . . ." [51] Contemporary with Buffon was the more speculative Maupertuis who suggested the "principle of least action" in physics, a man of whom the philosopher Hume (who had independently questioned the very logical foundation of that principle of the uniformity of nature which underlay inductive reasoning) [52] spoke with great admiration: [53] "It was especially Maupertuis who brought Leibniz to France," said Cassirer.[54] And Maupertuis likewise perceived the unsuitability of Newton's rule of reasoning for the understanding and interpretation of organic life. Most influential of all in developing the new philosophy of nature was Diderot, chief editor of the great *Encyclopedia* who published his *Thoughts on the Interpretation of Nature* in 1754 and who dwelt on the "mutation of matter and form" and on the fact that "this infinitely changeable universe can only be understood by means of a flexible manner of thinking." And it is Diderot's eminent contribution to the whole development that "he changes the very forms of thought which had made [previous] achievements possible and given them permanence." [55]

51. Buffon, *Histoire naturelle* (1750), 9, 455. For more extensive comment and translation see C. W. Hendel, "The Status of Mind in Reality," *Journal of Philosophy, 31,* No. 9 (April 26, 1934), 225 ff. For Cassirer's own observations on Buffon see *Philosophy of the Enlightenment,* pp. 35, 77 ff.

52. This was Hume's basic question and "discovery" in philosophy. See his later preoccupation (in the *Dialogues concerning Natural Religion,* Pt. VI to end) with the phenomena of organic nature. Hume knew Buffon, Maupertuis, and Diderot when he lived in Paris.

53. See *Letters of David Hume,* edited by J. Y. T. Greig (Oxford, Clarendon Press, 1932), *1,* 227 (To Abbé Le Blanc).

54. Cassirer, *Philosophy of the Enlightenment,* p. 86 ff. See also pp. 34–35, 55.

55. Ibid., pp. 90, 92.

SHAFTESBURY. In such new suggestions of "the mind of the Enlightenment" a "philosophy of form" is adumbrated. Moreover, Cassirer with his rich knowledge of the various developments occurring in a historical period was able to discern the remarkable affiliation of the new philosophy of organic form with a philosophy of aesthetics coming to the fore in the work of Shaftesbury. What Cassirer had in mind is shown in the following: that "Shaftesbury's purpose is so to state his concept of form that its intellectual, supersensible origin will be recognisable, retaining, however, the purely intuitive aspect of this concept." [56] And Shaftesbury, Cassirer goes on to say, had a "decisive influence" upon later German thought, particularly that of Herder and the early Goethe.[57]

Kant's Signal Contribution to the Development of Eighteenth-Century Thought in This Realm

Such were the characteristic "cultural developments of the eighteenth century" not only in Germany but also throughout all Europe. And Cassirer regarded Kant's *Critique of Judgment* as fundamentally related to this movement of thought of a whole epoch. Let us consider, now, Kant's contribution to the philosophy of nature which had started with interpretations of "natural history" and was to develop in the next century into a philosophy of biological science.

In the *Problem of Knowledge,* completed about 1940, Cassirer declared that "The *Critique of Judgment* marked a decisive break when it asserted the autonomy and the methodological independence of biology without giving up its connection with mathematical physics. Herewith there was posed a new question, which biological research, no matter what its school or trend, could not in the future neglect." [58] Now in a sense the break had been made previously by Buffon, Maupertuis, and Diderot nearly half a century earlier, all of whom at least had asserted the "methodological independence" of the mechanistic view of nature. The real break which Cassirer had in mind was internal to Kant's own thinking, like that which had occurred on other occasions as when Hume had "roused him from his

56. Ibid., p. 84.
57. Ibid., p. 85.
58. *Problem of Knowledge*, p. 118.

dogmatic slumber" or when Rousseau convinced him of the primacy of moral values. In the present case Kant had been holding to a conviction "that in any particular theory there was only as much real science as there was mathematics." [59] But he recognized the fact that an autonomous biological science was in the making, thanks to a new method of research and interpretation advanced by such men as Buffon, Maupertuis, and Diderot. As a "critical" philosopher he had to address himself to "the fact" of knowledge in whatever guise it appeared. Now what the new adventures in natural history and science were in fact doing was really to bring back the notion of purpose, not in the old sense of "final causes" which early modern science and philosophy had eschewed to the profit of the science of nature as well as philosophy, but in a new sense. Hence the basic question was "what sort of methodological value may be ascribed to the concept of purpose." And Kant in his own thinking

> asked simply whether it was possible and rational, at one and the same time, to conceive of phenomena as obedient to natural law, that is, to refer them to the universal dynamic principle of causality, and to regard them also from the point of view of purpose and organize and arrange them accordingly. The *Critique of Judgment* aims to prove that there is no antinomy whatsoever between these two *forms of order* in knowledge. . . . Causality has to do with knowledge of the objective temporal succession of events, the order in change, whereas the concept of purpose has to do with the *structure* of those empirical objects that are called living organisms. . . . Biology . . . considers nature under the aspect of a whole so formed that it determines the properties of its various parts. Then nature ceases to be a mere aggregate and becomes a system.[60]

"Kant limited the concept of purpose to this role of taking *cognizance* of nature, which must be distinguished from mathematical knowledge of it," and Cassirer quotes Kant directly: " 'The concept of purposive combinations and forms in nature is at least, then, *one principle more* for bringing the appearances under rules, where the laws of mechanistic causality do not suffice.' " [61] Thus "we must always make the presupposition that

59. Ibid.
60. Ibid., p. 121 (Cassirer's italics).
61. Ibid., p. 122.

nature as a whole not only behaves according to law, but also discloses a thoroughgoing organization in all details as well . . ." [62]

This "principle of formal purposiveness" is an a priori principle necessary for the knowledge of nature but it is still only "regulative" for the knowing, and not essentially "constitutive" of the known, the appearances or the phenomena.

Cassirer's Advance upon Kant

It should be noted later in this same work, the *Problem of Knowledge*, that the cautious position of Kant is called an *"attempted* solution of the antinomy of judgment." Kant "could dwell on the special rights and value of biology but could not assign it the same rank or the same objective value in the hierarchy of knowledge as mathematical and physical knowledge." He had misgivings about that but—and here Cassirer speaks for himself— "Such misgivings exist no longer." [63]

Cassirer believes that he is still faithful to the Kantian orientation and method when he takes the next step, which is to obliterate the distinction between "regulative" and "constitutive" principles. Nature, according to the critical view, is that structure of empirical reality which is conformable with the specific ways of knowing of the human understanding. If, then, phenomena of nature are actually understood and known in accordance with this organic conception of the whole as determining the properties and functions of the parts, then the character of organic form is as constitutive of nature in respect to life as causal order is in the case of physical science. Thus Cassirer has no hesitation in speaking of the "natural forms" with which biology deals.[64] It was not Kant's "attempted solution" then that was so significant for the future development of philosophy but the sheer fact that he made the problem of "form" all-important. In

62. Ibid., pp. 125–126.
63. Ibid., p. 211.
64. *Kants Leben*, pp. 369–370. In the *Problem of Knowledge*, Pt. II, Cassirer begins his study of biological knowledge with a chapter treating of the problem about the classification and systematization of "Natural Forms"—there is no question about their existence or the validity of the concept.

his attempt to solve this problem Kant was limited by the undeveloped state of biological science in his time. He "spoke as the *logician* of Linnaeus' descriptive science, just as . . . he had appeared as logician for the Newtonian system. He tracked down the hidden problem contained in Linnaeus' work." [65] That "problem of form" became the problem of knowledge in the subsequent century and, in Cassirer's opinion, it remains the essential problem today. "In this respect," he claims for his master, "Kant stood nearer to modern biology than he did to that of his own day . . . 'form-concepts' . . . must be retained." [66]

The Continuing Relevance of Kant's Emphasis on Form to Theoretical Biology in the Nineteenth and Twentieth Centuries

It is advisable to note in Cassirer's account of the later nineteenth- and twentieth-century developments in biological theory what he actually says in substantiation of his claim that Kant's philosophy is thus closely relevant. Our intention is not to trace out the far-flung ramification of the thought of Kant but to see what Cassirer himself saw there and related to the central inspiration of his own thinking.

When Cassirer concludes his chapter on "Developmental Mechanics and the Problem of Cause," he singles out the Kantian idea of form as the essential thought in the theory of Roux: "Developing organisms are, in substance, 'self-contained complexes of activities that are determining and productive of form . . .'" [67] Again, in dismissing the topic "vitalism" Cassirer says that "the theoretical biology of the past decade has begun to define the method and the goal with ever increasing clarity. Here we encounter chiefly the idea of 'wholeness' as a special category of biological knowledge." [68] More recently still Emil Ungerer urged that though much might be said against the metaphysical idea of purpose, nevertheless, "that character of maintaining wholeness *has* significance in the *realm of life* itself." [69] And Cassirer adds for his own part: "All this is in the Kantian

65. *Problem of Knowledge,* p. 127 (Cassirer's italics).
66. Ibid., p. 210
67. Ibid., p. 187 (quoting from Roux).
68. Ibid., p. 212.
69. Ibid., p. 213 (Cassirer's italics).

manner and leans on the *Critique of Judgment,* which Ungerer minutely analyzed in a work of his own, comparing the *Critique* with the results of modern biology. He arrived at the conclusion that the latest phase of biology more than any other prior to it has brought into currency the fundamental view which Kant had advocated." [70] Finally the contemporary Bertalanffy is quoted directly on this theme, declaring: " 'That phenomena in the organism are chiefly "whole-forming" or "system-forming" in character and that it is the task of biology to establish whether and to what extent they are so can hardly be a matter of dispute.' " [71]

As a student of modern biological science Cassirer held that the character of "whole-forming" or "system-forming" pertains to the world itself of living nature. "Form" in this case is no longer a regulative idea but a genuinely constitutive principle, no less original and valid than the intuitive forms of space and time and the intellectual forms or categories of understanding. The barriers had fallen down between the views of organic nature and empirical physical reality. There may be realms or different orders within the whole of what we call the Universe, but the acknowledgment of these "universes of discourse" does not involve us in an antinomy or conflict of reason. We have seen another case of the role of form in "making" nature—perhaps there are other cases and other realms where form is disclosed as an essential character of the experience and life of man.

Pure Concrete Forms and the Realm of Art

"The artist is just as much a discoverer of the forms of nature as the scientist is a discoverer of facts or natural laws." In that statement from the *Essay on Man* [72] one sees the connection in Cassirer's own thinking between the theme of art as human self-expression and the theme of organic life. In art man is the "maker" in a perfectly unmistakable sense, for culture is his own production and yet it is a discovery, too, of "forms of nature.' There is no gulf then between Nature and Culture—in respect to forms.

70. Ibid., p. 214.
71. Ibid., p. 215.
72. *Essay,* pp. 143–144.

Goethe

The movement of Cassirer's thought from a "critique of reason" to a "critique of culture" [73] is one of the most interesting aspects of his developing philosophy. It is foreshadowed in his earlier study of Kant relating the "cognizance" of organic nature to the aesthetic judgment. We noted, too, in Cassirer's study of the Enlightenment how Shaftesbury's aesthetic of form was brought into close relation with Leibniz' conception of form. But before Cassirer's own concept of form would be complete, the magic of Goethe's imagination had to weave its spell, revealing the inexhaustible significance, too, of Kant's notion of the schema, that union of the sensuous-intuitive and the intellectual concept. For the *Critique of Judgment* seemed to Cassirer an inevitable sequel to the other *Critiques* and in it were explored these great problems of the systematization of empirical physical science, the reality of purpose in nature and the peculiar character of art as being both human expression and revelation of reality. How Cassirer explored this last theme still remains to be studied.

The importance of Goethe to Cassirer cannot be overestimated. There was an "elective affinity" between them and a strange bond between Goethe himself and Kant through the medium of the *Critique of Judgment*. Goethe testified to this in words quoted by Cassirer:

> "Here I saw my most disparate preoccupations placed alongside one another, art and the works of nature dealt with as on a par, the aesthetic and the teleological judgments mutually illuminating each other. . . . I rejoiced to learn that the art of poesy and the science of nature with its comparative method are closely related, both of them coming under one and the same power of judgment." [74]

Perhaps Cassirer himself learned to read Kant's *Critique of Judgment* through the poetic imagination of Goethe.

It is the poet of *Dauer und Wechsel* who is recalled in Cassirer's words about Goethe's way of thought being exemplified in his biological theory of metamorphosis.

> In the connection and indissoluble correlation between permanence and change he sought the distinguishing characteristic of the "ideal way

73. See below, p. 76.
74. *Kants Leben*, p. 292.

of thinking," which he himself had adopted and which he contrasted sharply with the analytical method . . . The "ideal mode" of thought . . . is that which allows the "eternal to be seen in the transitory," and he said that through it we should be raised gradually to the proper viewpoint, "where human understanding and philosophy are one." . . . This peculiar intermingling of being and becoming, of permanence and change, was comprehended in the concept of form, which became for Goethe the fundamental biological concept.[75]

Form, in Goethe's conception of it, as relevant to living beings and their metamorphoses, has a peculiar characteristic. If one thinks of form one ordinarily has in mind a spatial or geometrical pattern which is illustrated in various examples that are the changes as it were upon the essence. This is static form. But Cassirer explains:

> Form belongs not only to space but to time as well, and it must assert itself in the temporal. . . . It is remarkable how everything developed logically and consistently from this one original and basic concept of Goethe.[76]

One may now recall that Kant's schema, too, is a form involved in time and that the further problem of the *Critique of Judgment* concerned that combination of sensuous intuition and the intellectual form. Cassirer also notes how Goethe appropriated a term used by Spinoza "intuitive knowing" and gave it an entirely new meaning to suit his own purposes.[77] In Spinoza "intuitive knowledge" is God's prerogative, but Goethe makes it available to man. It is thanks to this "intuitive understanding" which is tantamount to "genius" that man can apprehend the truth about nature and the life-forms.

And this accords well with the theory of aesthetic "genius" which Kant had developed. Cassirer credited Shaftesbury originally with the new conception of genius as the "productive, formative, creative" agency in art— a conception which directly influenced German intellectual history in the eighteenth century, "and notably Lessing and Kant." [78] Here, too, is " 'a purposive activity . . . a self-maintaining activity, and one which further

75. *Problem of Knowledge*, pp. 138–139.
76. Ibid., pp. 139–140.
77. Ibid., p. 141. See also the reference to Plotinus in *Kants Leben*, as well as to Spinoza, pp. 299, 373–376, and *Das Erkenntnisproblem, 3,* 15–16.
78. *Philosophy of the Enlightenment*, pp. 318–319.

strengthens those very powers of mind themselves.'" [79] Thus the aesthetic
activity in man and the teleological formation in nature are assimilated to
each other exactly as Goethe had said. And another sort of unity is disclosed here, a rapport between man and nature, both exhibiting the same
form-giving character and mutually expressing each other's meanings,
art in nature, nature in art. It is in Goethe's thought about genius, as that
which sees connections and unity in diversity, that Cassirer finds the fulfillment of Kant's intention, the "indissoluble correlation" not only of permanence and change but also of man and nature, form and content, intuition and intelligence. The nub of the matter is in this tribute to Goethe:

> There prevails in his writings a relationship of the "particular" to the
> "universal" such as can hardly be found elsewhere in the history of phi-
> losophy or of natural science . . . the particular and the universal are
> not only intimately connected but . . . they interpenetrate one another.
> The "factual" and the "theoretical" were not opposite poles to him, . . .
> "The highest thing would be . . . to realize everything factual as being
> itself theoretical." [80]

This thought of Goethe, the realization of the ideal in fact and the actuality of idea, is identical with what Kant had first pointed out in the "schema"
of empirical knowledge and then explored further in his discussion of purpose and art in the *Critique of Judgment* which Goethe liked so well.[81]
When Cassirer prepares the reader of his *Essay on Man* for the second
part treating of "Man and Culture," he chooses Goethe's language for the
title of his chapter, "Facts and Ideals."

Hegel

Inevitably the language and the project foreshadowed in this view of
Goethe remind one of Hegel: the Ideal is Actual and the Actual is Ideal.

79. *Problem of Knowledge*, p. 143 (quoting Kant), *Critique of Judgment*, Sec. 49.

80. *Problem of Knowledge*, p. 145 (quotation from Goethe's *Maximen und Reflexionen*,
No. 575).

81. Cassirer's view of the epochal importance of the *Critique of Judgment* should be recalled at this place—notably in *Kants Leben und Lehre* and in the opening section of the
third volume of *Das Erkenntnisproblem*. See above, pp. 14–15 and 21 ff.

The Hegel of the *Phenomenology of the Spirit* especially portrays man moving of necessity, in a dialectical manner, toward that goal of the identity of the factual and the theoretical. And Cassirer sees Hegel in this respect following out the thought of Kant toward the universal as the system that expresses the truth of the particulars, the "concrete universal" as it was called. Hegel, too, was moving under the spell of Goethe no less than following the argument of Kant or Schelling. It is organic nature that properly answers to man's quest, where spirit in man finds an objective manifestation that is akin to it and revelatory of it. The "world of understanding" is but a world of law, the physical world, but there is a realm of life in which the forms themselves become transformed and where we cannot think simply of absolute law and mechanical structure but must conceive of changing form that interprets temporal change. The organic order is abo the mathematical-physical order and it is a dialectical stage toward the completely spiritual order of existence. From sense perception to physical science, to biological knowledge, to the cultural expressions of spirit in art and in the ethical life, philosophy and religion—the dialectic carries one onward irresistibly toward that "highest thing" of Goethe, that absolute identity in and including difference, the concrete realization of spirit.[82]

What is the difference then between Cassirer and Hegel? It will help to define the philosophy of the former if we consider this question.

There is an obvious difference in respect of temper and spirit. Hegel unites in a remarkable way an enthusiasm and conviction with elaborate, subtle, rational argument. He is not merely rationalizing but discovering as he goes, and he carries the reader who can follow his inventions of language with him in an exciting adventure. But he *arrives—he* touches the goal of absolute knowledge, journey's end: the system of the spirit is complete. An inexhaustible enthusiasm, too, is ever present in Cassirer but it is as an undercurrent of his lifework, keeping him patiently studying the *Factum,* what has actually been achieved *by mankind,* the history, the culture, the art, religion, science, and many things besides which condition such achievements but which have little or no merit in the eyes of civilized man who appropriates the useful form of his cultural heritage but fails to appreciate the role of such things as myth and even of language, tending to regard the latter, for example, as only a medium for expressing something that exists beforehand and not realizing that language is formative of the very world we live in. Cassirer studies these phenomena of the spirit

82. See *Das Erkenntnisproblem, 3,* 291.

in situ, so to speak, and really seeks to find the form in each set of contents as an artist tends to appreciate the character of the material which he is to make expressive of a meaning. The striking difference between Cassirer and Hegel is symbolized in the phrase used above—Cassirer wants to *discover* the actual forms so far realized by man, whereas Hegel gives the impression that he knows it all. The very structure of Cassirer's book on *Symbolic Forms* shows that he believed himself only started on a program and that there was no end to the task because no one can determine the limits of the spirit and life itself. His book came out in parts—Part I, Language; Part II, Myth and Religion; Part III, Science—and additional parts were to be expected as one progressed far enough in the quest for truth. Cassirer's attitude is in essence that the philosopher has "an unending task" never to be regarded as complete.[83] The Ideal remains ideal and is not all made factual. This is Kantian in tone and meaning, and Cassirer when he compares Kant and Hegel gives us the best possible characterization of what philosophy meant to himself in contradistinction from Hegel. "Philosophy is not content [in Hegel] to reveal and make intelligible each distinctive and ideal formative principle obtaining in the various cultural forms: science, morality, religion, art; it superposes its own deliverances upon all of them as a higher and all-embracing form . . ." The fault here "is that philosophy deprives them of their autonomous and independent value and subordinates them to its own systematic purpose. Here is the point of contrast with Kant. . . ."[84]

There are, however, significant and illuminating points of agreement between Cassirer and Hegel. Both eschew further talk about "things in themselves" as if there could be something intelligible transcendent to the phenomena. Keep the unknown out of it; stick to the known and the knowable. Thus both thinkers prize rationality but they also conceive of reason as not at all separate from sensuous intuition. Hegel's logic, Cassirer declares appreciatively, is "the logic of intuitive understanding." And the "form of thinking," he continues, is rightly discerned to be that of proceeding "not from the parts to the whole but from the whole to the parts."[85]

It is reasonable to suppose from these commendatory words that Cassirer learned much from Hegel and that he realized his own position through

83. *Das Erkenntnisproblem, 3,* 369–370.
84. Ibid., p. 372.
85. Ibid., pp. 364–365.

a characteristically patient study of his work. Surely the memory of Hegel echoes in these words of the *Essay on Man:* "Our objective is a *phenomenology of human culture.*" The very words define his own position over against that of the "phenomenology of the Spirit." [86]

3. TOWARD THE DEVELOPMENT OF A PHENOMENOLOGY OF CULTURE

This development of Cassirer's thought into a phenomenology of culture was dictated in part by his artistic nature and interests. Sensitive to poetry and the fine arts, gifted in the understanding and effective use of various languages, humanist in spirit, he could hardly do otherwise than extend his view to these characteristic manifestations of human genius and thus move toward an even more comprehensive philosophy of form.

Besides the artistic Cassirer there was the historical-minded Cassirer. For he had a particular genius of his own which also led him toward such an ampler philosophy. This was the historical genius, the power of imagination that brings the forms and ways of human existence of the past into life again, effecting a "resurrection of the past," he called it when in an eloquent passage on the meaning of history he rendered a tribute to Herder which is fully deserved by Cassirer himself.[87] He had precisely such gifts and he employed them wonderfully well. In consequence whenever he treats of the various forms of human achievement and self-expression he presents them in a historical dimension that imparts depth and richness to his portrayal. "In order to possess the world of culture we must incessantly reconquer it by historical recollection." [88] He sought to possess that world. And his successful reconquest through "historical recollection" is a matter of record in his various studies of ancient culture and of the culture of the Renaissance as well as the eighteenth century. He made these

---

86. *Essay,* p. 52 (author's italics). The pertinence of Hegel's *Phenomenology of the Spirit* is emphasized in the essays in *The Philosophy of Ernst Cassirer* by Felix Kaufmann, p. 188; Robert S. Hartman, pp. 306, 310; M. F. Ashley Montagu, p. 376; W. M. Urban, pp. 421, 435; Helmut Kuhn, p. 571; Harry Slochower, p. 642; Walter M. Solmitz, p. 756; Fritz Kaufmann, p. 825; in Cassirer's " 'Spirit' and 'Life' in Contemporary Philosophy," ibid., p. 875; and the third volume of *Philosophie der symbolischen Formen,* Vorrede, vii.

87. *Essay,* p. 177.

88. Ibid., p. 185.

epochs live again in the present and included them in his vision of human existence.

The New Historical Point of View: Its Discoverers, Herder and Montesquieu

Cassirer's approach to the study of the phenomena of culture was made by way of history. He tells us plainly who was his guide—Herder who was very early one of his "rich sources of inspiration." All his life thereafter Cassirer paid his grateful homage to Herder. He regarded Herder's essay *Auch eine Philosophie der Geschichte zur Bildung der Menschheit* as a great pioneer work in the new art and science of history that was to flourish in the coming nineteenth century.[89] For "Herder definitely broke the spell of analytical thinking and of the principle of identity." [90] And "Herder's achievement is in fact one of the greatest intellectual triumphs of the philosophy of the Enlightenment" [91] (1932). Again in the last volume of the *Problem of Knowledge* [92] (1940), Cassirer ends his account of history with an endorsement of Friedrich Meinecke's view attributing the new direction to the genius of "the young Herder." [93]

What was this new direction? We may treat this question after the fashion of Cassirer himself *in more historico*. For Herder's insight was not wholly and absolutely new but the outcome itself of a considerable ferment of thought about the nature of history. A fresh interest in the subject had developed with the empirical turn of thought that gained ascendency in eighteenth-century Europe. Previously the older rationalistic ideal of knowledge had led to a relative disparagement of history because it had to do with so much that seemed utterly contingent and accidental. There could be no necessary truths in that sphere. But in spite of that inferiority of history as compared with science and metaphysics the human interest in it was very great. This was especially the case in matters political

89. Ibid., p. 177.
90. *Philosophy of the Enlightenment*, p. 231.
91. Ibid., p. 233.
92. Chap. 12, "The Rise of Historicism: Herder," pp. 217 ff.
93. Ibid., p. 225.

and social at a time when criticism of the existing forms of government was rife and men were wondering how human affairs had come to such a pass and what they themselves could do about the existing state of things. They devised a history of civilization by postulating an original "state of nature" and then tracing the rise or the fall of man from the original condition to that in which they found themselves. But they were more interested in the principles they could learn for their own guidance and practice than in what actually happened. Theirs was unhistorical history. This had been the case with Grotius, Hobbes, Locke, and Rousseau. In a sense it was partly true even of the empirical-minded Hume. Thucydides, Polybius, Machiavelli had been his models and yet Hume's essential interest like theirs was in the utility of history. He studied historically in order to learn some general truths of politics, economics, morals, the arts and sciences, and religion, all of which, as expressions of man's interest and life, threw valuable light upon the subject of "human nature." Thus in Hume the historical interest which was very real was still subordinate to the concern of the "moral philosopher."

But Hume was an interesting case of a man at a critical juncture in the progress of both philosophy and history. For he had discovered that no rational "demonstration" of any matter of fact is possible, or, to put it otherwise, that any inference to the existence of some event remote from the present, whether it be of something in the past or in the future, is *logically* without warrant from reason. Precisely because of that lack of reason which cannot guarantee the necessity of any belief as to fact or existence Hume saw an obligation to do thoroughgoing research for empirical evidence— and that meant historical research as well as the research in natural science. Men like Hume were thus led to explore the historical world with the same zest as once the humanists of the Renaissance explored the art, literature, and philosophy of the classical world.

Montesquieu

The first great inspiration in this field of historical study was Montesquieu. He was a genuine innovator. His *Greatness and Decline and Rome,* his

Persian Letters, and notably his last work, the *Spirit of the Laws* (1749), developed a new method and theory of history in the course of writing a history of institutions. On the score of method he warned those who worked in history against the inveterate "habit of mind" (as Hume called it) of expecting the uniform repetition elsewhere of any observed conjunction of circumstances in the present. "To transfer into far-off centuries all the ideas of the century in which one is living is the most fecund of all sources of error." [94] Montesquieu was interested in the fundamental laws or constitutions of political and social systems and he had the same moral concern as his contemporaries about the present plight of European society ruled by monarchies, but though he had a republican ideal he did not write in order to recommend it as an ideal but really searched for the "spirit" of each known system of government whether it be in the present or the past. He felt it abso ely necessary to visit various countries in Europe to study the actual working of their institutions, notably England where he spent two years. In regard to the past he searched for the facts of actual record. But he differed from most of those who ransacked the records in not taking his story from them, not even from a Thucydides or Polybius or Machiavelli. They were all interpreters and each historian must be his own interpreter in performing the role of seeing all the facts in relation to each other and in some kind of unity. This synthesis calls for imagination. Yet it has to be an imagination of what actually existed, not an illustration of a preconceived thesis of the historian. Thus each nation's laws should be studied in the total situation of time, place, and circumstance and by reference to what the people thought, felt, and believed about themselves and their world. "Many things govern men: climate, religion, laws, maxims of government, the examples of the past, morals, manners—whence there is formed a resultant general spirit of the nation." [95]

This thought of "a general spirit of the nation" was destined not long afterward to take wings. In Montesquieu it is still close to earth. This spirit of the nation or the spirit of its laws is a unity that emerges from a congeries of particulars and manifests itself in a form of government or constitution. Montesquieu limited himself to those determinate *political* forms

94. Montesquieu, *De l'Esprit des lois,* Oeuvres complètes (Paris, 1866), Bk. 1, Chap. 2, p. 191; Bk. 30, Chap. 14, p. 488. For a discussion of the common trend away from the mechanical conception of nature and toward the biological and historical in the thought of Hume, Buffon, and Montesquieu see C. W. Hendel, "The Status of Mind," *Journal of Philosophy, 31,* No. 9 (April 26, 1934), 228 ff.

95. Montesquieu, *op. cit.,* Bk. 19, Chap. 4.

that express each in its own destinctive way the spirit of each particular nation.[96]

Cassirer wrote pages of appreciation of Montesquieu and concluded with these words of high praise: "Of all the thinkers of his circle he has the most profound historical sense, the purest intuition of the manifold forms of historical phenomena." He noted, too, that while Herder attacked Montesquieu's method and his "premises," nevertheless he had "admired his 'noble gigantic work' . . ."[97]

Herder, "the Copernicus of History"

But Herder was the true genius who had "the clearest insight" into an even larger historical task of synthesis and shaping *disjecta membra* of the past into a living whole which will have meaning to the present.[98] Cassirer quotes a vivid passage from his favorite essay of Herder, *Another Philosophy of History for the Education of Humanity:* " 'I cannot persuade myself that anything in all the kingdom of God is only a mere means; all is at once means and end.' " That is a transference of Kant's "kingdom of ends" to the world of men. In such a world " 'every nation has its center of felicity in itself alone, as every sphere has its center of gravity. . . . Is not the good distributed throughout the whole world? Simply because no one form of humanity and no one spot of earth could contain it all, it was divided into a thousand forms, transformed—an eternal Proteus!—in every region of the world and in every century . . . and yet a plan of striving forward is always visible—my great theme.' "[99]

Enthusiasm and youthful dreams are in these words; and Cassirer as if in long-lingering sympathy saw fit to recall a still more intimate account of the magnificent intentions of Herder: " 'If I could venture to be a philosopher,' " Herder had written in his diary in 1769, " 'my book would be . . . living logic, aesthetics, history, and art! Develop a splendid art

96. See C. W. Hendel, Chap. "The Role of Philosophy in Civilization," in *Philosophy in American Education* (New York, Harper, 1945), pp. 182–184.

97. *Philosophy of the Enlightenment*, pp. 215–216. See the whole account of Montesquieu, pp. 209 ff.

98. *Essay*, p. 177.

99. *Problem of Knowledge*, pp. 221–222.

from every sense! Draw a science from every faculty of the mind! And make of them all a history of learning and science in general! And a history of the human spirit in general, throughout the ages and in all peoples! What a book!' " [100]

These eloquent passages reveal what Herder meant to Cassirer. His own first piece of philosophical work had been a study of Leibniz in whose philosophy he first saw the new conception of synthesis. As he later expressed it, "the new whole is organic, not mechanical: its nature does not consist in the sum of its parts but is presupposed by its parts and constitutes the condition of the possibility of their nature and being." In this thought of Leibniz, Cassirer went on to say, "the rigid concept of form . . . breaks down." [101] And Herder's "metaphysics of history is based on Leibniz's central doctrine." [102]

Herder united in his own thought, then, the joint influences of Leibniz and Kant who were so important likewise to Cassirer himself. As a fellow pupil separated as it were only by time and space, Cassirer felt a great partiality for Herder. Thus he commented on the undue severity of Kant, who had been Herder's teacher, for his two critical reviews of that essay of Herder on the philosophy of history, and he vindicated the younger man as a "philosopher-poet" who should be treated as such and not held to "rigor of proof." [103]

And Herder and that other poet Goethe had an affinity for each other, too, which gratified and inspired Cassirer, who quotes the enthusiastic letter Goethe had sent to Herder upon the perusal of his books: I "have regaled myself with them. God knows how you make one feel the reality of that world! A compost heap teeming with life! . . . Your way of gathering gold, not by just sifting it out of the dirt but by having the dirt itself brought to life again in the form of plants, is ever close to my heart." [104]

But the "books" here mentioned were not that work dreamed of in Herder's youth, the work which was to be a "living logic, aesthetic, history and art." The book was never written but the dream was to be Cassirer's own dream for years which he turned into a reality in the *Philosophy of Symbolic Forms*. And the congeniality of his own mind with that of Herder, together with his long-enduring admiration of his imaginative predecessor,

100. Ibid., p. 220.
101. *Philosophy of the Enlightenment*, pp. 31, 34.
102. Ibid., pp. 230–231. See also above, p. 23, and *Problem of Knowledge*, pp. 203–204.
103. *Kants Leben*, pp. 243–245.
104. *Problem of Knowledge*, p. 219.

evoked at last the characterization which places Herder in a seat of honor alongside of the master Kant, for Cassirer writes that "Herder may be called the Copernicus of history." [105]

Problems about the "History of the Human Spirit"

The Ranking of Logic with other Forms of the Spirit

How could Cassirer who held so tenaciously to the Kantian "critique of reason" have any traffic with Herder's notion of a "living logic," etc.? Could he abide a ranking of logic with aesthetics, history, and art when "transcendental logic" had been as fundamental to his own philosophy as it had been to that of Kant? If the forms of art and other forms of the cultural expression of man are to be assimilated with the "constitutive" forms of knowledge and experience, how can it be done except at the cost of lowering logic itself to the status of being simply an expression of man's subjectivity? This Cassirer would never do and his philosophy emerged out of his long struggle with this problem, always in an endeavor, it seems, to reconcile the disparate inspiration of his own thinking, the two Copernicuses, the one of philosophy, the other of history.

The Problem of the Ordering of Herder's Thousand Protean Forms and the Rejection of a Solution in National Terms

Another question had to have immediate attention before Cassirer could make any progress. It was not a question about the relation of the thought of Kant and that of Herder but lay entirely within the circle, so to speak, of Herder's philosophy of history. It was the problem created by Herder's generous figure of "a thousand Protean forms" of the spirit. This was a most unmanageable number for a philosophic mind which must seek order

105. Ibid., p. 218.

and unity in such a manifold—in art, history, religion, science, logic, and philosophy itself.

There was one tempting suggestion of a solution that was implicit in the passage where Herder imagined every nation as a sphere having its own center of gravity and being self-contained. The desired unity and organization might thus be national, with all the phenomena envisaged as the expression of the spirit of a nation. Previously Montesquieu, as we have seen, had introduced the idea of a national spirit in connection with the laws and constitution—and Hume had partly followed him in his own historical writing. Why not, then, treat all the phenomena, not only laws but also art, morals, history itself, as forms of the national spirit? Now as a matter of fact, Herder himself had no such "nationalist" point of view. While he was interested in and appreciative of the individuality of nations, laws, morals, systems of society, and beliefs, his goal was "a history of the human spirit in general." The influence of Herder then would never lead Cassirer to take a "national" approach to the solution of his problem. And Cassirer's great tribute to Lessing, whom he linked with Herder as he closed his account of the Enlightenment, is ample evidence of his own attitude, for Lessing was pre-eminent in judging all human affairs in terms of a universal perspective.[106]

Cassirer also had the warning example of Hegel before him. Hegel like Herder had been deeply impressed by Montesquieu, and in his own *Philosophy of Right* he developed the notion of the national constitution as the "concrete" realization of the spirit. Further he had demonstrated a phenomenology and dialectic of the spirit throughout universal history in his introduction to the *Philosophy of History*. But Cassirer eschewed Hegel's philosophy for the following explicit reason: "If philosophy is to be the authentic and complete consciousness which Spirit has of itself . . . it must truly grasp everything within itself, all creative spiritual achievement in the whole of 'objective spirit' as it presents itself in religion and in art, morality, law, in science and in the state. Philosophy must not limit itself only to designating the conditions of the culture of spirit but must possess itself of its entire content in the form of thought." [107] "On this view," Cassirer continues, "it follows that philosophy provides the foundation for the other culture-forms only in the sense that it forthwith dispenses with them and takes from them their own autonomous and in-

106. *Philosophy of the Enlightenment*, pp. 357 ff.
107. "Critical and Absolute Idealism," *Das Erkenntnisproblem, 3,* 365.

dependent worth and all this is done to make them subservient to its own systematic purpose. . . . The task of the critical philosophy, on the contrary, is to show the unity of reason precisely in the different basic lines along which the world is constructed and formed in its scientific, artistic, moral and religious aspects." [108] That was Cassirer's choice, the way of a Kantian, not Hegel's way.

The Hypothesis of Cultural Forms and the New Varieties of Form It Suggested

The concept of "culture-forms" provides the solution for the problem of Herder's "history of the human spirit in general." Those myriad expressions and activities of the protean human spirit must somehow be ordered through some principle or set of principles. National unity as a principle is rejected as well as Hegel's philosophy which makes all things merely phenomena of philosophy as if philosophy were not only a manifestation of spirit but the essential and complete manifestation thereof. What now appears as the true principle of organization for a phenomenology of spirit is the various culture-forms themselves. They are types of creative activity and expression. As types they maintain themselves through time and manifest themselves variously in many places. The type in this case is not to be thought of as a "substantial" thing but rather as a "function" of the human spirit. The universal function of art, for instance, is the same in an ancient and in a modern civilization and not only for man in the civilized condition but in prehistory as well. It is a human function and it persists in the history of mankind. Self-expression in art is thus recognizable *as* art and not as something else in many different modes of expression of different peoples of the world. And there is a permanence and a continuity of every such cultural form not only in art but also in religion, science, morality.

The concept of typical "function" was thus a key to the solution of the problems confronting Cassirer. It not only enabled him to organize the "thousand Protean forms" in accordance with a principle but, as any good theoretical concept would do, it disclosed a wider range of data or facts

108. Ibid., pp. 372–373.

to be taken into the reckoning. The types of cultural forms of art, history, religion, and science are all quite familiar to man already civilized and living in the state. But "long before man had discovered this form of social organization," the civilized state, Cassirer reminds us, man "had made other attempts to organize his feelings, desires, and thoughts. Such organizations and systematizations are contained in language, in myth, in religion, and in art." [109] Moreover, we must also remember that "Man lived in an objective world long before he lived in a scientific world." [110] We must have imagination enough to include in our study of cultural forms the prescientific and precivilized manifestations of man's genius. And Cassirer tells us in that same work that "The philosophy of symbolic forms starts from the presupposition" that the nature of man is defined by his work. "It is this work, it is the system of human activities, which defines and determines the circle of 'humanity.'" [111]

New fields for exploration thus appeared. There is the universe of myth, for example, to which the philosopher Schelling had drawn attention, and there is also magic. Are these phenomena of man to be regarded as merely primitive, as imperfect versions of forms which supplant them in the rational and civilized mode of existence—magic giving up the ghost as it were to science, and myth passing into religion? Or are these genuine autonomous forms? Has myth a discoverable function and logic of its own? [112] How are we to explain the persistence of the mythical consciousness even in highly developed civilization and culture? Myth may perhaps have a permanent use and value.

What shall we say, too, of language? It is another function of human existence wherever man is found. It may be too much taken for granted, being the means by which men live, work, and communicate with each other. But language is an art and through it men disclose meanings to each other. They even discover themselves to themselves through it. That philosopher-poet of antiquity Plato had compared thought itself to a conversation within the soul, and he regarded language as a subject worthy of the philosopher's inquiry, as his Seventh Letter and the dialogue *Cratylus* witness. The philosophers of the Enlightenment had also been aware of language as a philosophical problem, though they tended to interest them-

---

109. *Essay*, p. 63.
110. Ibid., p. 208.
111. Ibid., pp. 67–68.
112. Ibid., "Myth and Religion."

selves only in its role as the bearer of concepts for discursive reasoning and science. But what are we to think of language when it functions neither as the instrument of rational knowledge nor as a merely practical signal for action but in its interpretive capacity as an art for the communicating of meaning?

Some beginnings had been made in the study of this function of language. Herder himself was to be remembered for the suggestions of a theory though "it did not proceed from a general theory of knowledge, nor from an observation of empirical facts," but rested "on his profound intuition of the character and development of human culture." [113] However, a great philosopher-scientist, Wilhelm von Humboldt, had observed facts about language and conceived a suitable theory to interpret them, and his work, Cassirer declares, "was more than a notable advance in linguistic thought. It marked also a new epoch in the history of the philosophy of language." [114]

"Language" was the subject with which the *Philosophy of Symbolic Forms* would begin. The subject of "Mythical Thinking" followed. And after his own exploring of these new fields Cassirer returned to the former subject of the theory of knowledge, which was now regarded in the light of the phenomenology of culture which he had developed, so that the title of that third part became "The Phenomenology of Knowledge."

FURTHER PROBLEMS

The "Deduction" of the Culture-forms

But though we see adumbrated the structure of the work on the *Philosophy of Symbolic Forms,* we have not yet seen the final solution of the problems which Cassirer had been facing. Questions still remain for consideration and answer. One is raised by the discovery that language and myth are distinct and autonomous cultural forms. More such discoveries can doubtless be made. How is one to determine once and for all what are the forms? Their "specification" must be a matter of principle and not simply a work of im-

113. Ibid., p. 40.
114. Ibid., p. 121. See also Cassirer's "Naturalistische und humanistische Begründung der Kulturphilosophie," *Göteborgs Kungl. Vetenskaps-och Vitterhets-Samhällets Handlingar,* Ser. A, No. 3 (1939), p. 18.

agination. Can there be a "deduction," so to speak, of the cultural forms?

When Kant confronted a similar problem in regard to the logical forms he had recourse to Aristotle's table of categories, assuming that reason was able at one stroke to specify exhaustively its own forms of meaning. While there was no such comparable organon of meanings in the present case, a Kantian faith remained strong in Cassirer that all the forms are really organic with each other in the consciousness of man and that they are members of a logical system, a whole which specifies them as its constituent parts. The very nature of human consciousness is to seek unity and synthesis and to identify the parts as elements of a whole of which it is already in possession in Idea. Call this faith or call it a postulate, it inspires a research, "an inquiry which will accomplish for the *totality* of cultural forms what the transcendental critique has done for pure *cognition*." [115]

The Reconciliation of the Cognitive Forms and the Expressive Forms

But a second question stares us in the face as soon as we attempt to equate the "critique of culture" with Kant's "transcendental critique of cognition." What is the relation between the culture forms and the forms of knowledge? This was the still unsolved problem encountered earlier in connection with Herder's "living logic" and the logic of Kant. Which of the two is being assimilated to the other, the logical forms of cognition to language, myth, history, art, religion, or these forms to the forms of knowledge? The answer now is that this way of putting the question does not really do justice to the situation, for it is not a case of subordinating one to the other but of a mutual assimilation or even, to use an expression of Cassirer's, an "interpenetration" of the forms. Organized thought in its scientific form is an expression of man's spirit and in that aspect as a *mode of expression* it is one among many other cultural forms. On the other hand, all expression in language, art, history, religion is "making" something of the materials of experience, and primary experience is itself a "mode of knowledge." In its making are involved the categories of knowledge as well as the sensuous contents and forms. Thus the forms such as language, art, history which organize experience are also kinds of knowl-

115. See below, p. 84.

edge.[116] They articulate and reveal the world of experience. They offer many "universes of discourse." [117] Thus there is at one and the same time an extension of the meaning of knowledge to include the deliverances of culture and an inclusion of knowledge within man's total life of self-expression and discovery of his world. "Our perspectives widen, if we consider that cognition . . . is only one of the many forms in which the mind can apprehend and interpret being." [118] In this fashion the critique of culture and that of reason are finally reconciled by Cassirer.

But a question remains—what is the third thing or mediating factor between the cultural form and the form of knowledge that makes possible their assimilation with each other in the way indicated? They must participate in something which is common to both kinds of form. But there is nothing common in a "substantial" sense. That cannot be found among the cultural forms themselves other than the forms of knowledge. The solution of this problem is the key which would open the way to "a systematic philosophy of human culture in which each particular form would take its meaning solely from the *place* in which it stands . . . the *universitas* of the human spirit." [119]

4. THE SYMBOLIC FUNCTION AND THE FORMS

In the essay "Cassirer: His Life and Work," [120] Dimitry Gawronsky recalls that "Cassirer once told how in 1917, just as he entered a street car to ride home, the conception of the symbolic forms flashed upon him; a few minutes later, when he reached his home, the whole plan of his new voluminous work was ready in his mind, in essentially the form in which it was carried out in the course of the subsequent ten years." Now it is a matter of record that the concept of symbolic form had already been attained by Cassirer. In his *Substanzbegriff und Funktionsbegriff* (1910) the mathematical symbol was said to effect a transformation of the concrete sense impressions that

116. *Essay*, pp. 136, 167–170, 205–206.
117. *Kants Leben*, p. 305, and *Essay*, pp. 152, 211–213, 221.
118. See below, p. 77.
119. See below, pp. 82–83.
120. *Philosophy of Ernst Cassirer*, p. 25.

imparts to them whatever "objective" value they have in knowledge.[121] It was argued that in physics, too, the given individual impression is made to serve as a "symbol" of the whole pervasive system of things in which it has its place and membership.[122] In this symbolic function the old notion that knowledge is somehow representative of reality had "new meaning" and a tenable form. And here, toward the end of his argument in the book, Cassirer envisaged it as applying to "every particular phase of experience." [123] Now we can understand why he said at the very beginning of the *Philosophy of Symbolic Forms* that his project had its inception in the investigations to which he had been led in *Substanzbegriff und Funktionsbegriff.*

But the significance of the concept of symbolic form had also been seen in the province of art and in the realm of life. In his *Kants Leben und Lehre,* "the manuscript of which was ready for the printer in the spring of 1916" (though it was not published until 1918), Cassirer had said: "The work of art is a unique and detached thing, independent and possessing its own end within itself—and yet there is portrayed therein a new 'whole,' a new total image of reality and the spiritual cosmos itself. The individual does not refer in this instance to some static abstract universal beyond itself but is this very universal itself because it grasps the sum and substance of it symbolically." And "in the realm of objective existence" there is "in the phenomenon of the organism a *symbolic* counterpart (exactly as in the case of the work of art)." [124]

It was not until after that had been written that the symbolic function perceived earlier in science and in art could be conceived as a general theory relating to all the forms. What Cassirer had been waiting for, one may hazard the guess, was the spark of genius that bridged a gap where tension had been long developing. Whoever dares to speak of "mythical thinking" as "thinking," of art as "knowledge" and "insight" and "leading to an objective view of things," and of history too as objective truth and broadly that every such "feature of our experience has a claim to reality," is straining and stretching very far the meanings of knowledge and reality.[125] Is

---

121. *Substanzbegriff und Funktionsbegriff,* p. 197. Swabey trans., p. 149.

122. Ibid., p. 373. Swabey trans., p. 281. See the later argument in *Problem of Knowledge,* pp. 69, 71, 104–106, 109, 111, 114, 116.

123. *Substanzbegriff und Funktionsbegriff,* p. 376 ff. Swabey trans., pp. 284 ff.

124. *Kants Leben,* pp. 328 and 363.

125. The quoted phrases are taken from the finished expression of Cassirer's thought in the *Essay on Man* (pp. 77, 143, 169, 170, 187, 204–206), but the same ideas are expressed in

not history, for example, which comes nearest of all these to being called a "science," still only a "hermeneutic," a mode of interpretation—not knowledge in any adequate sense? It is "a branch of semantics."[126] As to art, is it not true merely symbolically? The religious life is of course replete with symbols. But symbolic representation and truth seem entirely different things. So the mind would stay fixed in this convention until the tension of its own thought broke through the distinction with the crucial questions. Is not all representation whatsoever symbolic, whether it be in language, myth, art, religion, history, or science? Why are they not all alike manifestations of a varying function of symbolizing which man practices and in which he follows intuitively and sometimes consciously the forms of human "creativity"?

The difficulty and the waiting may have been caused by that hard and fast separation between science as objective knowledge and the other features of human experience which seem to be only expressive of subjectivity. There was where the trouble lay. The solution would come with the realization that scientific knowledge is no less symbolic throughout and that it has to be interpreted accordingly. If such were the case Cassirer would then be obliged to recast his own theory of knowledge at the same time as he resolved the difficulty over the unity and system of the cultural forms as a whole. According to Gawronsky's understanding it was seven years then after Cassirer had first defined the function-concept that this flash of a solution came to him and it was another twelve years before he could bring out the third part of a new study of knowledge in the *Phenomenology of Knowledge*. It may have been the necessary rethinking and reformulation of his *views of scientific thought* that took the time. But above all it was also requisite that he define the general meaning of "symbol" so that it would be suitable for application to scientific knowledge, and in this process the study of science could contribute significantly to the understanding of the nature of symbolic function and form in general.

But it was the master Kant, too, who would have to be appeased in imagination. Cassirer now had his own position and he had won it by a magnificent labor of thought. He had studied advanced modern mathe-

the very last paragraph of the study *Zur Einsteinschen Relativitätstheorie* (1921) where the reference is to history, painting, architecture, music, alongside of mathematics and physics. (See Swabey trans., p. 456.) It should be recalled that the first volume of *Symbolic Forms* appeared shortly after, in 1923.

126. *Essay*, p. 195.

matics from within, as it were, traveling in that realm of knowledge with
the mathematicians themselves and taking his cues from them. Now Kant
had said that there was only as much science in anything as there was mathematics. Yet of all modes of knowledge mathematics is itself most clearly
a science of symbols. It is a "universal symbolic language" where "the pure
symbolism of number supersedes and obliterates the symbolism of common speech." [127] Cassirer, fortified with such modern knowledge, dared
then to place his philosophy in a dramatic contrast with that of his old
master Kant. We can see this in a passage of the *Essay on Man* where he tells
of the change he would make in the very language of Kant. He selected
for this purpose one of the most important and most difficult of passages
where Kant ruled out the possibility of an "intuitive understanding"
(Goethe, we recall, reasserted the possibility) and confined man to the "discursive understanding" which is dependent upon two heterogeneous elements. "Concepts without intuitions are empty; intuitions without concepts
are blind." Then Cassirer speaks for himself: "Instead of saying that the
human intellect is an intellect which is 'in need of images' [Kant had written ". . . ein der Bilder bedürftiger Verstand"] we should rather say that
it is in need of symbols." [128]

The words of this declaration of independence can be a trifle misleading,
however, if read out of context. Cassirer does not mean that one is to dispense with images and substitute instead "symbols." Both image and symbol are necessary to understanding. Both have a role in the symbolizing
function. They are distinct, as Cassirer says in the *Symbolic Forms,* and
the difference is precisely that between "passive images" of something
given and "symbols" created by the intellect itself.[129] Images are given but
symbols are made. Made of what? Of the images, the content of perception and experience. The intellect takes images and makes them serve as
symbols. This is quite plain in the case of language. Words are sensuous
images seen or heard but they are used with meaning and so they are employed as symbols. The very last sentence of the present book on *Language*
leaves the reader with this thought: "language shows itself to be *at once*
a sensuous and an intellectual form of expression." [130] Indeed, this combination obtains throughout the realm of the intellectual life: "And so we

127. *Essay,* pp. 213–215, 217.
128. *Ibid.,* pp. 56–57. See also Cassirer's attention to that passage in Kant in his *Kants Leben,*
p. 375, and *Erkenntnisproblem, 3,* 363 ff.
129. See below, pp. 75, 87, 107.
130. See below, p. 319.

see that the very highest and purest spiritual activity . . . is conditioned and mediated by certain modes of sensory activity." [131]

These statements reaffirm that unity of the sensuous and intellectual which Kant had signalized in the schema and which Cassirer has persisted in maintaining throughout his argument. It is with the *intellectual* part of this whole, however, that we are now concerned—what is involved when an image, or any content, is used to serve as a symbol? The function of symbolizing must therefore be examined.

There have been many prior notions of the nature of symbols. In regard to language, for instance, it had been supposed in the eighteenth century that the mind notes similar properties or things and pins the label of a word upon each one of the images; this word-label thenceforward serves to recall any one of them upon occasion. This is a word-for-thing symbolizing—the abstract, general idea being represented by the name or word. Here language only serves to recapitulate what has been given and never to reveal or to develop a meaning. But language actually serves man better than that—it is a means to new knowledge and discovery. And the reason is that much more is involved in the function of symbol in language than is realized. Nothing is really a symbol if it is only a mark of something already given and enabling us to talk about it again. The "it" we denote with a word is only perceived in the first instance in the light of our whole previous experience of the world. It is identified as what it is, even in space and time, by the relations of whatever is "given" with other known contents of experience. There is such a whole always present in the moment of remarking upon a given content, and any symbol derives its own significance from that whole of experience which in a manner it represents. [132]

The case of language only exemplifies what is universally the case. Such symbolic representation is universal because it is inherent in the very character of human consciousness. Cassirer retains here the Kantian conception of consciousness as a knowing of many contents of experience together in unity, but he adds to this notion of synthetic unity a symbolic intent to express the meaning of the experience in and through some particular content which is made representative of the whole. The particular symbol is full of meaning conferred upon it by the totality of man's experience. But the adjective "symbolic" does not belong solely to the image or content

131. See below, p. 88.
132. For detailed discussion of *Language* see the essays of M. F. Ashley Montagu and W. M. Urban in the *Philosophy of Ernst Cassirer*, pp. 361–367 and 401–432.

taken as representative or expressive of meaning, for it pertains no less to the forms in which meaning is intelligible so that they are "symbolic forms" in virtue of their part in the symbolizing function. Cassirer never forgets, it seems, the insight of Kant in the conception of schema. For every schema of understanding is a phenomenon of imagination which is at once intellectual and sensuous; thanks to the latter aspect there is sense or meaning (*Bedeutung*) through reference to objects; thanks to the former there is agreement with the categories or forms through which anything whatsoever has meaning to the human mind. The last sentence of Kant in the "Schematism" expresses it thus: "The meaning comes to the categories from the sensibility but the understanding is what realizes the meaning at the same time as it restricts such meaning to its natural forms." [133] The term "natural" has been inserted in this paraphrase of Kant because Cassirer himself introduces it in the text of the *Symbolic Forms*. "We have acquired a new foundation for [our] investigation. We must go back to 'natural' symbolism, to that representation of consciousness as a whole which is necessarily contained or at least projected in every single moment and fragment of consciousness, if we wish to understand the artificial symbols, the 'arbitrary' signs which consciousness creates in language, art and myth. The force and effect of these mediating signs would remain a mystery if they were not ultimately rooted in an original spiritual process which belongs to the very essence of consciousness. We can understand how a sensuous particular, such as the spoken sound, can become the vehicle of a purely intellectual meaning, only if we assume that the basic function of signification is present and active before the individual sign is produced, so that this producing does not create signification, but merely stabilises it, applies it to the particular case." [134] This basic symbolic function has various "natural" directions—and the symbolic forms are precisely those directions in which meaning is realized in human consciousness.

Susanne K. Langer's comment is here very apposite and revealing: Cassirer's "emphasis on the constitutive character of symbolic renderings in the making of 'experience' is the masterstroke." [135] It abolishes the Kantian disparity between the regulative ideas and the constitutive forms—all are constitutive.

133. *Critique of Pure Reason,* A147–148, B186–188.

134. See below, pp. 105–106.

135. *The Philosophy of Ernst Cassirer,* p. 393. But Carl H. Hamburg appears to differ, retaining a distinction between constitutive form and cultural form. Ibid., p. 94.

Seeing a "natural symbolism" in human consciousness and in the very constituting of all experience, Cassirer is ready to include science as one of the "artificial" symbolisms along with language, art, and myth. Thus he found Heinrich Hertz' theory of symbols in science a point of departure for the exposition of his own general theory in the present book.[136] While there are the basic forms, such as space, time, and the categories of understanding, there are special constructive forms for each science and every theoretical construction within a science. The meanings of concepts depend upon the whole structure of the scientific system in which they are used and they vary with the general theory within which they are conceived. The consequences of this view Cassirer expresses pithily in his later *Essay:* "The facts of science always imply a theoretical, which means a symbolic, element." [137] Later in the same work, in the chapter on "Science," the statement is expanded, that "We must refer our observations to a system of well-ordered symbols in order to make them coherent and interpretable in terms of scientific concepts." [138]

Thus in every case "symbolic form" is a condition either of the knowledge of meaning or of the human expression of a meaning. In art the image or the content has its significance in virtue of the formal structure according to which the creation of the work of art is made. There is the form of painting and the form of music, and so on. And besides the generic form of an art there is the "individual form" of a style, even of the individual artist. Always some "universe of discourse" is involved in anything that has significance. Here then, as it is in organic life, the "whole is prior to the parts." Thus "like all the other symbolic forms art is not the mere reproduction of a ready-made, given reality. . . . It is not an imitation but a discovery of reality." [139] "Myth combines a theoretical element and an element of artistic creation." [140] Mythical thinking has its own distinctive symbolic forms of construction: they are modes both of expressing a theory of life and of portraying it in the manner of an art.

And to return to language, the subject of the first book, it should be clearer now how fallacious were those older nominalist views of the function of language. Language is symbolic in the same way as myth, art, and

136. See the comment of Helmut Kuhn in the *Philosophy of Ernst Cassirer*, p. 559.
137. *Essay*, p. 59.
138. Ibid., p. 217.
139. Ibid., p. 143. Consult the entire chapter of the *Essay* on "Art."
140. Ibid., p. 75.

science are. It is not a case of a point-for-point correspondence of terms with each identified thing or property. The properties and objects are only definite by virtue of the system of thought and experience which lies behind the intent to designate the words that serve as symbols. A world of thought is drawn upon when a word is used with meaning. Hence the "diversity of language is that of world-outlook" and each language has its own "inner linguistic form" and forms even more particular still.[141]

In a sense language may be considered the basic activity or "artifice" to which all other cultural forms may be related. "Art may be defined as symbolic language." [142] History, too, is a "symbolic reconstruction" where the historian or artist "tries to penetrate into the sense of all the various symbolic idioms." [143] Of science itself it can be said "that all truly strict and exact thought is sustained by the *symbolics* and *semiotics* on which it is based." [144]

Nevertheless it is the symbolic concept that is the truly universal one, not the semantic.[145] To stress the latter would tend to rob the other symbolic forms of their autonomy of which Cassirer was so jealous, and for this reason too, that he would not confine within a philosopher's rubrics the varied creativity of the human mind and the ways in which men may find, discover, and have revealed to them things not dreamed of in their philosophy.

5. CONSEQUENCES FOR PHILOSOPHY

This essay in interpretation cannot claim to be an exact account of the way Cassirer progressed toward his goal in the philosophy of symbolic forms. The order in which the questions are here presented and the themes developed may not have been precisely those of his own experience. We have

141. See below, p. 159.
142. *Essay*, p. 168.
143. Ibid., p. 177.
144. See below, p. 86.
145. The comparison of Cassirer's idealistic theory of symbolism with other contemporary theories of language and symbolism is made by several authors in the *Philosophy of Ernst Cassirer:* Carl H. Hamburg, pp. 81–84; W. M. Urban, esp. pp. 408–411; David Bidney, pp. 502–506.

construed his own statements in various works to make a story, paying particular attention to the "rich sources of inspiration" which he so abundantly acknowledged. Least of all could one pretend that this portrayal catches Cassirer at his actual moments of original insight, for the process of origination is veiled from view. We have given here one "symbolic" rendering of the making of Cassirer's "image-world." To do full justice to the inspiration of this very philosophy itself one needs to study the other essays in interpretation available, notably those in the collective volume, *The Philosophy of Ernst Cassirer*.[146]

One further venture of interpretation may be taken which is quite in accord with Cassirer's own intention. In his foreword to the last volume of *Symbolic Forms*, dated July 1929, he said: "In the original plan of this book a special concluding section was contemplated in which the relationship of the basic ideas of 'the philosophy of symbolic forms' to the whole of contemporary philosophy would be presented in careful detail and the position critically established and justified." Then Cassirer added that he eventually felt obliged to renounce this discussion of other present-day philosophy because it would have made the whole work too large, though some comparative study would admittedly be very fruitful, indeed it seemed even necessary. He could promise one such study, however, for separate publication, to be entitled " 'Life' and 'Spirit'—Towards a Critique of the Philosophy of the Present." Here some "consequences" of his position would be shown.[147] This turned out to be a discussion of Scheler's philosophical anthropology as set forth in his work, *The Place of Man in the Cosmos*. The essay enabled Cassirer to state by contrast his own view of man and cosmos and of the relation of Spirit and Life. But such a single encounter with only one other philosopher was hardly sufficient to show the "consequences" of his thought generally for philosophy in the modern world. An attempt will be made, therefore, in the conclusion to the present essay, to indicate more of those consequences. The resultant views and posi-

146. See as especially relevant to "symbolic form" Carl H. Hamburg, pp. 73–119; Robert S. Hartmann, pp. 289–333; M. F. Ashley Montagu, pp. 361–377; Susanne K. Langer, pp. 381–400; W. M. Urban, pp. 403–441; Helmut Kuhn, pp. 547–574; Felix Kaufmann, pp. 201–213; Folke Leander, pp. 337–357; D. Gawronsky, pp. 24–27, 30, 32–35; David Bidney, pp. 512–515, 535–544; Harry Slochower, pp. 652–659; Konstantin Reichardt, pp. 682–688; J. H. Randall, Jr., pp. 726–728; W. H. Werkmeister, pp. 792–798; Fritz Kaufmann, pp. 805–811, 823–854.

147. Cassirer subsequently reversed the order of topics in the title to " 'Spirit' and 'Life.' " See the translation by R. W. Brettall and P. A. Schilpp in *Philosophy of Ernst Cassirer*, pp. 857 ff.

tions are to be gleaned from the *Symbolic Forms* and from some of the subsequent writings.

THE UNIVERSE OF FORM

The argument has traveled from the forms of intuition and the logical forms in their combination to "schemas" which imaginatively unite sense intuitions and intelligible forms, and thence to a unity of these two moments more "concrete" than in Kant's "abstract schema." These truly concrete forms are exemplified both in nature, that is, in the "natural forms" of the organic world which is studied scientifically in biology, and in the forms of art which also disclose living reality. Man and nature are thus affiliated through art and life, as in the vision of Goethe. For man ranges more widely than in the objective world of scientific law and he explores other worlds in imagination according to forms congenial to his consciousness. He articulates these worlds in objective form and expresses himself through a variety of cultural forms among which are art and science themselves. Language is a primordial form which is both expressive of man and revelatory of the nature of reality. Myth and religion have a twofold character, the character both of art and of theoretical knowledge. Science itself, too, seeming so purely theoretical by nature, is nevertheless an achievement representing man's persistent quest for unity and the comprehension of all that enters into his experience. Looking at the entire scene we have a system of cultural forms where all the distinct forms relate to each other while the whole sustains them all in mutually enhancing interrelationships.

THE SYMBOLIC FUNCTION OF CONSCIOUSNESS.

That system of forms is related to human consciousness which is in essence activity. For consciousness takes some given content as signifying a universe of meaning beyond itself and of which the content is a symbolic representation. The various forms are the different structures of such meaning. Consciousness functions in accordance with these forms which are characteristic of itself. It is "form-giving" to whatever is "given" to it.

THE REJECTION OF POSITIVISM AND EMPIRICISM

Some implications of this position are immediately apparent. From the very first, so to speak, consciousness is a symbolizing activity. Hence one never finds in it anything barely "given" without meaning and reference beyond itself. There is no content which is not construed according to some form. Whatever human consciousness appropriates for any purpose whatsoever, whether to gain knowledge or to handle imaginatively in art, is already possessed of form at the very taking. Hence Cassirer rejects the positivism which assumes that hard facts or sense data are given at the start and that they are both the bases for and the criterion of all constructions of thought which must be referred back to either the perceptions or the facts for their truth.[148] If the position here criticized be called by the name of empiricism it is also rejected in this guise because it involves a mistaken notion of experience as consisting simply of an array or aggregation of perceptions.[149] On that score the very first sentence of Kant's introduction to the *Critique of Pure Reason* remained absolutely valid for Cassirer: "Experience is without doubt the first product which our understanding brings forth. . . ."[150] The primary experience is itself form-constituted. Whatever we make of it thereafter has to be judged by reference to the form in which it is cast. This means that in knowledge truth is whatever is in accordance with the form of understanding.

NO PRIVILEGED STATUS FOR SCIENCE

But Cassirer extends the concept of the form-giving agency beyond "understanding" in Kant's sense. Experience serves as material for art as well as

148. See *Problem of Knowledge*, pp. 7, 38, 243, 246, 253–254.
149. Ibid., the comparison of Comte and Mill, pp. 7 ff., 113, 253–254, 319.
150. *Critique*, A 1–2.

for science. The symbolic function of consciousness is exercised in that case in producing works of art. Now just as scientific theory is not to be judged by referring back to the experience which it reconstructs but by its own standards of theoretical completeness, so art is not to be judged in terms of its "imitation" of perception. Nor is it properly judged by the criterion of theoretical knowledge. Each formation or construction must be evaluated according to its own criterion of satisfaction. It has its own autonomy of form. Hence there is no privileged status for science over art or any other symbolic formation which constitutes some kind of interpretation of experience.

THE VIEW OF REALITY

The old alternatives are gone. On the one hand sense perceptions had been taken to be the touchstone of reality; on the other, the theoretical ideas of scientific thought. Or else there was a choice posited between the real as phenomenal being and as the ideal. But there need be no more of these dualisms.

> The illusion of an original division between the intelligible and the sensuous, between "idea" and "phenomenon," vanishes. True, we still remain in a world of "images"—but these are not images which reproduce a self-subsistent world of "things"; they are [whole] image-worlds whose principle and origin are to be sought in an autonomous creation of the spirit. Through them alone we see what we call "reality," and in them alone we possess it: for the highest objective truth that is accessible to the spirit is ultimately the form of its own activity. . . . in all this, the human spirit now perceives itself and reality.[151]

THE PROBLEM OF OBJECTIVITY

This passage provokes a question: Is this not a repetition in new dress of the older idealism? What is this spirit if not the spirit of Hegel's "phe-

151. See below, pp. 110–111.

nomenology of spirit"? Or, is it not, perhaps, simply Berkeleyan idealism when one recalls other phrases, such as this one telling that the task of the whole work on symbolic form is "the specification . . . of pure subjectivity"? [152]

Let us consider the latter question first. It appears as if Cassirer were simply looking within the mind and then projecting outwardly into the objective world the forms discovered in inner consciousness. But that kind of subjectivism was farthest from Cassirer's intentions. He consistently proceeded by identifying the various significant forms of knowledge or culture in the historical world and then studying how such authentic and objective realities could be conceived to be possible. But over and above such evidently outward-looking procedure, Cassirer had profounder reasons for eschewing any subjectivism. He never relinquished the position of Kant's "Refutation of Idealism" in the *Critique of Pure Reason*, where it is argued that the possibility of our very consciousness of ourselves is conditioned by our consciousness of an object and that there is only a "self" in so far as there is a world of objects having objective unity and relationship with each other so as to constitute "one world." The consciousness of a subject and the consciousness of an object are absolutely correlative with and indispensable to each other. Consequently the first thing Cassirer insists upon in regard to all phenomena as understood or appreciated is their *objective* character. What is known or represented in symbolic form is objective because it "bears the stamp of inner necessity." [153] This was what Kant had demonstrated in respect to the scientific representation of phenomena in a space-time order which is characterized by such necessary connections as cause and effect. But even Kant himself, Cassirer avers, learned that "scientific objectivity" is "too narrow." [154] The concept of objectivity itself must be enlarged so as to be applicable to all "the many forms in which the mind can apprehend and interpret being." [155]

Now what determines the necessary and objective character of anything for consciousness is precisely the element of form. It is the "conformity" of the factual with the theoretical that enables the former to have its "inner" or rational necessity. Accordingly it is said later in the *Essay on Man*: "Every work of art has an intuitive structure, and that means a character of

152. See below, Foreword, p. 69.
153. See below, p. iii.
154. See below, p. 79.
155. See below, p. 77.

rationality." [156] Hence we can very properly speak of objectivity in art. Yet we should not measure the objective validity by the standard of cognition. Art has its own formal necessity. So does every other form in and through which humanity interprets experience—as in "the development of our ethical ideas and ideals" and "the civilizing process" to which Cassirer makes a passing, but very suggestive allusion. [157] There is also objectivity in ethics. Cassirer was, in fact, in most thoroughgoing opposition to every sort of subjectivism in philosophy.

THE MEANING OF SUBJECTIVITY AND SUBJECT

Nevertheless, Cassirer retained the concept of subjectivity. This might reasonably be thought a lingering trace of Kant's early subjectivism, as it has been called, when he ascribed the forms of intuition and understanding to the knowing subject because such formal elements of experience were not discoverably "given" in sense perception. But Cassirer, as we have seen, followed with the keenest interest Kant's development in the later Critiques and the second edition of the first *Critique* and he found good reason still to exalt the "subject," and especially the "freedom" of man. It is in the spirit of Kant that Cassirer writes: "The ethical world is never given; it is forever in the making." [158] And the making is man's work, when he prescribes for himself action out of respect for the law of his own conception. Here is the clearest and most striking manifestation of the free spontaneity of the human spirit. It is the being capable of such moral judgment and action who is also the judge that poses the questions to physical nature and then passes judgment on the resulting evidence from experience or experiment. Judgment in all its forms testifies to a "subject" not to be lost among the phenomena of the world which are objectively real for it. Here is something else essential, the subject or spirit.

156. *Essay*, p. 167.
157. Ibid., pp. 60, 61, 63.
158. Ibid., p. 61.

THE CORRELATION OF SUBJECT AND WORLD

Thanks to the symbolic forms through which consciousness is form-giving, man articulates his experience in an objective order. In science he knows a world of law. But he also knows *himself* with it. And in whatever form he makes, construes, creates—"in all this the human spirit now perceives itself and reality." There is here "a synthesis of world and spirit." [159]

"SPIRIT" AND "LIFE"

The term "spirit" is alone adequate to express the significance of man's own activity and being in this affair. First it had been "understanding" that had such importance, then the subject, now it is spirit. The order of thought here seems to parallel that of Hegel to whom Cassirer refers with appreciation in his critique of Scheler's theme of "man in the cosmos." Hegel had treated the relationship between spirit and life as a dialectical advance over the relationship between subject and object in the realm of nature. [160] In the philosophy of Scheler, however, life and spirit seemed to stand in an unresolved opposition to each other. But, Cassirer says, they cannot "belong to entirely disparate worlds," for "how is it possible that they nevertheless can accomplish a perfectly homogeneous piece of work, that they cooperate and interpenetrate in constructing the specifically human world, the world of 'meaning'? Is this interpenetration . . . nothing more than a 'happy accident'?" [161] The question is rhetorical: Cassirer himself maintains spirit and life to be cooperating and interpenetrating.

159. See below, p. 111. See the comment of M. F. Ashley Montagu, *Philosophy of Ernst Cassirer*, p. 376, on the pertinence of Hegel's *Phenomenology of Spirit*.
160. See above, p. 33.
161. *Philosophy of Ernst Cassirer*, p. 864.

CASSIRER AND HEGEL IN CONTRAST

Wherein lies the difference, then, between Cassirer and Hegel whose "objective idealism," as he says, "completely maintains its ground, in the face of all the criticism which the nineteenth and twentieth centuries' 'philosophy of life' has urged against it?" [162] He refers to the Hegel of the *Phenomenology of Spirit,* where it was written, " 'The strength of the Spirit is only as great as its expression; its depth only as deep as in its revelation it dares to expand and lose itself.' " [163] So far Cassirer agrees. He had also written in the foreword of his third volume on *Symbolic Forms* that in its "first approach" his own phenomenology was in agreement with that of Hegel, however much he "departed from him when it came to establishing his position and carrying it out into detail." [164]

The difference is seen, then, in what follows in the two respective philosophies. Hegel advances from the engagement of spirit with life to the ultimate resolution of the dialectic where Spirit has "absolute knowledge" of itself. But Cassirer keeps the twain ever twain, spirit and its other. It is never forgotten that in the constitution of whatever appears as "given" at any stage, even the highest, there is always a factor not contributed by the form-giving activity of consciousness.[165] Cassirer sees the unsolved problem of Kant, that the human understanding is "an image-needing one." Expand "understanding" to "spirit," and it still remains the case in every instance that the human spirit *needs images* which it uses symbolically to disclose meaning beyond them. There is no leaping clean out of an image-world so that spirit knows ultimately itself. There is always the added phrase "and reality," the reality of the phenomenal world. To Cassirer there is an "endless task" ahead, and the course for man is one of discovering the inexhaustible possibilities of the formative role of the human spirit in the course of experience and history.

162. Ibid., p. 875.
163. Ibid., p. 875.
164. *Philosophie der symbolischen Formen, 3,* vii.
165. See above, p. 57.

A Modified Philosophical Idealism

In the beginning of the first part of *Symbolic Forms* Cassirer identified his philosophy with classic idealism. It retained the essential concept of the relation of thought and being which Plato had introduced into philosophy, namely, that thought "no longer runs parallel to being, a mere reflection 'about' being, but by its own inner form it now determines the inner form of being." [166] This has been shown by Cassirer in the realm of knowledge and in the universes of art, myth and religion, language. The showing of it constitutes a kind of idealistic "phenomenology of culture."

Critique of Naturalistic Theory of Culture and a New Humanism

From the standpoint of this phenomenology Cassirer takes a critical view of the "naturalistic philosophy of culture" which started from the "world-image" of Darwin and Spencer and was chiefly represented by Taine, Comte, Spengler. This view tended toward a cultural determinism with its "laws" of history. Even though Hegel's philosophy of history was conceived as a phenomenology of freedom it offered no real opposition to this other trend because the freedom meant was, as Cassirer says, "only consummated for the absolute subject, not for the finite subject," that is, for man himself. [167] A "humanistic philosophy of culture" is needed, therefore, to do justice to man and his freedom. The whole gamut of cultural phenomena bears witness to man's "will to formations." "What man achieves is the objectification, the intuition of himself, in and through the theoretical, aesthetic, and ethical form which he gives to his existence. This is exhibited even in the very first promptings of human speech and it is unfolded and developed in rich and many-sided forms in poetry, in the fine arts, in religious consciousness, in philosophical concepts." [168] Such had

166. See below, p. 74.
167. "Naturalistische und humanistische Begründung der Kulturphilosophie" (1939), ibid., p. 14.
168. Ibid., pp. 15–17.

been the insight of Goethe, Herder, and Humboldt. They had all prized
the free personality of man and human individuality. They produced "the
new humanism."

THE ETHICAL TASK

Cassirer carries on the theme into the scene of the present world where
there is "once again an outbreak of uncertainty over the destiny and future
of human culture." A philosopher cannot avoid attending to such crises in
the life of mankind and must have some theory with which to meet the
need of the times. "All that can be said here," said Cassirer, writing in
Sweden in 1939, "is that culture will exist and progress only so long as we
do not renounce or cripple our own form-shaping powers, which in the last
analysis are to be brought out of ourselves." The mode of expression, "we"
and "ours," prepares us for the next admonition, "that we must learn our
own subjective responsibility in these affairs." [169] The Cassirer who wrote
that was moved by the deepest impulse of the thought of Plato and by the
ethical example of that great figure, the ideal philosopher, Socrates. Some
have said of Cassirer that he neglected to address himself to the actual
social and political exigencies of the contemporary world.[170] *The Myth
of the State* (1946) was something of an answer to that question. It was
written for the people of the American civilization in which Cassirer had
found a home and where he perceived work for him to do as a philosopher.
There was a current tendency to explain the second World War by reference solely to the evil purpose of foreign governments which had seemed
to gain and hold their power by false propaganda that enlisted the allegiance
of their several nations—but to the philosopher the source of the trouble
was deeper, and indeed universal, in a myth which had been recurrent
in western history and was not by any means confined to one or more nations of the present era. It behooved a free nation contending with the
potent effects of that "myth of the state" to understand it well and to realize
that it might become resurgent in any society if care be not taken with the

169. Ibid., p. 28.
170. See the remarks of Helmut Kuhn in *Philosophy of Ernst Cassirer*, pp. 573–574, of
Harry Slochower, ibid., p. 656, and Fritz Kaufmann, ibid., pp. 837–844.

culture and education of man. There was implicit in this book therefore that ethical imperative which had been expressed openly in the *Essay on Culture* written in Sweden four years earlier: We must learn our own personal responsibility in this matter. And the ideal to keep in mind was that of a genuinely "humanistic" culture. And it was the object of the *Essay on Man* to show what this meant in all the forms of human culture—myth, religion, language, art, history, science. Here Cassirer taught a different philosophical anthropology from that to which many in America were committed by their biological or naturalistic view of man.[171] He coined a new characterization of man as "the symbolic animal," insisting on man's active search for and creation of ideal meaning in human existence. He interpreted the record of history as itself a mode of self-discovery:—"History as well as poetry is an organon of our self-knowledge . . ."[172] And the last paragraph of his book contains a summons to an ethical task, for "Human culture taken as a whole may be described as the process of man's progressive self-liberation."[173]

171. Cassirer repeatedly drew attention to the biological view of Üxküll, on which he based his own conception of man. See especially *Problem of Knowledge*, pp. 200–203, 205, and *Essay on Man*, pp. 23 ff.

172. *Essay*, p. 206.

173. Ibid., p. 228.

The Philosophy of
Symbolic Forms

Foreword by the Author

I FIRST projected this work, whose first volume I am here submitting, at the time of the investigations summed up in my book *Substanzbegriff und Funktionsbegriff* (Berlin, 1910). These investigations dealt essentially with the structure of mathematical and scientific thought. When I attempted to apply my findings to the problems of the cultural sciences, it gradually became clear to me that general epistemology, with its traditional form and limitations, does not provide an adequate methodological basis for the cultural sciences. It seemed to me that before this inadequacy could be made good, the whole program of epistemology would have to be broadened. Instead of investigating only the general premises of scientific *cognition* of the world, it would also have to differentiate the various fundamental forms of man's "understanding" of the world and apprehend each one of them as sharply as possible in its specific direction and characteristic spiritual form. Only when such a "morphology" of the human spirit was established, at least in general outline, could we hope to arrive at a clearer and more reliable methodological approach to the individual cultural sciences. It seemed to me that the theory of scientific concepts and judgments which defines the natural "object" by its constitutive traits, and apprehends the "object" of cognition·as contingent on the function of cognition, must be amplified by an analogous specification of pure subjectivity. This subjectivity does not consist solely in the cognition of nature and reality, but is everywhere at work where the phenomenal world as a whole is placed under a specific spiritual perspective, which determines its configuration. It seemed necessary to show how each of these configurations fulfills its own function in the growth of the human spirit and how each one is subject to a particular law. From my work with this problem developed the plan of a general theory of cultural forms, which will be expounded more fully in my Introduction. As for the detailed arrangement of this study, this first part is limited to an analysis of linguistic form; a second volume which, I hope, will appear in approximately one year is designed to embody the sketch of a phenomenology of mythical and religious thinking; while in the third and last volume I expect to deal with epistemology proper, i.e., the morphology of *scientific* thinking.

A study of the purely philosophical content of *language* from the stand-point of a definite philosophical "system" is indeed a bold venture that has scarcely been undertaken since the first, fundamental works of Wilhelm von Humboldt. Humboldt, as he wrote to Wolf in 1805, thought he had discovered how to use language as a vehicle by which to journey through the heights and depths and diversity of the whole world. However, this pretension seems to have been largely nullified by the trends of linguistics and linguistic philosophy in the nineteenth century. At times, language seemed to be becoming the principal weapon of skepticism rather than a vehicle of philosophical knowledge. But even if we disregard those in-ferences of the modern critique of language, according to which the phi-losophy of language is synonymous with the negation of its spiritual con-tent, we find an increasing conviction that a philosophical elucidation of language, if possible at all, would have to be undertaken by psychological means. The ideal of an absolutely universal, "philosophical" grammar, which the empiricists and rationalists of the seventeenth and eighteenth centuries had pursued in different ways, seemed shattered once and for all since the emergence of scientific comparative linguistics: the unity of language could no longer be sought in its logical content, but only in its genesis and in the psychological laws governing this genesis. Wundt's great work on language, in which he once again attempted to subject the totality of linguistic phenomena to a specific interpretation, derives the principle of this interpretation from the concept and methodology of ethnic psychology. Along the same lines of thought Steinthal, in his *Einlei-tung in die Psychologie und Sprachwissenschaft* (1871), had attempted to use Herbart's concept of apperception as the foundation of inquiry into language. Subsequently Marty (1908), in conscious opposition to the view of Steinthal and Wundt, returned to the idea of a "universal grammar and philosophy of language," which he looked upon as the framework of a "descriptive theory of signification." But he too attempted to build this theory of signification by purely psychological means; indeed, he expressly limits the scope of linguistic philosophy to those problems of linguistic law which are "either of a psychological nature or which at least cannot be solved without having recourse primarily to psychology." Thus, despite the resistance to this view among linguists—particularly Karl Vossler—psy-chologism and positivism seemed to have been established as a methodolog-ical ideal, if not a universal dogma, in this field. To be sure, this dogma was still combatted by philosophical idealism which, however, did not restore language to the *autonomous* position it had enjoyed in the works of Humboldt. For, instead of regarding it as an independent cultural "form" with its specific underlying law, these philosophical idealists attempted to reduce it to the general aesthetic function. In this sense, Benedetto Croce subordinated the problem of linguistic expression to the problem of aesthetic expression, while Hermann Cohen's philosophical system treats logic, ethics, aesthetics and finally religion as independent links, but touches on the problems of language only occasionally and in connection with the problems of aesthetics.

From these circumstances it follows that in the present work I have not been able to pursue any charted philosophical course, but have been compelled throughout to seek my own methodological path. However, the development of *linguistic science* since the days of Wilhelm von Humboldt provided me rich sources of inspiration. In Humboldt the idea of a truly universal inquiry into language may still strike us as a mere postulate of idealistic philosophy, but since then it seems to have approached a concrete, scientific realization. True, this very wealth of empirical material creates an almost insuperable difficulty for philosophical inquiry. For it can neither disregard empirical particulars nor can it wholly submit to them and still remain entirely faithful to its own mission and purpose. In the face of this methodological dilemma, the only possibility was to formulate the *questions* asked of linguistics with systematic universality, but in each case to derive the *answers* from actual empirical inquiry. It was necessary to seek as broad as possible a view, and not only of one linguistic family, but of different families widely divergent in their logic and structure. The linguistic literature which it was necessary to consult became so vast that the goal I originally set myself receded farther and farther into the distance and I often doubted whether it lay within my reach. If I nevertheless continued, it is because, as the diversity of linguistic phenomena opened up before me, the particulars seemed more and more to cast light upon one another and to fit as though of their own accord into a general picture. The following investigation is concerned not with the study of any particular phenomena, but with the development and elucidation of this general picture. If the fundamental epistemological idea by which it is oriented is confirmed, if the description and characterization of the pure *form* of language, here attempted, proves sound, many particulars which I have overlooked or misinterpreted will easily be supplied or rectified in a future treatment of the subject. In working on this book I myself have become too keenly aware of the difficulty of the problem and the limitations of my own powers, not to welcome the criticism of experts in the field; in order to facilitate this criticism I have, in interpreting and evaluating linguistic data, always expressly indicated my authorities and sources so as to make immediate verification possible.

It remains for me only to express my thanks to all those who have helped me in the preparation of this book, either by the general interest they have taken in it or by their expert advice. In my attempt to gain a more accurate insight into the structure of the so-called "primitive" languages, I have been guided from the first by the works of Carl Meinhof, and by those of Boas and Seler on the American Indian languages. After my call to Hamburg in 1919 I had at my disposal the well-stocked library of Meinhof's Institute for African and South Sea Languages, and moreover, in many difficult problems I was able to avail myself of Professor Meinhof's cordially proffered and extremely helpful advice. I also owe thanks to my colleagues Professor Otto Dempwolff and Professor Heinrich Junker for insights gained through conversation with them. Finally Ernst Hoffmann in Heidelberg and Emil Wolff in Hamburg assisted me far beyond any matter of detail. Above all these two men, themselves in the midst of philological and linguistic inquiries, share with me the fundamental view on which this book rests: the conviction that language, like all basic functions of the human spirit, can be elucidated by philosophy only within a general system of philosophical idealism. I also owe heartfelt thanks to Ernst Hoffmann for reading the proofs of this first volume despite the heavy pressure of his own work. Unfortunately, certain important suggestions which he offered me in the process could not, for technical reasons, be included in the published book, but I hope to make use of them in a future treatment of the subject.

ERNST CASSIRER

Hamburg, April 1923

Introduction and Presentation of the Problem

1. The Concept of Symbolic Form and the System of Symbolic Forms

PHILOSOPHICAL speculation began with the concept of *being*. In the very moment when this concept appeared, when man's consciousness awakened to the unity of being as opposed to the multiplicity and diversity of existing things, the specific philosophical approach to the world was born. But even then man's thinking about the world remained for a long while imprisoned within the sphere of existing things, which it was seeking to relinquish and surpass. The philosophers attempted to determine the beginning and origin, the ultimate "foundation" of all being: the question was stated clearly, but the concrete, determinate answers given were not adequate to this supreme, universal formulation. What these thinkers called the essence, the substance of the world was not something which in principle went beyond it; it was a fragment taken from this very same world. A particular, specific and limited existing thing was picked out, and everything else was genetically derived from it and "explained by it." Much as these explanations might change in content, their general form remained within the same methodological limits. At first a particular material substance, a concrete *prima materia,* was set up as the ultimate foundation of all phenomena; then the explanations became more ideal and the substance was replaced by a purely rational "principle," from which everything was derived. But on closer inspection this "principle" hung in midair between the "physical" and "spiritual." Despite its ideal coloration, it was closely connected with the world of existing things. The number of the Pythagoreans, the atom of Democritus, though far removed from the original substance of the Ionians, remained a methodological hybrid, which had not found its true nature and had not, as it were, chosen its true spiritual home. This inner uncertainty was not definitely overcome until Plato developed his theory of ideas. The great systematic and historical achievement of this theory is that here, for the first time, the essential intellectual premise for any philosophical understanding and explanation of the world took on explicit form. What Plato sought for, what he

called "idea," had been effective as an immanent principle in the earliest
attempts to explain the world, in the Eleatic philosophers, in the Pythagoreans, in Democritus; but Plato was the first to be conscious of this principle
and its significance. Plato himself took this to be his philosophical achievement. In his late works, where he sees the logical implications of his doctrine most clearly, he characterizes the crucial difference between his
speculation and that of the Pre-Socratics: the Pre-Socratics identified being
with a particular existing thing and took it as a fixed point of departure,
while he for the first time recognized it as a *problem*. He no longer simply
inquired into the order, condition and structure of being, but inquired into
the concept of being and the meaning of that concept. Compared with
the sharpness of Plato's question and the rigor of his approach, all earlier
speculations paled to tales or myths about being.[1] It was time to abandon
these mythical, cosmological explanations for the true, dialectical explanation of being, which no longer clings to its mere facticity but discloses its intelligible *meaning,* its systematic, teleological order. And with this, thought,
which in Greek philosophy since Parmenides had appeared as a concept
interchangeable with that of being, gained a new and profounder meaning. Only where being has the sharply defined meaning of a *problem,*
does thought attain to the sharply defined meaning and value of a *principle.*
It no longer runs parallel to being, a mere reflection "about" being, but by
its own inner form, it now determines the inner form of being.

The same typical process was repeated at different stages in the historical
development of idealism. Where a materialist view of the world contented
itself with some ultimate attribute of things as the basis of all cognition—
idealism turned this very same attribute into a question for thought. And
this process is discernible not only in the history of philosophy but in the
specialized sciences as well. The road does not lead solely from "data" to
"laws" and from laws back to "axioms" and "principles": the axioms and
principles themselves, which at a certain stage of knowledge represent the
ultimate and most complete solution, must at a later stage become once
more a problem. Accordingly, what science designates as its "being" and
its "object," ceases to appear as a simple and indivisible set of facts; every
new type or trend of thought discloses some new phase in this complex.
The rigid concept of being seems to be thrown into flux, into general movement, and the unity of being becomes conceivable only as the aim, and no
longer as the beginning of this movement. As this insight develops and

1. Cf. especially *The Sophists* 243 C ff.

gains acceptance in science itself, the naïve *copy theory* of knowledge is discredited. The fundamental concepts of each science, the instruments with which it propounds its questions and formulates its solutions, are regarded no longer as passive images of something given but as *symbols* created by the intellect itself.

Mathematicians and physicists were first to gain a clear awareness of this symbolic character of their basic implements.[2] The new ideal of knowledge, to which this whole development points, was brilliantly formulated by Heinrich Hertz in the introduction to his *Principles of Mechanics*. He declares that the most pressing and important function of our natural science is to enable us to foresee future experience—and he goes on to describe the method by which science derives the future from the past: We make "inner fictions or symbols" of outward objects, and these symbols are so constituted that the necessary logical consequences of the images are always images of the necessary natural consequences of the imaged objects.

> Once we have succeeded in deriving images of the required nature from our past experience, we can with them as models soon develop the consequences which will be manifested in the outward world much later or as consequences of our own intervention. . . . The images of which we are speaking are our ideas of things; they have with things the one essential agreement which lies in the fulfillment of the stated requirement, but further agreement with things is not necessary to their purpose. Actually we do not know and have no means of finding out whether our ideas of things accord with them in any other respect than in this one fundamental relation.[3]

The epistemology of the physical sciences, on which the work of Heinrich Hertz is based and the theory of "signs" as first fully developed by Helmholtz, was still couched in the *language* of the copy theory of knowledge—but the concept of the "image" had undergone an inner change. In place of the vague demand for a similarity of content between image and thing, we now find expressed a highly complex logical relation, a general intellectual *condition,* which the basic concepts of physical knowledge must satisfy. Its value lies not in the reflection of a given existence, but in what it accomplishes as an instrument of knowledge, in a unity of phenomena,

2. This is discussed in greater detail in my book *Zur Einstein'schen Relativitätstheorie* (Berlin, B. Cassirer, 1921); cf. especially the first section on "Massbegriffe und Denkbegriffe."

3. H. Hertz, *Die Prinzipien der Mechanik* (Leipzig, F. A. Barth, 1894), p. 1 ff.

which the phenomena must produce out of themselves. A system of physical concepts must reflect the relations between objective things as well as the nature of their mutual dependency, but this is only possible in so far as these concepts pertain from the very outset to a definite, homogeneous intellectual orientation. The object cannot be regarded as a naked thing in itself, independent of the essential categories of natural science: for only within these categories which are required to constitute its form can it be described at all.

In this sense, Hertz came to look upon the fundamental concepts of mechanics, particularly the concepts of mass and force, as "fictions" which, since they are created by the logic of natural science, are subordinate to the universal requirements of this logic, among which the a priori requirement of clarity, freedom from contradiction, and unambiguousness of reference takes first place.

With this critical insight, it is true, science renounces its aspiration and its claim to an "immediate" grasp and communication of reality. It realizes that the only objectivization of which it is capable is, and must remain, mediation. And in this insight, another highly significant idealistic consequence is implicit. If the object of knowledge can be defined only through the medium of a particular logical and conceptual structure, we are forced to conclude that a variety of media will correspond to various structures of the object, to various meanings for "objective" relations. Even in "nature," the physical object will not coincide absolutely with the chemical object, nor the chemical with the biological—because physical, chemical, biological knowledge *frame their questions* each from its own particular standpoint and, in accordance with this standpoint, subject the phenomena to a special interpretation and formation. It might also seem that this consequence in the development of idealistic thought had conclusively frustrated the expectation in which it began. The end of this development seems to negate its beginning—the unity of being, for which it strove, threatens once more to disintegrate into a mere diversity of existing things. The One Being, to which thought holds fast and which it seems unable to relinquish without destroying its own form, eludes *cognition*. The more its metaphysical unity as a "thing in itself" is asserted, the more it evades all possibility of knowledge, until at last it is relegated entirely to the sphere of the unknowable and becomes a mere "X." And to this rigid metaphysical absolute is juxtaposed the realm of phenomena, the true sphere of the knowable, with its enduring multiplicity, finiteness and relativity. But upon closer scrutiny the fundamental postulate of unity is not discredited by this irreducible diversity of the methods and objects of knowledge; it merely assumes a new form. True, the unity of knowledge can no longer be made certain and secure by referring knowledge in all its forms to a "simple" common object which is related to all these forms as the transcendent prototype to the empirical copies. But instead, a new task arises: to gather the various branches of science with their diverse methodologies—with all their recognized specificity and independence—into one system, whose separate parts precisely through their necessary diversity will complement and further one another. This postulate of a purely functional unity replaces the postulate of a unity of substance and origin, which lay at the core of the ancient concept of being.

And this creates a new task for the philosophical critique of knowledge. It must follow the special sciences and survey them as a whole. It must ask whether the intellectual symbols by means of which the specialized disciplines reflect on and describe reality exist merely side by side or whether they are not diverse manifestations of the same basic human function. And if the latter hypothesis should be confirmed, a philosophical critique must formulate the universal conditions of this function and define the principle underlying it. Instead of dogmatic metaphysics, which seeks absolute unity in a substance to which all the particulars of existence are reducible, such a philosophical critique seeks after a rule governing the concrete diversity of the functions of cognition, a rule which, without negating and destroying them, will gather them into a unity of deed, the unity of a self-contained human endeavor.

But again our perspectives widen if we consider that cognition, however universally and comprehensively we may define it, is only one of the many forms in which the mind can apprehend and interpret being. In giving form to multiplicity it is governed by a specific, hence sharply delimited principle. All cognition, much as it may vary in method and orientation, aims ultimately to subject the multiplicity of phenomena to the unity of a "fundamental proposition." The particular must not be left to stand alone, but must be made to take its place in a context, where it appears as part of a logical structure, whether of a teleological, logical or causal character. Essentially cognition is always oriented toward this essential aim, the articulation of the particular into a universal law and order. But beside this intellectual synthesis, which operates and expresses itself within a system of scientific concepts, the life of the human spirit as a whole

knows other forms. They too can be designated as modes of "objectivization": i.e., as means of raising the particular to the level of the universally
valid; but they achieve this universal validity by methods entirely different
from the logical concept and logical law. Every authentic function of the
human spirit has this decisive characteristic in common with cognition:
it does not merely copy but rather embodies an original, formative power.
It does not express passively the mere fact that something is present but
contains an independent energy of the human spirit through which the
simple presence of the phenomenon assumes a definite "meaning," a particular ideational content. This is as true of art as it is of cognition; it is as
true of myth as of religion. All live in particular image-worlds, which do
not merely reflect the empirically given, but which rather produce it in
accordance with an independent principle. Each of these functions creates
its own symbolic forms which, if not similar to the intellectual symbols,
enjoy equal rank as products of the human spirit. None of these forms can
simply be reduced to, or derived from, the others; each of them designates
a particular approach, in which and through which it constitutes its own
aspect of "reality." They are not different modes in which an independent
reality manifests itself to the human spirit but roads by which the spirit
proceeds towards its objectivization, i.e., its self-revelation. If we consider
art and language, myth and cognition in this light, they present a common
problem which opens up new access to a universal philosophy of the cultural sciences.

The "revolution in method" which Kant brought to theoretical philosophy rests on the fundamental idea that the relation between cognition and
its object, generally accepted until then, must be radically modified. Instead of starting from the object as the known and given, we must begin
with the law of cognition, which alone is truly accessible and certain in a
primary sense; instead of defining the universal qualities of *being,* like
ontological metaphysics, we must, by an analysis of reason, ascertain the
fundamental form of *judgment* and define it in all its numerous ramifica-
tions; only if this is done, can objectivity become conceivable. According
to Kant, only such an analysis can disclose the conditions on which all
knowledge of being and the pure concept of being depend. But the object
which transcendental analytics thus places before us is the correlate of the
synthetic unity of the understanding, an object determined by purely
logical attributes. Hence it does not characterize all objectivity as such,
but only that form of objective necessity which can be apprehended and

described by the basic concepts of science, particularly the concepts and principles of mathematical physics. When in the course of the three critiques Kant proceeded to develop the true "system of pure reason," he himself found this objectivity too narrow. In his idealistic view, mathematics and physics do not exhaust all reality, because they are far from encompassing all the workings of the human spirit in its creative spontaneity. In the realm of ethical freedom, whose basic law is developed by the *Critique of Practical Reason,* in the realm of art and the realm of organic natural forms, as represented in the *Critique of Judgment,* a new aspect of this reality appears. This *gradual* unfolding of the critical-idealistic concept of reality and the critical-idealistic concept of the spirit is among the most characteristic traits of Kantian thinking, and is indeed grounded in a kind of law of style that governed this thinking. He does not set out to designate the authentic, concrete totality of the spirit in a simple initial formula, to deliver it ready-made, as it were; on the contrary, it develops and finds itself only in the progressive course of his critical analysis. We can designate and define the scope of the human spirit only by pursuing this analytical process. It lies in the nature of this process that its beginning and end are not only separate from each other, but must apparently conflict—however, the tension is none other than that between potency and act, between the mere "potentiality" of a concept and its full development and effect. From the standpoint of this latter, the Copernican revolution with which Kant began, takes on a new and amplified meaning. It refers no longer solely to the function of logical judgment but extends with equal justification and right to every trend and every principle by which the human spirit gives form to reality.

The crucial question always remains whether we seek to understand the function by the structure or the structure by the function, which one we choose to "base" upon the other. This question forms the living bond connecting the most diverse realms of thought with one another: it constitutes their inner methodological unity, without ever letting them lapse into a factual sameness. For the fundamental principle of critical thinking, the principle of the "primacy" of the function over the object, assumes in each special field a new form and demands a new and dependent explanation. Along with the pure function of cognition we must seek to understand the function of linguistic thinking, the function of mythical and religious thinking, and the function of artistic perception, in such a way as to disclose how in all of them there is attained an entirely determinate formation, not exactly of the world, but rather making for the world, for an objective, meaningful context and an objective unity that can be apprehended as such.

Thus the critique of reason becomes the critique of culture. It seeks to understand and to show how every content of culture, in so far as it is more than a mere isolated content, in so far as it is grounded in a universal principle of form, presupposes an original act of the human spirit. Herein the basic thesis of idealism finds its true and complete confirmation. As long as philosophical thought limits itself to analysis of *pure cognition,* the naïve-realistic view of the world cannot be wholly discredited. The object of cognition is no doubt determined and formed in some way by cognition and through its original law—but it must nevertheless, so it would seem, also be present and given as something independent outside of this relation to the fundamental categories of knowledge. If, however, we take as our starting point not the general concept of the world, but rather the general concept of culture, the question assumes a different form. For the content of the concept of culture cannot be detached from the fundamental forms and directions of human activity: here "being" can be apprehended only in "action." Only in so far as aesthetic imagination and perception exist as a specific pursuit, is there a sphere of aesthetic objects — and the same applies to all those other energies of the spirit by which a definite universe of objects takes on form. Even religious consciousness— convinced as it is of the "reality," the truth, of its object—transforms this reality into a simple material *existence* only at the lowest level, the level of purely mythological thinking. At higher levels of contemplation it is more or less clearly aware that it only possesses its object in so far as it relates itself to that object in a special way. What ultimately guarantees objectivity itself is the way in which it is approached, the specific direction that the spirit gives itself in relation to a proposed objective context. Philosophical thought confronts all these directions—not just in order to follow each one of them separately or to survey them as a whole, but under the assumption that it must be possible to relate them to a unified, ideal center. From the standpoint of critical thinking, however, this center can never lie in a given essence but only in a common *project.* Thus, with all their inner diversity, the various products of culture—language, scientific knowledge, myth, art, religion—become parts of a single great problem-complex: they become multiple efforts, all directed toward the one goal of transforming the passive world of mere *impressions,* in which the spirit seems at first imprisoned, into a world that is pure *expression* of the human spirit.

In seeking the proper starting point for a philosophical study of language, modern philosophy has devised the concept of "inner linguistic form." A similar "inner form" may be sought in religion and myth, in art and scientific cognition. And this form would not mean only a sum or retrospective compendium of the particular phenomena in these fields, but the law determining their structure. True, we can find this law only through the phenomena themselves from which we "abstract" it; but this very abstraction shows that the law is a necessary constituent factor of the content and existence of the particular.

Throughout its history philosophy has been more or less aware of the need for such an analysis and critique of the particular forms of culture; but it has directly undertaken only parts of this task, and then usually more with a negative than a positive intention. The purpose of this critique was often not so much to describe and explain the positive achievements of each particular form, as to refute false claims. Since the days of the Greek Sophists there has been a skeptical critique of language, as well as of myths and of rational knowledge. This essentially negative attitude becomes understandable when we consider that in the course of its development every basic cultural form tends to represent itself not as a part but as the whole, laying claim to an absolute and not merely relative validity, not contenting itself with its special sphere, but seeking to imprint its own characteristic stamp on the whole realm of being and the whole life of the spirit. From this striving toward the absolute inherent in each special sphere arise the conflicts of culture and the antinomies within the concept of culture.

Science had its origin in a form of thinking which, before it could operate in its own right, was compelled to work with those first intellectual associations and distinctions which found their earliest expression and deposit in language and general linguistic concepts. But though science uses language as a material and foundation, it must at the same time go beyond language. A new "logos," guided and governed by a principle other than that imbedded in the concepts of language, appears and becomes more and more sharply defined and independent. Beside this logos the products of language seem to be mere impediments and barriers, which must be progressively overcome by the force and specificity of the new principle.

The critique of language and of the linguistic form of thinking becomes an integral part of advancing scientific and philosophical thought.

And in the other fields this typical course of development is repeated. The particular cultural trends do not move peacefully side by side, seeking to complement one another; each becomes what it is only by demonstrating its own peculiar power against the others and in battle with the others. Religion and art are so close to one another in their purely historical development, and so permeate one another, that sometimes the two seem indistinguishable in content and in their inner formative principle. It has been said that the gods of Greece owed their origin to Homer and Hesiod. But as it progressed, the religious thought of the Greeks moved farther and farther away from its aesthetic beginning and source. After Xenophanes, it rebelled more and more resolutely against the mythical-poetic and the sensuous-plastic concepts of the gods, which it rejected as anthropomorphic. In such spiritual struggles and conflicts, which have increased in intensity and significance in the course of history, the ultimate decision seems to rest with philosophy alone, as the supreme authority and repository of unity. But the dogmatic systems of metaphysics satisfied this expectation and mission only in part. For they themselves usually stand in the midst of the battle, and not above it: despite the conceptual universality towards which they strive, they stand only for one side of the conflict, instead of encompassing and mediating the conflict itself in all its breadth and depth. For most of them are nothing other than metaphysical hypostases of a definite logical, or aesthetic, or religious principle. In shutting themselves up in the abstract universality of this principle, they cut themselves off from particular aspects of cultural life and the concrete totality of its forms. Philosophical thought might avoid this danger of occlusion only if it could find a standpoint situated above all these forms and yet not merely outside them: a standpoint which would make it possible to encompass the whole of them in one view, which would seek to penetrate nothing other than the purely immanent relation of all these forms to one another, and not their relation to any external, "transcendent" being or principle. Then we could have a systematic philosophy of human culture in which each particular form would take its meaning solely from the *place* in which it stands, a system in which the content and significance of each form would be characterized by the richness and specific quality of the relations and concatenations in which it stands with other spiritual energies and ultimately with totality.

Ever since the beginnings of modern philosophy and particularly since the emergence of modern philosophical idealism, there has been no lack of attempts to establish such a system. Though Descartes' programmatic *Discours de la méthode* and his *Regulae ad directionem ingenii* reject as futile the attempts of the old metaphysics to survey the totality of things and penetrate the ultimate secrets of nature, they insist all the more emphatically that it must be possible to deal exhaustively with the *universitas* of the human spirit and to survey it by means of thought. "Ingenii limites definire," to define the area and limits of the spirit—this maxim of Descartes has become the watchword of all modern philosophy. But the concept of "spirit" is still divided and ambiguous, for it is used sometimes in a broader, sometimes in a more restricted sense. The philosophy of Descartes starts from a new and comprehensive concept of *consciousness,* but then, with the term *cogitatio,* lets this concept relapse into synonymity with pure *thought.* For Descartes, and for all the rationalists, the systems of spirit and of reason coincide. They hold that philosophy can be said to encompass and permeate the universitas, the concrete totality of the spirit, only if it can be deduced from a *logical* principle. Thus the pure form of logic becomes again the prototype and model for every form of the human spirit. And just as in Descartes, with whom the systems of classical idealism began, so likewise in Hegel with whom they ended, this methodic relationship is still evident. More sharply than any thinker before him, Hegel stated that we must think of the human spirit as a *concrete* whole, that we must not stop at the simple concept but develop it in the totality of its manifestations. And yet in his *Phenomenology of Spirit,* with which he endeavored to fulfill this task, he intended merely to prepare the ground for *logic.* All the diverse forms of the spirit set forth in the *Phenomenology* seem to culminate in a supreme logical summit—and it is only in this end point that they attain to their perfect "truth" and essence. Rich and varied as they are in content, their structure is subordinated to a single and, in a certain sense, uniform law—the law of dialectical method, which represents the unchanging rhythm of the concept's autonomous movement. All cultural forms culminate in absolute knowledge; it is here that the spirit gains the pure element of its existence, the concept. All the earlier stages it has passed through are, to be sure, preserved as factors in this culminate state, but by being reduced to mere factors they are, on the other hand, negated. Of all cultural forms, only that of logic, the concept, cognition, seems to enjoy a true and authentic *autonomy.* The concept is not only a means of representing the concrete life of the spirit, it is also the truly substantial element in the spirit itself. So that, with all Hegel's endeavor to apprehend the specific differentiations of the spirit, he ultimately refers and reduces its whole content and capacity to a single dimension—and its profoundest content and true meaning are apprehended only in relation to this dimension.

Indeed, this ultimate reduction of all cultural forms to the *one* form of logic seems to be implied by the concept of philosophy itself and particularly by the fundamental principle of philosophical idealism. For if we renounce this unity, a strict *systematic* understanding of these forms would seem to be unattainable. The only counterpart to the dialectical method is pure empiricism. If we can find no universal law by virtue of which one cultural form necessarily issues from another, until at last the whole cycle of forms has been comprehended—then, it would seem, the totality of these forms can no longer be looked upon as a self-contained cosmos. Then the particular forms simply stand side by side: their scope and specific character can be described, but they no longer express a common ideal content. The philosophy of these forms would then necessarily amount to their history, which, according to its object, would define itself as history of language, history of religion and myth, history of art, etc. At this point a strange dilemma arises. If we hold fast to the postulate of logical unity, the universality of the logical form threatens ultimately to efface the individuality of each special province and the specificity of its principle—but if we immerse ourselves in this individuality and persevere in our examination of it, we run the risk of losing ourselves and of finding no way back to the universal. An escape from this methodological dilemma is possible only if we can discover a factor which recurs in each basic cultural form but in no two of them takes exactly the same shape. Then, in reference to this principle, we might assert the ideal relation between the individual provinces —between the basic functions of language and cognition, of art and religion —without losing the incomparable particularity of any one of them. If we can find a medium through which all the configurations effected in the separate branches of cultural life must pass, but which nevertheless retains its particular nature, its specific character—we shall have found the necessary intermediary link for an inquiry which will accomplish for the *totality* of cultural forms what the transcendental critique has done for pure *cognition*. Our next question must therefore be: do the diverse branches of cultural life actually present such an intermediate field and mediating func-

tion, and if so, does this function disclose typic
it can be recognized and described?

2. *Universal Function of the Sign. The Problem*

In seeking an answer to this question we shall first ⸻ ⸺ to the concept
of the "symbol," as Heinrich Hertz characterized it from the standpoint of
natural science. What the physicist seeks in phenomena is a statement of
their necessary connection. But in order to arrive at this statement, he must
not only leave behind him the immediate world of sensory impressions, but
must seemingly turn away from them entirely. The concepts with which
he operates, the concepts of space and time, of mass and force, of material
point and energy, of the atom or the ether, are free "fictions." Cognition
devises them in order to dominate the world of sensory experience and
survey it as a world ordered by law, but nothing in the sensory data themselves immediately corresponds to them, yet although there is no such correspondence—and perhaps precisely *because* there is none—the conceptual
world of physics is entirely self-contained. Each particular concept, each
special fiction and sign is like the articulated *word* of a *language* meaningful in itself and ordered according to fixed rules. In the very beginnings of
modern physics, in Galileo, we find the metaphor that the "book of nature"
is written in mathematical language and can be read only through mathematical ciphers. And since then, the entire development of exact natural
science shows that every step forward in the formulation of its problems
and concepts has gone hand in hand with the increasing refinement of its
system of signs. A clear understanding of the fundamental concepts of
Galileo's mechanics became possible only when the universal logical locus
of these concepts was, as it were, determined and a universally valid mathe-
matical-logical sign for them was created in the algorism of the differential
calculus. And then, taking as his point of departure the problems connected
with the discovery of the analysis of infinity, Leibniz was soon able to
formulate the universal problem inherent in the function of symbolism,
and to raise his universal "characteristic" to a truly philosophical plane. In
his view, the logic of things, i.e., of the material concepts and relations on
which the structure of a science rests, cannot be separated from the logic

sign is no mere accidental cloak of the idea, but its neces-
ntial organ. It serves not merely to communicate a complete
thought-content, but is an instrument, by means of which this
t develops and fully defines itself. The conceptual definition of a
ntent goes hand in hand with its stabilization in some characteristic sign.
Consequently, all truly strict and exact thought is sustained by the *symbolics* and *semiotics* on which it is based. Every "law" of nature assumes for our thinking the form of a universal "formula"—and a formula can be expressed only by a combination of universal and specific signs. Without the universal signs provided by arithmetic and algebra, no special relation in physics, no special law of nature would be expressible. It is, as it were, the fundamental principle of cognition that the universal can be perceived only in the particular, while the particular can be thought only in reference to the universal.

This mutual relation is not limited to science but runs through all the other fundamental forms of cultural activity. None of them can develop its appropriate and peculiar type of comprehension and configuration without, as it were, creating a definite sensuous substratum for itself. This substratum is so essential that it sometimes seems to constitute the entire content, the true "meaning" of these forms. Language seems fully definable as a system of phonetic symbols—the worlds of art and myth seem to consist entirely in the particular, sensuously tangible forms that they set before us. Here we have in fact an all-embracing medium in which the most diverse cultural forms meet. The content of the spirit is disclosed only in its manifestations; the ideal form is known only by and in the aggregate of the sensible signs which it uses for its expression. If it were possible to achieve a systematic survey of the various directions which this kind of expression has taken; if it were possible to show their typical and consistent features as well as their special gradations and inner differences, the ideal of a "universal characteristic," formulated by Leibniz for cognition, would be fulfilled for the whole of cultural activity. We should then possess a kind of grammar of the symbolic function as such, which would encompass and generally help to define its special terms and idioms as we encounter them in language and art, in myth and religion.

The idea of such a grammar implies a broadening of the traditional and historical concept of idealism. Idealism has always aimed at juxtaposing to the *mundus sensibilis* another cosmos, the *mundus intelligibilis,* and at defining the boundary between these two worlds. But the usual means of drawing this boundary was to say that the intelligible world is governed by the principle of pure action, while the sensible world is dominated by the principle of receptivity. The free spontaneity of the mind prevails in the former, the confinement, the passivity of the senses in the latter. But for the "universal characteristic" which now stands before us in the broadest outlines as problem and project, *this* opposition is no longer irreconcilable and exclusive. For the senses and the spirit are now joined in a new form of reciprocity and correlation. Their metaphysical dualism seems bridged, since it can be shown that precisely the pure *function* of the spirit itself must seek its concrete fulfillment in the sensory world. Within the sensory sphere, a sharp distinction must be made between mere "reaction" and pure "action," between "impression" and "expression." Dogmatic sensationalism underestimates the importance of the purely intellectual factors and moreover, though it insists on sensibility as the basic factor in the life of the spirit, it by no means encompasses either the whole concept of sensibility or its whole effect. Dogmatic sensationalism presents an inadequate and distorted picture of sensibility, which it limits to "impressions," to the immediate givenness of simple sensations. In so doing, it fails to recognize that there is also an activity of the sensibility itself, that, as Goethe said, there is also an "exact sensory imagination," which operates in the most diverse spheres of cultural endeavor. We find indeed that, beside and above the world of perception, all these spheres produce freely their own *world of symbols* which is the true vehicle of their immanent development—a world whose inner quality is still wholly sensory, but which already discloses a formed sensibility, that is to say, a sensibility governed by the spirit. Here we no longer have to do with a sensible world that is simply given and present, but with a system of diverse sensory factors which are produced by some form of free creation.

The process of language formation shows for example how the chaos of immediate impressions takes on order and clarity for us only when we "name" it and so permeate it with the function of linguistic thought and expression. In this new world of linguistic signs the world of impressions itself acquires an entirely new "permanence," because it acquires a new intellectual articulation. This differentiation and fixation of certain contents by words, not only designates a definite intellectual quality through them, but actually endows them with such a quality, by virtue of which they are now raised above the mere immediacy of so-called sensory qualities. Thus language becomes one of the human spirit's basic implements, by which we progress from the world of mere sensation to the world of intuition and ideas. It contains in germ that intellectual effort which is afterwards manifested in the formation of scientific concepts and in the logical unity of their form. Here lies the first beginning of that universal function of separation and association, which finds its highest conscious expression in the analyses and syntheses of scientific thought. And beside the world of linguistic and conceptual signs stands the world of myth and art, incommensurate with it and yet related in spiritual origin. For deeply rooted as it is in sensibility, mythical fantasy also goes far beyond the mere passivity of sensation. If we judge it by the ordinary empirical standards provided by our sensory experience, its creations cannot but seem "unreal," but precisely in this unreality lies the spontaneity and inner freedom of the mythical function. And this freedom is by no means arbitrary and lawless. The world of myth is no mere product of whim or chance, it has its own fundamental laws of form, which are at work in all its particular manifestations. And when we consider art, it is immediately clear that the conception of an aesthetic form in the sensible world is possible only because we ourselves create the fundamental elements of form. All understanding of spatial forms, for example, is ultimately bound up with this activity of their inner production and with the law governing this production. And so we see that the very highest and purest spiritual activity known to consciousness is conditioned and mediated by certain modes of sensory activity. Here again the authentic and essential life of the pure idea comes to us only when phenomena "stain the white radiance of eternity." We can arrive at a system of the manifold manifestations of the mind only by pursuing the different directions taken by its original imaginative power. In them we see reflected the essential nature of the human spirit—for it can only disclose itself to us by shaping sensible matter.

Another indication that the creation of the various systems of sensuous symbols is indeed a pure activity of the mind is that from the outset all these symbols lay claim to objective value. They go beyond the mere phenomena of the individual consciousness, claiming to confront them with something that is universally valid. This claim may possibly prove unwarranted in the light of subsequent critical inquiry with its more highly developed concept of truth; but the mere fact that it is made belongs to the essence and character of the particular cultural forms themselves. They themselves regard their symbols not only as objectively valid, but for the most part as the very core of the objective and "real." It is characteristic, for example, of the first seemingly naïve and unreflecting manifestations of linguistic thinking and mythical thinking, that they do not clearly distinguish between the content of the "thing" and the content of the "sign," but indifferently merge the two. The name of a thing and the thing itself are inseparably fused; the mere word or image contains a magic force through which the essence of the thing gives itself to us. And we need only transfer this notion from the real to the ideal, from the material to the functional, to find that it contains a kernel of justification. In the immanent development of the mind the acquisition of the *sign* really constitutes a first and necessary step towards knowledge of the objective nature of the thing. For consciousness the sign is, as it were, the first stage and the first demonstration of objectivity, because through it the constant flux of the contents of consciousness is for the first time halted, because in it something enduring is determined and emphasized. No mere *content* of consciousness as such recurs in strictly identical form once it has passed and been replaced by others. Once it has vanished from consciousness, it is gone forever as that which it was. But to this incessant flux of contents, consciousness now juxtaposes its own unity and the unity of its form. Its identity is truly demonstrated not in what it is or has, but in what it does. Through the sign that is associated with the content, the content itself acquires a new permanence. For the sign, in contrast to the actual flow of the particular contents of consciousness, has a definite ideal *meaning,* which endures as such. It is not, like the simple given sensation, an isolated particular, occurring but once, but persists as the representative of a totality, as an aggregate of potential contents, beside which it stands as a first "universal." In the symbolic function of consciousness—as it operates in language, in art, in myth—certain unchanging fundamental forms, some of a conceptual and some of a purely sensory nature, disengage themselves from the stream of consciousness; the flux of contents is replaced by a self-contained and enduring unity of form.

Here, however, we are not dealing with an isolated act, but with a progressive process of determination. At the first level, the fixation of the content through the linguistic sign, the mythical or artistic image, seems to do no more than hold it fast in the *memory,* it does not go beyond simple reproduction. At this level the sign seems to add nothing to the content to which it refers, but merely to preserve and repeat it. Even in the history of the psychological development of *art* it has been thought possible to identify a phase of mere "recollective art," in which all artistic endeavor was directed solely towards stressing certain features of what was perceived by the senses and presenting it to the memory in a man-made image.[4] But the more clearly the particular cultural forms disclose their specific energy, the more evident it becomes that all apparent "reproduction" presupposes an original and autonomous act of consciousness. The reproducibility of the content is itself bound up with the production of a sign for it, and in producing this sign the consciousness operates freely and independently. The concept of "memory" thus takes on a richer and deeper meaning. In order to remember a content, consciousness must previously have possessed itself of that content in a way differing from mere sensation or perception. The mere repetition of the given at another time does not suffice; in this repetition a new kind of conception and formation must be manifested. For every "reproduction" of a content embodies a new level of "reflection." By the mere fact that it no longer takes this content as something simply present, but confronts it in imagination as something past and yet not vanished, consciousness, by its changed *relation* to the content, gives both to itself and the content a changed ideal *meaning*. And this occurs more and more precisely and abundantly as the world of representations stemming from the "I" becomes differentiated. The "I" now exercises an original formative activity all the while developing a deeper understanding.

The limits of the "subjective" and "objective" worlds become for the first time really clear. One of the essential tasks performed by the general critique of knowledge is to ascertain the laws governing this delimitation in the purely *theoretical* sphere, where it is effected by the methods of scientific thought. This critique shows that the "subjective" and "objective" were not from the very beginning strictly separate spheres, fully defined in content, but that both became defined only in the process of cognition and in accordance with its methods and conditions. The categorical distinction between "I" and "not-I" proves to be an essential and constant function of theoretical thinking, whereas the manner in which this function is *fulfilled*, the boundary between the "subjective" and "objective" contents varies with the level of cognition. For theoretical science, the enduring and necessary elements in experience are "objective"—but which contents are said to be enduring and necessary depends on the general methodological standard applied to the experience and on the level of cognition at that time, that is, on the totality of its empirically and

4. Cf. W. Wundt, *Die Kunst*, Vol. *3* in *Völkerpsychologie*, 2d ed. pp. 115 ff.

theoretically assured insights. Seen in this context, the way in which we apply the conceptual opposition of "subjective" and "objective" in giving form to the world of experience, in constructing nature, appears to be not so much the *solution* to the problem of cognition, as its perfect *expression*.[5]

But this *opposition* is manifested in all its richness and diversity only when we follow it beyond the limits of theoretical thinking and its specific concepts. Not only science, but language, myth, art and religion as well, provide the building stones from which the world of "reality" is constructed for us, as well as that of the human spirit, in sum the World-of-the-I. Like scientific cognition, they are not simple *structures* which we can insert into a given world, we must understand them as *functions* by means of which a particular form is given to reality and in each of which specific distinctions are effected. Each function makes use of different instruments, each one presupposes and applies entirely different standards and criteria; and the result is different also. The scientific concept of truth and reality is different from that of religion—similarly, each sphere not only designates but actually creates its particular and irreducible basic relation between "inside" and "outside," between the I and the world. Before a *decision* can be reached with regard to all these diverse, overlapping and conflicting views and aspirations, they must first be differentiated with critical rigor and precision. The achievement of each one must be measured by itself, and not by the standards and aims of any other—and only at the end of this examination can we ask whether and how all these forms of conceiving the world and the I are compatible with one another—whether, though they are not copies of one and the same self-subsistent "thing," they do not complement one another to form a single totality and a unified system.

For the philosophy of *language* this approach was first envisaged and carried out with full clarity by Wilhelm von Humboldt. For Humboldt, the phonetic sign which represents the material of all language formation is in a sense the bridge between the subjective and objective, because in it the essential factors of the two are combined. For on the one hand the sound is spoken, that is, produced and formed by ourselves; but on the other hand, as a sound heard, it is a part of the sensible reality that sur-

5. For more detailed treatment see my book, *Substanzbegriff und Funktionsbegriff* (Berlin, B. Cassirer, 1910), ch. 6. Eng. trans. by Wm. C. and M. C. Swabey, *Substance and Function* (Chicago, Open Court Publishing Co., 1923).

rounds us. We apprehend and know it as something both "inward" and "outward"—as an inward energy which assumes objective form in the outward world.

In speech the energy of the mind breaks a path through the lips, but its product returns through our own ears. The idea is translated into true objectivity without being withdrawn from subjectivity. Only language can do this; and without this translation into an objectivity which returns to the subject—and such a translation occurs, even though silently, wherever language is at work—the formation of concepts and hence all true thought would be impossible. . . . For language cannot be regarded as a substance which is present, which can be apprehended as a whole or gradually communicated; it is something which must be constantly produced, and while the laws according to which it is produced are defined, its scope and in a certain sense the manner in which it is produced remains indeterminate. . . . Just as the particular sound mediates between the object and the man, so the whole language mediates between him and the nature that works upon him from within and without. He surrounds himself with a world of sounds in order to assimilate and elaborate the world of objects.[6]

In this critical, idealistic view of language, Humboldt mentions a factor which occurs in every type and form of symbolism. In each one of its freely projected signs the human spirit apprehends the object and at the same time apprehends itself and its own formative law. And this peculiar interpenetration prepares the way for the deeper determination both of subject and object. On the first level of this determination, it appears as though the two antithetical factors simply stood separately, side by side and juxtaposed. In its earliest formations, speech can equally well be interpreted as a pure expression of the inward or the outward, as an expression of *mere* subjectivity or mere objectivity. In the first case the spoken sound seems to be nothing other than an expression of excitement and emotion, in the second case it seems to be mere onomatopoeic imitation. The various speculations on the "origin of language" do indeed move between these two extremes, neither of which reach the core and essence of

6. W. V. Humboldt, "Einleitung zum Kawi-Werk," *Werke,* ed. Albert Leitzmann, *Gesammelte Schriften,* ed. Königlich Preussische Akademie der Wissenschaften, 7, No. 1, 55 ff. See *Über die Kawi-Sprache auf der Insel Java* (3 vols. Berlin, 1836–39), Vol. *1,* "Einleitung."

language itself. For what language designates and expresses is neither exclusively subjective nor exclusively objective; it effects a new mediation, a particular *reciprocal relation* between the two factors. Neither the mere discharge of emotion, nor the repetition of objective sound stimuli yields the characteristic meaning and form of language: language arises where the two ends are joined, so creating a new synthesis of "I" and "world." An analogous relation is created in every truly independent and original function and consciousness. Art can no more be defined as the mere expression of inward life than as a reflection of the forms of outward reality; in it, too, the crucial and characteristic factor is to be sought in how, through it, the "subjective" and "objective," pure emotion and pure form, merge with one another and so gain a new permanence and a new content. In all these examples we see more sharply than is possible if we limit ourselves to the purely intellectual function, that in analyzing the cultural forms we cannot begin with a rigid dogmatic distinction between the subjective and objective, but that they are differentiated and their spheres defined only through these forms themselves. Each particular cultural energy contributes to this definition in its particular way and plays its own characteristic part in establishing the concepts of the I and of the world. Cognition, language, myth and art: none of them is a mere mirror, simply reflecting images of inward or outward data; they are not indifferent media, but rather the true sources of light, the prerequisite of vision, and the wellsprings of all formation.

3. The Problem of "Representation" and the Structure of Consciousness

In analyzing language, art, myth, our first problem is: how can a finite and particular sensory content be made into the vehicle of a general spiritual "meaning"? If we content ourselves with considering the material aspect of the cultural forms, with describing the physical properties of the signs they employ, then their ultimate, basic elements seem to consist in an aggregate of particular sensations, in simple qualities of sight, hearing, or touch. But then a miracle occurs. Through the manner in which it is contemplated, this simple sensory material takes on a new and varied life.

When the physical sound, distinguished as such only by pitch and intensity and quality, is formed into a word, it becomes an expression of the finest intellectual and emotional distinctions. What it immediately is, is thrust into the background by what it accomplishes with its mediation, by what it "means." The concrete particular elements in a work of art also disclose this basic relation. No work of art can be understood as the simple *sum* of these elements, for in it a definite law, a specific principle of aesthetic formation are at work. The synthesis by which the consciousness combines a series of tones into the unity of a melody, would seem to be totally different from the synthesis by which a number of syllables is articulated into the unity of a "sentence." But they have one thing in common, that in both cases the sensory particulars do not stand by themselves; they are articulated into a conscious *whole*, from which they take their qualitative meaning.

If we attempt a broad initial survey of the basic relations which constitute the unity of consciousness, our attention is first drawn to certain mutually independent "modes" of combination. The factor of "juxtaposition" as it appears in the form of *space*, the factor of succession as in the form of *time*—the combination of material properties in such a way that one is apprehended as a *"thing,"* the other as an "attribute," or of successive events in such a way that the one appears as a *cause* of the other: all these are examples of such original types of relation. Sensationalism strives in vain to derive them from the immediate content of particular impressions. "Five tones on a flute" may, to be sure, according to Hume's well-known psychological theory, "add up to" the idea of time—but this result is possible only if "succession," the characteristic factor of relation and order, has been tacitly drawn into the content of the particular tones, so that the universal structure of time is taken as a premise. For psychological as well as epistemological analysis, the basic forms of relation prove to be just such simple and irreducible "qualities" of consciousness as the simple sensory qualities, the elements of sight, hearing or touch. And yet philosophical thought cannot content itself with accepting the diversity of these relations as such, as a simple given fact. In dealing with the sensations it may suffice to list their principal classes and consider them as an unconnected multiplicity; but when we come to the relations, it would seem that the operation of their particular forms becomes intelligible to us only when we think of them as connected by a higher synthesis. Since Plato in *The Sophists* formulated this problem of the κοινωνία τῶν γενῶν, the systematic "community" of pure ideas and formal concepts, it has remained alive throughout the history of philosophy. The critical and the metaphysical-speculative solutions to the problem differ in that they presuppose different concepts of the "universal" and hence a different notion of the logical system itself. The former view goes back to the concept of the analytic universal, the latter aims at a synthetic universal. In the critical view we content ourselves with gathering all the possible forms of connection into a systematic concept and thus *subordinating* them to definite fundamental laws; in the metaphysical view we seek to understand how the concrete totality of particular forms develops from a single original principle. The metaphysical view admits of only *one* initial point and *one* end point, which are connected with one another by the constant application of one and the same methodical principle to a synthetic-deductive demonstration—the critical view not only tolerates but encourages several different dimensions of inquiry. It raises the problem of a unity which from the outset makes no claim to simplicity. The different modes in which the human spirit gives form to reality are recognized as such, and no attempt is made to fit them into a single, simply progressing series. And yet, in such an approach we by no means abandon the idea of a connection between the particular forms as such; this approach sharpens, on the contrary, the idea of the system by replacing the concept of a simple system with the concept of a complex system. Each form, in a manner of speaking, is assigned to a special plane, within which it fulfills itself and develops its specific character in total independence—but precisely when all these ideal modes are considered together, certain analogies and certain typical relations appear, which can be singled out and described as such.

The first factor we encounter is a difference, which we may term the difference in the *quality* and *modality* of forms. By the "quality" of a given relation we here understand the particular type of combination by means of which it creates series within the whole of consciousness, the arrangement of whose members is subject to a special law. Thus, for example, the relation of simultaneity as opposed to succession constitutes such an independent quality. On the other hand, one and the same form of relation can undergo an inner transformation if it occurs within a different *formal context*. Each particular relation belongs—regardless of its particularity—to a *totality* of meanings which itself possesses its own "nature," its self-contained formal law. Thus, for example, the universal relation which we call "time" is just as much an element of theoretical scientific *cognition* as an essential factor in certain structures of the *aesthetic* consciousness. Time, as explained in the beginning of Newton's *Mechanics* as the stable basis of all motion and the uniform measure of all change, seems at first sight to have nothing more than the name in common with the time that governs a work of music and its rhythmic measures—and yet this unity of nomenclature involves a unity of meaning at least in so far as both posit that universal and abstract quality which we term "succession." But the consciousness of natural laws as laws of the temporal form of motion and the consciousness of musical measure have each their own specific mode of succession. Similarly, we can interpret certain spatial forms, certain complexes of lines and figures, in one case as an artistic ornament and in another as a geometrical figure, so endowing one and the same material with entirely different meanings. The spatial unity which we build in aesthetic vision and creation, in painting, sculpture and architecture, belongs to an entirely different sphere from the spatial unity which is represented in geometrical theorems and axioms. In the one case we have the modality of the logical-geometric concept, in the other the modality of artistic imagination—in the one case, space is conceived as an aggregate of mutually independent relations, as a system of "causes" and "consequences"; in the other, it is conceived as a whole whose particular factors are dynamically interlocked, a perceptual, emotional unity. And the consciousness of space can assume still other forms: for in *mythical thinking* we find again a very special approach to space, a manner of articulating and "orienting" the spatial world that differs sharply and characteristically from the spatial articulation of the cosmos in empirical thinking.[7] Likewise, the general form of *causality* appears in a totally different light accordingly as we consider it on the plane of scientific or of mythical thinking. Myth also knows the concept of causality, which it employs both in its general theogonies and cosmogonies and in its interpretations of all sorts of particular phenomena which it "explains" mythically on the basis of this concept. But the ultimate motive of this "explanation" is entirely different from that which governs the study of causality by theoretical, scientific concepts. The *problem* of the origin as such is common to science and myth; but the type and character, the modality of the origin changes as soon as we move from the one province to the other—as soon

7. Cf. my study, *Die Begriffsform in mythischen Denken, Studien der Bibliòthek Warburg*, Vol. *1* (Leipzig, Berlin, B. G. Teubner, 1922).

as we use the origin and learn to understand it as a scientific *principle,* rather than as a mythical *potency.*

We see, then, that in order to characterize a given form of relation in its concrete application and concrete meaning, we must not only state its qualitative attributes as such, but also define the system in which it stands. If we designate the various kinds of relation—such as relation of space, time, causality, etc.—as R_1, R_2, R_3, we must assign to each one a special "index of modality," μ_1, μ_2, μ_3, denoting the context of function and meaning in which it is to be taken. For each of these contexts, language as well as scientific cognition, art as well as myth, possesses its own constitutive principle which sets its stamp, as it were, on all the particular forms within it. The result is an extraordinary diversity of formal relations, whose richness and inner involvements, however, can be apprehended only through a rigorous analysis of each fundamental form. But even aside from such an analysis, the most general survey of consciousness as a whole reveals certain fundamental conditions of unity, prerequisites for synthesis, combination, and statement. It lies in the very nature of consciousness that it cannot posit any content without, by this simple act, positing a complex of other contents. Kant—in his treatise on negative quantities—once formulated the problem of causality as the endeavor to understand why because *something* is, *something else,* of a totally different nature, ought to be and is. If with dogmatic metaphysics we take the concept of absolute *being* as our starting point, this question must seem ultimately insoluble. For an absolute being implies ultimate absolute elements, each of which is a static substance in itself, and must be conceived for itself. But this concept of substance discloses no necessary or even intelligible transition to the multiplicity of the world, to the diversity of its particular phenomena. Even in Spinoza the transition from substance as that which *in se est et per se concipitur,* to the multiplicity of particular, dependent and changeable *modi* is not deduced but arrived at by stealth. Metaphysics, as its history shows, is confronted more and more by a logical dilemma. It must either take seriously the fundamental concept of being, in which case all relations tend to evaporate, all the multiplicity of space, time, causality threatens to disperse into mere illusion—or it must, in recognizing these relations, turn them into mere "accidents" of being. But here metaphysics encounters a characteristic difficulty, for it becomes increasingly apparent that it is these "accidents" which are accessible to *cognition,* which can be apprehended in its forms, while the naked "essence," which is supposedly the foundation of the particular qualities and relations, becomes lost in the void of mere abstraction. What is ostensibly the "whole of reality" contains nothing but its definition and proves ultimately to have lost all independent, positive concretion.

This dialectic of metaphysical ontology can be avoided only if, from the very start, "content" and "form," "element" and "relation" are conceived not as terms independent of one another, but as concurrent and mutually determining one another. The modern, "subjective" trend in speculation has brought this general methodological approach increasingly to the fore. For the question assumes a new form once it is removed from the realm of absolute being to the sphere of consciousness. Every "simple" quality of consciousness has a definite content only in so far as it is apprehended in complete unity with certain qualities but separately from others. The function of this unity and this separation is not removable from the content of consciousness but constitutes one of its essential conditions. Accordingly there is no "something" in consciousness that does not *eo ipso* and without further mediation give rise to "another" and to a series of others. For what defines each particular content of consciousness is that in it the whole of consciousness is in some form posited and represented. Only in and through this *representation* does what we call the "presence" of the content become possible. This is immediately evident when we consider even the simplest instance of this presence, the temporal relation and the temporal "present." Nothing seems more certain than that every truly *immediate* content of consciousness has reference to a definite "now" in which it is contained. The past is "no longer" in the consciousness, the future is "not yet" in it: neither seems to belong to its concrete reality, its true actuality, but to dissolve into mere logical abstractions. And yet the content which we designate as the "now" is nothing but the eternally fluid boundary dividing the past from the future. This boundary cannot be posited independently of what it bounds: it exists only in this act of division itself, not as something that could be thought before this division and detached from it. The temporal moment, in so far as we mean to define it *as* temporal, can be apprehended only as the fluid transition from past to future, from no-longer to not-yet, and not as static substantial being. Where the now is interpreted differently, that is, absolutely, it represents no longer an element of time, but the negation of time. It seems then to halt and so negate the movement of time. For a school of thought like that of the Eleatic philosophers, which is oriented toward an absolute being in which it strives to persist, the flying arrow is *at rest,* because in every indivisible "now" it has only one single, unequivocally defined and invisible "position." But if the temporal moment is to be conceived as *pertaining* to temporal motion, it must not be removed from it and opposed to it, but truly situated in it: and this is only possible if in thinking the moment as a particular, we concurrently think the process as a whole, and if both, moment and process, merge into a perfect unity for consciousness. The form of time itself can be "given" for us only when the temporal sequence is represented as running forward and backward. If we think a particular cross section of consciousness, we can apprehend it, not by dwelling exclusively in this cross section, but only by going beyond it into the various related directions by means of definite spatial, temporal, or qualitative ordering functions. Only because in this way we can ascertain in the actual content of consciousness something that is not, in the given something that is not given—does there exist for us that unity which on the one hand we designate as the subjective unity of consciousness, and on the other as the objective unity of the object.

The psychological and epistemological analysis of the spatial consciousness takes us back to the same original function of representation. We can apprehend a spatial "whole" only by presupposing the formation of various temporal series: even though the simultaneous synthesis of consciousness constitutes a specific and original part of consciousness in general, it can only be completed and represented on the basis of the successive synthesis. If specific elements are to be combined into a spatial whole, they must pass through the sequence of consciousness and be related to one another in accordance with a definite rule. Neither the sensationalist psychology of the English nor the metaphysical psychology of Herbart was able to explain intelligibly how the consciousness of spatial synthesis originates in the consciousness of temporal synthesis—how a consciousness of "togetherness" can be shaped from a mere sequence of visual, tactile and motor sensations, or from a complex of simple sequences of percepts. But despite their entirely different points of departure, these theories have one thing in common: they all recognize that space in its concrete configuration and articulation is not "given" as a ready-made possession of the psyche, but comes into being only in the process or, one might say, in the general movement of consciousness. However, this process itself would disintegrate into isolated and unrelated particulars, permitting no synthesis into *one* result, if there were not, here again, the general possibility of apprehending the whole in the part and the part in the whole. Leibniz defined consciousness as an "expression of the many in the one," and here again this *multorum in uno expressio* is the determining factor. We intuit spatial *configurations* only by combining into *one* idea complete groups of sensory perceptions which mutually displace one another in immediate sensory experience, and on the other hand by diffusing this unity through the diversity of its particular components. It is only by this interplay of concentration and analysis that spatial consciousness is constructed. Form then appears as potential motion, while motion appears as potential form.

In his inquiries into the theory of vision, which form the starting point of modern physiological optics, Berkeley compared the development of spatial perception to the development of language. There is a kind of natural language, i.e., a fixed relationship between signs and meanings, which alone, in his belief, makes spatial perception possible. It is not by copying a ready-made material model of "absolute space" in our minds, but by learning to use the different, intrinsically incommensurate impressions of the diverse sensory spheres, particularly those of sight and touch, as representatives and signs for one another, that we create our world of space as a world of systematically related perceptions. In line with his sensationalist approach, Berkeley interpreted this language of the mind, which he proved to be a condition of spatial perception, exclusively as a language of the *senses*. But on closer scrutiny this interpretation negates itself. For it lies in the very concept of language that it can never be purely sensuous, but represents a characteristic interpenetration and interaction of sensuous and conceptual factors; in language it is always presupposed that individual sensory signs be filled with general intellectual meaning content. The same is true of every other kind of "representation"—that is, of every instance where one element of consciousness is represented in and through another. We may suppose the sensory foundation of the idea of space to lie in certain visual, motor and tactile sensations, but the sum of these sensations contains no trace of that characteristic form of unity which we call "space." The notion of space is manifested rather in a kind of coordination which enables us to pass from any one of these qualities to their totality. In every element that we posit as spatial, our consciousness posits an infinite number of potential *directions,* and only the sum of these directions constitutes the whole of our spatial intuition. The spatial "picture" that we possess of a particular empirical object, a house for example, takes form only when we amplify a particular, relatively limited perspective view in this sense; employing the partial perspective only as a starting point and stimulus, we construct from it a highly complex totality of spatial relations. Understood in this light, space is by no means a static vessel and container into which ready-made "things" are poured; it is rather a sum of ideal functions, which complement and determine one another to form a unified result. Just as in the simple temporal "now" earlier and later are expressed as the basic temporal directions, similarly in every "here" we posit a "there." The particular place is not given prior to the spatial system but only in reference to it and in correlation with it.

A third form of unity which is situated above spatial and temporal unity is the form of *objectifying* synthesis. When we combine a sum of determinate properties into the whole of a constant thing with diverse and variable characteristics, this combination presupposes simultaneous and successive syntheses, but that is not all. The relatively constant must be distinguished from the variable—certain spatial configurations must be apprehended before the concept of the thing as the constant "vehicle" of the variable properties can take form. On the other hand, the idea of this "vehicle" adds to the intuition of spatial simultaneity and temporal succession a characteristic new factor of independent importance. Empiricist analysis has indeed attempted again and again to deny this independence. It sees in the idea of the thing nothing other than a purely outward form of combination and attempts to show that the content and form of the "object" are exhausted in the sum of its attributes. But here we find the same fundamental fallacy as in the empiricist dissection of the concept and consciousness of the I. When Hume explains the self as a "bundle of perceptions," this explanation—aside from the fact that it merely speaks of combination as such but says nothing whatsoever concerning the *particular* form and type of synthesis that constitutes the self—negates itself because in the concept of perception the concept of the self, which was supposedly analyzed and dissected, is contained in its undissected totality. What makes the particular perception a perception, what distinguishes it as a "perceptual" quality from any material quality is precisely its "appurtenance to the self." This relation to the self does not arise through the synthesis of a number of perceptions but is an original characteristic of each one. A closely analogous relation prevails in the synthesis of diverse "properties" into the unity of a "thing." When we combine the sensations of extension, sweetness, roughness, whiteness into the idea of "sugar" as a unified whole, this is possible only because each one of these qualities is originally thought in reference to this whole. The whiteness or sweetness, etc., is not apprehended merely as a condition within me, but as a "property" and objective quality, because I have already attained the desired function and perspective of the "thing." Thus the particular can be posited only on the basis of a universal schema which is merely filled with new concrete content as our experience of the "thing" and its "attributes" progresses. The point as a simple and particular position is possible only "in" space, i.e., logically speaking, under presupposition of a *system* comprising all designations of position; the idea of the temporal "now" can be defined only in relation to a *sequence* of moments and to the order of succession that we call "time"—and the same is true of the relation between the thing and its properties. All these relations (the detailed definition and analysis of which are the business of specialized epistemology) disclose the same fundamental characteristic of consciousness, namely, that the whole is not obtained from its parts, but that every notion of a part already encompasses the notion of the whole, not as to content, but as to general structure and form. Every particular belongs from the outset to a definite *complex* and in itself expresses the rule of this complex. It is the totality of these rules which constitutes the true unity of consciousness, as a unity of time, space, objective synthesis, etc.

The traditional language of psychology offers no entirely adequate term for this state of affairs, because it is only recently, in the development of the modern "gestalt psychology," that this discipline has torn itself away from a fundamental sensationalism. For the sensationalist approach, which sees all objectivity as encompassed in the "simple" impression, synthesis consists merely in the "association" of impressions. This term is broad enough to cover all relations that can possibly exist in the consciousness; but by its very breadth it obscures their specific character. It fails to distinguish between relations of the most diverse quality and modality. "Association" means the fusion of elements into the unity of time or of space, into the unity of the ego or the object, into the whole of a thing or of a sequence of events—into series whose members are connected by the criterion of cause and effect and into series whose members are connected by the criterion of "means" and "end." "Association" also passes as an adequate term for the logical law by which particulars are synthesized into the conceptual unity of *cognition,* or for the forms of configuration which prove effective in the development of the *aesthetic* consciousness. But here again, it is evident that this term designates only the naked fact of combination as such, but does not say anything whatsoever regarding its specific character and law. The diversity of the paths and directions by which consciousness arrives at its syntheses is totally obscured. If we designate the "elements" as a, b, c, d, etc., their combinations, as we have seen, form a precisely graduated and internally differentiated system of diverse functions: F (a, b), (c, d), etc. This system, however, is by no means stated in the alleged generic term "association" which, on the contrary, levels and hence negates it. And the term has still another essential failing. However closely they may combine and "fuse," the contents that are brought together in association remain *separable,* both as to meaning and origin. In the course of experience they are articulated into increasingly stable organizations and groups; however, their existence as such is not given by the group, but precedes it. Yet it is precisely this relation of the "part" to the "whole" that is fundamentally surpassed in the true syntheses of consciousness. Here the whole does not *originate* in its parts, it *constitutes* them and gives them their essential meaning. In thinking of any limited segment of space we also think of its orientation to the whole of space; in every particular moment of time we encompass the universal form of succession; and in positing any particular attribute we posit the general relation of "substance" and "accident," hence the characteristic form of the object. It is precisely this interpenetration, this interdetermination which association, since it states merely the contiguity of ideas, leaves unexplained. The empirical rules it sets up regarding the mere flow of ideas fail to make intelligible the specific and fundamental forms in which ideas combine, or the unity of "meaning" that arises among them.

The rationalistic theory of knowledge set out to save and demonstrate the independence of this "meaning." One of its essential historical achievements is to have established by one and the same intellectual operation a new and deeper view of consciousness as such and a new concept of the "object" of knowledge. It confirmed Descartes' dictum that the unity of the objective world, the unity of substance, could not be apprehended by perception, but only by the reflection of the mind on itself, by *inspectio mentis.* This fundamental theory of rationalism stands in the sharpest antithesis to the empiricist theory of "associations"—but it too fails to overcome the inner tension between two fundamentally different elements of consciousness, between its mere "matter" and its pure "form." For here too the *synthesis* of the contents of consciousness is based upon an activity which in some way approaches the particular contents from outside. According to Descartes, the "ideas" of outward perception, the ideas of lightness and darkness, roughness and smoothness, colored and resonant, are essentially given only as pictures (*velut picturae*) and, in this sense, as merely subjective events. What leads us beyond this stage, what enables us to progress from the diversity and variability of impressions to the unity and constancy of the object, is the function of judgment and "unconscious inference," which is totally independent of the impressions. Objective unity is a purely formal unity, which can neither be heard nor seen as such, but can be apprehended only in the logical process of pure thought. Descartes' *metaphysical* dualism is ultimately rooted in his *methodological* dualism: the theory of the absolute division between the substance of extension and the thinking substance, is merely a metaphysical expression for an antithesis which is discernible in his account of the pure function of consciousness.

And even with Kant, in the beginning of his *Critique of Pure Reason,* this antithesis between sensibility and thought, between the "material" and "formal" determinants of consciousness, retains its full force—though here he goes on to say that perhaps the two are connected in a common root unknown to us. The principal objection to this formulation is that the antithesis expressed in it is a product of abstraction; the particular factors of knowledge are logically evaluated, whereas the unity of the matter and form of consciousness, of the "particular" and the "universal," of sensory "data" and pure "principles of order," constitutes precisely that originally certain and originally known phenomenon which every *analysis* of consciousness must take as its point of departure. If we wished to characterize this process by a mathematical metaphor and symbol, despite the fact that it goes beyond the sphere of the mathematical, we might, in contradistinction to mere "association," choose the term "integration." The element of consciousness is related to the whole of consciousness not as an extensive part to a sum of parts, but as a differential to its integral. Just as the differential equation of a moving body expresses the trajectory and general law of its motion, we must think of the general structural laws of consciousness as given in each of its elements, in any of its cross sections —not however in the sense of independent contents, but of tendencies and directions which are already projected in the sensory particular. This, precisely, is the nature of a content of consciousness; it exists only in so far as it immediately goes beyond itself in various directions of synthesis. The consciousness of the moment contains reference to temporal succession; the consciousness of a single point in space contains reference to space as the sum and totality of all possible designations of position; and there are countless analogous relations through which the form of the whole is expressed in the consciousness of the particular. The "integral" of consciousness is constructed not from the sum of its sensuous elements (a, b, c, d . . .), but from the totality, as it were, of its differentials of relation and form (d r_1, d r_2, d r_3 . . .). The full actuality of consciousness is merely the unfolding of what was present as "potency" and general possibility in each of its separate factors. Here, in the most general terms, lies the critical solution of Kant's question as to how it is thinkable that because "something" is, something "other," totally different from it, must also be. The relation, which inevitably seemed more and more paradoxical the more sharply it was examined and analyzed from the standpoint of absolute being, becomes necessary and immediately intelligible when it is considered from the standpoint of consciousness. For here there is not from the very start an abstract "one," confronted by an equally abstract and detached "other"; here the one is "in" the many and the many is "in" the one: in the sense that each determines and represents the other.

4. Ideational Content of the Sign. Transcending the Copy Theory of Knowledge

So far we have aimed at a kind of critical "deduction," an explanation and justification of the concept of representation, in the belief that the representation of one content in and through another is an essential premise for the structure and formal unity of consciousness. The following study, however, will not deal with this general logical significance of the representative function. We shall seek to pursue the problem of signs, not backward to its ultimate "foundations," but forward to its concrete unfolding and configuration in the diverse cultural spheres.

We have acquired a new foundation for such an investigation. We must go back to "natural" symbolism, to that representation of consciousness as a whole which is necessarily contained or at least projected in every single moment and fragment of consciousness, if we wish to understand the artificial symbols, the "arbitrary" signs which consciousness creates in language, art, and myth. The force and effect of these mediating signs would remain a mystery if they were not ultimately rooted in an original spiritual process which belongs to the very essence of consciousness. We can understand how a sensuous particular, such as the spoken sound, can become the vehicle of a purely intellectual meaning, only if we assume that the basic function of signification is present and active before the individual sign is produced, so that this producing does not create signification, but merely stabilizes it, applies it to the particular case. Since every particular content of consciousness is situated in a network of diverse relations, by virtue of which its simple existence and self-representation contain *reference* to other and still other contents, there can and must be certain formations of consciousness in which the pure form of reference is, as it were, sensuously embodied. From this follows the characteristic twofold nature of these formations: their bond with sensibility, which however contains within it a freedom from sensibility. In every linguistic "sign," in every mythical or artistic "image," a spiritual content, which intrinsically points beyond the whole sensory sphere, is translated into the form of the sensuous, into something visible, audible or tangible. An independent mode of configuration appears, a specific activity of consciousness, which is differentiated from any datum of immediate sensation or perception, but makes use of these data as vehicles, as means of expression. Thus the "natural" symbolism which we have found embedded as a fundamental characteristic of consciousness is on the one hand utilized and retained, while on the other hand it is surpassed and refined. For in this "natural" symbolism, a certain partial content of consciousness, though distinct from the whole, retained the power to represent this whole and in so doing to reconstitute it in a sense. A present content possessed the power of evoking another content, which was not immediately given but merely conveyed by it. It is not the case, however, that the symbolic signs which we encounter in language, myth, and art first "are" and then, beyond this "being," achieve a certain meaning; their being arises from their signification. Their content subsists purely and wholly in the function of signification. Here consciousness, in order to apprehend the whole in the particular, no longer requires the stimulus of the particular itself, which must be given as such; here consciousness *creates* definite concrete sensory contents as an expression for definite complexes of meaning. And because these contents which consciousness creates are entirely in its power, it can, through them, freely "evoke" all those meanings at any time. When, for example, we link a given intuition or idea with an arbitrary linguistic sound, we seem, at first sight, to have added nothing whatever to its content. And yet, on closer scrutiny, the content itself takes on a different "character" for consciousness through the creation of the linguistic sign: it becomes more definite. Its sharp and clear intellectual "reproduction" proves to be inseparable from the act of linguistic "production." For the function of language is not merely to *repeat* definitions and distinctions which are already present in the mind, but to formulate them and make them intelligible as such. Thus in every sphere, it is through the freedom of spiritual action that the chaos of sensory impressions begins to clear and take on fixed form for us. The fluid impression assumes form and duration for us only when we *mould* it by symbolic action in one direction or another. In science and language, in art and myth, this formative process proceeds in different ways and according to different principles, but all these spheres have this in common: that the product of their activity in no way resembles the mere *material* with which they began. It is in the basic symbolic function and its various directions that the spiritual consciousness and the sensory consciousness are first truly differentiated. It is here that we pass beyond passive receptivity to an indeterminate outward material, and begin to place upon it our independent imprint which articulates it for us into diverse spheres and forms of reality. Myth and art, language and science, are in this sense configurations *towards* being: they are not simple copies of an existing reality but represent the main directions of the spiritual movement, of the ideal process by which reality is constituted for us as one and many—as a diversity of forms which are ultimately held together by a unity of meaning.

Only when we are oriented towards this goal do the specifications of the various systems of signs, and the use which the intelligence makes of them, become intelligible. If the sign were nothing but a repetition of a determinate and finished, particular intuitive or ideational content, we should be faced with two questions. What would be accomplished by a mere copy of something already present? And how could such an exact copy be accomplished? For it is obvious that a copy can never approach the original and can never replace it for the eye of the spirit. If we took an exact reproduction as our norm, we should be driven to an attitude of fundamental skepticism toward the value of the sign as such. If, for example, we regarded it as the true and essential function of language to express once again, but merely in a different medium, the very same reality that lies ready-made before us in particular sensations and intuitions—we should be struck at once by the vast inadequacy of all languages. Measured by the limitless richness and diversity of intuitive reality, all linguistic sym bols would inevitably seem empty; measured by its individual concretion, they would inevitably seem abstract and vague. If language attempts to compete with sensation or intuition in *this* respect, it cannot but fall far behind. The πρῶτον ψευδός of the skeptical critique of language is precisely that it takes this standard as the only valid and possible one. In reality the analysis of language—particularly if it starts not from the mere particular of the word, but from the unity of the *sentence*—shows that all linguistic expression, far from being a mere copy of the given world of sensation or intuition, possesses a definite independent character of "signification."

And the same relation applies to signs of the most diverse type and origin. In a sense it can be said of them all that their value consists not so much in what they stabilize of the concrete, sensuous content and its immediate factuality, as in the part of this immediate factuality which they suppress and pass over. Similarly, artistic delineation becomes what it is and is distinguished from a mere mechanistic reproduction, only through what it omits from the "given" impression. It does not reflect this impression in its sensuous totality, but rather selects certain "pregnant" factors, i.e., factors through which the given impression is amplified beyond itself and through which the artistic-constructive fantasy, the synthetic spatial imagination, is guided in a certain direction. What constitutes the true force of the sign, here as in other fields, is precisely this: that as the immediate, determinate contents recede, the general factors of form and relation become all the sharper and clearer. The particular as such is seemingly limited; but precisely thereby that operation which we have called "integration" is effected the more clearly and forcefully. We have seen that the particular of consciousness "exists" only in so far as it potentially contains the whole and is, as it were, in constant transition towards the whole. But the use of the sign liberates this potentiality and enables it to become true actuality. Now, *one* blow strikes a thousand connected chords which all vibrate more or less forcefully and clearly in the sign. In positing the sign, consciousness detaches itself more and more from the direct *substratum* of sensation and sensory intuition: but precisely therein it reveals its inherent, original power of synthesis and unification.

Perhaps this tendency is most clearly manifested in the functioning of the *scientific* systems of signs. The abstract chemical "formula," for example, which is used to designate a certain substance, contains nothing of what direct observation and sensory perception teach us about this substance; but, instead, it places the particular body in an extraordinarily rich and finely articulated complex of relations, of which perception as such knows nothing. It no longer designates the body according to its sensuous content, according to its immediate sensory data, but represents it as a sum of potential "reactions," of possible chains of causality which are defined by general rules. In the chemical formula the totality of these necessary relations fuses with the expression of the particular, and gives this expression of the particular an entirely new and characteristic imprint. Here as elsewhere, the sign serves as an intermediary between the mere "substance" of consciousness and its spiritual "form." Precisely because it is without any sensuous mass of its own, because, in a manner of speaking, it hovers in the pure ether of meaning, it has the power to represent not the mere particulars of consciousness but its complex general movements. It does not reflect a fixed content of consciousness but defines the direction of such a general movement. Similarly, the spoken word, considered from the standpoint of physical substance, is a mere breath of wind; but in this breath there lies an extraordinary force for the dynamic of ideas and thought. This dynamic is both intensified and regulated by the sign. It is one of the essential advantages of the sign—as Leibniz pointed out in his *Characteristica generalis,* that it serves not only to represent, but above all to *discover* certain logical relations—that it not only offers a symbolic abbreviation for what is already known, but opens up new roads into the unknown. Herein we see confirmed from a new angle the synthetic power of consciousness as such, by virtue of which every concentration of its contents impels it to extend its limits. The concentration provided by the sign not only permits us to look backward, but at the same time opens up new perspectives. It sets a relative limit, but this limit itself embodies a challenge to advance and opens up the road to this advance by disclosing its general rule. This is eminently borne out by the history of science, which shows how far we have progressed toward solving a given problem or complex of problems, once we have found a fixed and clear "formula" for it. For example: Most of the questions solved in Newton's concept of fluxion and in the algorism of Leibniz' differential calculus were known before Leibniz and Newton and approached from the most diverse directions—from the angles of algebraic analysis, geometry, and mechanics. But all these problems were truly mastered only when a unified and comprehensive symbolic *expression* was found for them: for now they no longer formed a loose and fortuitous sequence of separate questions; the common principle of their origin was designated in a definite, universally applicable *method,* a basic operation whose rules were established.

In the symbolic function of consciousness, an antithesis which is given and grounded in the simple concept of consciousness is represented and mediated. All consciousness appears to us in the form of a temporal process —but in the course of this process certain types of "form" tend to detach themselves. The factor of constant change and the factor of duration tend to merge. This universal tendency is realized in different ways in the products of language, myth and art, and in the intellectual symbols of science. All these forms seem to be an immediate part of the living, constantly renewed process of consciousness: yet, at the same time, they reveal a spiritual striving for certain fixed points or resting places in this process. In them consciousness retains a character of constant flux; yet it does not flow indeterminately, but articulates itself around fixed centers of form and meaning. In its pure specificity, each such form is an αὐτὸ καθ᾽ αὐτό in the Platonic sense, detached from the mere stream of ideas—but at the same time in order to be manifested, to exist "for us," it must in some way be represented in this stream. In the creation and application of the various groups and systems of symbolic signs, both conditions are fulfilled, since here indeed a particular sensory content, without ceasing to be such, acquires the power to represent a universal for consciousness. Here neither the sensationalist axiom, "Nihil est in intellectu, quod non ante fuerit in sensu," nor its intellectualistic reversal applies. We no longer ask whether the "sensory" precedes or follows the "spiritual," for we are dealing with the revelation and manifestation of basic spiritual functions in the sensory material itself.

What would seem to constitute the bias of "empiricism" as well as abstract "idealism" is precisely that neither of them fully and clearly develops this fundamental relation. One posits a concept of the given particular but fails to recognize that any such concept must always, explicitly or implicitly, encompass the *defining* attributes of some universal; the other asserts the necessity and validity of these attributes but fails to designate the medium through which they can be represented in the given psychological world of consciousness. If, however, we start not with abstract postulates but from the concrete basic form of spiritual life, this dualistic antithesis is resolved. The illusion of an original division between the intelligible and the sensuous, between "idea" and "phenomenon," vanishes. True, we still remain in a world of "images"—but these are not images which reproduce a self-subsistent world of "things"; they are image-worlds whose principle and origin are to be sought in an autonomous creation of the spirit. Through them alone we see what we call "reality," and in them alone we possess it: for the highest objective truth that is accessible to the spirit is ultimately the form of its own activity. In the totality of its own achievements, in the knowledge of the specific rule by which each of them is determined and in the consciousness of the context which reunites all these special rules into *one* problem and one solution: in all this, the human spirit now perceives itself and reality. True, the question of what, apart from these spiritual functions, constitutes absolute reality, the question of what the "thing in itself" may be in *this* sense, remains unanswered, except that more and more we learn to recognize it as a fallacy in formulation, an intellectual phantasm. The true concept of reality cannot be squeezed into the form of mere abstract being; it opens out into the diversity and richness of the forms of spiritual *life*—but of a spiritual life which bears the stamp of inner necessity and hence of objectivity. In this sense each new "symbolic form"—not only the conceptual world of scientific cognition but also the intuitive world of art, myth, and language—constitutes, as Goethe said, a revelation sent outward from within, a "synthesis of world and spirit," which truly assures us that the two are originally one.

And here new light is cast upon a last fundamental antithesis, with which modern philosophy has struggled since its beginnings and which it has formulated with increasing sharpness. Its "subjective" trend has led philosophy more and more to focus the totality of its problems in the concept of *life* rather than the concept of being. But though this seemed to appease the antithesis of subjectivity and objectivity in the form manifested by dogmatic ontology, and to prepare the way for its ultimate reconciliation —now, in the sphere of life itself, a still more radical antithesis appeared. The truth of life seems to be given only in its pure *immediacy*, to be enclosed in it—but any attempt to understand and apprehend life seems to endanger, if not to negate, this immediacy. True, if we start from the dogmatic concept of being, the dualism of being and thought becomes more and more pronounced as we advance in our investigations—but here there remains some hope that the picture of being developed by cognition will retain at least a remnant of the truth of being. Not all being, to be sure, but at least a *part* of it would seem to enter into this picture—the substance of being would seem to penetrate the substance of cognition and in it create a more or less faithful reflection of itself. But the pure immediacy of life admits of no such partition. It, apparently, must be seen wholly or not at all; it does not enter into our mediate representations of it, but remains outside them, fundamentally different from them and opposed to them. The original content of life cannot be apprehended in any form of *representation,* but only in pure *intuition.* It would seem, therefore, that any understanding of spiritual life must choose between the two extremes. We are called upon to decide whether to seek the substance of the human spirit in its pure originality, which *precedes* all mediate configurations— or whether to surrender ourselves to the richness and diversity of these mediate forms. Only in the first approach do we seem to touch upon the true and authentic center of life, which however appears as a simple, self-enclosed center; in the second, we survey the entire drama of spiritual developments, but as we immerse ourselves in it, it dissolves more and more manifestly into a mere drama, a reflected image, without independent truth and essence. The cleavage between these two antitheses—it would seem—cannot be bridged by any effort of mediating thought which itself remains entirely on one side of the antithesis: the farther we advance in the direction of the symbolic, the merely figurative, the farther we go from the primal source of pure intuition.

Philosophical mysticism has not been alone in its constant confrontation of this problem and this dilemma; the pure logic of idealism has repeatedly seen it and formulated it. Plato's remarks in his *Seventh Epistle* on the relation of the "idea" to the "sign" and on the necessary inadequacy of this relation, strike a motif which has recurred in all manner of variations. In Leibniz' methodology of knowledge, "intuitive knowledge" is sharply distinguished from mere "symbolic" knowledge. Even for the author of the *characteristica universalis,* all knowledge through mere symbols becomes "blind knowledge" (*cogitatio caeca*) when measured by intuition, as the pure vision, the true "sight" of the idea.[8] True, *human* knowledge can nowhere dispense with symbols and signs; but it is precisely this that characterizes it as human, i.e., limited and finite in contradistinction to the ideal of the perfect, archetypal and divine intellect. Even Kant, who assigned its exact logical position to this idea by defining it as a mere borderline concept of cognition, and who believed that in so doing he had criti-

---

8. Cf. G. W. Leibniz, "Meditationes de cognitione, veritate et ideis," *Die Philosophischen Schriften von Gottfried Wilhelm Leibniz,* ed. C. J. Gerhardt (Berlin, 1880), 4, 422 ff.

cally mastered it—even Kant, in a passage which constitutes the purely methodical climax of the *Critique of Judgment,* once again sharply develops the antithesis between the *intellectus archetypus* and the *intellectus ectypus,* between the intuitive, archetypal intellect and the discursive intellect "which is dependent on images." From the standpoint of this antithesis it would seem to follow that the richer the *symbolic content* of cognition or of any other cultural form becomes, the more its *essential content* must diminish. All the many images do not designate, but cloak and conceal the imageless One, which stands behind them and towards which they strive in vain. Only the negation of all finite figuration, only a return to the "pure nothingness" of the mystics can lead us back to the true primal source of being. Seen in a different light, this antithesis takes the form of a constant tension between "culture" and "life." For it is the necessary destiny of culture that everything which it creates in its constant process of configuration and education [9] removes us more and more from the originality of life. The more richly and energetically the human spirit engages in its formative activity, the farther this very activity seems to remove it from the primal source of its own being. More and more, it appears to be imprisoned in its own creations—in the words of language, in the images of myth or art, in the intellectual symbols of cognition, which cover it like a delicate and transparent, but unbreachable veil. But the true, the profoundest task of a *philosophy* of culture, a philosophy of language, cognition, myth, etc., seems precisely to consist in raising this veil—in penetrating from the mediate sphere of mere meaning and characterization to the original sphere of intuitive vision. But on the other hand the specific *organ* of philosophy—and it has no other at its disposal—rebels against this task. To philosophy, which finds its fulfillment only in the sharpness of the concept and in the clarity of "discursive" thought, the paradise of mysticism, the paradise of pure immediacy, is closed. Hence it has no other solution than to reverse the *direction* of inquiry. Instead of taking the road back, it must attempt to continue forward. If all culture is manifested in the creation of specific image-worlds, of specific symbolic forms, the aim of philosophy is not to go behind all these creations, but rather to understand and elucidate their basic formative principle. It is solely through awareness of this principle that the content of life acquires its true form. Then life is removed from the sphere of mere given natural existence: it ceases to be a part of this natural existence or a mere biological

9. The German *Bildung* means both formation and education. *Trans.*

process, but is transformed and fulfilled as a form of the "spirit." In truth, the negation of the symbolic forms would not help us to apprehend the essence of life; it would rather destroy the spiritual form with which for us this essence proves to be bound up. If we take the opposite direction, we do not pursue the idea of a passive intuition of spiritual reality, but situate ourselves in the midst of its activity. If we approach spiritual life, not as the static contemplation of being, but as functions and energies of formation, we shall find certain common and typical principles of formation, diverse and dissimilar as the forms may be. If the philosophy of culture succeeds in apprehending and elucidating such basic principles, it will have fulfilled, in a new sense, its task of demonstrating the unity of the spirit as opposed to the multiplicity of its manifestations—for the clearest evidence of this unity is precisely that the diversity of the *products* of the human spirit does not impair the unity of its *productive process*, but rather sustains and confirms it.

Chapter 1

The Problem of Language in the History of Philosophy[1]

*1. The Problem of Language in the History of Philosophical
Idealism (Plato, Descartes, Leibniz)*

PHILOSOPHICAL inquiry into the origin and nature of *language* is as old as
that into the essence and origin of *being*. For it is characteristic of the earliest conscious reflection on the world as a whole that there was as yet no
distinction between language and being, word and meaning, but that they
stil ormed an indivisible unity. Because language itself is a necessary condition of reflection, because philosophical awareness arises only in and
through language, the human spirit always finds language present as a
given reality, comparable and equal in stature to physical reality. From the
moment when man first turns his attention to it, the world of language
assumes for him the same specificity and necessity, the same "objectivity"
as the world of things. Like the world of things, it confronts him as a
whole, possessing its own self-contained nature and laws, in which there is
nothing individual or arbitrary. For this first level of reflection, the character and meaning of words, like the character of things or the immediate
character of sensory impressions, involves no free activity of the spirit. The

1. A comprehensive work on the history of the philosophy of language is still a desideratum:
the most recent (eleventh) edition (1920) of Friedrich Überweg's *Grundriss der Geschichte der
Philosophie* lists, in addition to the general works on the history of philosophy, an abundance
of monographs on the history of logic and epistemology, on the history of metaphysics, natural
philosophy, ethics, philosophy of religion, and aesthetics, but mentions no single work on
the history of the philosophy of language. The ancient period alone has been treated in any
detail, in the well-known works of Lersch and Steinthal and in the literature on classical
grammar and rhetoric. It goes without saying that the brief historical introduction that
follows makes no claim to fill this gap; it purports merely to trace the most important steps
in the philosophical development of the "idea of language" and suggest certain lines that
might be followed in a detailed study.

word is not a designation and denomination, or a spiritual symbol of reality; it is itself a very real part of reality. The mythical view of language which everywhere precedes the philosophical view of it is always characterized by this indifference of word and thing. Here the essence of every thing is contained in its name. Magical powers attach directly to the word. He who gains possession of the name and knows how to make use of it, has gained power over the object itself; he has made it his own with all its energies. All word magic and name magic is based on the assumption that the world of things and the world of names form a single undifferentiated chain of causality and hence a single reality. The same form of substantiality and the same form of causality prevail in both, linking them into one self-enclosed whole.

This characteristic "wholeness" of the mythical picture of the world, in which all the differentiations of things are dissolved into a mythical-magical chain of causality, carries with it a significant consequence for man's approach to language. As soon as myth rises above the level of the most primitive magical "practice," which strives to obtain a specific effect by the use of a specific means, which accordingly links one particular with another in immediate action—as soon as mythical thinking seeks, even in the crudest, most imperfect form, to *understand* its own activity, it has penetrated to the sphere of universality. Once it becomes a form of *knowledge,* the tendency towards unity is essential to it as to all other knowledge. If the spiritual entities and forces in which myth lives are to be susceptible of *domination* by man, they must disclose certain enduring and *determinate* features. Hence man's very first sensory and practical step toward the mastery of the things in his natural environment contains the germ of the idea that they are governed by a theoretical necessity. As mythical thinking advances, the particular demonic forces cease to be mere particular forces, mere "gods of the moment" or "particular gods"—a kind of hierarchical order appears among them. The mythical view of language develops in the same direction, rising from the perception of the particular force contained in the individual word and individual magical formula to the idea of a universal potency possessed by the word as such, by "speech" as a whole. It is in this mythical form that the concept of *language as a unity* is first engendered. It recurs with characteristic uniformity in the earliest religious speculation of the most disparate regions. Vedic religion looks upon the spiritual power of the word as one of its essential sources: his use of the holy word makes the sage or priest lord over all being, over gods and men. In the *Rigveda* the commander of the word ı equated with the soma, the all-nourishing force, and designated as "he who governs all things with power." For at the base of the human word which comes into being and passes away, lies the eternal, imperishable word, the celestial Vâc. "I go," says this Heavenly Discourse in a hymn, "with the Rudras, with the Vasus, I go with the Ādityas and the All-gods. . . . I am the queen, the assembler of treasures, the wise, the first of the worshipful ones. In manifold places did the Gods divide me, who dwell in many abodes, causing me to penetrate many regions. Through me he eats food who perceives, who breathes, who hears what is spoken. . . . I blow forth even as the wind, reaching all beings, beyond heaven, beyond this earth. Such have I become through my greatness." [2]

At first sight the concept of the logos as it first appears in Greek speculation seems closely related to this mythical view of the dignity and omnipotence of the heavenly word. For here too the word is eternal and imperishable; here too the unity and permanence of reality are built upon the unity and indestructibility of the word. For Heraclitus, the logos is the "helmsman of the cosmos." Like the cosmos which it governs, it was created by god and no man, but always was and always will be. Yet though Heraclitus still speaks the language of myth, an entirely new tone is discernible within it. For the first time the mythical view of the cosmic process is clearly and consciously confronted by the fundamental philosophical-speculative idea that the universe is subordinate to a unified and indivisible law. The world is no longer the plaything of demonic powers who govern it according to their whim and fancy, but is subject to a universal rule which binds together every particular reality and event and assigns to them their unchanging measure. "The sun will not transgress his measures; otherwise the Furies, ministers of Justice, will find him out." [3] And it is this one intrinsically immutable law of the cosmos which is expressed in the world of nature as in the world of language, in different form yet intrinsically the same. "That which is wise is one: to understand the purpose which steers all things through all things—

2. *Rigveda*, x, 125. Eng. trans. by Edward J. Thomas, *Vedic Hymns* (London, J. Murray, 1923), pp. 88–89. On the mythical and religious significance of the Vâc cf. particularly *Brihadâranyaka* Upanishad *1, 5*, 3 ff. in Deussen, *Sechzig Upanishad's des Veda* (3d ed. Leipzig, 1921), pp. 401 ff.

3. Heraclitus, Fragment 94, in H. Diels, *Die Fragmente der Vorsokratiker*. Eng. trans. by Kathleen Freeman, in *Ancilla to the Pre-Socratic Philosophers* (Cambridge, Harvard Univ. Press, 1948).

ἓν τὸ σοφόν, ἐπίστασθαι γνώμην, ὁτέη ἐκυβέρνησε πάντα διὰ πάντων
(Fragment 41). With this the magic-mythical field of forces has turned into
a context of meaning. But this context is not divulged to us as long as we
content ourselves with apprehending the One Being as broken into fragments, shattered into a multiplicity of particular "things," but only when we
perceive and apprehend it as a living whole. Language also combines both
views: according to our approach, it offers us a merely accidental and particular view of reality or a truly speculative and universal view. If we consider the logos of language only in the form in which it is represented and
crystallized in the particular *word*—we find that every word limits the object
it is meant to designate and by this limitation falsifies it. Through fixation
in the word, the content is lifted out of the continuous stream of becoming
in which it stands; hence it is not apprehended according to its totality but
only according to a onesided determination. If we wish to regain a deeper
knowledge of the true nature of the thing, there is no other way than to
supplant this particular determination by another, that is, to oppose to each
word embodying a specific individual concept, its own antithesis. Indeed
we find, in language taken as a whole, that every meaning is linked with
its opposite, and that only the two together become an adequate expression
of reality. The spiritual synthesis, the union that is effected in the word,
resembles the harmony of the cosmos in that it is a harmony "of opposing
tension": παλίντροπος ἁρμονίη ὅκωσπερ τόξου καὶ λύρης (Fragment 51).
And here, in an intensified form, we encounter the fundamental law of the
cosmos. For what in reality appears as an *opposition* becomes in the expression of language a *contradiction*—and only in such an interplay of thesis
and antithesis, of statement and contradiction is it possible to reproduce
the true law and the inner structure of reality. Thus, on the basis of
Heraclitus' general view of the world, we can understand the fundamental
form of his *style,* whose reputed "obscurity" is not accidental and arbitrary,
but the adequate and necessary expression of his thought. Heraclitus'
linguistic style and his style of thought condition one another: the two represent in different aspects the same basic principle of his philosophy, the
principle of the ἐν διαφερόμενον ἑαυτῷ. Both suggest that "invisible harmony" which, as Heraclitus says, is better than visible harmony, and it is
by this standard that they should be measured. Heraclitus situates the particular object in the constant stream of becoming, in which it is both preserved and destroyed; and for him the particular word is related to "speech"
as a whole in the same way. Consequently, even the ambiguity inherent

in the word is not a mere deficiency of language, but is an essential and positive factor in its power of expression. For in this ambiguity it is manifested that the limits of language, as of reality itself, are not rigid but fluid. Only in the mobile and multiform word, which seems to be constantly bursting its own limits, does the fullness of the world-forming logos find its counterpart. Language itself must recognize all the distinctions which it necessarily effects as provisional and relative distinctions which it will withdraw when it considers the object in a new perspective. "God is day-night, winter-summer, war-peace, satiety-famine. But he changes like (fire) which when it mingles with the smoke of incense, is named according to each man's pleasure" (Fragment 67). And similarly: "Immortals are mortal, mortals are immortal: (*each*) lives the death of the other, and dies their life" (Fragment 62). He who would speak with intelligence must not permit himself to be misled by the diversity of words but must penetrate behind them to that which is common to all, the ξυνόν καὶ θεῖον.[4] For only when contradictories are understood and linked in this way, can the word become the guide of knowledge. It becomes understandable that most of the "etymologies" with which Heraclitus plays embody this two-fold sense: they join word and thing *per antiphrasin* rather than by any similarity. "The bow is called Life, but its work is death" (τῶι οὖν τόξωι ὄνομα βίος, ἔργον δὲ θάνατος. Fragment 48). Every particular content of language both reveals and conceals the truth of reality; it is at the same time both pure definition and mere indication.[5] In this view of the world, language is like the sybil who, as Heraclitus said, utters unadorned, un-licensed words with raving mouth, but who nevertheless "reaches out over a thousand years with her voice, through the (*inspiration of the*) god" (Fragment 92). It contains a meaning which is hidden from it, which it can only surmise in image and metaphor.

This approach to language expresses a general conception of reality and spirit, which, though indefinite and unclarified, is fully self-contained—but the immediate successors of Heraclitus, who made his doctrine their own, gradually submerged this meaning which had originally been inherent in it. In the discursive approach to the problem of language, what

4. ξύν νόωι λέγοντας ἰσχυρίζεσθαι χρὴ τῶι ξυνῶι πάντων, ὅκωσπερ νόμωι πόλις, καὶ πολὺ ἰσχυροτέρως. τρέφονται γὰρ πάντες οἱ ἀνθρώπειοι νόμοι ὑπὸ ἑνὸς τοῦ θείου. κρατεῖ γὰρ τοσοῦτον ὁκόσον ἐθέλει καὶ ἐξαρκεῖ πᾶσι καὶ περιγινέται (Fragment 114).

5. Cf. in particular Fragment 32: ἓν τὸ σοφὸν μοῦνον λέγεσθαι οὐκ ἐθέλει καὶ ἐθέλει Ζηνὸς ὄνομα. ("That which alone is wise is one; it is willing and unwilling to be called by the name of Zeus.")

Heraclitus, with his profound metaphysical intuition, still sensed as an immediate unity, broke down into heterogeneous components, into separate and conflicting logical theses. The two principles which the Heraclitean metaphysics had seen as a compelling unity: the doctrine of the identity of word and being and the doctrine of the antithesis between word and being were now developed independently. For the first time the problem of language was formulated with true conceptual sharpness—but at the same time these philosophers shattered Heraclitus' fundamental thought and refashioned it as small negotiable coin, transferring it from the realm of symbolic signification to that of abstract concepts. What for him was a carefully guarded secret, at which he dared only hint remotely, now became the actual object of philosophical discussion and controversy. In his *Memorabilia* Xenophon shows us the Athenians of the fifth century discussing the ὀρθότης τῶν ὀνομάτων over their wine.[6]

Is there a natural or only a mediate and conventional connection between the form of language and the form of reality, between the essence of words and that of things? Is the inner structure of reality itself expressed in words, or do they reveal no law other than that imprinted on them by the caprice of the first coiners of speech? And if the latter is true, but some connection is still presumed to exist between word and meaning, between speech and thought, must not the arbitrary character which inevitably attaches to the word, also cast doubt upon the objective clarity and objective necessity of thought? In defending their thesis that all knowledge is relative and that man is the "measure of all things," the Sophists would therefore seem to have drawn their most effective weapons from the study of language. From the first, they were very much at home in that middle region of words that is situated *between* man and things; here they entrenched themselves for the struggle against the claims of pure, allegedly universal thought. Their audacious play with the ambiguity of words did indeed put the world of things at their mercy, enabling them to dissolve its determinateness in the free movement of the spirit. Thus the first conscious reflection on language and its first conscious mastery by the spirit resulted in the flowering of *eristics;* but this reflection on the meaning and origin of speech also gave rise to the reaction which brought about a new fundamental approach and a new methodology of the concept.

6. Xenophon, *Memorabilia*, Bk. 3, ch. 14, sec. 2; for further historical material on this question cf. Chajim Steinthal, *Geschichte der Sprachwissenschaft bei den Griechen und Römern* (2d ed. Berlin, 1890), *1,* 76 ff.

For while the Sophists emphasized the ambiguous and arbitrary factor in words, Socrates stressed the concrete, unequivocal factor which though not given in them as a *fact,* lies latent in them as a postulate. This supposed unity of the signification of words was the point of departure for his characteristic question, the question of τὶ ἔστι, the search for the identical and enduring meaning of the concept. Though the word may not immediately contain this meaning in itself, still, it constantly suggests it—and the aim of Socratic "induction" is to understand this suggestion, to follow it out, and so progress toward the truth. Behind the fluid, indeterminate form of the word one should strive to find the enduring identical concept, the *eidos* in which alone the possibility of speech as well as of thought is grounded. Plato's thinking is rooted in these basic Socratic assumptions. They determine his approach to words and language. In his youth he studied with Cratylus who, in opposition to the Sophists, represented the positive side of Heraclitean thought, since he looked upon words as the true and authentic instruments of knowledge, expressing and encompassing the essence of things. Heraclitus had asserted an identity between the *whole* of language and the *whole* of reason; Cratylus transferred this identity to the relation between the *particular* word and its conceptual content. But this transfer, this conversion of the metaphysical content of the Heraclitean logos into a pedantic and abstruse etymology and philology, was precisely that *reductio ad absurdum* which Plato was to develop with all his dialectical and stylistic mastery in the *Cratylus.* With surpassing irony Plato tears down the thesis that there is a "naturally" correct term for every existing thing (ονόματος ὀρθότητα εἶναι ἑκάστῳ τῶν ὄντων φύσει πεφυκυῖαν), eliminating it forever in this naïve form. But for Plato this insight does not end all relation between word and knowledge; rather, the immediate and untenable relation of similarity is replaced by a deeper, a mediated relation. In the structure and development of dialectical knowledge the word retains a unique place and value. The fluid boundaries of the word, the fact that its content at all times is only relatively fixed, spur the dialectician to raise himself, through opposition and the struggle with opposition, to the postulate of the pure concept with its absolutely fixed signification, to the βεβαιότης of the realm of ideas.[7] But it was only in his old age that Plato fully developed this fundamental view, in the positive as well as the negative sense. Perhaps the strongest argument for the authenticity of Plato's *Seventh Epistle* is that in this respect it ties in directly with the conclusion

7. Cf. particularly *Cratylus* 386A, 438D ff.

of the *Cratylus,* to which for the first time it brings full methodic clarity
and rigorous systematic proof.

The *Seventh Epistle* distinguishes four stages of knowledge which only
in their totality yield the vision of true being, of the object of knowledge, as
the γνωστὸν καὶ ἀληθῶς ὄν. The lower levels consist in the name, in the
verbal definition of the object, and in its sensory copy, ὄνομα, λόγος, and
εἴδωλον. For example, we can apprehend the nature of the circle in these
three ways: first, by uttering the *name* of circle; second, by *explaining* what
is meant by this name, let us say, by "defining" the circle as a figure whose
circumference is at all points equidistant from its center; and finally by
taking some sensuous figure, whether drawn in the sand or turned on a
lathe, as an image or model of the circle. None of these three representations, the word, the definition, or the model, attains to the true essence of
the circle, for they all belong not to the realm of being but to the realm of
becoming. The word is variable and ephemeral, it comes into being and
passes away; the drawing can be effaced, the turner's model destroyed—
all these determinate forms fail completely to capture the circle as such
(αὐτὸς ὁ κύκλος). And yet it is only *through* these inadequate preliminary
stages that the fourth and fifth stages, scientific cognition and its object,
are reached. In this sense, name and image, ὄνομα and εἴδωλον, are sharply
distinguished from rational insight, ἐπιστήμη—and yet they are its presuppositions, the vehicles and intermediaries by virtue of which we can
steadily progress to knowledge (δι᾽ ὧν τὴν ἐπιστήμην ἀνάγκη παρα-
γίγνεσθαι). The knowledge of the object and the object itself both surpass
and encompass, transcend and synthesize these three stages.[8]

In the *Seventh Epistle* Plato attempted, for the first time in the history
of thought, to define and delimit the cognitive value of language in a purely
methodical sense. Language is recognized as a first beginning of knowledge,
but as no more than a beginning. Its content is even more ephemeral and
variable than that of sensory perception; the phonetic form of the word
or of the sentence built out of ὀνόματα and ῥήματα grasps even less of the
true content of the *idea* than is captured by the material model or image.
And yet a certain *relation* between word and idea remains: just as sensory
contents are said to "strive" toward the ideas, a direction and spiritual

8. See *Seventh Epistle,* 342a ff.; concerning the authenticity of the *Seventh Epistle,* ci.
particularly Willamowitz, *Platon, 1,* 641 ff.; *2,* 282 ff., and the penetrating analysis of the
philosophical stage in Jul. Stenzel, "Über den Aufbau der Erkenntnis im VII. Platonischen
Brief," *Sokrates* (1847), pp. 63 ff., and E. Howald, *Die Briefe Platons* (Zurich, 1923), p. 34.

tendency towards the ideas is to be discerned in the formations of language. Plato's system was eminently suited to this appreciation of the relative value of language, because for the first time it fully recognized a basic principle essential to all language. All language as such is "representation"; it represents a specific "meaning" by a sensuous "sign." As long as philosophical thought confines itself to what is *merely existent,* it can find no analogy or adequate expression for this characteristic relationship. For in things themselves, whether we consider them in their facticity as aggregates of "elements," or whether we study the causal connections between them, there is nothing which corresponds to the relation of "word" to "meaning," of the "sign" to the "signification" intended in it. But for Plato, who, as he shows us in the *Phaedo,* had characteristically reversed the formulation of the question, the way of philosophical thinking leads not from πράγματα to λόγοι but from λόγοι to πράγματα, since the reality of things can be apprehended only in the truth of concepts [9]—for Plato, the concept of representation assumed for the first time a truly central importance, since it is precisely in this concept that the problem fundamental to the doctrine of ideas is ultimately epitomized, and through it the relation between "idea" and "phenomenon" is expressed. From the standpoint of idealism the "things" of common experience, sensuous, concrete objects themselves becomes "images," whose truth content lies not in what they immediately are, but in what they mediately express. And this concept of the image, of the εἴδωλον creates a new spiritual intermediary between the form of language and the form of cognition. In order to define the relation between the two clearly and sharply, in order to delimit the "sphere" of the word from the sphere of pure concepts, and at the same time to maintain the connection between them, Plato now need only invoke the central principle of the theory of ideas, the principle of "participation." The darkness surrounding Heraclitus' metaphysical doctrine of the unity of word and meaning and the opposition between them, seems dispelled at one stroke by this new methodic concept of μέθεξις.[10] Participation contains a factor of identity as well as a factor of nonidentity; it implies on the one hand a necessary relationship, a unity of the elements, and on the other hand a sharp fundamental division and distinction between them. The pure idea of

9. Cf. Plato, *Phaedo* 99D ff.

10. For the methodic position of the concept of μέθεξις in the *whole* of Plato's philosophy, cf. Ernst Hoffmann's excellent article, "Methexis und Metaxy bei Platon," in *Sokrates* (1919), pp. 48 ff.

"equality" remains something other than the equal stones or pieces of wood by which it is represented, an ἕτερον—and yet, from the standpoint of the relative, sensory view of the world, this "other" can be apprehended *only* in this representation. In the same sense, the physical-sensory content of the word becomes for Plato the vehicle of an ideal signification, which as such cannot be encompassed within the limits of language but remains outside them. Language and word strive for the expression of pure being; but they never attain to it, because in them the designation of something other, of an accidental "attribute" of the object, is mixed with the designation of this pure being. Accordingly, what constitutes the characteristic power of language is also its characteristic weakness, that makes it incapable of representing the supreme, truly philosophical content of cognition.[11]

The history of logic and epistemology shows, to be sure, that the sharp boundary which Plato drew between the two significations of the λόγος, between the concept "as such" and its representative in language, tends gradually to disappear. This is the case even in the first systematization of logic—although it is surely an exaggeration to say that Aristotle borrowed from language the fundamental distinctions underlying his logical doctrines. However, the very *word* "categories" indicates how closely the analysis of logical forms and that of linguistic forms were related for Aristotle. The categories represent the most universal relations of being, and at the same time the highest classifications of *statement* (γένη or σχήματα τῆς κατηγορίας). The categories are, from an ontological standpoint, the basic specifications of actuality, the ultimate "predicates" of being; however these predicates can be arrived at not only through things, but also through the universal form of predication. And indeed, the structure of the *sentence* and its division into words and classes of words seem, in large part, to have served Aristotle as a model for his system of categories. In the category of substance we clearly discern the grammatical signification of the "substantive"; in quantity and quality, in the "when" and "where," we discern the signification of the adjective and of the adverbs of time and place—and above all the four last categories, of ποιεῖν and πάσχειν, ἔχειν and κεῖσθαι, seem to become fully transparent only when

---

11. Cf. in particular *Seventh Epistle*, 342c–343a: "πρὸς γὰρ τούτοις ταῦτα [scil. ὄνομα, λόγος, εἴδωλον] οὐχ ἧττον ἐπιχειρεῖ τὸ ποῖόν τι περὶ ἕκαστον δηλοῦν ἢ τὸ ὂν ἑκάστου διὰ τὸ τῶν λόγων ἀσθενές. ὧν ἕνεκα νοῦν ἔχων οὐδεὶς τολμήσει ποτὲ εἰς αὐτὸ τιθέναι τὰ νενοημένα ὑπ' αὐτοῦ . . ."

we consider them in reference to certain fundamental distinctions which the Greek language makes in its designation of verbs and verbal action.[12] Here logical and grammatical speculation seemed to be in thoroughgoing correspondence, to condition one another—and mediaeval philosophy, basing itself on Aristotle, clung to this correspondence between the two.[13] However, when modern thinkers began to attack the Aristotelian logic, when they contested its right to be called "the" system of thought, the close alliance into which it had entered with language and universal grammar, proved to be one of its most vulnerable points. Assailing it at this point, Lorenzo Valla in Italy, Lodovico Vives in Spain, Petrus Ramus in France attempted to discredit the Scholastic-Aristotelian philosophy. At first the controversy was limited to the sphere of linguistic study: it was precisely the "philologists" of the Renaissance who, on the basis of their deepened understanding of language, demanded a new "theory of thought." They argued that the Scholastics had seen only the outward, grammatical structure of language, while its real kernel, which is to be sought not in grammar but in stylistics, had remained closed to them. The great stylists of the Renaissance attacked syllogistics and its "barbarous" forms, not so much from the logical as from the aesthetic angle. But gradually this battle of the rhetoricians and stylists against the mere "dialecticians"—exemplified by Valla's *Dialectical Disputations*—took on a new form. As Renaissance scholars went back to the actual classical sources, the Scholastic notion of dialectic was replaced more and more by the original Platonic conception. Invoking Plato's dialectic, the Renaissance thinkers now demanded a return from words to "things"—and among the "factual sciences" the fundamental view of the Renaissance, which was becoming more and more decisive, accorded primacy to mathematics and the mathematical study of nature. Thus even pure philosophers of language expressed an increasingly conscious and resolute demand for a new orientation, as opposed to the orientation toward grammar.[14] They held that a truly systematic conception and formation of language could be obtained only through the application of the method and standards of mathematics.

Descartes, who provided the universal philosophical foundation for the

12. Cf. particularly Fr. A. Trendelenburg, *De Aristotelis Categoriis* (Berlin, 1833) and "Geschichte der Kategorienlehre," *Historische Beiträge zur Philosophie, 1* (1846), 23 ff.

13. Cf., e.g., Joannes Duns Scotus, "Tractatus de modis significandi seu grammatica speculativa," *Opera omnia,* ed. L. Wadding (Paris, L. Vivès, 1891–95), Vol. *1.*

14. For historical documentation see my book, *Das Erkenntnisproblem in der Philosophie und Wissenschaft der neueren Zeit* (3d ed. Berlin, B. Cassirer, 1922), *1,* 120–135.

Renaissance ideal of knowledge, saw the theory of language in a new light. In his principal systematic works Descartes gives us no independent philosophical study of language—but in a letter to Mersenne, the only place where he touches on the problem, he shows a very characteristic approach, which was to be highly significant in the ensuing period. The ideal of the unity of knowledge, the *sapientia humana* which always remains one and the same, regardless of how many objects it encompasses, is here extended to language. To the demand for a *mathesis universalis* is added the demand for a *lingua universalis*. Since only the One identical, fundamental form of knowledge, the form of human reason, recurs in all branches of knowledge really deserving of the name, all speech must be based upon the one, universal, rational form of language, which, though cloaked by the abundance and diversity of verbal forms, cannot be hidden entirely. For just as there is a very definite order among the ideas of mathematics, e.g., among numbers, so the whole of human consciousness, with all the contents that can ever enter into it, constitutes a strictly ordered totality. And similarly, just as the whole system of arithmetic can be constructed out of relatively few numerical signs, it must be possible to designate the sum and structure of all intellectual contents by a limited number of linguistic signs, provided only that they are combined in accordance with definite, universal rules. True, Descartes refrained from carrying out this plan: for since the creation of the universal language would presuppose the analysis of all the contents of consciousness into their ultimate elements, into simple, constitutive "ideas," it could be undertaken successfully only after this analysis itself has been completed and the goal of the "true philosophy" thus attained.[15]

Descartes' immediate successors, however, did not let themselves be deterred by the critical caution expressed in these words of the founder of modern philosophy. In rapid sequence they produced the most diverse systems of artificial universal language, which, though very different in execution, were in agreement in their fundamental idea and the principle of their structure. They all started from the notion that there is a limited number of concepts, that each of these concepts stands to the others in a very definite factual relation of coordination, superordination or subordination, and that a truly perfect language must strive to express this natural hierarchy of concepts adequately in a system of signs. Starting from this

15. See R. Descartes' letter to Mersenne of November 20, 1629, in *Correspondance*, ed. Adam-Tannery, *1*, 80 ff.

premise, Delgarno for example, in his *Ars signorum,* classified all concepts under seventeen supreme generic concepts, each of which is designated by a specific letter; all the words falling under the category in question begin with this letter; similarly, the subclassifications distinguished within the common genus are each represented by a special letter or syllable affixed to the first letter. Wilkins, who strove to complete and perfect this system, established forty principal concepts in place of the original seventeen and expressed each of them by a special syllable, consisting of a consonant and a vowel.[16] All these systems pass rather hastily over the difficulty of discovering the "natural" order of fundamental concepts and of clearly and exhaustively determining their mutual relations. More and more their authors transformed the *methodic* problem of classifying concepts into a purely *technical* problem; they were satisfied to work with any purely conventional classification of concepts as a basis and, by progressive differentiation, make it serve for the expression of the concrete cognitive and perceptual contents.

It was only with Leibniz, who restored the problem of language to the context of *universal logic* (which he recognized to be the prerequisite for all philosophy and all theoretical cognition in general) that the problem of a universal language was seen in a new depth. He was fully aware of the difficulty to which Descartes had pointed, but he believed that the progress which philosophical and scientific knowledge had made since then provided him with entirely new means of surmounting it. Any "characteristic," which is not content to remain an arbitrary sign language but aspires to be a *characteristica realis,* representing the true fundamental relations of things, demands a logical analysis of the *contents* of thought. But this "alphabet of thought" no longer seems an unlimited, insoluble problem so long as one goes consistently along the road laid down by the newly established theory of combinations and the newly established mathematical analysis instead of starting with random, more or less accidental classifications of the whole conceptual substance. Algebraic analysis teaches us that every number is constructed from definite original elements, that it can be broken down into "prime factors" and represented as their product,

16. If for example the letter P designates the general category of "quantity," the concepts of size in general, of space and measure, are expressed by Pe, Pi, Po, etc. Cf. George Delgarno, *Ars signorum vulgo character universalis et lingua philosophica* (London, 1661), and Wilkins, *An Essay towards a Real Character and a Philosophical Language* (London, 1668). A brief outline of the systems of Delgarno and Wilkins is given by L. Couturat in *La Logique de Leibniz* (Paris, F. Alcan, 1901), nn. 3 and 4, pp. 544 ff.

and this applies to any content of cognition. The breakdown into prime numbers has its parallel in the breakdown into primitive ideas—and it is one of the basic tenets of Leibniz' philosophy that essentially the two can and must be effected in accordance with the same principle and method.[17] It is true that the form of a truly universal characteristic seems to presuppose the content and structure of knowledge as given, while on the other hand it is only through this same characteristic that the structure of knowledge is intelligible and comprehensible for us. But for Leibniz this vicious circle is resolved by the fact that we are not dealing with two separate problems, approached successively, but that the two are seen in pure, factual *correlation*. The progress of analysis and of characteristic demand and condition one another: for every logical position of unity and every logical differentiation effected by the intellect *exists* for it in true clarity and sharpness only when fixed in a specific sign. Leibniz grants Descartes that the true universal language of knowledge is dependent upon knowledge itself, i.e., upon the "true philosophy," but he adds that nevertheless the language need not await the completion of the philosophy and that the analysis of ideas and the system of signs would develop hand in hand.[18] Here he expresses only that general methodic conviction, one might say that methodic experience, which he had found confirmed in the discovery of the analysis of infinity. The algorism of the differential calculus had proved to be not merely a convenient means of representing what had already been discovered, but a true organ of mathematical inquiry, and Leibniz expected language in general to perform the same service for thought, not merely following in its footsteps, but progressively preparing its path.

Leibniz' *rationalism* achieves its ultimate confirmation and completion in the contemplation of language, which is seen purely as a means of cognition, an instrument of logical analysis; but at the same time this rationalism itself, in comparison to that of Descartes, gains a kind of concrete form. For the correlation here asserted between thought and speech, thrusts the relation between thought and sensation into a new light. True, sensation must be progressively transformed into the distinct ideas of the understanding—but on the other hand, from the standpoint of the finite

---

17. For further details see my book, *Leibniz' System in seinen wissenschaftlichen Grundlagen* (Marburg, N. G. Elwert, 1902), pp. 105 ff., 487 ff., and Couturat, especially chs. 3–5.

18. See Leibniz' remarks on Descartes' letter to Mersenne, *Opuscules et fragments inédits de Leibniz,* ed. Couturat (Paris, F. Alcan, 1903), pp. 27 ff.

spirit, the converse relation also applies. Even our "most abstract" ideas always contain an admixture of imagination, and though it is true that we can further analyze this element of imagination, yet our analysis never arrives at an ultimate limit but rather can and must continue ad infinitum.[19] Here we are at the juncture where the fundamental idea of Leibniz' logic merges with the fundamental idea of his *metaphysics*. For this metaphysics the hierarchy of being is determined by the hierarchy of cognition. The monads, the only truly substantial entities, are differentiated only by the varying degree of clarity and distinctness of their perceptual contents. Only the supreme, divine being is characterized by perfect cognition, which is no longer in any sense representative but purely intuitive, i.e., which no longer contemplates its objects mediately through signs, but intuits them immediately in their pure and original essence. By comparison, even the highest stage to which the knowledge of the finite spirit can raise itself, even the distinct cognition of figures and numbers, appears only as inadequate knowledge: for instead of apprehending the spiritual contents themselves, it must, for the most part, content itself with their signs. In any mathematical demonstration of any length, we must have recourse to such representation. If for example we think of a regular thousand-sided figure, we do not constantly have in mind the nature of the sides, their equality and number; we rather use these words, whose meaning is only dimly and imperfectly present to us, instead of the ideas themselves, since we remember having known their meaning, and do not regard a closer explanation as necessary for the moment. Here then we are dealing not with a purely intuitive cognition but with a "blind" or symbolic cognition which, like algebra and arithmetic, governs almost all the rest of our knowledge.[20] Thus we see how according to Leibniz' project of universal characteristic, language, in striving more and more to encompass the totality of knowledge, both limits this totality and draws it into its own contingency. But this contingency has by no means a purely negative character; it contains within it a very positive factor. Just as every sense perception, however obscure and confused, includes within it a true, rational content

19. "Les plus abstraites pensées ont besoin de quelque imagination: et quand on considère ce que c'est que les pensées confuses (qui ne manquent jamais d'accompagner les plus distinctes que nous puissions avoir) comme sont celles de couleurs, odeurs, saveurs, de la chaleur, du froid etc. on reconnoist qu'elles enveloppent toujours l'infini." Réponse aux réflexions de Bayle, *Philos. Schriften*, ed. Gerhardt, 4, 563.

20. See Leibniz, "Meditationes de cognitione, veritate et ideis" (1684), *Philos. Schriften*, 4, 422 ff.

of cognition, which merely requires to be unfolded and "developed," so every sensuous symbol is the vehicle of a purely spiritual signification, which to be sure is given only "virtually" and implicitly in it. The true ideal of the "Enlightenment" consists not in casting off these sensuous cloaks at one stroke, not in casting away these symbols, but in gradually learning to understand them for what they are, in being master of them and permeating them with the human spirit.

But so broad and universal is the logical and metaphysical function which Leibniz here attributes to language that the specific content of language itself is in danger of being submerged in this very universality. The plan of a "universal characteristic" is not limited to any single field; it is meant to encompass all types of groups and signs, from the simple phonetic signs and word signs to the numerical signs of algebra and the symbols of mathematical and logical analysis. It seeks to embrace both those forms of expression that seem to originate in a natural, involuntarily erupting "instinct," and those which have their source in a free and self-conscious creation of the spirit. With this however the specific character of language as a language of sounds and words, seems not so much acknowledged and explained, as ultimately negated. If the aim of the universal characteristic were achieved, if every simple idea were expressed by a simple sensuous sign and every complex idea by a corresponding combination of such signs, the specific and accidental character of the particular languages would be dissolved into a single, universal basic language. Leibniz does not locate this basic language, this *lingua adamica,* as he calls it, borrowing an old term of the mystics and of Jacob Boehme,[21] in a paradisiacal human past; he looks upon it as an ideal concept, which our cognition must progressively approach in order to attain to the goal of objectivity and universality. In his opinion, it is in this ultimate, supreme, definitive form that language will appear as what it essentially is: the word will no longer be a veil over the meaning, it will appear as a true witness to the *unity of reason* which is a necessary postulate underlying the philosophical understanding of any particular spiritual reality.

21. On the idea of the lingua adamica, cf. Leibniz, *Philos. Schriften,* 7, 198–199, 204–205; *Nouveaux essais sur l'entendement,* Bk. 3, ch. 2 (*Philos. Schriften, 5,* 260).

2. The Position of the Problem of Language in the Systems of Empiricism (Bacon, Hobbes, Locke, Berkeley)

Philosophical *empiricism* seems to open up a new approach to language, for, in accordance with its fundamental tendency, it strives, not to relate the fact of language to a logical ideal, but rather to understand it in its sheer facticity, in its empirical origin and purpose. Instead of losing language in a logical or metaphysical utopia, it seeks to know it solely in its psychological reality and function. Yet even empiricism in its formulation of the problem borrowed an essential presupposition from the rationalistic systems it opposed, since at first it considered language exclusively as an instrument of *cognition*. Locke explicitly stresses that his plan for a critique of the understanding did not originally call for special critique of language, that it became evident to him only gradually that the question of the meaning and origin of concepts could not be separated from the question of the origin of names.[22] But once he had recognized this relationship, language became for him one of the most important witnesses to the truth of the fundamental empiricist attitude. Leibniz once said that nature loved to reveal its ultimate secrets at some point, to set them before our eyes in visible demonstrations, as it were. Locke looked upon language as such a demonstration of his general view of spiritual reality. "It may also lead us a little towards the original of all our notions and knowledge," he begins his analysis of words,

if we remark how great a dependence our words have on common sensible ideas; and how those which are made use of to stand for actions and notions quite removed from sense, have their rise from thence, and from obvious sensible ideas are transferred to more abstruse significations, and made to stand for ideas that come not under the cognizance of our senses: e.g., to "imagine, apprehend, comprehend" . . . , etc., are all words taken from the operations of sensible things and applied to certain modes of thinking. Spirit, in its primary signification, is "breath"; angel, a "messenger": and I doubt not but, if we could trace them to their sources, we should find, in all languages, the names which stand

22. John Locke, *An Essay Concerning the Human Understanding*, Bk. 3, ch. 9, sec. 21.

for things that fall not under our senses to have had their first rise from sensible ideas. By which we may give some kind of guess what kind of notions they were, and whence derived, which filled their minds who were the first beginners of languages; and how nature, even in the naming of things, unawares suggested to men the originals and principles of all their knowledge . . . we having, as has been proved, no ideas at all but what originally come either from sensible objects without, or what we feel within ourselves from the inward workings of our own spirits, of which we are conscious to ourselves within.[23]

Here we have the fundamental systematic thesis upon which all empiricist discussion of the problem of language is directly or indirectly based. Once again the analysis of language is not an end in itself, but is intended to prepare the way for the main undertaking, the analysis of ideas. For linguistic denominations never immediately express things themselves, but refer solely to the ideas of the spirit, to the speaker's own perceptions. This universal principle of language had already been formulated by Hobbes, who believed that with this formulation he had definitively withdrawn the philosophy of language from the sphere of metaphysics. Since names are signs for concepts and not signs for objects themselves, the whole question as to whether they designate the matter or the form of things, or something composed of the two, could be set aside as empty metaphysical speculation.[24] Locke bases his investigations on this decision, to which he returns again and again and which he amplifies in all its aspects. The nature of objects—as he too stresses—is never expressed in the unity of the word; what is expressed is only the subjective operation by which the human spirit proceeds to collect its simple sensory ideas into one concept. In so doing, the spirit is not bound by any substantial model, by any real property of things. It can arbitrarily stress one or another perceptual content, or combine different groups of simple elements into complex ideas. It is the diversity of these subjective lines of connection and division that differentiates the various classes of linguistic concepts and significations. Hence these can never be anything more than reflection of the subjective process of combination and separation; they can not reflect the objective character of reality and its structure according to real or logical-metaphysical genera and species.[25] The theory of definition thus takes a

23. Locke, *Essay*, Bk. 3, ch. 1, sec. 5.
24. Th. Hobbes, *Elementorum philosophiae, sectio prima. De corpore*, Pt. I, ch. 2, sec. 5.
25. Locke, *Essay*, esp. Bk. 3, chs. 2 and 6.

new form contrasting with that of rationalism. The antithesis between nominal definition and real definition, between verbal explanation and factual explanation vanishes: for a definition can only claim to give the denotation of the name of the thing, not to portray its ontological reality and structure. For not only is the nature of every particular thing unknown to us, but we cannot connect any specific representation with the general concept of what a thing as such should be. The only concept of the "nature" of a thing to which we can attach a clear meaning, has no absolute, but only a relative signification; it contains within it a reference to ourselves, to our psychological organization and our powers of cognition. To define the nature of a thing means for us nothing other than to develop the simple ideas which are contained in it and which enter as elements into the general idea of it.[26]

In its *expression* this fundamental attitude seems to go back to the Leibnizian form of analysis and the postulate of a universal "alphabet of thought"—but behind this identity of expression a sharp systematic opposition is concealed. For between the two conceptions of language and cognition stands the crucial change of signification that has taken place in the term "idea." On the one side the idea is understood in its objective-logical sense, on the other side, in its subjective-psychological sense; on the one side stands its original Platonic concept, on the other, its modern empiricist and sensationalist concept. Among the rationalists, the reduction of all contents of cognition to their simple ideas and the designation of these ideas signifies a return to ultimate and universal *principles* of knowledge; among the empiricists, it stands for the derivation of all complex intellectual notions from the immediate data of the inward or outward senses, from the elements of "sensation" and "reflection." But with this, the *objectivity* of language, as of all cognition, has become a problem in an entirely new sense. For Leibniz and all rationalists the ideal being of concepts and the real being of things are indissolubly correlated: for "truth" and "reality" are one in their foundation and ultimate root.[27] All empirical existence and all empirical events are related and ordered in accordance with the demands of the intelligible truths—and herein consists their reality, herein consists what distinguishes being from appearance,

26. Cf. especially J. d'Alembert, "Essai sur les éléments de philosophie ou sur les principes des connoissances humaines," *Oeuvres, 1,* sec. 4.

27. ". . . la vérité étant une même chose avec l'être." Descartes, *Meditationes de prima philosophia . . . ,* Vol. 5.

reality from dream.[28] For the empiricists this mutual relation—this "pre-established harmony" between the ideal and the real, between the realm of the universal, necessary truths and the realm of particular, factual reality —is suspended. The more sharply they defined language not as an expression of things but as an expression of *concepts*, the more imperiously the question was bound to rise as to whether the new spiritual medium here recognized did not falsify rather than designate the ultimate, "real" elements of being. From Bacon to Hobbes and Locke we can progressively follow the development and increasing acuteness of this question, until at last in Berkeley it stands before us in full clarity. In the case of Locke, even though cognition was founded in the particular data of sensory perception and the perception of self, it embodied a tendency towards "universality": and the universality of the word corresponded to this tendency toward the universal in cognition. The abstract word becomes the expression of the "abstract universal idea," which, beside the particular sensations, is here still recognized as a psychological reality of a specific type and of independent importance.[29] However, the progress and implications of the sensationalist view led beyond this relative recognition, and at least indirect toleration, of the "universal." The universal now has no more real foundation in the realm of ideas than in the realm of things. But this, in a manner of speaking, places the word and all language totally in the void. Neither in physical nor psychological reality, neither in things nor ideas, is there any model or "archetype" for what is expressed in them. All reality—psychological as well as physical—is by nature concrete and individually determined: in order to apprehend it, we must therefore free ourselves above all from the false and illusory, the "abstract" universality of the word. This inference is resolutely drawn by Berkeley. Every reform of philosophy must primarily base itself upon a critique of language, must above all dispel the illusion in which the human mind has from time immemorial been confined.

28. Cf. e.g. Leibniz, *Hauptschriften zur Grundlegung der Philosophie*, ed. Cassirer-Buchenau, *1*, 100, 287, 349; 2, 402 ff., etc.

29. "A distinct name for every particular thing would not be of any great use for the improvement of knowledge, *which, though founded in particular things, enlarges itself by general views;* to which things reduced into general names are properly subservient. . . . Words become general by separating from them the circumstances of time and place, and any other ideas that may determine them to this or that particular existence. By this way of abstraction they are made capable of representing more individuals than one; each of which, having in it a conformity to that abstract idea, is (as we call it) of that sort." Locke, *Essay,* Bk. 3, ch. 3, secs. 4–6.

It cannot be denied that words are of excellent use, in that by their means all that stock of knowledge which has been purchased by the joint labours of inquisitive men in all ages and nations may be drawn into the view and made the possession of one single person. But at the same time it must be owned that most parts of knowledge have been so strangely perplexed and darkened by the abuse of words, and general ways of speech wherein they are delivered, that it may almost be made a question whether language has contributed more to the hindrance or advancement of the sciences . . . It were, therefore, to be wished that every one would use his utmost endeavors to obtain a clear view of the ideas he would consider; separating from them all that dress and incumbrance of words which so much contribute to blind the judgment and divide the attention. In vain do we extend our view into the heavens and pry into the entrails of the earth, in vain do we consult the writings of learned men and trace the dark footsteps of antiquity. We need only draw the curtain of words to behold the fairest tree of knowledge, whose fruit is excellent, and within the reach of our hand.[30]

But on closer scrutiny, this radical critique of language contains within it a critique of the sensationalist *ideal of cognition* upon which it is based. From Locke to Berkeley there was a peculiar reversal in the empiricist position on the problem of knowledge. Locke found in language a confirmation of his fundamental approach to knowledge, and invoked it as a witness to his general thesis that there could be nothing in the understanding which was not previously in the senses: but now it becomes evident that the distinctive and essential *function* of the word has no place within the sensationalist system. The system could be sustained only by negating and excluding this function. The structure of language is no longer used to elucidate the structure of cognition, but constitutes its exact antithesis. Far from having even a conditional and relative truth content, language is a magic mirror which falsifies and distorts the forms of reality in its own characteristic way. Empiricism had undergone a dialectical development which is strikingly illustrated by a comparison of the two historical extremes in the empiricist philosophy of language. Berkeley, on the one hand, strives to negate the truth content and cognition content of language, which he regards as the root of all the human spirit's error and self-

30. G. Berkeley, *A Treatise Concerning the Principles of Human Knowledge,* Introduction, pars. 21–24.

deception; Hobbes, on the other hand, had imputed not only truth, but *all* truth to language. Hobbes' concept of truth culminates in the thesis that truth lies not in things, but solely in words and the use of words: *veritas in dicto, non in re consistit.*[31] Things are and subsist as real particulars which are manifested to us in concrete, particular sensations. However, neither the particular thing nor the particular sensation can ever constitute the true object of *knowledge:* for knowledge deserving of the name is not mere historical knowledge of the particular, but philosophical, i.e., necessary knowledge of the universal. Hence, while sensation and memory are limited to *material facts,* all science is oriented toward general relations and inferences, toward *deductive* combinations.[32] And the organ and instrument it employs can be none other than the word. For our spirit can obtain deductive insight only into those contents which are not, like things or sensations, *given* to it from outside but only into those which it *creates* and freely produces out of itself. It does not enjoy such freedom toward the real objects of nature, but only toward their ideal representatives or denominations. Thus, not only is the creation of a system of names prerequisite to any system of knowledge—but all true knowledge consists in creating names and combining them into sentences and judgments. Truth and falsehood are not attributes of things, but attributes of language—a spirit deprived of language would consequently lack all power over these attributes and would be unable to distinguish and juxtapose the "true" and the "false." [33] In Hobbes' nominalistic view, language is a source of error only to the extent that it is also the condition of conceptual knowledge in general, the source of all universality and all truth.

Berkeley's critique of language, however, seems to have deprived universality of its last support, and thus the rationalistic method, which is still unmistakable throughout the writings of Hobbes, seems at last to have been definitively confuted and eradicated. But as Berkeley strove to extend his system from these first beginnings, a new and characteristic reversal took place within it. The living "logos" in language, which he had at first denied and forcibly suppressed, seems to have gradually freed itself from the constraint of the sensationalist schema into which Berkeley attempted to force all speech and thought. Through his study and analysis of the

---

31. Hobbes, *De corpore,* Pt. 1: "Computatio sive logica," ch. 3, sec. 7.

32. Hobbes, *Leviathan,* Pt. 1: "De homine," ch. 5, sec. 6.

33. "De homine," ch. 4: *"Verum* et *Falsum* attributa sunt non rerum, sed Orationis; ubi autem Oratio non est, ibi neque *Verum* est neque *Falsum.*"

function of the *sign,* and through the new positive evaluation which the sign acquired for him, Berkeley was led, step by step and unawares, to a new fundamental view of cognition. He himself, particularly in his last work, the *Siris,* took the decisive step: he freed the "idea" from all its sensationalist-psychological implications and restored it to its fundamental Platonic signification. And in this last phase of his system, language also regained a dominant, truly central position. Whereas previously the value of language had been contested on general grounds implicit in Berkeley's psychology and metaphysics, we now witness, in the final form of this same metaphysics, a dramatic and noteworthy reversal: all reality, spiritual as well as sensory, is *transformed* into language; the sensationalist view of the world has gradually changed into a purely symbolic view. What we designate as the reality of perceptions and bodies is, more profoundly understood, nothing other than the sensuous sign language in which an all-embracing, infinite spirit communicates itself to our finite spirit.[34] In the struggle between metaphysics and language, language has come off victorious—in the end, language which had at first been driven from the threshold of metaphysics is not only readmitted, but becomes the crucial determinant of metaphysical form.

3. The Philosophy of the French Enlightenment (Condillac, Maupertuis, Diderot)

Yet in the history of empiricism the last phase of Berkeley's system remained an isolated episode The general development was in a different direction, tending more and more clearly to replace the logical and metaphysical perspectives in which the relation of speech to thought had for the most part been considered up until then, by purely psychological perspectives. This meant an indubitable gain for the concrete study of language; instead of merely considering the nature of language as a *whole,* thinkers began to take an increasing interest in the *individuality,* the spiritual specificity of the *particular* languages. While the logical approach, as though impelled by its method, turned persistently to the problem of

34. For more detailed discussion and documentation, see my book, *Das Erkenntnisproblem,* 2, 315 ff.

a universal language, psychological analysis chose the opposite road. Even Bacon, in the treatise *De dignitate et augmentis scientiarum,* had called for a universal form of "philosophical grammar" in addition to the usual empirical study of language and *grammatica litteraria.* But this philosophical grammar should not strive to disclose any necessary relationship between words and the objects they designate: tempting as such an undertaking may seem, it would prove exceedingly dangerous and elusive in view of the elasticity of words and the uncertainty of all purely etymological investigations. However, it would provide the most noble form of grammar, if someone versed in a large number of languages, popular as well as learned, were to treat of their various peculiarities, and show wherein consisted the advantages and deficiencies of each. A study of this sort would make it possible to establish an ideal plan for a perfect language by comparison of the individual languages, and would also provide the most significant insights into the spirit and customs of the various nations. In his development of this idea, and in his brief characterizations of the Greek, Latin and Hebrew languages, Bacon anticipated a project which was to be fully realized only with Wilhelm von Humboldt.[35] The philosophical empiricists, however, followed this lead only in so far as they looked more and more closely into the specific character of concepts within each particular language. If the concepts of langue are not simply signs for objective things and processes, but signs for the idea that we form of them, they must reflect not so much the nature of things as the individual type and direction of our apprehension of things. This is particularly true where it is not a question of stabilizing simple sensory impressions in words, but where the word serves to express a complex total perception. For every such perception, and accordingly every name which we ascribe to such "mixed modes," as Locke calls them, goes back ultimately to the free activity of the spirit. The spirit is purely passive in relation to its simple impressions, and need merely receive them in the form given from outside, but when it comes to combining these simple ideas, it represents its own nature far more than that of the objects outside it. There is no need to inquire after the real model of these combinations; the types and species of the "mixed modes" and the names we give them are created by the understanding without models, without any immediate link with real

35. See F. Bacon, *De dignitate et augmentis scientiarum,* Bk. 6, ch. 1: "Innumera sunt ejusmodi, quae justum volumen complere possint. Non abs re igitur fuerit grammatica philosophantem a simplici et litteraria distinguere, *et desideratam ponere.*"

existing things. The same freedom which Adam possessed when he created the first names for complex perceptions according to no model other than his own thoughts—this same freedom has existed ever since for all men.[36]

Here, as we see, we have come to the point where the system of the empiricists accorded a certain recognition to the *spontaneity* of the spirit, though, for the present this recognition was only conditional and mediate. And this essential curtailment of the *copy theory* of knowledge could not but react immediately upon the *general view* of language. If language, in its complex conceptual terms, is not so much a reflection of material *reality*, as a reflection of mental *operations,* this reflection can and must be effected in an infinite diversity of ways. If the content and expression of the concept are not dependent on the substance of the particular sensory percepts, but rather on the form of their combination, every new linguistic concept fundamentally represents a new spiritual creation. Consequently, no concept of one language is simply "transferable" to another. Locke already had insisted on this inference; he stressed that in a close comparison of different languages one almost never found words which fully corresponded to one another, and which fully coincided in their whole sphere of meaning.[37] Thus from a new angle, the idea of a "universal" grammar is exposed as a delusion. More and more resolutely, thinkers declared that instead of seeking a universal grammar, one should seek out and strive to understand the specific *stylistic* of each separate language. The emphasis in the study of language shifted from logic to psychology and aesthetics. This is particularly evident in that thinker who, as no other empiricist, combined the sharpness and clarity of logical analysis with the keenest feeling for individuality, for the finest shadings and nuances of aesthetic expression. In his "Letter on the Deaf and Dumb" Diderot develops Locke's observation; but what in Locke had been in isolated aperçu is now supported by an abundance of concrete examples from the field of linguistic and particularly of literary expression, and set forth in a style which is itself an immediate proof that every truly original spiritual form creates its proper linguistic form. Beginning with a specific stylistic problem, the problem of linguistic "inversion," Diderot progresses methodically and yet with the freest movement of thought to the problem of the individuality of linguistic form. In characterizing the incomparable uniqueness of poetic genius, Lessing had recalled the saying that one might sooner take from Hercules

36. Locke, *Essay,* Bk. 2, ch. 22, secs. 1 ff.; Bk. 3, ch. 5, secs. 1–3; ch. 6, sec. 51, etc.
37. Locke, *Essay,* Bk. 2, ch. 22, sec. 6; Bk. 3, ch. 5, sec. 8.

his club than from Homer or Shakespeare a single verse—and Diderot also starts from this dictum. The work of a true poet is and remains untranslatable—we may render the thought, we may even have the good fortune to find here and there an equivalent expression; but the general treatment, the tone and sound of the whole, remains a single, subtle and untranslatable "hieroglyph." [38] And such a hieroglyph, such a formal and stylistic law, is not only realized in each particular art, in music, painting, sculpture, but also dominates each particular language, setting upon it its spiritual seal, its intellectual and emotional stamp.

Here the study of language comes into direct contact with the central problem which dominated the cultural sciences throughout the seventeenth and eighteenth centuries. The concept of *subjectivity* underwent the same characteristic transformation that we encounter in the theory of art and artistic creation. Out of the narrow, empiricist-psychological conception of subjectivity there gradually arose a deeper and more comprehensive view, which removed subjectivity from the sphere of mere accidental facticity and arbitrary action and recognized its specific spiritual "form," i.e., its specific necessity. In the aesthetic theory of the seventeenth and eighteenth century this whole current of thought was focused more and more clearly and consciously in a single center. Both in thought and language, the new notion of a spiritual life far surpassing mere empirical-psychological reflection was epitomized in the concept of genius. In Diderot's "Lettre sur les sourds et muets" the concept of genius, though not explicitly stressed, constitutes the animating principle of all theoretical discussion of language and art; it is the point of ideal unity toward which such discussion is oriented. And this is merely one example: in the most diverse quarters this concept was introduced into the study of language. In England the empirical-psychological method which strove to dissect spiritual processes into their sensory and material factors had, by the late seventeenth century, ceased to dominate all intellectual life; it shared the field with another view, which was oriented towards the "form" of these processes and strove to apprehend them in their original and indivisible *totality*. From the standpoint of systematic philosophy this attitude found its center in English Platonism, in Cudworth and the Cambridge school; it achieved its finished literary expression in Shaftesbury. All outward formation of sensuous material things—Shaftesbury held this conviction in common

38. D. Diderot, "Lettre sur les sourds et muets," *Oeuvres*, ed. Naigeon (Paris, 1798), 2, 322 ff.

with the English Platonists—must be based on certain inner proportions, or "interior numbers" as Shaftesbury called them, for form can never be created from matter, it is and remains unborn and imperishable, a pure ideal unity, which imprints itself upon multiplicity and so gives it definite form. It is these inner spiritual *proportions,* and not the accidental existence and accidental properties of empirical *things,* that the true artist represents in his work. Such an artist is indeed a second creator, a true Prometheus under Jupiter. "Like that sovereign artist or universal plastic nature, he forms a whole, coherent and proportional in itself, with due subjection and subordinacy of constituent parts. . . . The moral artist who can thus imitate the Creator, and is thus knowing in the inward form and structure of his fellow-creature, will hardly, I presume, be found unknowing in himself, or at a loss in those numbers which make the harmony of a mind." What the study of every natural organism reveals to us, becomes irrefutable certainty as soon as we consider our own self, the unity of our consciousness: namely, that truly self-subsistent being does not take its form from its parts, but is and operates as a formed whole prior to any division. In his self, each one of us can immediately apprehend an individual principle of form, his own characteristic *"genius,"* which he finds again, in the particular as in the whole, as the always different and yet intrinsically identical form-giving power, the "genius of the universe." The two ideas are parallel and interdeterminant—correctly understood and interpreted, empirical subjectivity necessarily surpasses itself and culminates in the concept of the "universal spirit." [39]

The part played by this aesthetic-metaphysical concept of "inner form" in the philosophy of language can be seen in a work emanating from the immediate circle of the English Neoplatonists and clearly reflecting their general approach. In its general plan, Harris' *Hermes or a philosophical inquiry concerning universal grammar* (1751) seems to remain within the tradition of the rationalistic theories of language, to pursue for example, the same ideal as the *Grammaire générale et raisonnée* of Port Royal. Once again, Harris strives to create a grammar which, without regard for the particular idioms of the diverse languages, will lay down universal principles identical for all languages. He strives to base the organization of language upon a general logic and a general psychology which will make

39. See Shaftesbury "Soliloquy or Advice to an Author," *Characteristics of Men, Manners, Opinions, Times, etc.,* ed. J. M. Robertson (London, G. Richards, 1900), *1,* 135 ff.; cf. "Moralists," ibid., Vol. 2, sec. 5.

this organization seem necessary. Our psychological faculties, for example, disclose an original division into those of representation and those of appetition; accordingly, every sentence must either be a "sentence of assertion or a sentence of volition." On the basis of this logic and psychology, it must in general be possible to demonstrate unequivocally why language contains precisely these and no other parts of speech and why these parts take this form and no other. Of particular interest is Harris' attempt to derive a general schema of tense formation from a logical and psychological analysis of the perception of time.[40] But the farther he proceeds, the more evident it becomes that the psychology upon which he relies for his study and classification of linguistic forms is a pure "structure psychology," sharply opposed to the sensationalist psychology of elements. In his defense of "universal ideas" against their empiricist critics, Harris shows his kinship with the Cambridge school:[41] "For my own part," he remarks, "when I read the detail about Sensation and Reflection, and am taught the process at large how my Ideas are all generated, I seem to view the human Soul in the light of a Crucible, where Truths are produced by a kind of logical Chemistry. They may consist (for aught we know) of natural materials, but are as much creatures of our own, as a Bolus or Elixir."[42] To the empiricist belief in the production of "form" out of matter he opposes his own, based on Plato and Aristotle, in which he insists on the absolute primacy of form. All sensible forms must be based on pure, intelligible forms, which are "prior" to the sensible forms.[43] And in this connection Harris—who, as Shaftesbury's nephew, had no doubt long been close to his ideas—goes back to Shaftesbury's central concept, the concept of "genius." Every national language has its own spirit; each contains a characteristic formative principle: "We shall be led to observe, how Nations, like single Men, have their peculiar Ideas; how these peculiar Ideas become the genius of their language, since the Symbol must of course correspond to its Archetype; how the wisest nations, having the most and best Ideas, will consequently have the best and most copious Languages." Just as there is a nature, a genius of the Roman, the Greek, the English people,

40. J. Harris, *Hermes* (3d ed. London, 1771), Bk 1, ch. 6, pp. 97 ff.; on the above see especially Bk. 1, ch. 2, pp. 17 ff.; ch. 3, pp. 24 ff.

41 Ibid., Bk. 3, ch. 4, pp. 350 ff. Compare with R. Cudworth, *The True Intellectual System of the Universe* (London, 1678), Bk. 1, ch. 4.

42. Harris, Bk. 3, ch. 5, pp. 404 ff.

43. Bk. 3, ch. 4, pp. 380 ff.

there is a genius of the Latin, the Greek, the English language.[44] Here we encounter, perhaps for the first time so explicitly formulated, the new notion of the "spirit of language," which was soon to dominate the whole philosophical approach to language. In Rudolf Hildebrand's masterly articles on *Geist* and *Genie* in Grimm's *Lexicon* we can follow step for step how this concept entered into German cultural history and gained recognition in German linguistics.[45] A direct road leads from Shaftesbury and Harris to Hamann and Herder. As early as 1768, Hamann wrote to Herder in Riga that he had ordered *Hermes* for him from the publisher and speaks of it as "a work which struck me as indispensable for your plan" (the discussion of language in the fragments on recent German literature).[46] And Herder himself, who in his *Kritisches Wäldchen* invokes Harris' *aesthetic* theory in attacking Lessing's *Laokoon,* also refers repeatedly to his theory of language. In his preface to the German translation of Monboddo's work on the origin and development of language he expressly states that Monboddo and Harris had opened up a new and certain approach to language: "Enough . . . the path is broken: the principles of our author and his friend Harris strike me as the only true and secure ones, and moreover, his first attempts at comparing the languages of several different peoples at different cultural levels, will always remain the pioneer work of a master. Some day (though certainly not too soon) a *philosophy of the human understanding,* developed out of its most characteristic work, the different languages of the earth, will be a possibility." [47]

Perhaps Herder was most attracted to Harris' ideas on language by the very feature which he had stressed in his judgment of Harris' aesthetic theory. In his dialogue on art, to which Herder expressly refers in his earliest discussion of aesthetic problems,[48] Harris restored the Aristotelian distinction between ἔργον and ἐνέργεια to the center of artistic theory.

44. Bk. 3, ch. 5, pp. 409 ff.

45. Cf. Jacob Grimm, *Deutsches Wörterbuch,* 4, No. 1, sec. 2, cols. 2727 ff. and 3401 ff.

46. J. G. Hamann to Herder, September 7, 1768, *Schriften,* ed. Fr. Roth (Berlin, 1821–43), 3, 386.

47. J. G. V. Herder, "Vorrede zur Übersetzung des Monboddo" (1784), *Werke,* ed. B. Suphan (Berlin, 1877–1900), 15, 183; Herder expresses a similar judgment on Harris in his *Metakritik* (1799), ed. B. Suphan, 21, 57. As early as 1772, Herder in his *Allgemeine deutsche Bibliothek,* ed. B. Suphan, 5, 315, expressed the desire for a German version of excerpts from *Hermes.*

48. Herder, *Kritische Wälder, 3,* 19 (ed. Suphan, *3,* 159 ff.), in conjunction with J. Harris, "Concerning Music, Painting and Poetry," *Three Treatises* (London, 1744).

Thence it was taken into the theory of language, where at length it was rigorously formulated by Wilhelm von Humboldt. Language like art cannot be conceived as a mere work of the spirit, but must be regarded as a form of spiritual *energy*. The "energetic" theory of language and the energetic theory of art fused in the concept of *genius* as it developed in the seventeenth and eighteenth centuries. For the decisive factor in this development was the tendency to trace all cultural reality back to the original creative process in which it is rooted, to reduce all cultural "products" to basic forms and formative trends.[49] At first glance this tendency seems to have been operative in those empiricist and rationalist theories of the origin of language which, instead of regarding language as a divine work springing ready-made from the hand of God, interpreted it as a free creation of human reason. But since in these theories reason retains the character of subjective, arbitrary reflection, the "formation" of language becomes tantamount to its "invention." In inventing the first linguistic signs, in developing them into words and sentences, man effects a conscious, purposive process. The French Enlightenment liked to draw a direct comparison between this gradual progress of language and the methodic development which mankind accomplishes in science, particularly in mathematics. For Condillac all the special sciences are merely a continuation of the same process of analyzing ideas which begins with the formation of language. The initial language of phonetic signs is augmented by a language of general symbols, particularly of an arithmetical and algebraic character, the "language of calculation"; in both these languages, ideas are analyzed, combined, and ordered according to the same principle. The sciences as a whole are nothing other than well-ordered languages (*langues bien faites*), and similarly, our language of words and sounds is merely the first science of reality, the first manifestation of that original impulse towards knowledge, which moves from the complex to the simple, from the particular to the universal.[50] In his "Philosophical Reflections on the Origin of Languages" Maupertuis attempted to follow this development of language in detail, to show how, from its first primitive beginnings, when language possessed only a few terms for complex sense perceptions, it progressively increased its store of denominations, word forms and parts of speech by conscious comparison and differentiation of the parts of

49. Cf. my book, *Freiheit und Form, Studien zur deutschen Geistesgeschichte* (Berlin, B. Cassirer, 1922), especially chs. 2 and 4.

50. E. B. de Condillac, "La Langue des calculs," *Oeuvres* (Paris, 1798), Vol. 23.

these perceptions.[51] To this view of language, which makes it the product of abstract ratiocination, Herder opposes a new conception of "linguistic reason." Here again the profound relation between the fundamental cultural problems appears with surprising sharpness: for the struggle which now begins corresponds blow for blow with the battle which Lessing had waged in the field of art against Gottsched and French classicism. Though the formations of language are also "regular" in the highest sense, they cannot be derived from, or measured by, an objective, conceptual rule. They too, through the agreement of the parts to a whole, are purposively constructed throughout—but they are governed by that "purposiveness without purpose" which precludes all mere fancy and all merely subjective "intention." Consequently, in language as in artistic creation, the factors which shun one another in mere abstract reflection interpenetrate to form a new unity—a unity which for the present, to be sure, merely confronts us with a new problem, a new *task*. The antitheses of freedom and necessity, individuality and universality, "subjectivity" and "objectivity," spontaneity and causality, themselves required a deeper definition and a new fundamental explanaton before they could be employed as philosophical categories by which to elucidate the "origin of the work of art" and the "origin of language."

4. Language as an Expression of Emotion. The Problem of the "Origin of Language" (Giambattista Vico, Hamann, Herder, Romanticism)

Despite all their essential differences, the empiricist and rationalist, the psychological and the logical theories of languages, as formulated up to this point, have one basic trait in common. They all consider language essentially in its *theoretical* content, in its relation to knowledge as a whole and its contribution to the development of knowledge. Whether it is interpreted as the immediate work and indispensable organ of reason, or as a mere veil which conceals the basic contents of knowledge, the true and "original" perceptions of the spirit: in either case the goal of language, by

51. P. L. de Maupertuis, "Reflexions philosophiques sur l'origine des langues et la signification des mots," *Oeuvres* (Lyon, 1756), *1*, 259 ff.

which its positive or negative value is determined, is seen as theoretical cognition and its expression. Words are signs for *ideas*—which are regarded either as objective and necessary contents of cognition or as subjective representations. But as philosophy brought a new breadth and depth to the concept of "subjectivity"; as this concept gave rise, more and more clearly, to a truly universal view of the *spontaneity* of the spirit, which proved to be as much a spontaneity of feeling and will as of cognition—it became necessary to stress a new factor in the achievement of language. For when we seek to follow language back to its earliest beginnings, it seems to be not merely a representative sign for ideas, but also an emotional sign for sensuous drives and stimuli. The ancients knew this derivation of language from emotion, from the πάθος of sensation, pleasure and pain. In the opinion of Epicurus, it is to this primal source, which is common to man and beast and hence truly "natural," that we must return, in order to understand the origin of language. Language is not the product of a mere convention or arbitrary decree; it is as necessary and natural as immediate sensation itself. Sight, hearing, and the feelings of pleasure and pain are characteristic of man from the very first, and so likewise is the expression of our sensations and emotions. Men's sensations varied with their physical spiritual and ethnic constitution and accordingly different sounds necessarily arose, which only gradually with a view to simplification and mutual understanding were contracted into more general types of words and languages.⁵² In the same way, Lucretius traces the supposed wonder of the creation of language back to the general and particular laws of human nature. The special field of language develops from the general impulse for sensory-mimic expression, which is innate in man, which is not a product of reflection but unconscious and unwilled.⁵³

In its theory of language as in its natural philosophy and epistemology, modern philosophy hearkened back to Epicurus. In the seventeenth century the old "theory of natural sounds" underwent a highly remarkable renewal, equally original in its form and in its theoretical justification, particularly with that thinker who first attempted a comprehensive, sys-

52. Cf. Diogenes Laertius, Bk. 10, sec. 24, par. 75: ὅθεν καὶ τὰ ὀνόματα ἐξ ἀρχῆς μὴ θέσει γενέσθαι, ἀλλ' αὐτὰς τὰς φύσεις τῶν ἀνθρώπων, καθ' ἕκαστα ἔθνη ἴδια πασχούσας πάθη καὶ ἴδια λαμβανούσας φαντάσματα, ἰδίως τὸν ἀέρα ἐκπέμπειν, στελλόμενον ὑφ' ἑκάστων τῶν παθῶν καὶ τῶν φαντασμάτων, ὡς ἄν ποτε καὶ ἡ παρὰ τοὺς τόπους τῶν ἐθνῶν διαφορὰ εἴη· ὕστερον δὲ κοινῶς καθ' ἕκαστα ἔθνη τὰ ἴδια τιθῆναι, πρὸς τὸ τὰς δηλώσεις ἧττον ἀμφιβόλους γενέσθαι ἀλλήλοις καὶ συντομωτέρως δηλουμένας.

53. See Lucretius, *De rerum natura*, Bk. 5, ll. 1026 ff.

tematic outline of the cultural sciences. In his *Principi di scienza nuova d'intorno alla commune natura delle nazioni,* Giambattista Vico posed the problem of language within the sphere of a general metaphysic of the spirit. Beginning with the "poetic metaphysic" which was intended to disclose the origin of poetry and of mythical thinking, he passed through the intermediary link of "poetic logic," in which he strove to explain the genesis of poetic tropes and metaphors, to the question of the origin of language, which for him was synonymous with the question of the origin of "literature" and of the sciences in general. He too rejected the theory that the original words of language were attributable solely to convention; he too insisted on a "natural" relation between them and their meanings. If the present phase in the development of language, if our *lingua volgare* no longer reveals this relation, the reason is simply that it has moved farther and farther away from its true source, the language of the gods and heroes. But even in the present obscurity and fragmentation of language, the original relation of words to what they mean is apparent to the truly philosophical eye. Since nearly all words are derived from natural properties of things or from sensory impressions and feelings, the idea of a "universal dictionary," showing the meanings of words in all the different languages and tracing them all back to an original unity of ideas, is not presumptuous. Vico's own attempts in this direction reveal, to be sure, all the naïve fancy of a purely speculative "etymology," totally unhampered by critical or historical scruples.[54] All the original words were monosyllabic roots, which either reproduced a natural sound by onomatopoeia, or immediate expressions of emotion, interjections of pain or pleasure, joy or grief, surprise or terror.[55] Vico found support for this theory that the first words were simple monosyllabic interjections, in the German language which he—

---

54. How widespread this naïve conception of the meaning and purpose of "etymology" remained even among the philologists of the eighteenth century is shown, for example, by the reconstruction of the original language undertaken by Hemsterhuis and Ruhnken of the celebrated Dutch school of philologists. For details, see Th. Benfey, *Geschichte der Sprachwissenschaft* (Munich, 1869), pp. 255 ff.

55. Cf. the characteristic example in Vico, *La Scienza nuova* (Napoli, 1811), 2, 70 ff., Bk. 2: "Della sapienza poetica" sec. 2, ch. 4: "Seguitarono a formarsi le voci umane con *l'Interjezione,* che sone voci articolate all empito di passioni violente, che 'n tutte le lingue sono *monosillabe.* Onde non è fuori del verisimile, che da primi fulmini incominciata a destarsi negli uomini la *maraviglia,* nascese la *prima Interjezione* da quella di *Giove,* formata con la voce *pa,* e che poi restò raddoppiata *pape,* Interjezione di maraviglia; onde poi nacque a *Giove* il titolo di Padre degli uomini et degli Dei," etc. Eng. trans. by T. G. Bergin and M. H. Fisch, *The New Science of Giambattista Vico* (Ithaca, Cornell Univ. Press, 1948), p. 135.

like Fichte after him—regarded as a true original language, a *lingua madre,*
because the Germans had never succumbed to foreign conquerors and had
so kept the purity of their nation and language intact from time immemorial. The formation of interjections is followed by that of pronouns
and particles, which in their primitive form also go back to monosyllabic
roots; next the nouns developed, and only then the verbs, the ultimate
creation of language. In Vico's view the speech of children and persons
afflicted with pathological speech disturbance makes it clear that nouns precede verbs and belong to an earlier linguistic stratum.[56]

Strange and baroque as this theory may seem if we consider only its
particular interpretations, it embodies an approach which was to prove
extremely fruitful for future inquiry into the problem of language. A
static relation between sound and meaning had been replaced by a dynamic
relation: language was considered in terms of the dynamics of speech,
which in turn was related to the dynamics of feeling and emotion. As the
eighteenth century turned from reason to feeling, in which it came to
see the true foundation, the original creative potency of spiritual life, there
was a revival of interest in Vico's theory of the origin of language. It is no
accident that Rousseau should have been first to take up this theory and
attempt to develop it in detail.[57] But in another and profounder sense,
Vico's ideas influenced that eighteenth-century thinker who stood closest
to his symbolic metaphysic and his symbolic view of history, and who
like him regarded poetry as the mother tongue of the human race. Although this man, Johann Georg Hamann, sought no rational foundation
for his views, though his ideas seem to defy all logical system, they nevertheless in spite of him, one might say, shaped themselves into an immanent
system, since he persistently related all problems to the *one* basic problem
of language. Here from the very first Hamann's thinking, although with
its emphasis on immediate feeling and momentary impression it stood in
constant danger of losing itself in peripheral particulars and accidents,
found a specific center which it not so much defined as continuously cir-
cumscribed. "I speak," he himself said, "neither of physics nor of theology;
with me *language* is the mother of reason and revelation, its A and Ω."
"Even if I were as eloquent as Demosthenes, I would merely have to repeat a single maxim three times: reason is language, λόγος. This is the
bone I gnaw on, and on it I will gnaw myself to death. For me these depths
are still shrouded in darkness; I am still waiting for an apocalyptic angel

56. Ibid., 2, 73 ff.
57. J. J. Rousseau, "Essai sur l'origine des langues," *Oeuvres* (Paris, 1877), Vol. *1.*

with a key to this abyss." [58] Here lies for Hamann the true essence of reason, with its unity and inner contradiction. "What Demosthenes calls *actio,* Engel mimicry, Batteaux imitation of nature's beauty, is for me language, the organon and criterion of reason, as Young puts it. Here lies pure reason and at the same time its critique." [59] But this reality, through which the divine logos seems to manifest itself to us, evades everything that we call "reason." Of language as of history we can say that it is "like nature a sealed book, a veiled testimony, a riddle that cannot be solved unless we plough with a heifer other than our reason." [60] For language is not a collection of discursive conventional signs for discursive concepts, but is the symbol and counterpart of the same divine life which everywhere surrounds us visibly and invisibly, mysteriously yet revealingly. For Hamann as for Heraclitus, everything in it is at once expression and concealment, veiling and unveiling. All creation, nature as well as history, is nothing other than a message of the creator to the creature through the creature.

It belongs to the unity of divine revelation, that the *spirit* of God should have abased itself and divested itself of its majesty through the human stylus of the holy men who were driven by it, just as the *Son* of God condescended by taking the form of a servant, and just as all creation is a work of supreme humility. To admire the all-wise God only in nature is perhaps an insult similar to that shown an intelligent man by the rabble who judge his value by his cloak. . . . The opinions of the philosophers are variants of nature and the dogmas of the theologians are variants of Scripture. The author is the best interpreter of his words; he may speak through creatures—through events—or through blood and fire and incense, wherein consists the language of the godhead. . . . The unity of the author is reflected even in the *dialect* of his works; in all of them there is One tone of immeasurable sublimity and depth.[61]

Into these depths which, according to his own admission, remained in darkness for Hamann, Herder cast new light. Herder's prize "Essay on

58. Hamann an Jacobi, *Briefwechsel mit Jacobi,* ed. Gildemeister (Gotha, 1868), p. 122; an Herder, August 6, 1784, *Schriften,* ed. Fr. Roth, 7, 151 ff.

59. Hamann an Scheffner, February 11, 1785, *Schriften, 7,* 216.

60. Hamann, "Sokratische Denkwürdigkeiten," *Schriften, 2,* 19.

61. Hamann, "Kleeblatt hellenistischer Briefe," *Schriften, 2,* 207, "Aesthetica in nuce," *Schriften, 2,* 274 ff. Concerning Hamann's theory of language and its position within the whole of his "symbolic philosophy," see R. Unger's excellent *Hamanns Sprachlehre im Zusammenhang seines Denkens* (Munich, 1905).

the Origin of Language" exerted a crucial influence on the cultural history of the eighteenth century, primarily because in it he arrived at an entirely new *methodic* synthesis of two sharply antagonistic interpretations of cultural life. Herder was influenced by Hamann; but in the period preceding the prize essay he had been a disciple of Kant and through him of Leibniz. In speaking of his treatise *Vom Erkennen und Empfinden der menschlichen Seele* (On the Cognition and Feeling of the Human Soul), which is close to the prize essay both in conception and development, Haym writes that it is imbued with the spirit of Leibnizian philosophy from one end to the other, indeed, that it is nothing other than a summation of this philosophy as reflected in Herder.[62] But how was it possible to unite the two extreme poles in the approach to language, how was it possible to reconcile Hamann and Leibniz? How could the opinion that language was the supreme achievement of the analytic mind, the specific organ for the formation of "distinct" concepts, be fused with the belief that its origin evades all reflective understanding and must rather be sought in the darkness and unconscious poetic creation of feeling? Here Herder's problem begins and he solves it by a new approach to the problem of language. Even if all language is rooted in feeling and its immediate, instinctive manifestations, even if it originates not in the need for communication but in cries, tones, and wild, articulated sounds—even so, such an aggregate of sounds can never constitute the specific "form" of language. This form comes into being only with the operation of a new "human function," which from the very outset distinguishes the man from the beast. Herder's conception of this specifically human faculty of "reflection," and the role he assigns to it, are clearly derived from that fundamental concept which connects Leibniz' logic with his psychology. According to Leibniz, the unity of consciousness is made possible only by the unity of spiritual *action,* the unity of synthesis by which the spirit apprehends itself as an enduring and identical monad, and by which, when it encounters the same content at different times, it recognizes it to be one and the same. It is this form of "recognition" that Leibniz calls apperception, Herder "reflection," and Kant "synthesis of recognition."

> Man demonstrates reflection when the force of his soul works so freely that in the ocean of sensations that flows into it from all the senses, he can, in a manner of speaking, isolate and stop One wave, and direct his attention toward this wave, conscious that he is so doing. He dem-

62. R. Haym, *Herder* (Berlin, 1880–85), *I,* 665.

onstrates reflection when, emerging from the nebulous dream of images flitting past his senses, he can concentrate upon a point of wakefulness, dwell voluntarily on One image, observe it calmly and lucidly, and distinguish characteristics proving that this and no other is the object. He demonstrates reflection when he not only knows all attributes vividly and clearly, but can *recognize* one or more distinguishing attributes: the first act of this recognition yields a clear concept; it is the soul's First judgment—and what made this recognition possible? A characteristic which he had to isolate and which came to him clearly as a characteristic of reflection. Forward! Let us cry εὕρηκα! The first characteristic of reflection was the word of the soul. With it human speech was invented! [63]

In this way, it is possible for Herder to interpret language entirely as a product of immediate sensation and at the same time entirely as a product of reflection: because reflection is not something external that is merely added to the content of feeling; it enters into feeling as a constitutive factor. It is "reflection" which makes the ephemeral sensory stimulus into a determinate, differentiated and hence spiritual "content." Here perception is not, as in Maupertuis and Condillac, a ready-made, self-contained psychological content, to which expression in word and concept is merely appended; here the mere impressions are synthesized into "ideas" and named in one and the same act. An artificial system of signs is no longer juxtaposed to perceptions considered as natural data; here perception itself, by virtue of its spiritual character, contains a specific factor of form which, when fully developed, is represented in the form of words and language. Hence language—though Herder goes on to speak of its "invention"—is never merely *made,* but *grows* in a necessary process from within. It is a factor in the synthetic structure of consciousness itself, through which the world of sensation becomes a world of *intuition:* it is not a thing that is produced but a specific type of spiritual generation and formation.

Here the general concept of linguistic form has undergone a decisive transformation. Herder's prize essay marks the transition from the older rationalistic concept of "reflective form," which dominated the philosophy of the Enlightenment, to the Romantic concept of "organic form." The new concept was first definitely introduced into philology in Friedrich Schlegel's essay *Über die Sprache und Weisheit der Indier* (On the Language and Wisdom of India). It would be unjust to suppose that the

63. Herder "Über den Ursprung der Sprache" (1772), *Werke,* ed. B. Suphan, 5, 34 ff.

designation of language as an organism was a mere image or poetic metaphor. Pale and vague as this term may seem to us today, Friedrich Schlegel and his epoch formed a very concrete picture of the position of language within man's spiritual life as a whole. The Romantic concept of the organism did not refer to a single *fact* of nature, a specific, limited group of objective phenomena, with which, it is true, linguistic phenomena can be compared only very indirectly and inaccurately. For them, the "organism" signified not a particular class of phenomena, but a universal speculative principle, a principle which indeed constitutes the ultimate goal and systematic focus of Romantic speculation. The problem of the organism was a center to which the Romantics repeatedly found themselves drawn back from the most diverse fields. Goethe's theory of metamorphoses, Kant's critical philosophy, Schelling's "system of transcendental idealism" and the beginning of his natural philosophy, seemed to move together in this *one* point. In the *Critique of Judgment* this concept seems to be the true *medius terminus* resolving the dualistic opposition within the Kantian system. Nature and freedom, being and moral law, which previously had been considered not only as separate but as antagonistic, were now related to one another through this middle link—and this relation disclosed a new content in both of them. Kant saw this content in *systematic* terms, primarily he considered the two extremes from a critical-transcendental point of view, as "perspectives" from which to contemplate and interpret the whole phenomenal world; for Schelling, however, the concept of the organic became the vehicle for an all-embracing speculative metaphysic. Nature and art, like nature and freedom, were united in the idea of the organic. This idea bridged the chasm that seemed to divide the unconscious growth of nature from the conscious creation of the spirit—here for the first time man gained an intimation of the true unity of his own nature, in which intuition and concept, form and object, ideal and material are originally one and the same. "Hence the unique radiance surrounding these problems—a radiance which the mere philosophy of reflection, concerned only with analysis, can never develop, whereas pure intuition, or rather the creative imagination, long ago invented the symbolic language which we need only interpret in order to discover that the less merely reflective thought we give nature, the more comprehensibly it speaks to us." [64]

64. F. W. v. Schelling, *Ideen zu einer Philosophie der Natur* (1797) *Sämmtliche Werke* (Stuttgart and Augsburg, 1857), 2, 47.

It is only in the light of this general systematic significance which the idea of the organic assumed for the philosophy of Romanticism, that we can understand the role it was destined to play in philological speculation. The philosophy of language had also revolved around sharp antagonisms; but now there was a new intermediary between "subjectivity" and "objectivity," between "individuality" and "universality." In connection with organic life the concept of "individual form" had already been coined by Leibniz—and Herder had extended it to the whole breadth of cultural life, from nature to history, from history to art and the concrete study of art styles. Everywhere, a "universal" was sought: however, this universal is not conceived as a self-contained reality, as the abstract unity of a genus juxtaposed to its individuals, but as a unity which exists only in a totality of specific individuals. This totality and the law, the inner relationship expressed in it: these have become the true universal. For the philosophy of language this new conception of the universal meant abandonment of the quest for a basic, original language behind the diversity and historical contingency of the individual languages; it also meant that the true universal "essence" of language was no longer sought in abstraction from differentiation, but in the *totality* of differentiations. It was through this fusion of the idea of organic form with the idea of totality that Wilhelm von Humboldt arrived at his philosophical view which implied a fundamental new approach to the problem of language.[65]

5. Wilhelm von Humboldt

Early in his career, language became the center of Wilhelm von Humboldt's cultural interests and endeavors. "Fundamentally," he wrote as early as 1805 in a letter to Wolf, "everything I do is language study. I believe that I have discovered the art of using language as a vehicle by which to explore the heights, the depths and the diversity of the whole world." Humboldt practiced this art in a vast number of monographs on language and the history of language, culminating in the brilliant introduction to his

---

65. The following discussion of Wilhelm von Humboldt's philosophy of language is based in part on my monograph "Die Kantischen Elemente in Wilhelm von Humboldt's Sprachphilosophie," published in *Festschrift zu Paul Hensels 60. Geburtstag.*

work on the Kavi language. It is true that Humboldt does not, in all parts of his writings on the philosophy and science of language, seem fully aware of the implications of his "art." Not infrequently it goes beyond anything that he himself defines in sharp and clear concepts. But even the much criticized obscurity of certain of his ideas always carries a productive content, which often cannot be captured in a simple formula, an abstract definition, but proves fruitful only when considered in the context of Humboldt's whole concrete view of language.

In any exposition of Humboldt's ideas it is, therefore, necessary to group them around certain systematic centers, even when he himself did not signalize these centers as such. Fundamentally, Humboldt was a thoroughly systematic thinker; but he was hostile to any purely external technique of systematization. In his endeavor to set the *whole* of his view of language before us at every point of his inquiry, he resists any clear and sharp analysis of this whole. His concepts are never the pure, detached products of logical analysis, they embody a note of aesthetic feeling, an artistic mood, which animates his work but at the same time cloaks the articulation and structure of his ideas. If we seek to disclose this structure, we find three great fundamental antitheses which determine Humboldt's thinking, and for which he hoped to find a critical and speculative synthesis in the study of language.

For Humboldt language primarily represents the opposition between the individual and the "objective" spirit, and its resolution. Each individual speaks his own language—and yet, precisely in the freedom with which he employs it, he is aware of an inner spiritual constraint. Language is everywhere an intermediary, first between infinite and finite nature, then between one individual and another—simultaneously and through the same act, it makes union possible and arises from this union.

> We must free ourselves completely from the idea that it can be separated from what it designates, as for example the name of a man from his person, and that like a conventional cipher it is a product of reflection and agreement or in any sense the work of man (as we tend to think of concepts in common experience), not to say the work of the individual. Like a true, inexplicable wonder, it bursts forth from the mouth of a nation, and no less amazingly, though this is repeated every day and indifferently overlooked, it springs from the babble of every child; it is the most radiant sign and certain proof that man does not possess

an intrinsically separate individuality, that I and Thou are not merely complementary concepts, but that if we could go back to the point of separation, they would prove to be truly identical, that in this sense there are spheres of individuality, from the weak, helpless, perishable individual down to the primeval clan of mankind, because otherwise all understanding would be eternally impossible.[66]

In this sense a *nation* is also a cultural form of mankind, characterized by a specific language and individualized in relation to ideal totality.

Individuality is shattered, but in so miraculous a way that by its very division it arouses a sense of unity, indeed it appears as a means of creating unity, at least in the idea . . . For striving deep within him after that unity and totality, man seeks to surpass the barriers of his individuality, but since, like the giant who obtains his strength only from contact with mother earth, he possesses power only in his individuality, he must enhance it in this higher striving. Thus he continuously progresses in an inherently impossible striving. And here, in a truly miraculous way he is aided by language, which binds as it individualizes, and beneath the cloak of the most individual expression holds the possibility of universal understanding. The individual, wherever, whenever and however he lives, is a fragment broken off from his whole race, and language demonstrates and sustains this eternal bond which governs the destinies of the individual and the history of the world.[67]

Elements of Kant and Schelling are strangely intermingled in this first metaphysical sketch of Humboldt's philosophy of language. On the basis of the critical analysis of the cognitive faculties, Humboldt seeks to arrive at the point where the antitheses, subjectivity and objectivity, individuality and universality, resolve themselves in pure indifference. But he does not seek this ultimate unity by the intellectual approach which aspires to raise us immediately over all the barriers of the "finite," analytical-discursive concept. Like Kant as a critic of cognition, Humboldt as a critic of language stands in the "terrible bathos of experience." Again and again he stresses that if it is not to be chimerical, the philosophy of language, though destined to lead us into the ultimate depths of humanity, must begin with

66. Humboldt, "Über die Verschiedenheit des menschlichen Sprachbaues" ["Vorstudie zur Einleitung zum Kawi-Werk"], *Werke, Gesammelte Schriften* (Akademie ed.), 6, No. 1, 125 ff.
67. Ibid.

the dry mechanical analysis of its physical aspect. For that original accord between world and man, upon which depends all possibility of a knowledge of truth, and which we must consequently presuppose as a universal postulate in any investigation of particular objects, can only be regained bit by bit, through the study of *phenomena*. In this sense the objective is not the given but always remains to be achieved.[68] Here Humboldt applies the Kantian critique to the philosophy of language. The metaphysical opposition between subjectivity and objectivity is replaced by their transcendental correlation. In Kant the object, as "object in experience," is not something outside of and apart from cognition; on the contrary, it is only "made possible," determined and constituted by the categories of cognition. Similarly, the subjectivity of language no longer appears as a barrier that prevents us from apprehending objective being but rather as a means of forming, of "objectifying" sensory impressions. Like cognition, language does not merely "copy" a given object; it rather embodies a spiritual attitude which is always a crucial factor in our perception of the objective. Since the naïve-realistic approach lives and moves among objects, it takes too little account of this subjectivity; it does not readily conceive of a subjectivity which transforms the objective world, not accidentally or arbitrarily but in accordance with inner laws, so that the apparent object itself becomes only a subjective concept, yet a concept with a fully justified claim to universal validity. In this view with its orientation towards *things,* the diversity of languages is merely a diversity of sounds, which are regarded as mere means of entering into a relation with things. But it is precisely this empirical-realistic approach which obstructs the extension of our knowledge of language, and makes what knowledge we have dead and barren.[69] The true *ideality* of language exists only in its *subjectivity*. Hence it was and always will be futile to attempt to exchange the words in the various languages for universally valid signs such as mathematics possesses in its lines, numbers, and algebraic symbols. For such a system would express only a small part of what can be thought, it would serve only to designate such concepts as are formed by purely rational construction. But the substance of inner perception and sensation can be stamped into concepts only by man's individual rep-

68. Humboldt, "Über das vergleichende Sprachstudium in Beziehung auf die verschiedenen Epochen der Sprachentwicklyng" (1820) *Werke, 4,* 27 ff.

69. Humboldt, "Über die Verschiedenheit des menschlichen Sprachbaues," *Werke, 6,* No. 1, 119 ff.

resentative faculty, and that is inseparable from his language. "The word which is required to make the concept into a citizen of the world of thought adds to it some of its own signification, and in defining the idea, the word confines it within certain limits. . . . Because of the mutual dependency of thought and word, it is evident that the languages are not really means of representing the truth that has already been ascertained, but far more, means of discovering a truth not previously known. Their diversity is not a diversity of sounds and signs, but of world outlook." For Humboldt this idea provides the foundation and ultimate aim of all philosophy of language. Historically, it discloses a noteworthy process which once again teaches us how the truly fruitful philosophical ideas propagate themselves even outside the immediate formulation given to them by their authors. For here Humboldt, through the intermediary of Kant and Herder, had found his way back from Leibniz' narrow view of language to a deeper, more comprehensive, universal-idealistic view implicit in the general principles of the Leibnizian philosophy. For Leibniz the universe is given only in its reflection by the monads, and each one of them represents the totality from an individual "point of view"; while on the other hand it is precisely the totality of these perspective views and the harmony among them that constitutes what we call the objectivity of appearances, the reality of the phenomenal world. Similarly for Humboldt each single language is such an individual view of the world, and only the totality of these views constitutes the objectivity attainable by man. Accordingly, language is subjective in relation to the knowable, and objective in relation to man as an empirical-psychological subject. For each language is a note in the harmony of man's universal nature: "once again the subjectivity of *all* mankind becomes intrinsically objective." [70]

This conception of objectivity, not as a given which need merely be described but as a goal which must be *achieved* by a process of spiritual formation, brings us to the second basic idea underlying Humboldt's view of language. Any inquiry into language must proceed "genetically": this does not mean that we must pursue its temporal genesis and seek to explain its development by specific empirical-psychological "causes," but that we must recognize the finished structure of language as something derived and mediated, which we can understand only if we are able to reconstitute

70. Humboldt, "Über das vergleichende Sprachstudium," *Werke*, 4, 21 ff.; cf. "Grundzüge des allgemeinen Sprachtypus," *Werke*, 5, 386 ff., and "Einleitung zum Kawi-Werk," *Werke*, 7, No. 1 59 ff.

it out of its factors and determine the type and direction of these factors. Language broken down into words and rules remains a dead product of scientific analysis—for the essence of language never resides in those elements isolated by abstraction and analysis, but solely in the spirit's eternally repeated endeavor to make the articulated sound an expression of thought. In each particular language this endeavor begins at certain specific centers, from which it spreads out in different directions—and yet these diverse products ultimately join to form, not indeed the material unity of one product, but the ideal unity of a lawful activity. The content of the spirit can be conceived only in activity and as activity—and the same is true of every particular content which only the spirit makes knowable and possible. What we call the essence and form of a language is consequently nothing other than the enduring, uniform element which we can demonstrate not in any one phenomenon, but in the endeavor of the spirit to raise the articulated sound to the level of an expression of thought.[71] Even what might seem to be the actual substance of language, the simple word detached from the context of the sentence, does not like a substance communicate something already produced, or constitute a self-contained concept, but merely stimulates us to form such a concept, independently and in a specific way.

> Men do not understand one another by relying on the signs for things, nor by causing one another to produce exactly the same concept, but by touching the same link in each other's sense perceptions and concepts, by striking the same key in each other's spiritual instrument, whereupon corresponding, but not identical concepts arise in each of them. . . . When . . . the link in the chain, the key of the instrument is touched in this way, the whole organism vibrates and the concept that springs from the soul stands in harmony with everything surrounding the individual link, even at a great distance from it.[72]

Thus, here too objectivity is guaranteed by harmony in the infinitely varied production of words and concepts, and by the simplicity of the reality they reproduce. Hence the true vehicle of linguistic meaning is never to be sought in the particular word, but only in the sentence; for the sentence reveals the original force of *synthesis* upon which all speech and all understanding are essentially based. This general view is most sharply and suc-

71. Humboldt, "Einleitung zum Kawi-Werk," *Werke*, 7, No. 1, 46 ff.
72. Ibid., pp. 169 ff.

cinctly expressed in Humboldt's famous dictum that language is not a work (*ergon*) but an activity (*energeia*) and that consequently the only true definition of it must be a genetic one. In a strict sense this definition applies to every particular instance of speech: but fundamentally it is only the totality of these instances that we can regard as language; it is only in the function and its general exercise in accordance with certain specific laws that we can find its substantiality and ideal essence.[73]

With the concept of *synthesis* we reach the third of the great oppositions in the light of which Humboldt considers language. This distinction, the differentiation of *matter* and *form,* which dominates Humboldt's general view, is also rooted in Kantian thought. For Kant, form is a mere expression of relation, but for this very reason, since all our knowledge of phenomena ultimately dissolves into a knowledge of temporal and spatial relations, it constitutes the truly objectifying principle of knowledge. The unity of form is the synthetic unity in which the unity of the object is grounded. "The conjunction of a manifold can never be given us by the senses," it is always "a spontaneous act of the faculty of representation . . . we cannot represent anything as conjoined in the object without having previously conjoined it ourselves. Of all mental notions, that of conjunction is the only one which cannot be given through objects, but can be originated only by the subject itself." [74] In order to characterize this form of conjunction, grounded in the transcendental subject and its spontaneity, yet strictly "objective," because necessary and universally valid, Kant himself had invoked the unity of judgment and so indirectly that of the *sentence.* For him judgment is "nothing but the mode of bringing given cognitions under the objective unity of apperception": but in language this unity is expressed in the copula of judgment, in the little word of relation "is," which conjoins subject and predicate. Only by this "is" do we posit a necessary *content* of our judgment, do we state that the representations in question necessarily belong to each other and are not merely connected by fortuitous, psychological associations.[75] Humboldt's concept of form extends what is here said of a single linguistic term to the whole of language. In every complete and thoroughly formed language the act of designating

73. Ibid., p. 46.

74. I. Kant, "Transzendentale Deduktion der reinen Verstandesbegriffe," § 15, in *Kritik der reinen Vernunft* (2d ed.), pp. 129 ff. Eng. Trans. by J. M. D. Meiklejohn, Everyman ed. (London, Dent, 1950), § 11, p. 93.

75. Ibid., § 19, pp. 141 ff.; Eng. Trans. § 15, p. 99.

a concept by definite material characteristics must be augmented by a specific endeavor and a specific formal determination which place the concept in a definite *category of thought*, designating it for example as substance, attribute or activity. This transference of the concept to a definite category of thinking is "a new act of the linguistic self-consciousness, through which the particular instance, the individual word, is related to the totality of possible instances in language or speech. Only by this operation, carried out with the greatest possible purity and depth and firmly embedded in the language itself, is an adequate fusion and articulation created between its independent activity, arising from thought and that purely receptive activity which follows from outward impressions." [76] Here again matter and form, receptivity and spontaneity—like the above-mentioned antitheses "individual" and "universal," "subjective" and "objective"—are not disjoined parts out of which the process of language is composed, but factors in the genetic process itself, which necessarily belong together and can only be separated in our analysis. The priority of form over matter, which Humboldt asserts with Kant and which he finds most clearly and sharply expressed in the inflected languages, is hence regarded as a priority of value and not as a priority of empirical-temporal existence, since in actual language, even in the so-called "isolating" languages, both determinants, the formal and the material, necessarily operate conjointly, not one without the other or before the other. [77]

Here we have suggested only the bare outline of Humboldt's view of language, its intellectual frame as it were. What gave this view its fertility and importance was the manner in which it was filled out by Humboldt's linguistic researches, the twofold movement by which he persistently passed from the phenomenon to the idea, from the idea to the phenomenon. The basic principle of the transcendental method: the universal application of philosophy to science, which Kant had demonstrated for mathematics and mathematical physics, now seemed confirmed in a totally new field. The new philosophical view of language demanded and made possible a new approach to linguistic science. Throughout his general survey of language, Bopp reverts to Humboldt—the very first sentences of his *Comparative Grammar*, published in 1833, invoke Humboldt's concept of

76. Humboldt "Vorwort zum Kawi-Werke," *Werke*, 7, No. 1, 109.

77. Cf. Humboldt's remarks on the Chinese language in "Lettre à M. Abel Rémusat sur la nature des formes grammaticales en général et sur le génie de la langue chinoise en particulier," *Werke*, 5, 284 ff.; on the grammatical structure of the Chinese language, *Werke*, 5, 309 ff.

the "linguistic organism" in defining the function of the new science of comparative linguistics.[78]

6. August Schleicher and the Development of the Scientific View of Language

However, as philological speculation gave way to the empirical study of language, it was felt that the very breadth of the concept of the organism gave it a vagueness and ambiguity which threatened to make it unfit for specific, concrete tasks. Philosophical speculation had seen this concept essentially as a mediation between opposite extremes, so that it appeared to partake of the nature of both extremes. Could such a concept, which seemed to take on all colors, continue to be used as a foundation, no longer of a general metaphysic of language, but of a specific methodology? When it came to deciding whether, from the standpoint of method, the laws of language should be designated as scientific or historical laws; to determining the relative importance of material and of spiritual factors in language formation; and finally, to defining the part played by conscious and unconscious factors in language formation—the mere concept of a linguistic organism seemed inadequate. For precisely its hovering middle position between "nature" and "spirit," between unconscious action and conscious creation, enabled it to move back and forth between the two perspectives. Only a slight shift in emphasis in either direction was required to disturb its fluid equilibrium and give it a changed, or indeed an opposite methodological significance.

The history of linguistics in the nineteenth century reveals concretely the process which we have here attempted to suggest in a general, schematic form. In this period the science of language passed through the same transition as did history and the cultural sciences. The concept of the "organic" retained its central position; but its meaning changed radically once the biological concept of development prevailing in modern natural

78. "In this book I intend to give a comparative description of the organism of the languages named in the title, a compendium of all their related features, an inquiry into their physical and mechanical laws, and into the origin of the forms designating grammatical relations." F. Bopp, *Vergleichende Grammatik des Sanskrit, Zend, Griechischen*, etc. (Berlin, 1833), p. 1.

science was opposed to the concept of development dominant in Romantic philosophy. In the field of biology, the speculative concept of organic form was gradually replaced by its purely scientific concept, and this immediately affected the study of language. This transformation is most clearly and typically reflected in the scientific development of August Schleicher. In his view of language and its history, Schleicher not only took the step from Hegel to Darwin, but also passed through all the intermediary stages. In him we see not only the beginning and the end, but also the separate phases of that process by which the speculative study of language became a purely empirical study, and by which for the first time the concept of linguistic law acquired distinct content.

In his first important work, the *Sprachvergleichende Untersuchungen* (investigations in Comparative Philology), Schleicher starts from the proposition that the true essence of language as articulated sound expressing spiritual life, is to be sought in the relationship between expression of signification and expression of relation. Each language is characterized by the manner in which it expresses signification and relation—no third essential element of language is conceivable. On this presupposition, languages are divided into three main types: the isolating (monosyllabic), agglutinative, and inflected languages. Signification is the material element, the root; relation is the formal element, the change effected in the root. Both factors are necessary constituents which must be contained in a language; but although neither can be totally lacking, the *relation* between the two can vary exceedingly, it can be merely implicit, or more or less explicit. The isolating languages express only signification in words, while relation is expressed by the position of the words and by the stress; the agglutinative languages possess specific syllables of relation in addition to the syllables of signification, but the two are connected only outwardly, for the designation of relation is attached only materially and superficially to the root, which undergoes no internal change. Only in the inflected languages are the two basic elements not merely attached to one another, but truly combined and intermingled. The first is characterized by the undifferentiated identity of relation and signification, or one might say, by pure relation; the second is characterized by differentiation into syllables of relation and syllables of signification, relation merges into a distinct phonetic existence of its own; in the third, finally, this difference is negated and bridged: here there is a return to unity, but to a unity which is far higher because it presupposes the difference out of which it grew, and contains within it this surpassed difference. So far, Schleicher has strictly followed Hegel's dialectical schema, which dominates his view both of language as a whole and of its inner articulations. But even in *Sprachvergleichende Untersuchungen* this attempt at a dialectical classification is accompanied by an attempt at classification in the spirit of the natural sciences. From the systematic standpoint, Schleicher expressly points out, linguistics shows an unmistakable similarity to the natural sciences. The habitus of a family of languages can, like that of a family of plants or animals, be reduced to certain specific criteria. "In botany certain characteristics—seed-leaves, types of blossom—prove valuable as bases of classification, precisely because these characteristics usually run parallel to others, and the *phonetic laws* seem to fulfill this function in the classification of languages within a single linguistic family, e.g., the Semitic or Indo-Germanic family." For the present, however, his investigation does not follow this empirical path, but takes a purely speculative direction. The monosyllabic languages, in which the word is in no way articulated, resemble the simple crystal which in contrast to the higher, articulated organisms appears as a strict unity; the agglutinative languages, which have achieved articulation into parts, but have not yet fused these parts into a true whole, correspond to the organic realm of plants; while the inflected languages, in which the word is unity in the diversity of its articulations, correspond to the animal organism.[79] For Schleicher this is no mere analogy but a highly significant objective definition, springing from the very essence of language and determining the *methodology* of philological science. If the languages are natural entities, the laws according to which they develop must be not historical, but scientific laws. The historical process and the process of language formation are utterly divergent, temporally as well as in content. History and language formation do not proceed concomitantly but successively. For history is the work of the self-conscious spirit, while language is the work of an unconscious necessity. History represents human freedom, creating true reality for itself; language partakes of man's unfree, natural aspect. "Language, it is true, also reveals a *development,* which in the broader sense of the word may be called history: a successive emergence of forces; but this development is so little characteristic of the free spiritual sphere, that it is manifested most clearly in nature." Once history begins and the spirit ceases to produce the word, but confronts it

79. August Schleicher, *Sprachvergleichende Untersuchungen* (Bonn, 1848–50), *1,* 7 ff; *2,* 5 ff.

and uses it as an instrument, language can no longer develop, but merely refines itself. Language formation occurs before history, the decline of the languages begins in the historical period.[80]

Language is for the human spirit what nature is for the World Spirit: the condition of its otherness. "Its accord with history begins with its spiritualizations; from then on it gradually loses its corporeal element, its form. Consequently, the scientific, and not the historical, part of linguistics is the systematic part." The *philologist,* who uses language only as a means by which to enter into the spirit and cultural life of the peoples, deals with history; the object of linguistics, on the other hand, is language, whose character can no more be determined by the human will than a nightingale can exchange its song for that of the lark: "That which can no more be organically changed by man's free will than his own physical constitution, does not belong to the sphere of the free spirit, but to that of nature. Consequently, the method of linguistics is totally different from the method of any cultural science and is essentially similar to that of the other natural sciences. . . . Like the natural sciences, it aims to investigate a field in which we discern the rule of unalterable natural laws which man's will and whim are powerless to change in any way." [81]

From here on, only one step was needed to dissolve linguistics completely into natural science and linguistic laws into pure natural laws; this step was taken twenty-five years later by Schleicher himself in his *Darwinian Theory and Linguistic Science.* In this work, which takes the form of an "open letter to Ernst Haeckel," the *opposition* between "nature" and "spirit," which had hitherto governed Schleicher's view of language and its position in the system of the sciences, was dropped as obsolete. Schleicher notes that the direction of thought in the modern period is "unmistakably toward monism." Dualism, construed as an opposition of spirit and nature, content and form, essence and appearance, had, he declared, been entirely superseded in the outlook of the natural sciences. For the scientific view, there was no matter without spirit, no spirit without matter: or rather, there was neither spirit nor matter in the usual sense, but only one entity that was both at once. From this, linguistic science must draw the plain inference therefore, that it too must renounce any sort of special position for its laws. The theory of evolution which Darwin showed valid for the species of animals and plants, must apply no less to the organisms of the

80. Ibid., 2, 10 ff.; cf. *1,* 16 ff.
81. Ibid., 2, 2 ff.; cf. 2, 21 ff. and *1,* 24 ff.

languages. To the species of a genus correspond the languages of a family, to the subspecies correspond the dialects of a language, to the varieties correspond the subdialects, and finally, to the individuals corresponds the speech of the particular men who speak the language. In the linguistic sphere we also find the origin of species by gradual differentiation and the survival of the more highly developed organisms in the struggle for existence. Darwin's idea seems to have been confirmed far beyond its original province, and shown to be the basic principle both of the natural and the cultural sciences.[82]

Here, from a methodological standpoint, we find ourselves at the opposite extreme from Schleicher's original point of departure. Anything that is constructed a priori—he now expressly declares—is at best an ingenious game, but utterly useless for science. Once it is recognized that "observation is the foundation of our present knowledge," once empiricism is granted unlimited rights, everything that has hitherto passed for philosophy of language is as dead as the dialectical philosophy of nature: it belongs to a past phase of thought, whose questions, like its solutions, lie behind us.

True, Schleicher himself, even in this last formulation of the problem of language, fulfilled his stated aim only in small part:—it is easy to see that in turning from Hegel to Haeckel he merely exchanged one form of metaphysics for another. The actual step into the promised land of positivism was reserved for a later generation of scholars who, instead of attempting a total monistic or evolutionistic explanation of all reality, strove to apprehend the methodological problems of linguistic science in their special character, in their sharp and clear isolation.

7. Definition of Modern Linguistic Science and the Problem of Phonetic Laws

This limitation, however, does not mean that the problem of language was suddenly removed from all its involvements with the methodological problems of historical and natural science. This would not have been possible, for even positivism, to which the solution of this problem now seemed to have been entrusted once and for all, remained a philosophy precisely

82. Schleicher, *Die Darwinsche Theorie und die Sprachwissenschaft* (Weimar, 1873).

in its rejection of metaphysics. And as a philosophy, it could not content itself with a multiplicity of mere facts or special laws governing facts, but was compelled to seek in this diversity a unity which can be found only in the *concept* of law itself. That this concept has a single *signification,* identical for the diverse spheres of knowledge, was for the present simply assumed: but as the method was more closely defined, this assumption inevitably took on the character of a problem. When we speak of linguistic, historical and scientific "laws," we assume that a certain logical structure is common to all of them—but what seems more important from the standpoint of method is the specific imprint and nuance which the concept of law acquires in each special field. If the sciences are to be apprehended as a truly systematic whole, a universal problem of knowledge must be found present in all of them, but it must also be shown that in each of them this problem demands a special solution under definite particular conditions. The development of the concept of law in modern linguistic science has been determined by both these considerations. If we now follow the transformations of this concept in the light of the general history of science and of general epistemology, it becomes evident in a very remarkable and characteristic way how the different branches of knowledge exerted an ideal influence on one another even where we cannot speak of any immediate influence. The concept of *linguistic* law passed, almost without exception, through all the same phases as the concept of *natural law*. And this is no matter of superficial transference, but of profound kinship, resulting from the workings in widely divergent fields of the fundamental intellectual trends of the time.

The principles which dominated the exact natural sciences in the middle of the nineteenth century were most suggestively expressed in those celebrated sentences with which Helmholtz introduced his treatise *Über die Erhaltung der Kraft* (On the Conservation of Energy). While Helmholtz indicated that the intent of this work was to prove that all happenings in nature can be reduced to attractive and repellent forces, whose intensity depends only on the distance between the points affecting one another, he did not mean to state this proposition as a mere *fact,* but rather to derive its validity and necessity from the *form* of our understanding of nature. The principle that any change in nature must have an adequate cause, is, according to him, truly fulfilled only if we can reduce all events to ultimate causes which act in accordance with an absolutely immutable law, which consequently produce *the same* effect at all times under the same outward conditions. The discovery of these ultimate immutable causes is the true aim of all the theoretical natural sciences. "Now whether all events can really be reduced to such causes, whether nature is fully comprehensible, or whether there are changes in it which evade the laws of a necessary causality, that is to say, which fall into the province of spontaneity or freedom, need not be decided here; in any case it is clear that science, whose purpose it is to understand nature, must assume it to be intelligible and continue to investigate and draw inferences under this assumption until perhaps compelled by irrefutable facts to recognize its limitations." [83] It is well known how this assumption that nature can be understood only if it can be fully explained on the basis of mechanical principles spread from the field of "inorganic" reality to the study of *organic* processes, and how descriptive natural science came to be wholly dominated by it. The "limits of natural knowledge" now coincided with the limits of the mechanical view of the world. To gain knowledge of any process in inorganic or organic nature meant nothing other than to dissolve it into its components and ultimately into the mechanical motion of atoms: anything that did not lend itself to such a breakdown seemed destined to remain an absolutely transcendent problem for the human mind.

Applied to language, this fundamental view—which within the natural sciences was stated most clearly by Du Bois-Reymond in his celebrated lecture *Über die Grenzen des Naturerkennens* (1872) (On the Limits of our Knowledge of Nature)—implies that we can speak of an understanding of language only if we succeed in reducing its complex phenomena to simple changes of ultimate elements and establish universally valid rules for these changes. Such an inference was far removed from the older speculative conception of language as an organism, which situated the organic process *between* nature and freedom, hence subjected it to no absolute necessity but left a certain amount of free play between the different possibilities. Bopp had sometimes expressly remarked that in language one should not seek laws offering more solid resistance than the shores of rivers and oceans.[84] Here Goethe's conception of the organism prevails: language is subordinated to a rule which, as Goethe put it, is firm and eternal, but also living. Now, however, since in natural science itself the idea of

---

83. H. v. Helmholtz, *Über die Erhaltung der Kraft* (1847), pp. 2 ff.

84. Cf. B. Delbrück, *Einleitung in das Sprachstudium* (Leipzig, 1880), p. 21. Authorized trans. by Eva Channing, *Introduction to the Study of Language* (Leipzig and London, 1882), p. 21.

the organism seemed to have dissolved utterly into the concept of the mechanism, no room remained for such a view. It was held that though the absolute necessity governing all linguistic development may be very much obscured in complex phenomena, it must stand out clearly in the elementary phenomena, i.e., phonetic changes. "If we admit of accidental deviations which cannot be brought into relation with one another"—wrote one linguist of this period, "we are, fundamentally, saying that the object of our investigation, language, is inaccessible to scientific knowledge." [85] Here again a specific conception of linguistic law is built upon a general assumption regarding knowledge and intelligibility *as such,* upon a specific epistemological ideal. This postulate of elementary, exceptionless laws was given its sharpest formulation in the *Morphological Investigations* of Brugmann and Osthoff. "All phonetic change, in so far as it occurs mechanically, follows laws without exception, i.e., the direction of the phonetic movement . . . is always the same in all members of a linguistic family, and all words in which the syllable subjected to the phonetic movement appears under like conditions, will without exception be affected by the change." [86]

But even though this view of the neogrammarians became more and more firmly entrenched and set its characteristic stamp on all scientific linguistics in the second half of the nineteenth century, the concept of phonetic law nevertheless gradually underwent the same transformations as we discern in the same period in the *general* concept of natural law. As the pure positivist ideal came to be more strictly formulated in science, the insistence on *explaining* the natural process by the universal laws of mechanics receded in favor of the more modest endeavor to *describe* it in such laws. Mechanics itself—according to Kirchhoff's famous definition —now consisted merely in a complete and unambiguous description of the dynamic processes occurring in nature.[87] What it yields is not the ultimate and absolute causes of the process, but only the *forms* which the process takes. Accordingly, if the analogy between linguistic science and natural science is asserted, we should expect and demand nothing more

85. Aug. Leskien, *Die Deklination im Slawisch-Litauischen und Germanischen* (Leipzig, 1876).

86. H. Osthoff and K. Brugmann, *Morphologische Untersuchungen* (6 vols. Leipzig, 1878–1910), *1*, xiii; Leskien, p. xxviii.

87. G. Kirchhoff, *Vorlesungen über mathematische Physik;* Vol. *1, Mechanik* (Berlin, 1876), p. 1.

from the laws of language than just such a comprehensive expression of empirically observed regularities. Here again, if we remain strictly within the sphere of given facts, we shall not seek to disclose the ultimate forces of language formation, but merely to establish certain *similarities of form* by observation and comparison. Hence the supposed "natural necessity" of phonetic laws takes on a different character. As late as 1878 Osthoff was formulating the principle that phonetic laws were without exception: "Everything that we have learned from the methodologically stricter studies of our own day makes it more and more apparent that the phonetic laws of language work blindly, with a blind natural necessity, that there are simply no exceptions to them or exemptions from them."[88] A scholar like Hermann Paul, however, took a far soberer and more critical view of the phonetic laws. "Phonetic law," he stresses, "does not state what *must* repeatedly happen under certain general conditions, it merely notes regularity within a group of specific historical manifestations."[89] A view of this sort, which interpreted law merely as an expression of certain *facts* of linguistic history but not as an expression of the ultimate factors of all language formation, was free to ascribe observed similarities of form to quite divergent forces. Side by side with the elementary physical processes of phonetic development, the complex psychological conditions of speech were once more acknowledged. The constant uniformities of phonetic change were now generally attributed to the physical factors, while the apparent exceptions were imputed to psychological factors. Over against the strict and uniform workings of the physiological laws of phonetic change this school emphasized a tendency to form linguistic *analogies,* to create a phonetic link between words of a *formal* grouping and to assimilate them to one another. Yet for the present this recognition of the psychological or "spiritual" factors in language formation remained within relatively narrow bounds. For the concept of the spirit no longer meant what it had meant for Humboldt and idealistic philosophy, but itself bore

---

88. H. Osthoff, *Das Verbum in der Nominalkomposition im Deutschen, Griechischen, Slawischen und Romanischen* (Jena, 1878), p. 326.

89. Hermann Paul, *Principien der Sprachgeschichte* (2d ed. Halle, M. Niemeyer, 1886, 3d ed., 1898), p. 61, Eng. trans. by H. A. Strong, *Principles of the History of Language* (New York, Macmillan, 1889), p. 57. In B. Delbrück we occasionally find a paradoxical formulation of the same idea, namely that the "pure phonetic laws" are without exception but not the "empirical phonetic laws." See "Das Wesen der Lautgesetze" in Ostwald, *Annalen der Naturphilosophie, 1* (1902), 294.

an unmistakable naturalistic imprint, having been influenced by the concept of mechanism. The "fundamental laws of the spirit" had been replaced by psychological laws governing the "mechanism of representations." It mattered little in principle whether these laws were formulated in terms of Herbart's (as in the case of Hermann Paul) or of Wundt's psychology. In either case the ultimate aim was to derive linguistic laws from "laws of association" and to understand them on this basis.[90] The two heterogeneous factors in language formation would then stand on the same methodological plane and pertain, one might say, to the same dimension of inquiry. Language, it was held, is built up in the individual's mind by the interaction of the various physiological mechanisms of sound production on the one hand and of the psychological mechanism of associations on the other; it becomes a whole, but a whole which we can understand only by dissecting it into physical and psychological elements.[91]

Here language is classified as a natural process, but the mechanistic concept of nature has been replaced by a broader concept, the "psychophysical" nature of man. In the most comprehensive and consistent discussions of linguistic phenomena from the standpoint of modern psychology, this development is expressly emphasized. The constant interaction of phonetic laws and analogy formation—writes Wundt—becomes far more comprehensible when we consider them not as disparate and opposing forces, but as conditions, both of which are in some way ultimately rooted in the unitary psychophysical organization of man.

So it is that, because of the memory-like reproduction of forms governed by phonetic law, we must presuppose on the one hand a concurrence of the verbal associations that have been brought in to explain the formation by analogy, and on the other hand that associations, like all psychological processes, are modified by repetition into automatic connections, so that those phenomena which at the outset are characterized as psychological factors come in time to be numbered among the physical factors. And the change is not merely successive as here illustrated, where a psychological factor thus called by us on the basis of certain obvious characteristics is transformed into a physical factor and vice versa, but from the very first the two are so intimately

90. On this dominant position of the concept of association and of the laws of association see, in addition to Wundt's work, e.g., H. Paul, 3d ed., pp. 23 ff., 96 ff., etc.

91. Cf. Osthoff, *Das physiologische und psychologische Moment in der sprachlichen Formenbildung* (Berlin, 1879).

intertwined that they cannot be separated, because with each factor of one type a factor of the other type would have to be eliminated.[92]

Here the idealistic postulate of "totality," according to which language cannot be pieced together out of disparate elements but must be seen as an expression of the "whole" man and of his spiritual-natural being—seems to recur in a new form: but it soon becomes apparent that for the present this postulate is only vaguely formulated and inadequately fulfilled in what is here designated as the unity of man's "psychophysical nature." If we look back over the whole development of the philosophy of language from Humboldt to the neogrammarians, from Schleicher to Wundt, we see that with all its increased special knowledge and insight it has, from the purely methodological point of view, moved in a circle. The attempt was made to relate linguistics to natural science, to orient it by reference to the structure of natural science, in order to find the same inner certainty and to acquire a similar stock of exact and inviolable laws. But the concept of nature that was chosen as a basis proved more and more to be a unity only in appearance. The more sharply it was analyzed, the more apparent it became that this concept concealed within itself factors of quite diverse significance and origin. So long as the relation between these factors was not understood and plainly defined, the various naturalistically colored concepts of language were in danger of a dialectical shift into their opposite. This development can be followed in the concept of phonetic law, which at first designated a strict, uniform *necessity* governing all linguistic changes, but became more and more alien to this signification. Phonetic change and development ceased to be regarded as an expression of "blind" necessity, and were referred back to mere "statistical rules of chance." In this view the supposed laws of nature become mere laws of fashion, created by some individual arbitrary act, stabilized by habit and extended by imitation.[93] Thus, the very concept which was expected to provide a unified foundation for linguistic science, remained fraught with unmediated antagonisms which created new problems for the philosophy of language.

How this not only shook but finally shattered the positivist schema of

92. Wundt, *Die Sprache*, Vol. *1* in *Völkerpsychologie* (2d ed. Leipzig, Engelmann, 1904), *1*, 369.

93. This essentially is the view of phonetic law advocated by B. Delbrück, *op. cit., Annalen der Naturphilosophie, 1*, 277 ff., 297 ff. On phonetic laws seen as "laws of fashion," see also Fr. Müller, "Sind die Lautgesetze Naturgesetze?" in Techmer's *Zeitschrift, 1* (Leipzig and New York, 1884), 211 ff.

linguistics is shown with particular clarity by the writings of Karl Vossler. In his two books *Positivismus und Idealismus in der Sprachwissenschaft* (1904) (*Positivism and Idealism in Linguistic Science*) and *Sprache als Schöpfung und Entwicklung* (1905) (*Language as Creation and Development*) Vossler shows unmistakable Hegelian influence; but no less distinct is the line connecting him with Wilhelm von Humboldt. Humboldt's idea that language must never be considered as a mere work (*ergon*) but as an activity (*energeia*), that the "facts" of language become fully comprehensible only if we trace them back to the spiritual actions from which they arise, is revived here under changed historical conditions. Even in Humboldt this principle is intended to indicate not so much the psychological "origin" of language as its enduring form that is effective through all the phases of its growth. This growth does not resemble the mere unfolding of a given natural germ, but everywhere bears the character of a spiritual spontaneity which is manifested in a new way at every new stage. In the same sense Vossler sets the concept of language as *creation* over against the intrinsically ambiguous concept of linguistic development. What is taken to be the given lawfulness of a definite state of affairs, is a mere petrefaction; behind this sheer fact of existence stand the true constitutive acts of becoming, the constantly renewed acts of spiritual generation. And it is in these acts, which are the essential foundation of language as a *whole,* that the true explanation of particular linguistic phenomena should be sought. The positivist approach, which seeks to progress from the elements to the whole, from syllables to words and sentences and thence to the characteristic "meaning" of language, is accordingly reversed. We must start with the "sense" and with the universality of meaning determination, Vossler declared, in order to understand the particular phenomena of linguistic development and history. The spirit that lives in human discourse constitutes the sentence, the phrase, the word and the syllable. If this "idealistic principle of causality" is taken seriously, all the phenomena described by such lower disciplines as phonetics, theory of inflection, morphology and syntax, must find their ultimate and true explanation in the supreme discipline, i.e., stylistics. The grammatical rules of each language, the "laws," as well as the "exceptions" in morphology and syntax, are to be explained by the "style" that dominates its structure. Linguistic usage, in so far as it is convention, i.e., petrified rule, is represented by syntax; the linguistic usage that is living creation and formation, is the concern of stylistics; the road must run from the latter to the former, not from the former to the latter, since in all cultural matters it is the form of growth that enables us to understand the form of the existing product.[94]

In so far as we are concerned with the mere communication of the facts of linguistic history, with knowledge of the given, a "methodological positivism" can, said Vossler, be accepted as a principle of inquiry. What he rejected was merely that positivistic metaphysics which believes that in communicating facts it has also fulfilled the task of interpreting them. In its place he set a metaphysic of idealism, in which aesthetics forms the central link. "If the idealistic definition: language = spiritual expression —is justified," Vossler concludes, "the history of linguistic development can be nothing other than the history of spiritual forms of expression, that is to say, a *history of art* in the broadest sense of the term."[95] However, this conclusion, in which Vossler joins Benedetto Croce, represents a new problem and a new danger for the philosophy of language. Once again linguistics is taken into the whole of a philosophical system, but apparently on condition that language be identified with one of the members of this system. As in the universal grammar of rationalism the specificity of language was ultimately dissolved in universal logic, it is now in danger of being submerged in aesthetics, considered as the universal science of expression. But is aesthetics, as Vossler assumes with Croce, really *the* science of expression, or is it not rather *one* of the sciences of expression, a "symbolic form," beside others of equal stature? In addition to the relations between language and art, are there not analogous relations between language and other forms which, like myth, build up their own world of spiritual meaning through the medium of their own image world? This question again confronts us with the fundamental methodological question from which we started. Language stands in a focus of cultural life, a point at which rays of quite diverse origin converge and from which lines of influence radiate to every sphere of culture. From this it follows that the philosophy of language can be designated as a special branch of aesthetics only if aesthetics has previously been detached from all *specific* relation to artistic expression, if, in other words, the scope of aesthetics is interpreted so universally that it expands to what we have here attempted to define as a "philosophy of symbolic forms." If language should be shown

94. Cf. K. Vossler, *Positivismus und Idealismus in der Sprachwissenschaft* (Heidelberg, C. Winter, 1904), pp. 8 ff.
95. Ibid., pp. 10 ff.; cf. pp. 24 ff.

to be a truly original and independent energy of the human spirit, it must take its place in the totality of these forms, but it must not be thought to coincide with any of the others. Despite any systematic *combination* into which it may enter with logic and aesthetics, we must assign to it a *specific* and autonomous position within this whole.

Chapter 2

Language in the Phase of Sensuous Expression

1. Language as Expressive Movement. Sign Language and Sound Language

In DEFINING the distinctive character of any spiritual form, it is essential to measure it by its own standards. The criteria by which we judge it and appraise its achievement, must not be drawn from outside, but must be taken from its own fundamental law of formation. No rigid "metaphysical" category, no definition and classification of being derived elsewhere, however certain and firmly grounded these may seem, can relieve us of the need for a purely immanent beginning. We are justified in invoking a metaphysical category only if, instead of accepting it as a fixed datum to which we accord priority over the characteristic principle of form, we can *derive* it from this principle and understand it in this light. In this sense every new form represents a new "building" of the world, in accordance with specific criteria, valid for it alone. The dogmatic approach, which starts from the being of the world as from a fixed point of unity, is of course disposed to subsume all these inner diversities of the spirit's *spontaneity* under some universal concept of the world's "essence" and so to lose them. It creates rigid segments of being, distinguishing, for example, between an "inward" and "outward," a "psychic" and a "physical" reality, between a world of "things" and a world of "representation"—and within these spheres further divisions of the same sort are made. Consciousness, the reality of the "soul," is also dissected into a number of separate and independent "faculties." It is only through the advancing critique of knowledge that we learn not to take these divisions and distinctions as absolute distinctions, inherent once and for all in things themselves, but to understand them as *mediated* by knowledge itself. Such a critique shows particularly that the opposition of "subject" and "object," of "I" and "world," is not simply to be accepted but must be grounded in the presuppositions of knowledge, by which its meaning is first determined. And this is true not only in the world of cognition; in some sense it holds good for all the truly independent basic functions of spiritual life. Philosophical inquiry into artistic as well as mythical and linguistic expression is in danger of missing its mark if, instead of immersing itself freely in the particular forms and laws of expression, it starts from dogmatic assumptions regarding the relation between "archetype" and "reproduction," "reality" and "appearance," "inner" and "outer" world. The question must rather be whether these distinctions are not determined *through* art, *through* language and *through* myth, and whether each of these forms must not draw its distinctions according to different perspectives, and consequently set up different dividing lines. The idea of a rigid substantial differentiation, of a sharp dualism between "inner" and "outer" world, is in this way thrust more and more into the background. The spirit apprehends itself and its antithesis to the "objective" world only by bringing certain distinctions inherent in itself into its view of the phenomena and, as it were, injecting them into the phenomena.

Language also reveals a noteworthy indifference toward the division of the world into two distinct spheres, into an "outward" and an "inward" reality; so much so, indeed, that this indifference seems inherent in its nature. Spiritual *content* and its sensuous expression are united: the former is not an independent, self-contained entity preceding the latter, but is rather completed in it and with it. The two, content and expression, become what they are only in their interpenetration: the signification they acquire through their relation to one another is not outwardly added to their being; it is this signification which constitutes their being. Here we have to do not with a mediated product but with that fundamental synthesis from which language as a whole arises and by which all its parts, from the most elementary sensuous expression to the supreme spiritual expression, are held together. And not only the formed and articulated language of words, but even the simplest *mimetic* expression of an inner process shows this indissoluble involvement, shows that the process does not in itself form a finished, closed-off sphere, out of which consciousness emerges only accidentally, as it were, for the purpose of conventional communication to others, but that this seeming externalization is an essential factor in its own formation. In this sense the modern psychology of language was right in assigning the problem of language to the general *psychology of expressive movements*.[1] From the purely methodological standpoint this presents an important step forward, since this emphasis on the act of movement and the feeling of movement meant that fundamentally the concepts of the traditional *sensationalist* psychology had already been surpassed. From the sensationalist standpoint, the rigid "state" of consciousness is the first given, indeed in a sense, it is all that is given: the *processes* of consciousness, in so far as they are acknowledged at all in their own character, are reduced to a mere sum, a "combination" of states. However, to regard movement and feeling of movement as an element and a fundamental factor in the structure of consciousness itself,[2] is to acknowledge that here again the dynamic is not based on the static but the static on the dynamic—that all psychological "reality" consists in processes and changes, while the fixation of states is merely a subsequent work of abstraction and analysis. Thus mimetic movement is also an immediate unity of the "inward" and "outward," the "spiritual" and the "physical," for by what it directly and sensuously is, it signifies and "says" something else, which is nonetheless present in it. Here there is no mere "transition," no arbitrary addition of the mimetic sign to the emotion it designates; on the contrary, both emotion and its expression, inner tension and its discharge are given in one and the same act, undivided in time. By a process that can be described and interpreted in purely physiological terms, every inner stimulation expresses itself originally in a bodily movement—and the progressive development consists only in a sharper differentiation of this relation: *specific* movements come to be linked more and more precisely with *specific* stimulations. It is true that at first this form of expression does not seem to be anything more than a "reproduction" of the inward in the outward. An outward stimulus passes from the sensory to the motor function, which however seems to remain within the sphere of mere mechanical reflexes, giving no indication of a higher

1. As early a writer as J. J. Engel attempted, in his "Ideen zur Mimik," *Schriften* (Berlin, 1801), vols. 7 and 8, to establish a complete system of expressive movements on the basis of the psychological and aesthetic investigations of the eighteenth century; on the interpretation of language as expressive movement see Wundt, *Die Sprache, Völkerpsychologie*, 2d ed., *1*, 37 ff.

2. This idea of the "primacy of movement" was put forward with particular force and sharpness in the psychology of Hermann Cohen; cf. in particular Cohen's *Ästhetik des reinen Gefühls* (Berlin, 1912), *1*, 143 ff.

spiritual "spontaneity." And yet this reflex is itself the first indication of an activity in which a new form of concrete consciousness of the I and of the object begins to develop. In his work on *The Expression of the Emotions in Man and Animals* Darwin attempted to create a biological theory of expressive movements by interpreting them as a vestige of actions which originally served a practical purpose. According to this theory, the expression of a specific emotion would be merely an attenuated form of a previous purposive action; the expression of anger, for example, would be merely a pale, attenuated image of a former movement of aggression, the expression of fear would be the image of a movement of defense, etc. This view is susceptible of an interpretation which leads beyond the restricted sphere of Darwin's biological formulations and places the question in a more general context. Every elementary expressive movement does actually form a first step in spiritual development, in so far as it is still entirely situated in the immediacy of sensuous life and yet at the same time goes beyond it. It implies that the sensory drive, instead of proceeding directly towards its object, instead of satisfying itself and losing itself in the object, encounters a kind of inhibition and reversal, in which a new *consciousness* of this same drive is born. In this sense the reaction contained in the expressive movement prepares the way for a higher stage of action. In withdrawing, as it were, from the immediate form of activity, action gains a new scope and a new freedom; it is already in transition from the merely "pragmatic" to the "theoretical," from physical to ideal activity.

In the psychological theory of *sign language,* two forms of gesture are usually distinguished, the *indicative* and the *imitative;* these classes can be clearly delimited both as to content and psychological genesis. The indicative gesture is derived biologically and genetically from the movement of grasping. "The arms and hands," Wundt writes,

> have from the earliest development of man been active as the organs with which he grasps and masters objects. From this evidently original use of the grasping organs, in which man is superior only in degree but not in kind to the higher animals with analogous activities, there follows one of those gradual transformations, which are at first regressive, but in their consequences provide important components of a progressive development, leading to the first primitive form of pantomimic movement. Genetically considered, this is nothing other than the

grasping movement attenuated to an indicative gesture. We still find it among children in every possible intermediary phase from the original to the later form. The child still clutches for objects that he cannot reach because they are too far away. In such cases, the clutching movement changes to a pointing movement. Only after repeated efforts to grasp the objects, does the pointing movement as such establish itself.[3]

And this seemingly so simple step toward the independence of gesture, constitutes one of the most important stages in the development from the animal to the specifically human. For no animal progresses to the characteristic transformation of the grasping movement into the indicative gesture. Even among the most highly developed animals, "clutching at the distance," as pointing with the hand has been called, has never gone beyond the first, incomplete beginnings. This simple genetic fact suggests that "clutching at the distance" involves a factor of general spiritual significance. It is one of the first steps by which the perceiving and desiring I removes a perceived and desired content from himself and so forms it into an "object," an "objective" content. In the primitive instinctual stage, to "apprehend" an object is to grasp it immediately with the senses, to take possession of it. The foreign reality is brought into the power of the I—in a purely material sense it is drawn into the sphere of the I. Even the first beginnings of sensory *knowledge* are still entirely within this stage of "pointing there": at this stage man believes, in Plato's characteristic and pregnant term, that he can clutch the object with his hands ($\dot{\alpha}\pi\rho\grave{\iota}\xi\ \tau\alpha\hat{\iota}\nu\ \chi\epsilon\rho\sigma\hat{\iota}\nu$).[4] All progress in conceptual knowledge and pure "theory" consists precisely in surpassing this first sensory immediacy. The object of knowledge recedes more and more into the distance, so that for knowledge critically reflecting upon itself, it comes ultimately to appear as an "infinitely remote point," an endless task; and yet, in this apparent distance, it achieves its ideal specification. In the logical concept, in judgment and inference develops that mediate grasp which characterizes "reason." Thus both genetically and actually, there seems to be a continuous transition from physical to conceptual "grasping." Sensory-physical grasping becomes sensory interpretation, which in turn conceals within it the first impulse toward the higher functions of signification manifested in language and thought. We might suggest the scope of this development by saying that it leads from the sensory extreme of mere "indication" (*Weisen*)

3. Wundt, *Die Sprache, Völkerpsychologie,* 2d ed., *1,* 129 ff.
4. Cf. Plato, *Theaetetus* 155E.

to the logical extreme of "demonstration" (*Beweisen*). From the mere indication by which an absolutely single thing (a τόδετι in the Aristotelian sense) is designated, the road leads to a progressively general specification: what in the beginning was a mere deictic function becomes the function of "apodeixis." Language itself seems to preserve this connection in the relation between the terms for speaking and saying and those for showing and indicating. In the Indo-Germanic languages, most verbs of "saying" are derived from verbs of "showing": *dicere* stems from the root contained in the Greek δείκνυμι (Gothic * *teihan, ga-teihan,* Old High German *zeigôn*), while the Greek φημί φίσκω goes back to the root φα (Sanskrit *bhâ*), which originally designated glitter, appear, and "make to appear." (Cf. φαέθω, φῶς, φαίνω, Lat. *fari, fateri,* etc.) [5]

It would seem, however, that we shall have to take a different view of the language of gestures if we start, not with the gestures of indication but with the second fundamental class, those of *imitation.* For imitation as such forms a counterpart to any free form of spiritual activity. In imitation the I remains a prisoner of outward impression and its properties; the more accurately it repeats this impression, excluding all spontaneity of its own, the more fully the aim of imitation has been realized. The richest and most highly differentiated sign languages, those of the primitive peoples, show the strongest bond with outward impression. Along with the immediately sensuous, imitative signs, the sign languages of civilized peoples tend to include an abundance of so-called "symbolic gestures," which do not directly mimic the object or activity to be expressed, but designate it only indirectly. However, such languages—for example that of the Cistercian monks or the Neapolitan sign language described in detail by Jorio [6]—are obviously not primitive forms but highly complex constructions strongly influenced by the spoken language. But as we go back to the true and independent content of the sign languages, mere "concept signs" seem to give way to "thing signs." The ideal of a purely "natural" language in which all arbitrary convention is excluded seems thus to be realized. It is reported that in the sign language of the North American Indians, few gestures are "conventional" in origin, while by far the greater

5. Cf. Fr. Kluge, *Etymologisches Wörterbuch der deutschen Sprache* (5th ed., Strassburg, 1894), p. 415 (s.v. *zeigen*); G. Curtius, *Grundzüge der griechischen Etymologie* (5th ed. Leipzig, B. G. Teubner, 1878), pp. 115, 134, 296.

6. Andrea de Jorio, *La Mimica degli antichi investigata nel Gestire Napolitano* (Napoli, 1832); on the language of the Cistercian monks, see Wundt, *Die Sprache, Völkerpsychologie,* 2d ed., *1,* 151 ff.

number consist in a simple reproduction of natural phenomena.[7] If we consider only this factor of pantomimic imitation of given objects of sense perception, we do not seem to be on the road to *language* as a free and original activity of the human spirit. However, it must be borne in mind that neither "imitation" nor "indication"—neither the "mimetic" nor the "deictic" function represents a simple, uniform operation of consciousness, but that elements of diverse origin and significance are intermingled in both of them. Even Aristotle calls the sounds of language "imitations," and says that the human voice is of all organs the best suited to imitation.[8] But for him this mimetic character of the word is not opposed to its purely symbolic character; on the contrary, Aristotle stresses the symbolic character of the word by pointing out that the inarticulate sound expressing sensation, such as we find in the animal world, becomes *linguistic sound* only through its use as a symbol.[9] The two terms merge, for Aristotle here uses "imitation" in a broader, deeper sense: for him it is not only the origin of language, but also of artistic activity. Thus understood μίμησις itself belongs to the sphere of ποίησις, of creative and formative activity. It no longer implies the mere repetition of something outwardly given, but a free project of the spirit: the apparent "reproduction" (*Nachbilden*) actually presupposes an inner "production" (*Vorbilden*). And indeed, it becomes evident on closer scrutiny that this factor which is pure and independent in the form of artistic creation, extends down to the elementary beginnings of all apparently passive reproduction. For this reproduction never consists in retracing, line for line, a specific content of reality; but in selecting a pregnant motif in that content and so producing a characteristic "outline" of its form. But with this, imitation itself is on its way to becoming *representation,* in which objects are no longer simply received in their finished structure, but built up by the consciousness according to their constitutive traits. To reproduce an object in this sense means not merely to compose it from its particular sensuous characteristics, but to apprehend it

---

7. Cf. G. Mallery, *Sign Language among North American Indians* (Smithsonian Institution, Bureau of American Ethnology, Washington, Govt. Print. Off., 1881), Annual Report, No. 1, p. 334.

8. Cf. Aristotle, *Rhetoric* iii. 1. 1404a 20: τὰ γὰρ ὀνόματα μιμήματά ἐστιν, ὑπῆρξε δὲ καὶ ἡ φωνὴ πάντων μιμητικώτατων τῶν μορίων ἡμῖν.

9. Cf. περὶ ἑρμηνείας (2. 16a 27): φύσει τῶν ὀνομάτων οὐδέν ἐστιν ἀλλ' ὅταν γένηται σύμβολον ἐπεὶ δηλοῦσί γέ τι καὶ οἱ ἀγράμματοι ψόφοι, οἷον θηρίσον, ὧν οὐδέν ἐστιν ὄνομα. A definite distinction between "imitation" and "symbol" (ὁμοίωμα and σύμβολον) is also found for example in Ammonius' *Commentary on Aristotle's* "De interpretatione," ed. A. Busse (Berlin, 1897), p. 100, 15b.

in its structural relations which can only be truly understood if the consciousness constructively produces them. Sign language represents the germ of this higher form of reproduction; the more highly developed sign languages disclose a transition from the merely imitative to the *representative* gesture, in which, according to Wundt, "the image of an object is more freely formed, in the same sense as creative art is freer than mere mechanical imitation." [10]

But this function of representation emerges in an entirely new freedom and depth, in a new spiritual actuality when for the gesture it substitutes the *word* as its instrument and sensuous basis. In the historical development of language this process of substitution does not take place all at once. Even today, among primitive peoples, the language of gestures not only continues to exist side by side with the language of words, but still decisively affects its formation. Everywhere we find this characteristic permeation, in consequence of which the "verbal concepts" of these languages cannot be fully understood unless they are considered at the same time as mimetic and "manual concepts." The hands are so closely bound up with the intellect that they seem to form a part of it.[11] Likewise in the development of children's speech, the articulated sound breaks away only very gradually from the totality of mimetic movements; even at relatively advanced stages, it remains embedded in this totality.[12] But once the separation is accomplished, language has acquired a new fundamental principle in the new element in which it now moves. Its truly spiritual spontaneity develops only in the physical medium of articulated sound. The articulation of sounds now becomes an instrument for the articulation of thoughts, while the latter creates for itself a more and more differentiated and sensitive organ in the elaboration and formation of these sounds. Compared to all other means of mimetic expression, the spoken sound has the advantage that it is far more capable of "articulation." Its very fluidity, which differs from the sensuous concreteness of the gesture, gives it an entirely new capacity for configuration, making it capable of expressing not only rigid representative contents, but the most subtle vibrations and nuances

10. Wundt, *Die Sprache, Völkerpsychologie*, 2d ed., *1*, 156.

11. Regarding the "manual concepts" of the Zuñi Indians, see Cushing, "Manual Concepts," *American Anthropologist, 5*, 291 ff.; on the relation between sign language and verbal language among primitive peoples, see the copious material in L. Lévy-Bruhl, *Les Fonctions mentales dans les sociétés inférieures* (Paris, 1910). Eng. trans., *How Natives Think* (London and New York, 1926).

12. Cf. Clara and William Stern, *Die Kindersprache* (2d ed. Leipzig, 1920), pp. 144 ff.

of the representative *process*. If with its plastic imitation the gesture seems better adapted to the character of "things" than the disembodied element of the spoken sound, the word gains its inner freedom by the very fact that in it this connection is broken off, that it is a mere becoming, which can no longer immediately reproduce the being of objects. On the objective side, it now becomes capable of serving, not only as an expression of contents and their qualities, but also and above all as an expression of formal relations; on the subjective side, the dynamic of feeling and the dynamic of thought are imprinted upon it. For this dynamic the language of gestures, which is restricted to the medium of space and thus can designate motion only by dividing it into particular and discrete spatial forms, has no adequate organ. In the language of words, however, the particular, discrete element enters into a new relation with speech as a whole. Here the element exists only in so far as it is constantly regenerated: its content is gathered up into the act of its production. But now this act of sound production itself becomes more and more sharply differentiated. To the qualitative differentiation and gradation of sounds is added a dynamic gradation by stress and rhythm. Attempts have been made to prove that this rhythmic articulation, as particularly manifested in primitive work songs, represents an essential factor both of artistic and linguistic development.[13] Here the spoken sound is still immediately rooted in the purely sensuous sphere; yet since what it springs from and serves to express is not merely passive feeling, but a simple sensory activity, it is already on its way to surpassing this sphere. The mere interjection, the expression of emotion produced by an overwhelming momentary impression, now passes into a coherently ordered phonetic sequence, in which the context and order of the activity are reflected. "The ordered unfolding of spoken sounds," writes Jacob Grimm in his essay "On the Origin of Language," "requires us to articulate, and the human language appears as an articulated language; this is borne out by the Homeric epithet for men: οἱ μέροπες, μέροπες ἄνθρωποι or βροτοί—from μείρομαι or μερίζω, those who divide, articulate their voice." [14]

13. Cf. Karl Bücher, *Arbeit und Rhythmus* (4th ed. Leipzig, 1909); for the influence of work and "working rhythms" on the development of language cf. Ludwig Noiré, *Der Ursprung der Sprache* (Mainz, 1877); idem, *Logos-Ursprung und Wesen der Begriffe* (Leipzig, 1885).

14. "Über den Ursprung der Sprache" (1851), in *Kleinere Schriften*, Berlin, 1864, *1*, 266. The etymological connection set forth by Grimm is, to be sure, contested: for details see Curtius, *Grundzüge der griechischen Etymologie*, 5th ed., pp. 110 and 330.

Only now is the material of language so constituted that a new form can become imprinted upon it. The sensory-affective state transposes and dissolves itself into mimetic expression; it discharges itself in mimetic expression and therein finds its end. It is only when this immediacy is superseded in the course of further development that the content comes to be stabilized and formed in itself. A higher stage of awareness, a sharper grasp of its inner differentiations is now needed before it can be manifested clearly and concretely in the medium of articulated sounds. Inhibition of the direct outbreak into gestures and inarticulate cries gives rise to an inner measure, a movement within the sphere of sensory appetition and representation. The road leads upwards, more and more clearly, from the mere reflex to the various stages of "reflection." The genesis of the articulated sound, "the noise rounding itself into a tone"—as Goethe put it— presents us with a universal phenomenon which we encounter in different forms in the most divergent fields of cultural life. Through the particularity of the linguistic function, we perceive the universal *symbolic* function, as it unfolds in accordance with immanent laws, in art, in the mythical-religious consciousness, in language and in cognition.

2. Mimetic, Analogical, and Symbolic Expression

It is true that, like the theory of art and the theory of knowledge, linguistic theory freed itself only gradually from the constraint of the concept of imitation and the copy theory. The problem of the κυριότης τῶν ονομάτων stands at the center of the ancient philosophy of language. And the question of whether language should be regarded as a φύσει or a νόμῳ ὄν was primarily concerned not with the genesis of language but with its truth and reality content.[15] Do language and the word belong exclusively to the sphere of subjective representation and judgment, or is there a profounder bond between the world of names and the world of true being; is there an inner "objective" truth and rightness in names themselves? The Sophists denied and the Stoics affirmed such an objective validity of the word; but

15. For further material concerning this original meaning of the opposition φύσει and νόμῳ, for which φύσει and θέσει were substituted in the Alexandrian period, see Steinthal, *Geschichte der Sprachwissenschaft*, 2d ed., *1*, 76 ff., 114 ff., 319 ff.

whether the answer was positive or negative, the form of the *question* itself remained the same. The basic assumption underlying both answers is that the aim of cognition is to reflect and reproduce the essence of things, while the aim of language is to reflect and reproduce the essence of cognition. The Sophists strive to show that both aims are unattainable: if there is being, says Gorgias, it is inaccessible and unknowable; if it is knowable, it is inexpressible and incommunicable. Just as by their nature, the senses of sight and hearing are restricted to their specific sphere of qualities; just as the one can perceive only brightness and colors and the other can perceive only tones—similarly speech can never transcend itself to apprehend something "other," standing over against it, that is to apprehend "being" and truth.[16] The Stoics sought vainly to avoid this consequence by asserting a natural kinship between being and cognition and a natural accord κατὰ μίμησιν between word and meaning. The view that the word partly or wholly reflected reality, forming its true ἔτυμον, reduced itself to the absurd by shifting into its opposite in its subsequent development. Not only the relationship of "similarity," but also its converse was now admitted as a basis for etymological explanation: not only ἀναλογία and ὁμοιότης, but also ἐναντίωσις and ἀντίφρασις passed as formative principles of language. *Similitudo* became *contrarium;* "analogy" became "anomaly." The devastating effects of this "explanation by opposites" on the subsequent development of etymology are well known:[17] on the whole, they make it very plain that any explanation of language built on the postulate of similarity must necessarily end in its antithesis and so negate itself.

Even where words are interpreted as imitations not of things but of subjective states of feeling, where, as in Epicurus, they are said to reflect not so much the nature of objects as the ἴδια πάθη of the speaker,[18] the philosophy of language, though it has changed its norm, is still essentially subordinated to the same principle. If the postulate of reproduction as such is sustained, it becomes ultimately indifferent whether what is reproduced is "inward" or "outward," whether it is a complex of things or of feelings and representations. Indeed, under the latter assumption a recurrence of

16. Cf. "Sextus adv. mathematicos," VII, 83 ff. (Diels, *Die Fragmente der Vorsokratiker*, 76B, 554–555): ὧι γὰρ μηνύομεν, ἔστι λόγος, λόγος δὲ οὐκ ἔστι τὰ ὑποκείμενα καὶ ὄντα· οὐκ ἄρα τὰ ὄντα μηνύομεν τοῖς πέλας ἀλλὰ λόγον, ὃς ἕτερός ἐστι τῶν ὑποκειμένων.

17. For characteristic examples see Curtius, *Grundzüge der griechischen Etymologie*, 5th ed., pp. 5 ff.; Steinthal, *op. cit.*, I, 353 ff.; L. Lersch, *Sprachphilosophie der Alten* (Bonn, 1838–41), *3*, 47 ff.

18. Cf. above, pp. 148 ff.

skepticism toward language is inevitable, and in its sharpest form. For language can claim to apprehend the immediacy of *life* far less than the immediacy of things. The slightest attempt to express this immediacy merely negates it. "Once the soul speaks, alas, the soul speaks no more." Thus language, by its pure *form* alone is the counterpart of the abundance and concretion of the world of sensation and emotion. Gorgias' contention that "it is the speaker who speaks, not the color or the thing," [19] applies to a heightened degree if we replace "objective" by "subjective" reality. Subjective reality is characterized by extreme individuality and concretion; while the world of words is characterized by the universality, and that is to say, the indeterminacy and ambiguity, of merely schematic signs. Since the "universal" signification of the word effaces all the differences which characterize real psychological processes, the road of language seems to lead us, not upward into spiritual universality, but downward to the commonplace: for only this, only what is not peculiar to an individual intuition or sensation, but is common to it and others, is accessible to language. Thus language remains a pseudo-value, the mere rule of a game, which becomes more compelling as more players subject themselves to it, but which, as soon as it is critically understood, must renounce all claim to represent, let alone know and understand, any reality, whether of the "inner" or "outer" world.[20]

Fundamentally, however, in the critique of knowledge as of language, this radical skepticism contains within it the transcending of skepticism. Skepticism seeks to expose the nullity of knowledge and language—but what it ultimately demonstrates is rather the nullity of the *standard* by which it measures them. In skepticism the "copy theory" is methodically and consistently demolished by the self-destruction of its basic premises. The farther negation is carried in this point, the more clearly a new positive insight follows from it. The last semblance of any mediate or immediate *identity* between reality and symbol must be effaced, the *tension* between the two must be enhanced to the extreme, for it is precisely in this tension that the specific achievement of symbolic expression and the content of the particular symbolic forms is made evident. For this content cannot be revealed as long as we hold fast to the belief that we possess "reality" as

19. De Melisso, *Xenophane et Gorgia*, ch. 6, 980 a 20: ὃ γὰρ εἶδε, πῶς ἄν τις, φησί, τοῦτο εἴποι λόγῳ; ἢ πῶς ἂν ἐκείνῳ δῆλον ἀκούσαντι γίγνοιτο, μὴ ἰδόντι; ὥσπερ γὰρ οὐδὲ ἡ ὄψις τοὺς φθόγγους γιγνώσκει, οὕτως οὐδὲ ἡ ἀκοὴ τὰ χρώματα ἀκούει, ἀλλὰ φθόγγους· καὶ λέγει ὁ λέγων ἀλλ' οὐ χρῶμα οὐδὲ πρᾶγμα.

20. Cf. Fr. Mauthner, *Beiträge zu einer Kritik der Sprache*, especially *1*, 25 ff., 70, 175, 193.

a given, self-sufficient being, as a totality whether of things or of simple sensations, prior to all spiritual formation. If this were true, the forms would indeed have no other purpose than mere reproduction, and such reproduction would inevitably be inferior to the original. In truth, however, the meaning of each form cannot be sought in what it expresses, but only in the manner and modality, the inner law of the expression itself. In this law of formation, and consequently not in proximity to the immediately given but in progressive *removal* from it, lie the value and the specific character of linguistic as of artistic formation. This *distance* from immediate reality and immediate experience is the condition of their being perceived, of our spiritual awareness of them. Language, too, *begins* only where our immediate relation to sensory impression and sensory affectivity *ceases*. The uttered sound is not yet speech as long as it purports to be mere repetition; as long as the specific factor of signification and the will to "signification" are lacking. The aim of repetition lies in identity—the aim of linguistic designation lies in difference. The synthesis effected can only be a synthesis of different elements, not of elements that are alike or similar in any respect. The more the sound resembles what it expresses; the more it continues to "be" the other, the less it can "signify" that other. The boundary is sharply drawn not only from the standpoint of spiritual content, but biologically and genetically as well. Even among the lower animals we encounter a great number of original sounds expressing feeling and sensation, which in the development to the higher types become more and more differentiated, developing into definitely articulated and distinct "linguistic utterances," cries of fear or warning, lures or mating calls. But between these cries and the sounds of designation and signification characteristic of human speech there remains a gap, a "hiatus" which has been newly confirmed by the sharper methods of observation of modern animal psychology.[21] The step to human speech, as Aristotle stressed, has been taken only when the pure significatory sound has gained primacy over the sounds of

---

21. For the "language" of the highest apes cf., e.g., B. W. Köhler, "Zur Psychologie des Schimpansen," *Psychologische Forschung*, 1 (1921), 27: "It is not easy to describe in detail how animals make themselves understood. It is absolutely certain that their *phonetic* utterances without any exception express 'subjective' states and desires, that they are so-called affective sounds and never aim to delineate or designate the objective. However, so many 'phonetic elements' of human speech occur in the chimpanzee phonetics that it is assuredly not for peripheral reasons that they have remained without language in our sense. The same is true of the facial expression and gestures of animals: nothing about them designates anything objective or fulfills any 'representative function.'" Cf. Eng. ed., *The Mentality of Apes* (New York, Harcourt, Brace, 1925), App., p. 317.

affectivity and stimulation: a primacy which in the history of language is expressed by the circumstance that many words of the highly developed languages, which at first sight seem to be mere interjections, prove, on close analysis, to be regressions from more complex linguistic structures, from words or sentences with a definite conceptual signification.[22]

In general, language can be shown to have passed through three stages in maturing to its specific form, in achieving its inner freedom. In calling these the mimetic, the analogical, and the truly symbolical stage, we are for the present merely setting up an abstract schema—but this schema will take on concrete content when we see that it represents a functional law of linguistic growth, which has its specific and characteristic counterpart in other fields such as art and cognition. The beginnings of phonetic language seem to be embedded in that sphere of mimetic representation and designation which lies at the base of sign language. Here the sound seeks to approach the sensory impression and reproduce its diversity as faithfully as possible. This striving plays an important part in the speech both of children and "primitive" peoples. Here language clings to the concrete phenomenon and its sensory image, attempting as it were to exhaust it in sound; it does not content itself with general designations but accompanies every particular nuance of the phenomenon with a particular phonetic nuance, devised especially for this case. In Ewe and certain related languages, for example, there are adverbs which describe only *one* activity, *one* state or *one* attribute, and which consequently can be combined only with *one* verb. Many verbs possess a number of such qualifying adverbs pertaining to them alone, and most of them are phonetic reproductions of sensory impressions. In his *Grammar of the Ewe Language* Westermann counts no less than thirty-three such phonetic images for the single verb "to walk," each designating a particular manner of walking: slouching or sauntering, limping or dragging the feet, shambling or waddling, energetic or weary. But this, as he adds, does not exhaust the number of adverbs that qualify walking; for most of these can occur in a doubled, usual, or diminutive form, depending or whether the subject is big or little.[23] Although this type of sound painting recedes as language

22. Examples of this in A. H. Sayce, *Introduction to the Science of Language* (2 vols., London, 1880) *1*, 109; for the Indo-Germanic languages see particularly K. Brugmann, *Verschiedenheit der Satzgestaltung nach Massgabe der seelischen Grundfunktionen in den indogermanischen Sprachen* (Leipzig, 1918), pp. 24 ff.

23. D. Westermann, *Grammatik der Ewe-Sprache* (Berlin, D. Reimer, 1907), pp. 83 ff., 129 ff.; Eng. trans. by A. L. Bickford-Smith, *A Study of the Ewe Language* (London, Oxford

develops, there is no language, however advanced, that has not preserved numerous examples of it. Certain onomatopoeic expressions, occur with striking uniformity in all the languages of the globe. They demonstrate extraordinary vitality, resisting phonetic changes which are otherwise almost universal; and moreover, new forms have appeared even in modern times, in the bright light of linguistic history.[24] In view of all this, it is understandable that particularly the empirical linguists have often been inclined to champion the principle of onomatopoeia, so severely chastised by philosophers of language, and to attempt at least a limited rehabilitation of that principle.[25] The sixteenth- and seventeenth-century philosophers of language still supposed that phenomena of onomatopoeia offered the key to the basic and original language of mankind, the lingua adamica. Today, to be sure, the critical progress of linguistics has more and more dispelled this dream; but we still occasionally encounter attempts to prove that in the earliest period of language formation the significatory classes and the phonetic classes corresponded to one another—that the original words were divided into distinct groups, each of which was linked to certain phonetic materials and built up out of them.[26] And even where the hope of arriving in this way at a true reconstruction of the original language has been abandoned, the principle of onomatopoeia is recognized as a means of arriving indirectly at an idea of the relatively oldest strata of language formation. "Despite all change," remarks G. Curtius with regard to the Indo-Germanic languages,

> a conservative instinct is also discernible in language. All the peoples
> of our family from the Ganges to the Atlantic designate the notion of

---

Univ. Press, 1930), pp. 107 ff., 187 ff. Very similar phenomena are found in the languages of the American natives; cf., e.g., the transition from purely onomatopoeic sounds to universal verbial or adverbial terms, described by Franz Boas in the Chinook language, in *Handbook of American Indian Languages*, (Smithsonian Institution, Washington, Govt. Print. Off., 1911), Bulletin No. 40, Pt. 1, pp. 575, 655 ff.

24. A list of such relatively late onomatopoetic creations in the German language has been given by Hermann Paul in *Principien der Sprachgeschichte*, 3d ed., pp. 160 ff.; for examples from the Romance languages see W. Meyer-Lübke, *Einführung in das Studium der romanischen Sprachwissenschaft* (2d ed., Heidelberg, 1909), pp. 91 ff.

25. See for example W. Scherer, *Zur Geschichte der deutschen Sprache* (Berlin, 1868), p. 38.

26. Thus Täuber in "Die Ursprache und ihre Entwicklung," *Globus*, Vol. 97 (1910), distinguishes six main groups: liquid food, solid food, atmospheric liquids, wood and forest, forage and watering place, animal world, and seeks to show that in the most divergent languages of the world, e.g., in Sanskrit and Hebrew, they were originally designated by similar phonetic combinations (m + vowel; p + vowel; n + vowel; t + vowel; l or r; k + vowel).

standing by the phonetic group *sta;* in all of them the notion of flowing is linked with the group *plu,* with only slight modifications. This cannot be an accident. Assuredly the same notion has remained associated with the same sounds through all the millennia, because the peoples felt a certain inner connection between the two, i.e., because of an instinct to express this notion by these particular sounds. The assertion that the oldest words presuppose some relation between sounds and the representations they designate has often been ridiculed. It is difficult, however, to explain the origin of language without such assumptions. In any case, the representation lives like a soul even in the words of far more advanced periods.[27]

Since the Stoics, the search for this soul of the individual sounds and sound classes has tempted innumerable linguists and philosophers of language. As late a thinker as Leibniz attempted to investigate the original meanings of particular sounds and sound groups.[28] And after him the subtlest and profoundest students of language attempted to demonstrate the symbolic value of certain sounds, not only in the material expression of certain isolated concepts, but even in the formal representation of certain grammatical *relations.* Humboldt found this relationship confirmed in the choice of certain sounds for the expression of certain feeling values—he held, for example, that the phonetic group *st* regularly designates the impression of the enduring and stable, the sound *l* that of the melting and fluid, the sound *v* the impression of uneven, vacillating motion. He also saw it in the elements of inflection and gave special attention to this "symbolic character in grammatical sounds." [29] Jacob Grimm also attempted to show that the sounds used in the Indo-Germanic languages for forming words of question and answer were closely related to the spiritual significations of question and answer.[30] The use of certain differences and

27. G. Curtius, *Grundzüge der griechischen Etymologie,* 5th ed. p. 96.

28. See Leibniz, *Nouveaux essais,* Bk. 3, ch. 3.

29. Cf. Humboldt, "Einleitung zum Kawi-Werk," *Werke,* 7, No. 1, 76 ff., and the work itself: *Über die Kawi-Sprache auf der Insel Java* (hereafter cited as *Kawi-Werk*), 2, 111, 153, and elsewhere.

30. See Jacob Grimm, *Deutsche Grammatik,* Bk. 3, ch. 1: "Among all the sounds of the human voice, none is so capable of expressing the essence of the question, which is perceived at the very beginning of the word, as k, the fullest consonant of which the throat is capable. A mere vowel would sound too indefinite, and the labial organ is not as strong as the guttural. T can be produced with the same force, but it is not so much expelled as pronounced and has something more solid about it; it is therefore suited to the expression of the calm, even an indicative *answer.* K questions, inquires, calls; T shows, explains, answers."

gradations of vowels to express specific objective gradations, particularly to designate the greater or lesser distance of an object from the speaker, is a phenomenon occurring in the most diverse languages and linguistic groups. Almost always *a, o, u* designate the greater distance, *e* and *i* the lesser.[31] Differences in time interval are also indicated by difference in vowels or by the pitch of vowels.[32] In the same way certain consonants and consonantal groups are used as "natural phonetic metaphors" to which a similar or identical significatory function attaches in nearly all language groups—e.g., with striking regularity the resonant labials indicate direction toward the speaker and the explosive linguals direction away from the speaker, so that the former appear as a "natural" expression of the "I," the latter of the "Thou." [33]

But although these last phenomena seem to retain the color of immediate sensory expression, they nevertheless burst the limits of mere mimicry and imitation. No longer is a single sensuous object or sense impression reproduced by an imitative sound; instead, a qualitatively graduated phonetic sequence serves to express a pure relation. There is no direct material similarity between the form and specificity of this relation and the sounds with which it is represented, since the mere material of sound as such is in general incapable of reflecting pure relational determinations. The context is rather communicated by a *formal* analogy between the phonetic sequence and the sequence of contents designated; this analogy makes possible a *coordination* of series entirely different in content. This brings us to the second stage which we call the stage of *analogical* as opposed to mere mimetic *expression*. The transition from one to the other is perhaps most clearly revealed in those languages which employ musical tones to differentiate word meanings or express grammatical relations. We still seem close to the mimetic sphere in so far as the pure function of signification remains inextricably bound up with the sensuous sound. Humboldt tells us that in the Indo-Chinese languages the differentiations of pitch and accent between syllables makes speech a kind of song or recitative,

31. Examples from various language groups in Fr. Müller, *Grundriss der Sprachwissenschaft* (Vienna, 1876–88), *1*, Pt. 2, 94 ff.; *3*, sec. 1, 194, etc.; Humboldt, *Kawi-Werk*, *2*, 153; also see below, Chapter 3.

32. See Fr. Müller, *1*, II, 94. Steinthal, *Die Mande-Neger-Sprachen* (Berlin, 1867), p. 117.

33. In the Ural-Altaic languages, for examples, which strikingly resemble the Indo-Germanic languages in this respect, the phonetic elements *ma, mi, mo*, or *ta, ti, si* serve as the basic elements of the personal pronouns: cf. Heinrich Winkler, *Das Uralaltaische und seine Gruppen* (Berlin, 1885), p. 26; for the other linguistic groups, see Wundt's compilation (op. cit, *1*, 345) on the basis of the material in Fr. Müller, *Grundriss der Sprachwissenschaft*.

and that the tonal gradations in the Siamese, for example are quite comparable to a musical scale.[34] And particularly in the Sudanese languages, the most diverse shades of meaning are expressed by tonal variations, by a high, middle, or low tone, or by composite shadings, such as the low-high rising tone, or high-low falling tone. These variations serve as a basis both for etymological distinctions—i.e., the same syllable serves, according to its tone, to designate entirely different things or actions—and for spatial and quantitative distinctions, i.e., high-pitched words, for example, express long distances and rapidity while low-pitched words express proximity and slowness, etc. . . .[35] And purely formal relations and oppositions can be expressed in this same way. A mere change in tone can transform the affirmative into the negative form of a verb.[36] Or it may determine the grammatical category of a word; for example, otherwise identical syllables may be identified as nouns or verbs by the manner in which they are pronounced.[37] We are carried one step further by the phenomenon of *vowel harmony* which dominates the whole structure of certain languages and linguistic groups, particularly those of the Ural-Altaic family. Here vowels fall into two sharply separate classes, hard and soft. When a root is augmented by suffixes, the suffix vowel must belong to the same class as that of the root syllable.[38] Here the phonetic assimilation of the components of a word, hence a purely sensuous means, creates a formal link between these components by which they are enabled to progress from relatively loose "agglutination" to a linguistic whole, to a self-contained word or sentence formation. In becoming a phonetic unit through the principle

34. Humboldt, "Einleitung zum Kawi-Werk," *Werke*, 7, No. 1, 300.

35. Cf. Westermann, *Die Sudansprachen* (Hamburg, 1911), pp. 76 ff.; *Die Gola-Sprache in Liberia* (Hamburg, 1921), pp. 19 ff.

36. Cf. Westermann, *Die Gola-Sprache*, pp. 66 ff.

37. In Ethiopian, for example, according to August Dillmann, *Grammatik der äthiopischen Sprache* (Leipzig, 1857), pp. 115 ff. Eng. trans. by J. A. Crichton (2d ed., London, 1907), pp. 140 ff. verbs and nouns are distinguished solely by the pronunciation of the vowels. Intransitive verbs of a passive character are also distinguished from verbs of pure action by the same means.

38. On the principle of vowel harmony in the Ural-Altaic languages see O. v. Böthlingk, *Über die Sprache der Jakuten* (Petersburg, 1851), pp. xxvi, 103, and H. Winkler, *Das Uralaltaische und seine Gruppen*, pp. 77 ff. Grunzel points out that the tendency to vowel harmony is common to *all* languages, though it has achieved regular development only in the Ural-Altaic. Here vowel harmony has in a certain sense resulted also in a "consonant harmony." See Josef Grunzel, *Entwurf einer vergleichenden Grammatik der altaischen Sprachen* (Leipzig, 1895), pp. 20 ff., 28 ff. Examples of vowel harmony in other languages: for the American languages Boas, *Handbook*, Pt. 1, p. 569 (Chinook); for the African languages C. Meinhof, *Lehrbuch der Nama-Sprache* (Berlin, 1909), pp. 114 ff.

of vowel harmony, the word or word-sentence gains its true significative unity: a relationship which at first applies solely to the quality and physiological production of the particular sounds, becomes a means of combining them into a spiritual whole, a unit of "signification."

This "analogical" correspondence between sound and signification is shown even more distinctly in the function of certain widespread and typical means of language formation, as for example, in the part played by *reduplication* both in morphology and syntax. Reduplication seems at first sight to be governed entirely by the principle of imitation: the doubling of the sound or syllable seems to serve the sole purpose of reflecting as faithfully as possible certain objective characteristics of the thing or event designated. The phonetic repetition conforms closely to a repetition given in the sensuous reality or impression. Reduplication is most at home where a thing presents itself repeatedly to the senses with the same characteristics, or where an event presents a sequence of identical or similar phases. But on this elementary foundation a system of astonishing diversity and subtlety arises. The sensory impression of "plurality" first breaks down into an expression of "collective" and "distributive" plurality. Certain languages, which have no designation for the plural in our sense, have instead developed the idea of distributive plurality to the utmost sharpness and concreteness by meticulously distinguishing whether a specific act presents itself as an indivisible whole or falls into several separate acts. If the latter is true, and the act is either performed by several subjects or effected by the same subject in different segments of time, in separate stages, this distributive division is expressed by reduplication. In this exposition of the Klamath language Gatschet has shown how this distinction has actually become the basic category of the language, permeating all its parts and determining its whole "form." [39] In other language groups we can also see how the duplication of a word, which in the beginnings of linguistic history was a simple means of designating quantity, gradually became an intuitive expression for quantities that do not exist as a cohesive whole but are divided into separate groups or individuals.[40] But this is far from exhausting the uses of reduplication. In addition to expressing plurality and repeti-

39. A. S. Gatschet, *Grammar of the Klamath Language, Contributions to North American Ethnology*, 2 (Washington, Govt. Print. Off., 1890), Pt. 1, pp. 259 ff. On the significance of the "ideal of severalty or distribution," as Gatschet calls it, see below, Chapter 3.

40. Cf. in particular the examples from the Semitic languages in C. Brockelmann, *Grundriss der vergleichenden Grammatik der semitischen Sprachen* (New York, Lemke & Buechner, 1908–13), 2, 457 ff.

tion, it can serve to represent many other relations, particularly relations of space and size. Scherer calls it an original grammatical form serving essentially to express three basic intuitions: those of force, space and time.[41] By a ready transition the iterative signification develops into a purely intensive signification, as in the comparative and superlative of adjectives, and in the case of verbs the intensive forms which often subsequently change to causatives.[42] Extremely subtle *modal* differences in an action or event can also be suggested by the very simple means of reduplication: in certain American Indian languages, for example, the reduplicated form of the verb is used to designate a kind of "unreality" in an action, to indicate that it exists only in purpose or "idea" and is not practically realized.[43] In all these cases reduplication has clearly passed far beyond the phase of mere sensory description or of a pointing to objective reality. One factor that makes this evident is a peculiar *polarity* in its use: it can be the expression and vehicle not only of different but of directly opposed modalities of signification. Side by side with the intensive signification we often find the exact opposite, an attenuative signification, so that it is used in constituting diminutive forms of adjectives and limitative forms of verbs.[44] In designating temporal stages of an action, it can serve equally well to designate present, past or future.[45] This is the clearest indication that it is not so much a reproduction of a fixed and limited perceptual content as the expression of a specific *approach*, one might say a certain perceptual movement. The purely formal accomplishment of reduplication becomes even more evident where it passes from the sphere of quantitative expression to that of pure relation. It then determines not so much the signification of the word as its general grammatical category. In languages

41. Scherer, *Zur Geschichte der deutschen Sprache*.

42. For examples, see particularly A. F. Pott, *Doppelung (Reduplikation, Gemination) als eines der wichtigsten Bildungsmittel der Sprache* (1862); see also the abundant material in R. Brandstetter, *Die Reduplikation in den indianischen, indonesischen und indogermanischen Sprachen* (Lucerne, 1917).

43. "Reduplication is also used to express the diminutive of nouns, the idea of a playful performance of an activity, and the endeavor to perform an action. It would seem that in all these forms we have the fundamental idea of an approach to a certain concept without its realization," in Boas, "Kwakiutl," *Handbook*, Pt. 1, pp. 444–445; cf. 526 ff.

44. Examples from the South Sea languages in R. H. Codrington, *The Melanesian Languages* (Oxford, Clarendon Press, 1885), p. 147; Sidney R. Ray, "The Melanesian Possessive and a Study in Method," *American Anthropologist*, 21 (1919), 356, 446; for the American Indian languages see Boas, *Handbook*, *1*, 526, and elsewhere.

45. As for example in the tense formation of verbs in Tagalog. Humboldt, *Kawi-Werk*, 2, 125 ff.

which do not make this category recognizable in the mere word form, a word is often transferred from one category to another, a noun changed to a verb, for example, by the mere reduplication of a sound or syllable.[46] All these phenomena, to which we might easily add others of like nature, make it evident that even where language starts as purely imitative or "analogical" expression, it constantly strives to extend and finally to surpass its limits. It makes a virtue of necessity, that is, of the ambiguity inevitable in the linguistic sign. For this very ambiguity will not permit the sign to remain a mere individual sign; it compels the spirit to take the decisive step from the concrete function of "designation" to the universal and universally valid function of "signification." In this function language casts off, as it were, the sensuous covering in which it has hitherto appeared: mimetic or analogical expression gives way to purely symbolic expression which, precisely in and by virtue of its otherness, becomes the vehicle of a new and deeper spiritual content.

46. Examples from Javanese in Humboldt's *Kawi-Werk*, 2, 86 ff.

Chapter 3

Language in the Phase of Intuitive Expression

1. The Expression of Space and Spatial Relations

IN LINGUISTICS as in epistemology it is not possible to divide the sensory and the intellectual into two distinct spheres, each with its own self-sufficient mode of "reality." The critique of knowledge shows that mere sensation, i.e., a sensory quality without form or *order*, is not a fact of immediate experience but a product of abstraction. The matter of sensation is never given purely in itself, "prior" to all formation; the very first perception of it contains a reference to the form of space and time. But in the continuous progress of knowledge this indefinite reference becomes more specific: the mere "possibility of juxtaposition and succession" unfolds into the whole of space and time, into an order that is both concrete and universal. We may expect that language, as a reflection of the spirit, will also reflect this fundamental process in some way. And indeed Kant's statement that concepts without intuitions are empty, applies as much to the linguistic designation of concepts as it does to their logical determination. Even the most abstract terms of language still reveal their link with the primary intuitive foundation in which they are rooted. Here again, "meaning" is not distinct from "sensibility"; the two are closely interwoven. Thus the step from the world of sensation to that of "pure intuition," which the critique of knowledge shows to be a necessary factor of the I and the pure concept of the object, has its exact counterpart in language. It is in the "intuitive forms" that the type and direction of the spiritual synthesis effected in language are primarily revealed, and it is only through the medium of these forms, through the intuitions of space, time and number that language can perform its essentially logical operation: the forming of impressions into representations.

It is the intuition of *space* which most fully reveals this interpenetration of sensuous and spiritual expression in language. The essential role of spatial representation is most clearly shown in the universal terms which language has devised for the designation of spiritual processes. Even in the most highly developed languages we encounter this "metaphorical" rendition of intellectual conceptions by spatial representations. In German this relationship is manifested in such terms as *vorstellen* and *verstehen*, *begreifen*, *begründen*, *erörtern*, etc.,[1] and it is found not only in the related languages of the Indo-Germanic group but in linguistic families far removed from it. Particularly the languages of primitive peoples are distinguished by the precision, the almost mimetic immediacy, with which they express all spatial specifications and distinctions of processes and activities. The languages of the American Indians, for example, seldom have a general term for "going," but instead possess special terms for "going up" and "going down" and for countless other shadings of motion; and states of rest—position, standing below or above, inside and outside a certain limit, standing near something, standing in water, in the woods, etc.—are similarly differentiated. Whereas these languages attach little importance to many distinctions which we make in our use of verbs, often failing to express them altogether, all specifications of place, situation and distance are meticulously designated by particles of original local signification. The strictness and precision with which this is done is often regarded by specialists as the basic and characteristic principle of these languages.[2] Crawford tells us that in the Malayo-Polynesian languages the different positions of the body are so sharply distinguished as to provide an anatomist, painter or sculptor with useful indications—the Javanese, for example, renders ten different varieties of standing and twenty of sitting, each with its own specific word.[3] Various American Indian languages can express a thought such as "The man is sick" only by stating at

1. " 'Begreifen' like simple 'greifen' goes back originally to touching with hands and feet, fingers and toes." Grimm, *Deutsches Wörterbuch*, Vol. *1*, col. 1307. On the spatial origin of *erörtern* (to discuss) cf. Leibniz, "Unvorgreifliche Gedanken betreffend die Ausübung und Verbesserung der teutschen Sprache," *Deutsche Schriften,* ed. G. E. Guhrauer (Berlin, 1838), *1*, 468, § 54; see also *Nouveaux essais*, Bk. 3, ch. 1.

2. E.g., Boas on Kwakiutl: "The rigidity with which location in relation to the speaker is expressed, both in nouns and in verbs, is one of the fundamental features of the language." *Handbook*, Pt. 1, p. 445. Gatschet expresses the same opinion in his *Klamath Language;* see especially pp. 396 ff., 433 ff., 460.

3. Crawford, *History of the Indian Archipelago, 2,* 9; cf. Codrington, *The Melanesian Languages,* pp. 164 ff.; "Everything and everybody spoken of are viewed as coming or going, or in some relation of place, in a way which to the European is by no means accustomed or natural."

the same time whether the subject of the statement is at a greater or lesser distance from the speaker or the listener and whether he is visible or invisible to them; and often the place, position and posture of the sick man are indicated by the form of the word sentence.[4] All other specifications are thrust into the background by this spatial characterization, or are represented only indirectly through it. This is equally true of temporal, qualitative and modal distinctions. In concrete intuition, the purpose of an action, for example, is always closely related to its spatial *goal* and the direction in which this goal is pursued: accordingly, the "final" or "intentional" form of the verb is often formed by the addition of a local particle.[5]

Here we encounter a common characteristic of linguistic thinking which is highly significant for the critique of knowledge. For Kant the concepts of the pure understanding can be applied to sensory intuitions only through the mediation of a third term, in which the two, although totally dissimilar, must come together—and he finds this mediation in the "transcendental schema," which is both intellectual and sensory. In this respect he distinguishes the schema from the mere image: "The image is a product of the empirical faculty of the productive imagination—the schema of sensuous conceptions (of figures in space, for example) is a product, and, as it were, a monogram of the pure imagination a priori, whereby and according to which images first become possible, which, however, can be connected with the conception only mediately by means of the schema which they indicate, and are in themselves never fully adequate to it."[6] Language possesses such a "schema"—to which it must refer all intellectual representations before they can be sensuously apprehended and represented —in its terms for spatial contents and relations. It would seem as though logical and ideal relations became accessible to the linguistic consciousness only when projected into space and there analogically "reproduced." The relations of "together," "side by side," "separate" provide it with a means of representing the most diverse qualitative relations, dependencies and oppositions.

This relationship can be recognized and clarified by an inquiry into the formation of the most elementary spatial terms known to language. They are still entirely rooted in immediate sensory impression; but, on

4. Cf. Boas, *Handbook*, pp. 43 ff., 446.

5. Examples in Westermann, *Die Sudansprachen*, p. 72; *Die Gola-Sprache in Liberia*, p. 62, and elsewhere.

6. Kant, *Kritik der reinen Vernunft*, 2d ed., pp. 177 ff.; Everyman ed., p. 119.

the other hand, they contain the first germ from which the terms of pure relation will grow. They are oriented both toward the "sensuous" and the "intellectual." For though they are entirely material in their beginnings, it is they that open up the characteristic form world of language. The sensuous factor is evident in their phonetic formation. Aside from mere interjections, which "say" nothing, which still carry no objective signification, there is scarcely any class of words in which the character of "natural sounds" is so pronounced as in those which designate here and there, the near and the distant. In most languages, nearly all the demonstrative particles which serve to designate these distinctions can still be recognized as echoes of direct "phonetic metaphors." Since in the various types of showing and indication, sound serves merely to intensify the gesture, it remains here entirely within the sphere of vocal *gesture*. Thus, we find that in the most diverse languages certain spatial specifications are almost always designated by the same sounds. Vowels of different quality and tone are used to designate degrees of distance, but it is above all in certain consonants and groups of consonants that a specific sensuous tendency is manifested. In the very first babblings of children a sharp distinction is evident between sound groups of essentially "centripetal" and essentially "centrifugal" tendency. The *m* and *n* clearly reveal the inward direction, while the explosive sounds *p* and *b*, *t* and *d* reveal the opposite trend. In the one case the sound indicates a striving back to the subject; in the other, a relation to the "outside world," a pointing or rejection. The one corresponds to the gestures of grasping, of attempting to draw close, the other to the gestures of showing or thrusting away. By this original distinction we can account for the astonishing similarity between the first "words" of children all over the world.[7] And the same phonetic groups are found in essentially identical or similar functions when we inquire into the origin and earliest phonetic form of the demonstrative particles and pronouns in different languages. For the beginnings of Indo-Germanic language, Brugmann distinguishes a threefold form of indication. "I-deixis" is distinguished, both in content and linguistic expression, from "thou-deixis" which in turn merges with the more general form of "that-deixis." Thou-deixis is indicated by its direction and by the characteristic sound corresponding to this direction, the ur-Indo-Germanic demonstrative root *to. At first it implies no reference to distance and proximity but merely estab-

7. Cf. Wundt, *Völkerpsychologie*, 2d ed., *1*, 333 ff., and Clara and William Stern, *Die Kindersprache*, 2d ed., pp. 300 ff.

lishes opposition to the "I," the general relation to the object as *object;* in it
for the first time the sphere outside one's own body is distinguished and
delimited. Subsequent development leads to a limitation of subsidiary
spheres within this general sphere,[8] to a differentiation of this and that,
here and there, the nearer and the more distant. By the simplest conceivable
means language had achieved an articulation of spatial intuition which
was to prove of incalculable importance for man's cultural development.
A first framework was created, in which all subsequent differentiations
could take their place. To understand how all this could be accomplished
by a mere group of "natural sounds," we must bear in mind that the indicative act stabilized in these sounds possesses a purely spiritual aspect side
by side with its sensuous aspect, that it bears the imprint of a new independent energy of consciousness, extending beyond the mere feeling of
which the animal is also capable.[9]

The demonstrative pronouns in particular spring then from one of
those "elementary" linguistic ideas which are similarly manifested in the
most diverse languages. Everywhere certain differences in the situation
or distance of the object referred to are expressed by a mere change of
vowel or consonant. For the most part, the soft vowels express the place
of the person addressed, the "there," while the place of the speaker is indicated by a sharper vowel.[10] As for the consonantal elements, the role
of pointing to the distance falls almost exclusively to the groups *d* and *t*,
k and *g*, *b* and *p*. In this respect, the Indo-Germanic, Semitic and Ural-
Altaic languages show an unmistakable similarity.[11] In certain languages
one demonstrative serves to indicate what lies within the speaker's sphere

8. Cf. K. Brugmann, "Die Demonstrativpronomina der indogermanischen Sprachen,"
Abhandlungen der Königlich Sächsischen Gesellschaft der Wissenschaften, Philol.-hist. Klasse,
Vol. 22 (Leipzig, 1904), No. 6; cf. also K. Brugmann and B. Delbrück, *Grundriss der vergleichenden Grammatik der indogermanischen Sprachen* (2d ed., Strassburg, K. J. Trübner,
1897–1916), 2, Pt. 2, 302 ff.

9. See above, pp. 177–178 ff.

10. As for example in the language of Tahiti (see Humboldt, *Kawi-Werk* 2, 153); for
the African languages see, e.g., Meinhof, *Lehrbuch der Nama-Sprache*, p. 61; also Steinthal,
Die Mande-Neger-Sprachen, p. 82; for the American Indian languages cf. Gatschet, *Klamath
Language*, p. 538.

11. This similarity becomes particularly evident if we compare Brugmann's indications on
the Indo-Germanic languages (see note 8 above) with those of Brockelmann and Dillmann
for the Semitic group (see Brockelmann, *Grundriss, 1*, 316 ff. and Dillmann, *Grammatik der
äthiopischen Sprache*, pp. 94 ff. [Eng. trans., 2d ed., pp. 115 ff.]); for the Ural-Altaic languages see H. Winkler, *Das Uralaltaische und seine Gruppen*, pp. 26 ff.

of perception, another what lies in the sphere of perception of the person addressed; or one form is used for an object close to the speaker, another for an object equally distant from the speaker and the person addressed, a third for an absent object.[12]

Thus for language as for cognition, the precise differentiation of spatial *situations* and *distances* represents a point of departure from which it proceeds to build objective reality, to define objects. The differentiation of places serves as a basis for the differentiation of contents, of the I, Thou and He on the one hand, and of physical objects on the other. The general *critique of knowledge* teaches us that the act of spatial position and differentiation is the indispensable condition for the act of objectivization in general, for "relating the representation to the object." This is the central idea underlying Kant's "Refutation of Idealism" in the sense of an empirical-psychological idealism. The very *form* of spatial intuition itself bears within it a necessary reference to an objective *existence*, a reality "in" space. The opposition of "inward" and "outward," on which the representation of the empirical I is based, is itself possible only because an empirical object is represented at the same time: for the I can become aware of the changes in its own states only by referring them to something permanent, to space and something enduring in space.

It is possible to perceive a determination of time only by means of a change in external relations (motion) to the permanent in space (for example, we become aware of the sun's motion by observing the changes in its relation to the objects of this earth). But this is not all. We find that we possess nothing permanent that can correspond and be submitted to the conception of a substance as intuition, except *matter*. . . . In the representation I, the consciousness of myself is not an intuition, but a merely intellectual representation produced by the spontaneous

12. The difference in the designation of a *visible* and an *invisible* object is particularly pronounced in many American Indian languages (cf. in particular the indications on the Kwakiutl, Ponca, and Eskimo languages in Boas, *Handbook*, pp. 41 ff., 445 ff. and Gatschet, *Klamath Language*, p. 538). The Bantu languages possess demonstratives in three different forms: one indicates that the thing shown is close to the speaker; the second that it is already known, that is, has entered into the speaker's sphere of vision and thought; the third that it is far removed from the speaker or not visible (C. Meinhof, *Grundzüge einer vergleichenden Grammatik der Bantusprachen* [Berlin, D. Reimer, 1906], pp. 39 ff.). For the South Sea languages see Humboldt's indications with regard to Tagalog (*Werke 6*, No. 1, 312 ff.).

activity of a thinking subject. It follows that this I has no predicate of intuition, which in its character of *permanence* could serve as correlate to the determination of time in the internal sense.[13]

The fundamental principle of Kant's proof lies in his demonstration that the specific function of space is a necessary instrument and vehicle for the universal function of substance and for its empirical and objective application. Only through the interpenetration of both functions do we gain the intuition of a "nature," a self-sufficient, comprehensive order of objects. It is only when a content is determined in space, when it is distinguished by fixed boundaries from the undifferentiated totality of space, that it gains its own real form: the act of "setting out" and differentiating, of *exsistere* first gives it the form of independent "existence." And this logical fact is marked out in the construction of language, where the concrete designation of situation and space also serves as an instrument for defining the category of the "object." This process can be followed in various branches of linguistic development. If it is true that the nominative endings in the masculine and neuter of the Indo-Germanic languages are derived from certain demonstrative particles,[14] this means that an instrument for designating place served to express the characteristic function of the nominative, its position as a "subjective case." It could become the "vehicle" of an action only when a specific local characteristic, a spatial determination was attached to it. But there is another linguistic phenomenon which seems to have grown directly out of this interpenetration of the two factors, this spiritual interaction between the category of space and the category of substance. Wherever language has produced a definite *article*, its manifest purpose is to constitute a representation of substance, while its origin unmistakably pertains to spatial representation. Since the definite article is a relatively late product, such a transition in its function can be plainly seen on many occasions. In the Indo-Germanic languages, the genesis and distribution of the article can be followed historically. The article is lacking in Old-Indian, Old-Iranian and Latin, and also in archaic Greek, specifically in Homer; it first came into regular use only with Attic prose. Similarly in the Germanic group, the use of the article was not established until the Middle High German period. The Slavic languages never developed

13. *Kritik der reinen Vernuft*, 2d ed., pp. 277 ff.; Everyman ed., p. 172.

14. In Brugmann & Delbrück, *Grundriss*, 2d ed., 2, Pt. 2, 475, expresses the belief that the nominative -s is identical with the demonstrative pronoun *so (ai: sa) and the -m of the neuter probably also goes back to a distant-deitic particle.

the consistent use of an abstract article.[15] The situation is similar in the Semitic languages; the article is in general use, but certain languages, like the Ethiopic, which in this respect has remained at an earlier stage, make no use of it.[16] Wherever the definite article has developed, it can clearly be recognized as an offshoot of the demonstrative pronouns. It grows out of the form of "that-deixis," designating the object to which it refers as "outside" and "there," and distinguishing it spatially from the "I" and the "here." [17]

This genesis of the article makes it clear that it did not acquire its universal linguistic function of expressing the idea of substance immediately, but through a series of intermediaries. The power of "substantiation" peculiar to it developed only gradually. In the languages of primitive peoples there are certain demonstrative pronouns that are used quite in the sense of the definite article; but they do not necessarily refer to the class of "substantives." In Ewe the article, which here follows the word it modifies, is used not only with substantives but also with the absolute pronoun, with adverbs and conjunctions.[18] And even where it does refer to things, where it remains within the strict sphere of "objective" representation, the general expression of "objectivization" which it embodies, develops only gradually from the more special meanings. The farther back we follow the use of the article, the more "concretely" it seems to be used: instead of a universal form of the article, we find diverse types, which vary according to the quality of the particular objects or object classes. The general *function* which it serves both in language and thought, is not yet detached from the particularity of the *contents* to which it is applied. In addition to the neuter article, the Indonesian languages have a special personal article, which stands before the names of individuals and tribes, and also before designations of kinship, not in order to qualify them in any way, but merely to identify them as personal names.[19] The language of the Ponca Indians draws a sharp distinction between the

15. Cf. the section "Vom Artikel" in Grimm, *Deutsche Grammatik*, *1*, 366 ff.; on the Slavic languages see Miklosich, *Vergleichende Grammatik der slawischen Sprachen*, 2d ed., *4*, 125.

16. See Dillmann, *Grammatik der äthiopischen Sprache*, pp. 333 ff. (Eng. trans., 2d ed., pp. 424 ff.), Brockelmann, *Grundriss*, *1*, 466.

17. Cf. Brugmann and Delbrück, *Grundriss*, 2d ed., *2*, Pt. 2, 315.

18. Cf. Westermann, *Grammatik der Ewe-Sprache*, p. 61. Eng. trans. by Bickford-Smith, pp. 66–67.

19. See Codrington, *The Melanesian Languages*, pp. 108 ff.; cf Brandstetter, *Der Artikel des Indonesischen verglichen mit dem des Indogermanischen* (Leipzig, 1913).

articles used for animate and inanimate objects: among the latter, such
classes as horizontal and round objects, scattered objects or collectives each
have an article of their own; and when an article is used for an animate
being, a sharp distinction is made as to whether this being is sitting, standing or moving.[20] A noteworthy and highly instructive indication of the
article's original concrete signification is to be found in the Somali language. Somali possesses three forms of the article, which are distinguished
from one another by the final vowel (-a, -i and -o [or u]). The factor determining the use of one or the other form is the spatial relation of the
person or thing in question to the speaker. The article ending in -a designates a person or thing in immediate proximity to the speaker, visible to
him and actually seen by him; the article ending in -o refers to a person or
thing more or less removed from the speaker but usually visible to him;
while the article ending in -i indicates a person or thing known to the
speaker in some way, but not visibly present.[21] Here we can see almost
tangibly how the universal form of "substantiation," the forming of a
"thing," expressed in the article, springs from the function of spatial indication, and at first remains attached to it; how it adheres to the various
modes of demonstration and their variations until finally, at a relatively late
stage, the pure category of substance frees itself from the special forms of
spatial intuition.

If we attempt to follow still farther the ways by which language progresses from its first sharply defined local distinctions to general spatial
specifications and terms, we seem to find here again that the direction of
this development is outward from the center. The "differentiation of
locations in space" starts from the situation of the speaker and spreads in
concentric circles until the objective whole, the sum and system of local
specifications has been articulated. At first local distinctions are closely
linked with specific material distinctions—and it is eminently the differentiation of the parts of his own body that serves man as a basis for all other
spatial specifications. Once he has formed a distinct representation of his
own body, once he has apprehended it as a self-enclosed and intrinsically
articulated organism, it becomes, as it were, a model according to which
he constructs the world as a whole. In this perception of his body, he
possesses an original set of coordinates, to which in the course of develop-

20. Boas and Swanton, "Siouan," *Handbook*, *1*, 939 ff.

21. See Maria von Tiling, "Die Vokale des bestimmten Artikels im Somali," *Zeitschrift für
Kolonialsprachen*, *9*, 132 ff.

ment he continually returns and refers—and from which accordingly he draws the terms which serve to designate this development.

Indeed, a close connection has been almost universally observed between the expression of spatial *relations* and certain concrete nouns, among which once again words designating parts of man's body are most prominent. "Inside" and "outside," "before" and "behind," "above" and "below" are associated with a specific part of one's own body. Where the more highly developed languages tend to use prepositions for the expression of spatial *relations,* the languages of primitive peoples use almost exclusively nouns, which are themselves either names for parts of the body or clearly derived from such names. According to Steinthal, the Mandingan languages express our prepositional concepts in "a very material way": "behind" is expressed by an independent substantive meaning "back" or "rear end," "in front of" by a word meaning "eye," while "on" is designated by "neck" and "in" by "belly," etc.[22] In other African languages and in the South Sea languages, such words as "face" and "back," "head" and "mouth," "loin" and "hip" perform the same function.[23] And if at first sight this seems a peculiarly "primitive" mode of designation, we find that it has its exact analogy and counterpart in far more advanced stages of language formation.[24] Yet language does not content itself with using the names of limbs and organs of the human body as "spatial substantives," but progresses to a more general application of the principle. Instead of "back," such a word as "track" may be used to indicate "behind"; while "under" may be designated by "ground" or "earth," "over" by such a word as "air."[25] Now the terms are no longer drawn exclusively from man's own body; but the method by which language represents spatial relations has remained the same. The representation of concrete spatial objects dominates the

22. Steinthal, *Die Mande-Neger-Sprachen,* pp. 245 ff.

23. See Westermann, *Die Sudansprachen,* pp. 53 ff.; *Die Gola-Sprache,* pp. 36 ff.; L. Reinisoh, *Die Nuba-Sprache,* Vols. 2–3 in *Sprachen von Nord-Ost-Afrika* (Vienna, 1879), pp. 123 ff.; for the South Sea languages cf. H. C. v. d. Gabelentz, *Die melanesischen Sprachen,* pp. 158, 230 ff.; Ray, "The Melanesian Possessive, *American Anthropologist, 21,* 352 ff.

24. In Egyptian, which has developed true prepositions, their original nominal character is shown by their combination with possessive suffixes; an analysis of these "prepositions" often leads back to names for parts of the body. Cf. G. A. Erman, *Ägyptische Grammatik* (3d ed., Berlin, 1911), pp. 231, 238 ff.; G. Steindorff, *Koptische Grammatik* (2d ed., Berlin, 1904; New York, Lemke & Buechner, 1904), pp. 173 ff. For the original nominal character of the Semitic prepositions see Brockelmann, *Grundriss, 1,* 494 ff.

25. Ewe, for example, has developed a great number of special and general "local substantives"; cf. Westermann, *Grammatik der Ewe-Sprache,* pp. 52 ff.; Eng. trans. by Bickford-Smith, pp. 51 ff.

expression of spatial relations. This appears with remarkable clarity in the formation taken by the words of spatial relation in most of the Ural-Altaic languages. Here, for example, nominal terms such as "top" or "summit," "bottom," "trace," "middle," "circle," are used to designate "over" and "under," "before" and "behind," "around," etc.[26]

And even where language has arrived at great freedom and abstract clarity in the expression of purely logical relations, the old spatial and hence sensuous origin of its terms for these relations is usually evident. That "prepositions" were originally independent words in the Indo-Germanic languages is made evident by the fact that in their combination with verbal roots the connection remains extremely loose, so that, for example, augment and reduplication are placed *between* the preposition and the verbal form.[27] And the development of certain Indo-Germanic languages, such as the Slavic, shows the constant appearance of new "pseudo-prepositions" whose material signification either remains alive in the linguistic consciousness or can be demonstrated by linguisitic research.[28] In general we find that the Indo-Germanic *case forms* served originally to express spatial, temporal or other outward intuitions, and only later acquired an "abstract" sense. Thus the instrumental was at first the "with" case; when the intuition of spatial *togetherness* passed into that of the accompanying and modifying circumstance, the case came to indicate the means or basis of an action. From spatial "whence" the causal "whereby" develops, from "whither" the general idea of aim and purpose.[29] It is true that the *localist theory of cases* has been attacked not only in terms of the history of language but also on the basis of general epistemological considerations, just as it has been defended on similar grounds. Those holding the localist view have pointed out that, since the whole development of language as of thought in general must proceed from the intuitive, from the "concrete and vital" to the conceptual, the originally spatial origin of

26. Examples from Yakut in Böthlingk, *Über die Sprache der Jakuten*, p. 391; from Japanese in E. Hoffmann, *Japanische Sprachlehre* (Leiden, 1877), pp. 188 ff., 197 ff.; see also Heinrich Winkler, *Der uralaltaische Sprachstamm* (Berlin, Dümmlers, 1909), pp. 147 ff.

27. See G. Curtius, *Das Verbum der griechischen Sprache*, 2d ed., *1*, 136.

28. Cf. Miklosich, *Vergleichende Grammatik der slawischen Sprachen*, 2d ed., *4*, 196. Such new forms are common in other inflected languages, such as the Semitic; cf., for example, the list of "new prepositions" which developed in the Semitic out of the names of *parts of the body*, in Brockelmann, *Grundriss*, 2d ed., *2*, 421 ff.

29. Cf. Brugmann and Delbrück, *Grundriss*, 2d ed., *2*, Pt. 2, 464 ff., 473, 518, etc.; cf. B. Delbrück, *Vergleichende Syntax der indogermanischen Sprachen* (Strassburg, 1893 ff.), *1*, 188.

all case determinations was in a sense proved a priori.[30] In answer to this argument it has been contended that there is no justification for narrowing down the concept of intuition to the one specific field of *spatial* intuition, since not only motion in space, but various other dynamic relations, such as victory and defeat, cause and effect, are given immediately and intuitively and are actually seen.[31] This objection however, which was raised by B. Delbrück, is untenable, at least in the form he gave it. For since Hume's analysis of the concept of causality it is certain that there is no sensory impression and no immediate intuition of what we call "causality." All that is ever "given" to us in the relation between cause and effect reduces to certain spatial and temporal relations, relations of juxtaposition and succession. Likewise Wundt, who opposes the localist view on the ground that spatial relations are far from exhausting all the sensuous, intuitive characteristics of objects, blunts his own objection by recognizing that spatial characteristics have one essential distinction over all others, namely that all other relations are also spatial, while only spatial relations can by themselves form the content of an intuition.[32] And this would make it probable a priori that language can proceed to the expression of purely "intellectual" relations only after it has detached and as it were "abstracted" them from their involvement with spatial relations. In the finished structure of our inflected languages, each of the principal case forms reveals a specific logical-grammatical function which it essentially serves. The nominative represents the agent of the action, the accusative or genitive designates its object, accordingly as it is entirely or partly affected by the action —and even the local cases in the more restricted sense can be fitted into this schema, since in addition to their specific local sense, they express a general relation of the substantive concept to the verbal concept.[33] But although, in this light, the logical-grammatical sense may appear to be the πρότερον τῇ φύσει rather than the spatial-intuitive sense, epistemological and linguistic considerations lead us to regard the latter as the true πρότερον πρὸς ἡμᾶς. Indeed, the more we consider those languages which have shown the greatest fertility in the formation of "case forms," the more we become convinced of the priority of the spatial over the grammatical-

30. Cf. Whitney, "General Considerations on the European Case-system," *Transactions of the American Philological Association, 13* (1888), 88 ff.

31. B. Delbrück, *Grundfragen der Sprachforschung* (Strassburg, 1901), pp. 130 ff.

32. Wundt, *Völkerpsychologie, 2,* 79 ff.

33. Cf. the account of the Indo-Germanic case system in Delbrück, *Vergleichende Syntax, 1,* 181 ff.

logical signification. Aside from the American Indian languages,[34] those
of the Ural-Altaic family show the most elaborate inflection of nouns. Yet
they have not succeeded in forming the three "strictly grammatical" cases;
in them, the relations which are expressed in the Indo-Germanic languages
by the nominative, genitive and accusative are indicated solely by the
context. A true nominative or subjective case is lacking, while the genitive
either has no formal expression or is represented by a pure "adessive" form,
which designates nothing but local presence. On the other hand, the development of terms for purely spatial indications is positively luxuriant.
We find the greatest diversity and precision in general designations of
locality, and in special designations for the situation of a thing and the
direction of a movement. There are allative and adessive, inessive and
illative, translative, delative and sublative cases, expressing rest within an
object, being with it, penetration into it, issuing from it, etc.[35] "These languages," writes Friedrich Müller "do not simply stop outside the object,
but penetrate, one might say, into the object and create a formal opposition between its inside and outside, its top and its bottom. The three conditions of rest, motion toward the object and motion away from the object,
combine with the categories of 'inside,' 'outside' and in some languages
'above,' to create an abundance of case forms for which our languages
have no feeling at all, and which we can therefore not adequately render." [36]
Considering how close this purely *intuitive* expression of case relations
remains to mere sensuous expression, it is worthy of note that subtly as
spatial *relations* are differentiated, they are still rendered throughout by
concrete substantives.

The expression of *direction* and differences of direction, however sensuous its form, implies a new spiritual factor not to be found in the mere expression of fixed position. In many languages spatial verbs as well as
spatial substantives serve to designate relations which we render by means
of prepositions. Humboldt illustrates this use of spatial verbs by examples

34. On the case formation of the American languages see the compilation from the Eskimo
language by Thalbitzer in Boas, *Handbook, 1,* 1017 ff.: here, among other cases, an allative,
locative, ablative, prosecutive are distinguished. Gatschet's *Klamath Language* distinguishes
an "inessive" and "adessive," a "directive" and "prosecutive" as well as an abundance of
other relations, each expressed by a local case ending (op. cit., pp. 479 ff., 489).

35. See the copious material in H. Winkler, *Das Uralaltaische und seine Gruppen* (especially
pp. 10 ff.), and the section "Indogermanische und uralaltaische Kasus" in *Uralaltaische Völker
und Sprachen* (Berlin, 1884), pp. 171 ff.; cf. also Grunzel, *Vergleichende Grammatik der
altaischen Sprachen,* pp. 49 ff.

36. Fr. Müller, *Grundriss, 2,* Pt. 2, 204.

from the Javanese and remarks that it seems to disclose a subtler linguistic sense than the use of spatial substantives, since the concept of action is freer from material mixture when expressed by a verb than when expressed by a mere concrete noun.[37] And indeed spatial relations do here take on a greater fluidity, as it were, than in substantivist expression, which is always characterized by a certain rigidity. The expression of a pure action, though still fully intuitive, prepares the way for the abstract expression of pure relations. Here again, the representation is still closely linked to one's own body, but now it is no longer the parts of the body but its movements, or, one might say, it is no longer its purely material existence but its activity, which forms the foundation of language. And historical considerations indicate that in certain languages where spatial verbs appear side by side with spatial substantives the nouns are the earlier forms.[38] Verbs are first used to express differences of "sense" in the movement, the difference between movement from a place and movement to that same place. These verbs then appear in attenuated form in the type of suffixes by which the type and direction of motion are characterized. The American Indian languages use such suffixes to indicate whether the motion occurs within or outside of a certain space, particularly inside or outside of the house, whether over the sea or over land, whether through the air or through the water, whether from inland toward the coast, or from the coast inland, whether from the fire site toward the house or from house to fire site.[39] But of all these many distinctions based on the source and goal of a motion and the manner and means of its execution, there is *one* which assumes greater and greater importance for the structure of language. The natural, in a certain sense "absolute" system of coordinates for all representation of motion in language is evidently provided by the situation of the speaker and the situation of the person addressed. Frequently language distinguishes sharply whether a particular movement is effected from the speaker to the person addressed, from the person addressed to the speaker, or from the speaker to a third person or thing, not addressed.[40] On the basis of such concrete distinctions in reference to some material thing or

37. Humboldt, *Kawi-Werk*, 2, 164 ff., 341, etc.

38. For the Melanesian languages, cf. Codrington, *The Melanesian Languages*, p. 158.

39. See the examples from Athapascan given by Goddard, from Haida given by Swanton, and from Tsimshian by Boas, *Handbook*, *1*, 112 ff., 244 ff., 300 ff.

40. For examples, see particularly Humboldt who was first to point out this distinction in "Über die Verwandtschaft der Ortsadverbien mit dem Pronomen in einigen Sprachen," *Werke, 6*, No. 1, 311 ff.); cf. also Fr. Müller, *Reise der österreichischen Fregatte Novara, 3*, 312.

to the "I" or "thou," language goes on to develop more general and more "abstract" designations. It creates definite groups and schemata of suffixes of direction, which classify all possible movements according to certain principal spatial division, particularly the cardinal points.[41] Different languages seem to employ very different methods in distinguishing between expressions of rest and expressions of motion. The accents may be distributed between the two in the greatest variety of ways. Languages of the purely "objective" or nominal type give priority to local terms over terms of direction, to the expression of rest over the expression of motion, while in the verbal types the opposite relation generally prevails. A middle position is perhaps occupied by those languages which give priority to the expression of rest, but lend it a verbal as well as a nominal form. Thus, for example, the languages of the Sudan employ only substantives to designate spatial relations such as above and below, inside and outside, but these substantives contain within them a verb which designates fixed position. This "local verb" is always used to express an activity occurring in a specific place.[42] Evidently, the intuition of *activity* cannot be detached from that of purely local *presence*, but remains in a sense imprisoned in it,[43] but on the other hand, this presence, this mere existence in a place appears as a kind of activity on the part of its subject. Here again we see how tenaciously language clings to its original intuition of a "given" space, yet is impelled to surpass the spatial datum as soon as it undertakes to represent motion and pure activity. As man turns his attention to activity and apprehends it as such, he must transform the purely objective, substantial unity of space into a dynamic-functional unity; he must, as it were, construct space as a totality of the directions of action. Here a new factor enters into the development of the perceptual world, which up to now we have followed essentially in its objective aspect. This special field of language

41. See, for example, a list of such suffixes in Nicobarese, in P. W. Schmidt, *Die Mon-Khmer-Völker, ein Bindeglied zwischen Völkern Zentralasiens und Austronesiens* (Braunschweig, 1906), p. 57.

42. In these languages the use of the "verb of locality and rest," expressing "being in a place," gives a sentence such as "He is working in the field" a form such as the following: "He works, is the inside of the field"; "The children are playing on the street" becomes "The children play, are the surface of the street." See Westermann, *Die Sudansprachen*, pp. 51 ff.

43. In the Sudan and Bantu languages, as in most of the Hamitic languages, a movement which we designate according to its aim and result is designated according to its beginning and local *starting point*. See examples in Meinof, *Die Sprachen der Hamiten* (Hamburg, 1912), p. 20 n. On analogous phenomena in the South Sea languages see Codrington, *The Melanesian Languages*, pp. 159 ff.

formation confirms the general law that the content and achievement of every spiritual form consist, not simply in reproducing something objectively present, but in creating a new relation, a unique correlation between "I" and "reality," between the "subjective" and the "objective" sphere. In language, as in the other forms, the "road outward" becomes at the same time a "road inward." For it is only as its outward intuition becomes more determinate, that its inner intuition can truly unfold: the formation of spatial terms becomes the medium for designating the I and defining it against other subjects.

Even the oldest stratum of spatial terms discloses this relationship. In nearly all languages, spatial demonstratives provided the foundation for the *personal pronouns*. Historically, the link between the two classes of words is so close that it is hard to decide which to regard as earlier or later, original or derived. In his basic treatise "On the relation of local adverbs to pronouns in several languages," [44] Humboldt attempted to prove that the personal pronouns in general go back to words of local signification and origin; many modern linguists, on the other hand, tend to reverse the relation, tracing the characteristic trichotomy of the demonstratives, found in most languages, to the natural trichotomy of the persons "I," "thou," and "he." However this genetic question may ultimately be decided, it is evident that the personal and demonstrative pronouns, the original designations of persons and of space, are closely related in their whole structure and belong as it were to the same stratum of linguistic thought. It is the same half-mimetic, half-linguistic act of indication, the same fundamental forms of "deixis," which gave rise to the opposition of *hier, da* and *dort* [45] and to that of "I," "thou" and "he." "Here," remarks G. v. d. Gabelentz, "is always where I am, and what is here I call *this*, in contrast to *das* and *jenes*, which are *da* and *dort*. This accounts for the Latin usage: *hic, iste, ille = meus, tuus, eius;* and, in Chinese, for the coincidence of the second person pronouns with conjunctions of local and temporal proximity and of similarity." [46] In the above-mentioned treatise Humboldt demonstrated the same relation for the Malayan languages, for Japanese, and Armenian. And in the whole development of the Indo-Germanic languages the third-person pronoun reveals a close

44. Humboldt, "Über die Verwandtschaft der Ortsadverbien mit dem Pronomen," *Werke*, 6, No. 1.

45. The German *da* occupies a middle position between here and there (*Trans.*).

46. G. v. d. Gabelentz, *Die Sprachwissenschaft* (Leipzig, T. O. Weigel, 1891), pp. 230 ff.

formal link with the corresponding demonstrative pronoun—the French *il* goes back to Latin *ille*, Gothic *is* (modern German *er*) corresponds to the Latin *is*. And often the I-thou pronouns also show an unmistakable connection with demonstrative pronouns.[47] Exactly corresponding relations are found in the Semitic and Altaic languages [48] as well as the languages of the American Indians and the Australian aborigines.[49] In this connection the Australian languages reveal a highly distinctive trait. It is reported that when certain South Australian languages express an action in the third person, they attach a spatial qualifier both to the subject and the object of this action. In order, for example, to express the thought that a man has struck a dog with a spear, one must say approximately that the man "up front" has struck the dog "back there" with this or that weapon.[50] In other words there is no general and abstract term for "he" or for "this"; the word used for this signification is still fused with a certain deictic phonetic gesture, from which it cannot be detached. The same is true in those languages which have terms for designating an individual in a definite situation, sitting, lying or standing, coming or going, but lack a unitary third-person pronoun. The language of the Cherokees, in which such distinctions are particularly pronounced, possesses nine third-person pronouns instead of one.[51] Other languages distinguish in the first as well as the second and third person whether the subject is visible or invisible, and use a different pronoun accordingly.[52] In addition to spatial distinctions of situation or distance, temporal presence or nonpresence is often expressed by a special form of the pronoun; and still other characteristics may be expressed in the same manner.[53] In all these cases, as we see, the terms for the purely "spiritual" differentiation of three persons retain an

47. Cf. Brugmann, *Die Demonstrativpronomina*, pp. 30 ff., 71 ff., 129 ff.; and Brugmann and Delbrück, *Grundriss*, 2d ed., 2, Pt. 2, 307 ff., 381 ff.

48. For the Semitic languages see Brockelmann, *Grundriss*, *1*, 296 ff. and his *Kurzgefasste vergleichende Grammatik der semitischen Sprachen* (Berlin, 1908), pp. 142 ff.; Dillman, *Grammatik der äthiopischen Sprache*, pp. 98 f. (Eng. trans., 2d ed., pp. 120 f.); for the Altaic languages see Grunzel, *Vergleichende Grammatik der altaischen Sprachen*, pp. 55 ff.

49. Cf. Gatschet, *Klamath Language*, pp. 536 ff.; S. Matthews, "Languages of the Bungandity Tribe in South Australia," *J. and Proc. of the Roy. Soc. of N. S. Wales*, *37* (1903), 151.

50. Matthews, *37*, 61.

51. Cf. Humboldt, "Über den Dualis," *Werke*, *6*, No. 1, 23; Fr. Müller, *Grundriss*, *2*, I, 224 ff.

52. Boas, "Kwakiutl," in *Handbook*, *1*, 527 ff.

53. Goddard, "Hupa," in Boas, *Handbook*, *1*, 117; Boas, "Chinook," in *Handbook*, *1*, 574, 617 ff.

immediately sensuous, above all a spatial coloration. According to Hoffmann, the Japanese has created a word for "I" from a local adverb whose proper meaning is "center" and a word for "he" from another word meaning "there." [54] In phenomena of this sort we see how language draws as it were a sensuous-spiritual circle round the speaker, designating the center of the circle as "I," the periphery as "thou" and "he." The characteristic "schematism" of space, which we have previously observed in the building of the objective world, here operates in the converse direction—and the representation of space is fully constituted only in this twofold function.

2. The Representation of Time

The precise distinction and designation of time relations present language with a far more difficult and complex problem than the development of its spatial conceptions and terms. The simple coordination of spatial form and temporal form that has often been attempted in epistemological inquiries, finds no confirmation in language. Language shows rather that thought in general and linguistic thought in particular must perform an operation of a different type and one might say of a higher dimension, in building up the representation of time, in differentiating directions and intervals of time. For "here" and "there" can be subsumed much more simply and immediately in an intuitive unity than is the case with the temporal factors "now," "earlier," and "later." What characterizes these factors as *temporal* is precisely that they are never, like things of objective intuition, given to the consciousness simultaneously. The units, the parts, which in spatial intuition seem to *combine* of themselves into a whole, here exclude one another: the existence of one specification signifies the nonexistence of the others and vice versa. Accordingly, the whole fact of the representation of time is never contained in immediate intuition; differentiation and combination, analytical and synthetic thought consequently play a larger part than in spatial representation. Since the elements of time exist as such only because consciousness "runs through" them and in so doing differentiates them, this act of running through, this *"discursus"* enters into the characteristic form of the concept of time itself. Thus the

54. Hoffmann, *Japanische Sprachlehre*, pp. 85 ff.

form of "being" which we designate as succession, as time, appears to occupy a far higher level of ideality than mere locally determined existence. Language cannot arrive at this level immediately but here too is subject to the same inner law that governs its entire formation and progress. It does not create new means of expression for every new sphere of signification that is opened up to it; on the contrary, its strength consists in giving new spiritual form to a specific given material which it employs for new purposes without at first changing its content.

We have seen that language employed the simplest possible means in forming its original spatial terms. The transposition from the sensuous to the ideal is so gradual that at first one scarcely perceives the decisive change in general spiritual attitude, which it embodies. From a very limited sensuous material, from shadings in vowel coloration and from the phonetic and affective quality peculiar to certain consonants and consonant groups, the designations for local distinctions and differences of direction are formed. The same process is manifested in a new aspect of linguistic development, when we investigate the manner in which it arrives at its original *temporal particles*. We have seen the fluidity of the dividing line between imitative or affective sounds and the simplest spatial terms—and we encounter the same continuous, imperceptible transition between the linguistic spheres embracing local and temporal determinations. Even in our modern civilized languages these two often form an inseparable unity; it is common to find one and the same word used to express both spatial and temporal relations. And still more abundant examples of this relationship are found in the languages of primitive peoples, which often seem to possess no other means of expressing the temporal idea. The simple local adverbs are used indifferently in a temporal sense, so that, for example, the word for "here" merges with the word for "now," the word for "there" with that for "earlier" or "later." [55] Attempts have been made to explain this on the ground that spatial and temporal proximity or distance condition one another objectively; that an event which has occurred in a distant place tends to be long past at the moment when it is spoken of. But apparently the relation is not so much a practical one of this sort as a purely ideal one, pertaining to a level of *consciousness* that is still relatively undifferentiated and not yet sensitive to the specific difference between the forms of space

55. Cf. the examples from the Klamath language in Gatschet, pp. 582 ff. and from the Melanesian languages in Codrington, pp. 164 ff.

and time. In the languages of primitive peoples even relatively complex temporal relations, for which the highly developed languages have created specific expressions, are often designated by the most primitive spatial terms.[56]

As long as this material bond remains in force, the distinctive character of the temporal *form* cannot be manifested. Involuntarily, language transposes the structural relations of time into relations of space. Spatial "here" and "there" stand to one another in a simple relation of distance; two points in space are merely differentiated, there is in general no preferred direction in the passage from one to the other. As spatial factors, the two points are "potentially co-existent" and in a sense equivalent; a simple movement can transform "there" into "here," and "here," after ceasing to be such, can be restored to its previous form by the reverse movement. Time however reveals, in addition to the distinction and distance between its elements, a unique and irreversible "sense" in which it proceeds. The directions from past to future and from future to past are not interchangeable—each is peculiar to itself. But where consciousness is limited to spatial intuition and apprehends temporal relations only through spatial analogies—this unique character of the direction of time must remain obscure. As in the intuition of space, everything is here reduced to the simple distinction of near and far. The only essential difference that is grasped and clearly expressed is that between "now" and "not-now"—between the immediate present and that which lies "outside" it. This present should not, to be sure, be conceived as a strict mathematical abstraction but as a psychological "now," encompassing all those contents which can be intuited as an immediate temporal unity, which can be condensed into an elementary unity of experience. It is no mere logical borderline, dividing earlier from later, but possesses in itself a certain duration, extending as far as the immediate, concrete memory. For this form of primary temporal intuition, the whole of consciousness and its contents falls, as it were, into two spheres: a bright sphere, illumined by the light of the "present," and another, dark sphere; and between these two basic levels, there are as yet no mediation of transition, no shadings or degrees.

---

56. The Sudanese languages generally express the thought that a subject is occupied in an action by a turn of phrase which means literally that he is inside this action. But since this "inside" is usually designated very materially, phrases result such as "I am in the inside of going," "I am the belly of going," for "I am in the process of going." See Westermann, *Die Sudansprachen*, p. 65; *Die Gola-Sprache*, pp. 37, 43, 61.

The fully developed consciousness, perticularly the consciousness of scientific *cognition*, does not content itself with this simple opposition of "now" and "not-now" but raises it to its richest logical development. It produces abundant *gradations of time*, all encompassed in a unitary temporal order in which every moment has its specific position. Epistemological analysis shows that this order is not "given" by sensation and cannot be derived from immediate intuition. It is rather a work of the understanding —particularly of causal inference. It is the category of cause and effect which transforms the mere intuition of succession into the idea of a unitary temporal order of events. The simple distinction of separate points in time must be transformed into the concept of a mutual dynamic dependence between them, time as a form of pure intuition must be permeated with the function of causal judgment, before this idea can be developed and stabilized, before the immediate feeling of time can be transformed into the systematic concept of time as a condition and content of knowledge. How long the road is from one to the other and through what difficulties and paradoxes it leads has been shown most clearly by the development of modern physics. Kant regarded the "analogies of experience," the three synthetic principles of substantiality, causality, and reciprocity, as the intellectual condition and foundation for the representation of the three possible relations of time: permanence, succession, and simultaneity. The progress of physics to the general theory of relativity and the transformation which the concept of time has undergone in this theory show that this relatively simple schema, which is drawn from the basic form of the Newtonian mechanics, must be replaced epistemologically by more complex determinants.[57] In general, the development from the feeling to the concept of time reveals three different stages, which are also of crucial importance for the linguistic reflection of the consciousness of time. At the first stage the consciousness is dominated by the opposition of "now" and "not-now," which has undergone no further differentiations; at the second, certain temporal "forms"—completed and incompleted, continued and momentary action—begin to be distinguished so that a definite distinction of temporal *modes* is developed; the final stage is characterized by the pure concept of time as an abstract *concept of order*, and the various stages of time stand out in their contrast and interdetermination.

For it is even more true of temporal than of spatial relations that they do

57. For a more detailed discussion of this matter see my book *Zur Einstein'schen Relativitäts-theorie*.

not come to consciousness at once as relations, but that their purely relational character is always mingled with and concealed by other specifications, particularly those of things and qualities. Although local specifications possess certain traits that distinguish them from other sensuous qualities by which things are differentiated, they nevertheless stand on one and the same plane with them as qualities. "Hereness" and "thereness" are just as much a part of an object as any other "thisness" and "thatness." Thus, all designations of spatial *form* must take certain material designations as their starting point. When this relationship is extended from space to time, the differences of temporal signification first appear as pure qualitative differences. Characteristically, these differences are expressed not only in the verb but also in the noun. For the consciousness governing our highly developed languages, the specification of time adheres essentially to those parts of speech which express a process or activity. The meaning of time and the diversity of the relations it implies can be apprehended and identified only in the phenomenon of change. The verb, as expression of a specific condition, from which change begins or as an expression of the act of change itself, seems consequently to be the only true vehicle of temporal specifications: it seems to be the *Zeitwort* [58] κατ᾽ ἐξοχήν. In the introduction to the *Kawi-Werk* Humboldt was still attempting to show that this was a necessary relationship arising from the specific nature of man's conception of time and of the verb. In the verb, he held, an energetic (not merely qualitative) attributive is comprised with being. The energetic attributive contains the stages of action, being encompasses the stages of time.[59] In the *Kawi-Werk* itself, however, Humboldt himself shows that not all languages express this relation with equal distinctness: Although we tend to conceive of time relations only in connection with the verb and its conjugation, the Malay languages, for example, have developed a usage indicating that they connect them with the noun.[60] This phenomenon is particularly apparent where language designates time relations by the same means which it has developed for the designation of local relations. Somali uses the above-mentioned variations in the vowels of the definite article not only to express differences of spatial position and situation, but also to represent temporal differences. Here the development and designation of temporal representations run exactly parallel to those of local

58. Verb, literally "time-word" *Trans.*
59. Humboldt, "Einleitung zum Kawi-Werk," *Werke*, 7, No. 1, 223.
60. *Kawi-Werk*, 2, 286.

representations. Pure *nouns*, which to our way of thinking embody not the slightest temporal reference, e.g., words such as "man" or "war," can be provided with a certain temporal index by changes of the vowel in their article. The vowel -a serves to designate the temporally present, the vowel -o designates the temporally absent, and no distinction is made between the future and the not yet distant past. On the basis of this separation, there is only an indirect differentiation in the expression of *action* as to whether it is complete or incomplete, momentary, or of greater or lesser duration.[61] Such a marking out of purely temporal characteristics in the noun might easily be interpreted as proof of a particularly acute and subtle sense of time, if it were not evident on the other hand that temporal sense and local sense were here quite undifferentiated, since the consciousness of the specific *directions* of time is totally undeveloped. A sharp distinction is made between the *contents* of now and not-now, as between those of here and there, but the distinction of past and future lags far behind, so that the very factor that is decisive for the consciousness of the pure temporal *form* and its distinctive nature is lacking.

The development of *child language* shows that adverbs of time are formed appreciably later than those of place, and that terms such as "today," "yesterday," "tomorrow" have at first no sharply defined temporal sense. "Today" is the expression of the present generally, "tomorrow" and "yesterday" for the future and past in general: thus certain specific temporal qualities are distinguished, but a quantitative measure, a measure of time intervals, is not attained.[62] We seem to be carried back one more step by the study of certain languages in which the qualitative differences of past and future are often totally blurred. In Ewe, one and the same adverb serves to designate both "yesterday" and "tomorrow." [63] In the Shambala language, the same word refers both to the earliest time and the distant future. "This phenomenon, which for us is so striking"—remarks one of the students of this language very aptly,

---

61. Cf. M. v. Tiling, "Die Vokale," *Zeitschrift für Kolonialsprachen,* 9, 145 ff. Such temporal indices in the noun are found frequently in the languages of the American Indians; see Boas, *Handbook, 1,* 39; Goddard, "Athapascan " ibid., *1,* 110, etc.

62. Cf. Clara and William Stern, *Die Kindersprache,* pp. 231 ff.

63. Westermann, *Grammatik der Ewe-Sprache,* p. 129; Eng. trans. by Bickford-Smith, p. 185. The same phenomenon occurs in many American languages; cf. Karl von den Steinen, *Die Bakaïri-Sprache* (Leipzig, 1892), p. 355. In Tlingit one and the same prefix *gu-* or *ga-* is used to designate future and past (Boas, *Handbook, 1,* 176), just as the Latin *olim* (from *ille*) designates the remote past and the distant future (cf. German: *einst*).

finds its natural explanation in the fact that the Ntus regard time as a thing, so that for them there is only a today and a not-today; whether the latter was yesterday or will be tomorrow is all the same to them; they do not reflect about it, since this would require not only intuition, but thought and a conceptual idea of the nature of time. . . . The concept of "time" is alien to the Shambala, they know only the intuition of time. How hard it was for us missionaries to emancipate ourselves from our concept of time and to understand the temporal intuition of the Shambala, can be seen from the fact that for years we searched for a form which designated only the future; how often we rejoiced at having found this form, only to recognize later, sometimes after a period of months, that our joy was premature, since in each instance it developed that the form we had found was also used for the past.[64]

One indication of this intuition of time as a *thing* is that time relations are expressed by *nouns* with an original spatial signification.[65] Only that segment of time as a whole which is present in consciousness at any particular time is apprehended, in opposition to other nonpresent segments, and the same material fragmentation occurs in the representation of action and activity. The unity of an action literally breaks into bits. At this stage, language can represent an action only by dissecting it into all its particulars and rendering each one separately. And this fragmentation is not a logical *analysis*—for analysis goes hand in hand with and is correlate to synthesis, in which the form of the whole is apprehended—here, on the contrary, the action is, as it were, broken materially into its components, each of which is regarded as an objective substance existing in itself. In many African languages, for example, every action is split into its parts, each of which is rendered by an independent sentence. The action is described in all its particulars, and each of these particular actions is expressed by a special verb. An event, for example, which we should express by the single sentence: "he drowned," must here be rendered by the sentences, "he drank water, died"· ;"to cut off" becomes "to cut, to fall"; the action of "bringing" becomes "take, go there." [66] Steinthal has attempted a psychological ex-

64. K. Roehl, *Versuch einer systematischen Grammatik der Schambalasprache* (Hamburg, 1911), pp. 108 ff.

65. Cf. Codrington, *The Melanesian Languages*, pp. 164 ff.

66. For examples from the Ewe and other Sudanese languages see Westermann, *Grammatik der Ewe-Sprache*, p. 95 (Eng. trans. by Bickford-Smith, p. 126), and *Die Sudansprachen*, pp. 48 ff.; from Nuba, see Reinisch, *Die Nuba-Sprache*, p. 52.

planation of this phenomenon, for which he cites examples from the Mandingan, imputing it to a "deficient condensation of representations." [67] This "deficient condensation," however, points to a fundamental peculiarity of the time representation in these languages. Since they only make the simple distinction between now and not-now, only the relatively small segment of consciousness that is immediately illumined by the light of the now, can truly exist for them. Hence the whole of an action cannot be apprehended either in thought or language unless the consciousness literally "actualizes" it in all its details, thrusting each of its stages, one after another, into the light of the now. Thus a great number of designations arise; one mosaic tile is set beside another: the product, however, has not the unity but only the variegated colors of a picture. For each detail is taken for itself and only punctually determined: such a mere aggregate of punctual presents cannot yield the percept of a true temporal continuum.

Zeno's paradox applies to the form in which these languages express motion and action; the flying arrow is fundamentally at rest, because in every moment of its motion, it possesses only *one* fixed position. The developed consciousness of time frees itself from this difficulty and paradox by creating entirely new means of apprehending a temporal "whole." Time is a substantial aggregate, pieced together from distinct moments, but is apprehended as a functional and dynamic whole: as a unity of relation and causality. The intuition of the temporal unity of action encompasses both the subject of the action and the aim toward which it is directed. The two factors are situated on entirely different planes; but the synthetic force of the concept of time consists precisely in its ability to transform their opposition into a reciprocal relation. The process of an action can no longer break down into disjoined phases, since from the very outset it now has behind it the unitary energy of the active subject and before it the unitary aim of the action. It is only when the moments of action thus join in a causal and teleological *whole*, in the unity of a dynamic synthesis and a teleological meaning, that a unified representation of time becomes possible. Where the linguistic consciousness is fully developed, language, in order to designate the whole of an action, need not represent all the details of its *course*, but contents itself with fixating the beginning and end of the action, the subject from which it emanates and the objective goal toward which it is directed. Encompassing the whole scope of this opposition in a single glance, language can now mediate it: the tension

67. Steinthal, *Die Mande-Neger-Sprachen*, p. 222.

between the two extremes has been intensified, but at the same time a spiritual spark, as it were, leaps the gap and reconciles them.

This view of the relatively complex and mediate character of the pure concept of time seems at first sight to be contradicted by our information concerning the grammar of "primitive" languages. The grammar of "primitive" peoples is reported to contain an almost inconceivable wealth of "tense forms." In the Sotho language, Endemann lists 38 affirmative tense forms, 22 potential forms, 40 conditional, 4 optative or final forms, a great number of participial forms, etc.; Roehl's grammar distinguishes 1,000 forms in the active indicative alone in Shambala.[68] The difficulty which these observations seem to raise vanishes however when we consider that according to the indications of the grammarians themselves, these forms express anything but strictly temporal nuances. We have seen that in Shambala the fundamental temporal distinction between past and future is in no way developed, and as for the so-called "tenses" in the Bantu languages, the grammars expressly state that they cannot be regarded as tenses in the strict sense since the only temporal distinction which they take into account is that of earlier or later. What all these verb forms express is not pure temporal characteristics of action, but certain qualitative and modal differences in that action. "A temporal difference," writes Seler regarding the verb in the American Indian languages, "is expressed by various particles or by combination with other verbs, but is far from playing the role in the language which the conjugations drawn up by the various clerical grammarians would lead us to suppose. And because distinctions of tense are unessential and accessory, we find the greatest differences in tense formation in otherwise closely related languages." [69] But even where language begins to express temporal specifications more clearly, it does not do so by building up a sharp, logical system of time distinctions. The first distinctions it makes are not relative, but in a sense absolute. To speak in psychological terms, it first apprehends certain temporal "gestalt qualities" in an action. It makes distinctions as to whether an action be-

68. Roehl, *Grammatik der Schambalasprache*, pp. 111 ff., and C. Meinhof, *Grammatik der Bantusprachen*, pp. 68, 75.

69. Ed. Seler, *Das Konjugationssystem der Maya-Sprachen* (Berlin, 1887), p. 30. Similarly K. v. d. Steinen says that the Bakairi language (op. cit., pp. 371 ff.) definitely does not possess tenses in our sense but uses modal terms for its verb inflexions, whose exact meaning, it must be admitted, cannot be determined from the available material and perhaps is altogether inaccessible to a European. A clear picture of the abundance of these modal shadings can be gained from Roehl's survey (pp. 111 ff.) of the verb forms in Shambala.

gins "suddenly" or develops gradually, whether it is abrupt or continuous, whether it constitutes a single undivided whole or takes place in similar, rhythmically recurrent phases. But for the concrete orientation which language still retains, these differences are not so much conceptual as intuitive, not so much quantitative as qualitative. Before proceeding to a sharp differentiation of "tenses" as true expressions of time relation, language represents the diverse "modes of action." Here time is by no means considered as a universal form of relation and order, embracing *all* events, as a totality of moments each ot which stands to the others in a specific and unambiguous relation of "before" and "after," "earlier" and "later." On the contrary, every single event expressed by a specific mood has, one might say, a "time of its own"—certain formal characteristics and modes of which are stressed. Languages vary appreciably in their relative emphasis on time distinctions and on pure modal distinctions. The Semitic languages start, not with the trichotomy of past, present and future, but with the simple dichotomy of completed and incompleted action. The "perfect," the tense of completed action can be used equally well to express the past and the present, for example it may designate an action which has begun in the past but extends into the present—on the other hand, the "imperfect," which designates an incompleted action still in process, can be used for a future, as well as a present or past action.[70] But even that linguistic family in which the pure relative concept of time and the expressions of pure temporal distinctions have achieved their highest development, did not attain to this level without numerous intermediary stages. The history of the Indo-Germanic languages shows that here too modes of action were differentiated before "tenses" proper. In the prehistoric period, writes Streitberg for example, the Indo-Germanic languages had no "tenses" at all, i.e., no formal categories whose original function it was to designate time distinctions.

The formal classes which we are accustomed to call tenses have essentially nothing whatever to do with time distinctions. All classes of present, all aorists, all perfects in all their moods are timeless, distinguished from one another only by the type of action which they desig-

---

70. For the use of "tenses" in the Semitic languages see Brockelmann, *Grundriss, 2,* 144 ff. With regard to the Ural-Altaic languages, H. Winkler points out (*Das Uralaltaische und seine Gruppen,* p. 159) that the abundance of determinative and modal qualificatives contained in the "verbal noun" so much overshadowed tense formation, the strictly verbal element, that the latter seemed secondary and almost incidental.

nate. Compared to this abundance of forms which served to differentiate modes of action, the means by which the Indo-Germanic designates time distinctions, seem modest in the extreme. For the present there was no special designation whatsoever, timeless action sufficed. The past was expressed by a temporal adverb attached to the verbal form: the augment . . . The future, finally, does not seem to have been expressed in any uniform way in the prehistoric period of the Indo-Germanic languages. One of the means of expressing it, perhaps the most original, was a modal form of probably *voluntative* significa-tion.[71]

This priority in the designation of modes of action over degrees of time is also evident, though in varying degree, in the development of the *in-dividual* Indo-Germanic languages.[72] Many of these languages have devel-oped a specific phonetic instrument for differentiating momentary and continued action; the momentary forms use the simple root vowel, while the continued forms use an intensified vowel.[73] Since G. Curtius, "punc-tual" action has generally been distinguished from "cursive" action in the Indo-Germanic languages, and more recent classifications include perfec-tive, iterative, intensive, terminative action, etc.[74] The individual Indo-Germanic languages vary considerably in the sharpness with which they make these distinctions and in the degree to which they have developed purely temporal designations;[75] but in all of them it is evident that the

71. Streitberg, "Perfektive und imperfektive Aktionsart," *Paul-Braune-Beiträge, 15* (1891), 117 ff.

72. For the Greek language cf. Brugmann, *Griechische Grammatik,* 3d ed., p. 469: "From the ur-Greek period down, every verbal concept had to enter into some relation with the mode of action, not with the category of time relation. Since the ur-Indo-Germanic period there had been many tenseless verb forms, but none without mood." A comparison of the Homeric with the old Attic language shows that it became the rule only very gradually to express clear time relations by means of the verb (ibid.).

73. In the Greek for example, roots like λαβ, πιθ, φυγ are used in the first function, while λαμβ, πειθ, φευγ are used in the second. Cf. G. Curtius, "Zur Chronologie der indoger-manischen Sprachforschung," *Abhandlungen der Königlich Sächsischen Gesellschaft der Wissenschaften,* Philol.-hist. Classe, Vol. 5 (Leipzig, 1867), No. 3, 229 ff.

74. Cf. G. Curtius, "Die Bildung der Tempora und Modi im Griechischen und Latein-ischen," *Sprachvergleichende Beiträge, 1* (1846), 150 ff.

75. In the Germanic system of inflections, modal distinctions diminish in importance at an early date, although they remain clearly discernible in certain isolated phenomena. Cf. H. Paul, "Die Umschreibung des Perfektums im Deutschen mit haben und sein," *Abhand-lungen der Königlich Bayerischen Akademie der Wissenschaften,* Classe 1, Vol. 22 (Munich, 1902), Pt. 1, 161 ff. However, they still play a prominent part in the Baltic-Slavic languages, which have preserved the distinction between "perfective" and "imperfective" action and

precise designation of time distinctions is a relatively late product, while the expression of the general "temporal gestalt" of a process or action seems to belong to an early stratum of thought and speech.

Farthest removed from the primary level of temporal intuition are those linguistic terms which presuppose a form of time *measurement* and consequently consider time as a sharply determined quantity. Here, to be sure, we face a problem which points beyond the sphere of language and which can only find its solution in the "artificial" systems of signs developed by scientific reflection. And yet language provides a decisive groundwork for this new achievement: for the numerical signs which constitute the foundation of all exact mathematical and astronomical measurement, could not have developed without numerical *words*. In three diverse but closely related phases, language develops the three basic intuitions of space, time and number and so creates the indispensable condition for all intellectual mastery of phenomena and for every synthesis of these phenomena into the unity of a "world concept."

3. The Linguistic Development of the Concept of Number

In progressing from the idea of space to that of time, and from these two in turn to the idea of *number*, we seem to round out the world of intuition and at the same time to be referred to something beyond it. The world of tangible *forms* seems to recede, and in its place a new world gradually arises: a world of intellectual *principles*. In this sense, the "nature" of number was determined by its true philosophical and scientific discoverers, the Pythagoreans. Proclus says that Pythagoras first raised geometry to the level of a free science by arriving at its principles deductively ($\check{\alpha}\nu o\theta\epsilon\nu$) and representing its theorems in immaterial and purely rational terms ($\dot{\alpha}\dot{\nu}\lambda\omega\varsigma$ $\kappa\alpha\grave{\iota}$ $\nu o\epsilon\rho\hat{\omega}\varsigma$).[76] The universal tendency thus imprinted upon scientific mathematics by its first founder has since then been further intensified and deepened. Through Plato, Descartes and Leibniz it has been imparted to modern mathematics. And in trying to construct geometry

---

divide all verbs into two classes accordingly. Cf. Leskien, *Grammatik der altbulgarischen (altkirchen-slawischen) Sprache* (Heidelberg, 1909), pp. 215 ff.

76. Proclus in *Euclid*, p. 64, ed. G. Friedlein.

and analysis out of *one* principle, the modern interpretation finds itself forced back—even more than was ancient mathematics—upon the concept of number as its true center. More and more clearly, the work devoted to the conceptual foundation of mathematics turns toward this central point. And nineteenth-century mathematicians strove increasingly to arrive at a concept of number as a logically autonomous formation. This aim was pursued along different paths by Dedekind and Russell, by Frege and Hilbert. Russell attempted to reduce all the basic factors underlying number to pure "logical constants"; Frege saw number as an "attribute," but an immaterial attribute attaching to an immaterial content, not so much the attribute of a "thing," as of a pure *concept*. In laying the groundwork and derivation of the concept of number, Dedekind just as resolutely avoided any link with intuitive relations or measurable quantities. The realm of number, he held, is not to be built on the intuition of space and time; it is just the reverse; the concept of number, an "immediate emanation of the pure laws of thought," can alone enable us to gain precise concepts of space and time. It is only by creating the pure and continuous realm of numbers through a finite system of simple logical operations, free from any representation of measurable quantities, that the spirit develops a clear representation of continuous space.[77] All these tendencies are rooted in the exact sciences; critical logic merely sums them up when it proceeds from the assumption that the first prerequisite for the understanding of number lies in the insight that number deals not with any given things but with pure laws of thought. "To derive number from things," writes Natorp, "is clearly circular reasoning if by derive we mean explain. For the concepts of things are complex concepts, into which number enters as one of their indispensable components. . . . For thought there can be nothing more fundamental than thought itself, that is: the positing of relations. Whatever else might be claimed as the foundation of number would include precisely this positing of relations and can only appear to be the foundation of number because it contains as a presupposition this true foundation, this positing of relations."[78]

But, however firmly "pure," scientific thought stands its ground and con-

77. R. Dedekind, *Was sind und was wollen die Zahlen* (1887); cf. G. Frege, *Die Grundlagen der Arithmetik* (Breslau, 1884); B. Russell, *The Principles of Mathematics, 1* (Cambridge, 1903).

78. P. Natorp, *Die logischen Grundlagen der exakten Wissenschaften* (Leipzig and Berlin, B. G. Teubner, 1910), pp. 98 ff.

sciously rejects all support and assistance from sensation and intuition, it seems nevertheless to retain strong ties with language and its concepts. The reciprocal bond between language and thought is once again manifested in the logical and linguistic development of *numerical concepts,* which are perhaps its clearest and most characteristic expression. Only the formation of number as a *verbal sign* opens the road to an understanding of its pure conceptual nature. Thus the numerical signs created by language represent the indispensable prerequisite for the "numbers" of pure mathematics; and yet, between linguistic and purely intellectual symbols there remains an inevitable tension and an *opposition* that can never be fully reconciled. Though language prepares the way for these symbols, it cannot pursue this road to its end. The form of "relational" thought which makes possible the representation of pure numerical concepts, constitutes for language an ultimate goal, which it continuously approaches in its development but can never fully attain.[79] For language cannot take the decisive step which mathematical thought demands of numerical concepts, namely their characteristic detachment and emancipation from the foundations of intuition and the intuitive representation of things. It clings to the designation of concrete objects and concrete processes and cannot free itself from them even when it seeks mediately to express pure relations. But again the dialectical principle of progress is confirmed: the more language, in the course of its development, seems to immerse itself in the expression of sensuous things, the more effectively it contributes to the spiritual process of liberation from the sensuous. It is through material enumerable things, however sensuous, concrete and limited its first representation of these things may be, that language develops the new form and the new logical force that are contained in number.

But this form does not appear all at once as a self-contained whole, it must gradually be built up from its separate factors. It is precisely this fact that makes inquiry into the origin and development of the numerical concepts in language valuable to logical analysis. The logical content of number derives from an interpenetration of quite different methods and requirements of thought. In number multiplicity seems to merge with unity, analysis with synthesis, thorough differentiation with pure similarity. Before the "exact" concept of number could take form, all these oppositions had to be placed in purely intellectual balance with one another. This, language cannot do; nevertheless, we can follow plainly how in lan-

79. Cf. Chapter 5, below.

guage those threads which are ultimately woven into the intricate mesh of number tie in with one another and form themselves in detail before they constitute a logical whole. In different languages this development takes different forms. Different factors of number formation are favored and emphasized—but the aggregate of all these particular and in a sense one-sided insights, which language gains into the concept of number, constitutes a relatively unitary whole. Although language of itself cannot fill out the intellectual circle in which the concept of number lies, it can circumscribe it in all its scope and thus mediately prepare the way for a definition of its content and limits.

This process begins in very much the same way as the approach of language to simple spatial relations. The differentiation of numbers starts, like that of spatial relations, from the human body and its members, thence extending over the whole of the sensuous, intuitive world. Everywhere man's own body provides the model for the first primitive enumeration: the first "counting" consists merely in designating certain differences found in external objects, by transferring them, as it were, to the body of the counter and so making them visible. All numerical concepts, accordingly, are purely mimetic hand concepts or other body concepts before they become verbal concepts. The counting gesture does not serve as a mere accompaniment to an otherwise independent numeral, but fuses in a sense with its signification and substance. The Ewe, for example, count on their outstretched fingers; beginning with the little finger of the left hand and turning back the counted finger with the pointer of their right hand: after the left hand, they do the same with the right hand; then they either begin again from the beginning or squat on the ground and continue counting on their toes.[80] In Nuba the gesture that accompanies counting usually consists in pressing first the little finger, then the ring finger, middle finger, index and thumb of the left hand into the fist of the right hand and then reversing the hands. At the number twenty, the two fists are pressed together horizontally.[81] Similarly, v. d. Steinen reports that among the Bakairi the simplest attempt at counting was doomed to failure unless the object counted, a handful of corn kernels, for example, was immediately present to the touch. "The right hand felt . . . the left hand reckoned. Even where there were only three kernels, it was absolutely impossible for them to count the grains on the fingers of the left

80. Westermann, *Grammatik der Ewe-Sprache*, p. 80; Eng. trans. by Bickford-Smith, p. 101.
81. Reinisch, *Die Nuba-Sprache*, pp. 36 ff.

hand merely by looking at them." [82] As we see, it does not suffice at this stage for counted objects to be *referred* to the parts of the body; in order to be counted, they must in a sense be immediately *transposed* into parts of the body or bodily sensations. Thus the numerals do not so much designate objective attributes or relations of objects, as embody certain directives for the bodily gesture of counting. They are terms and indices for positions of the hands or fingers, and are often couched in the imperative form of the verb. In Sotho, for example, the word for "five" means literally "complete the hand," that for "six" means "jump," i.e., jump to the other hand.[83] This active character of the so-called "numerals" is particularly evident in those languages where the form of the numeral indicates the manner in which the objects counted are placed or grouped. The Klamath language, for example, has a variety of "numerals" formed from verbs of setting, laying, placing, each indicating a particular type of arrangement, according to the specific character of the objects to be counted. One class of objects must be spread out on the ground in order to be counted, another must be piled in layers, one must be divided into heaps, another arranged in rows—and to each specific arrangement of the objects corresponds a different "numeral classifier." [84] By this method, the motions of arranging the objects are coordinated with certain bodily motions which are conceived as running in a certain order. These motions need not be limited to the hands and feet, the fingers and toes, but can extend to other parts of the body. In British New Guinea, the sequence in counting runs from the fingers of the left hand to the wrist, the elbow, the shoulder, the left side of the neck, the left breast, the chest, the right breast, the right side of the neck, etc.; in other regions the shoulder, the clavicular hollow, the navel, the neck, or the nose, eye, and ear are used.[85]

The intellectual value of primitive counting methods has often been disparaged. Steinthal writes for example in his discussion of the counting methods of the Mandingos:

82. K. v. d. Steinen, *Unter den Naturvölkern Zentral-Brasiliens* (2d ed., Berlin, D. Reimer, 1897), p. 86.

83. Cf. Meinhof, *Grammatik der Bantusprachen*, p. 58; similar examples from the Papuan languages in Ray, *Torres Straits Expedition*, p. 373, etc. In the Eskimo language the number 20 is expressed by the sentence "a man is completed," i.e., all his fingers and toes are counted. See W. Thalbitzer in Boas, *Handbook, 1*, p. 1047.

84. J. W. Powell, *The Evolution of Language* (Smithsonian Institution, Washington), *Annual Report*, No. 1, p. 21; Gatschet, *Klamath Language*, pp. 532 ff.

85. See Ray, *Torres Straits Expedition*, p. 364; cf. in particular the abundant material in Lévy-Bruhl, *How Natives Think* (London, 1926), pp. 181 ff.

The intellectual guilt which burdens the spirit of the Negro is that once arrived at the toe he did not depart from this material prop and multiply the toe by his own free creation, extending the short series to a long one; that instead, clinging to the body, he descended from the hand, that noble instrument of instruments, the servant of the spirit, to the dust-burrowing foot, the slave of the body. Thus number adhered to the body and did not become an abstract numerical concept. The Negro has no number but only a sum of fingers, fingers of the hand and foot; his is not the spirit which, impelled by a striving for the infinite, always passes beyond the specific number, adding one from out of itself; no, the existing particulars, the things of nature, led him from one to one, from the little finger to the thumb, from the left to the right hand, from the hand to the foot, from one man to another; never did his spirit intervene, creating freely, but crawled around in nature. . . . That is not the act which our spirit performs when it counts.[86]

But in the half-poetical, half-theological pathos of his diatribe, Steinthal forgets that it is far more fruitful to seek out and recognize the intellectual content of this method, however slight, than to measure it by our fully developed concept of number. Here, of course, we cannot speak of any system or general organization of numeric concepts. But one thing is accomplished: a very definite order is observed in passing from one member of a manifold to another, even though this manifold is determined in a purely sensuous way. In the act of counting, one part of the body does not follow another arbitrarily, the right hand follows the left, the foot follows the hand, the neck, breast, shoulder follow the hands and feet in accordance with a schema of succession which is conventional, to be sure, but is in any case strictly observed. The instituting of such a schema, though far from exhausting the content of what more highly developed thought understands by "number," nevertheless provides its indispensable groundwork. For even pure mathematical number resolves ultimately into a system of positions, into an "order in progression," as Hamilton has called it. True, the crucial weakness of the primitive counting method seems to be that it does not freely create this order in accordance with a spiritual principle but draws it solely from given things, particularly the articulation of the counter's own body. But even this method with its undeniable passivity, manifests

86. Steinthal, *Die Mande-Neger-Sprachen*, pp. 75 ff.

a characteristic spontaneity, though indeed only in germ. In apprehending material objects not only according to what they individually and immediately *are*, but according to the manner in which they are *ordered*, the spirit begins to advance from the concretion of objects to the concretion of acts: and through these acts, the acts of combination and differentiation which it performs, it will ultimately arrive at the new "intellectual" principle of number.

For the present, however, the ability to observe an order in progression from one object to another remains merely an isolated factor, which has not yet been attuned to the other factors necessary for the formation of the pure concept of number. There is indeed a certain coordination between the counted objects and the parts of the human body which function as expressions of number: but this coordination remains vague, it remains a kind of wholesale coordination, until the series compared can themselves be broken down into distinct "units." This can only be done, however, if the elements to be counted are regarded as strictly *similar*—so that each element is distinguished from the others through the *position* it occupies in the counting and by no other material attribute. For the present, however, we are far removed from the abstraction of such a "homogeneity." The counted objects must be present in all their tangible concretion, so that they can be immediately touched and felt, and the counting units themselves are differentiated only by concrete sensuous characteristics. In place of purely abstract, uniform *conceptual* units, we have only such natural things as the articulation of the human body offers. Primitive "arithmetic" finds its elements only in such natural groups. One system is distinguished from another by the material standard on which it is based. The use of one hand as a model gives rise to the quinary system, the use of both hands to the decimal system, the use of hands and feet, to the vigesimal system.[87] And there are other counting methods which are inferior even to these simplest attempts at group and system formation. However, such limitations in "counting" should not be interpreted as an inability to recognize and differentiate concrete groups. Even where actual counting has not progressed beyond the first meager beginnings, the differentiation of such groups can be highly developed—for this requires only that each specific group be recognized by some general qualitative characteristic, and not that the group itself be articulated and quantitatively defined as a

87. A rich collection of examples is to be found in A. F. Pott, *Die quinare und die vige-simale Zählmethode bei Völkern aller Weltteile* (Halle, 1847).

"sum of units." The Abipones, whose faculty of counting was only partially developed, are reported to have been extremely expert at distinguishing concrete groups. If a single member of the large packs of dogs which they took with them on hunting expeditions were lacking, it was noticed at once, and likewise the owner of a herd of four to five hundred cattle could recognize even at a distance whether any were missing and which ones.[88] Here individual groups are recognized and differentiated by some individual characteristic: in so far as one can speak of "number," it appears not in the form of a specific measured magnitude, but as a kind of concrete *numerical gestalt,* an intuitive quality adhering to a totally unarticulated general impression of quantity.[89]

This fundamental conception is clearly reflected in language which originally had no *universal* numerals applicable to all enumerable objects, but used different numerical designations for different classes of objects. As long as number is seen as a quality of things, there must fundamentally be as many diverse numbers and groups of numbers as there are different classes of things. If the number of a quantity of objects is regarded only as a qualitative attribute, belonging to the things in exactly the same way as a specific spatial formation or sensuous property, language cannot abstract it from other attributes and give it a universal form of expression. At primitive levels of language formation we do actually find that the designation of number is fused with the designation of things and attributes. The same term serves to express the nature of the object and its numerical character. There are words which express at the same time a particular class of objects and a particular group character of these objects. In the language of the Fiji Islands, for example, different words are used to designate groups of two, ten, a hundred, a thousand coconuts, or a group of ten canoes, ten fish, etc.[90] And even after the numeral has become independent of the designation of things and attributes, it continues to attach itself as far as possible to the manifold diversity of things and attributes.

---

88. M. Dobrizhoffer, *Historia de Abiponibus* (Vienna, 1784), Eng. trans., *An Account of the Abipones* (London, 1822); cf. Pott, pp. 5, 17, etc.

89. Regarding this qualitative character of the first numbers and of counting, cf. the excellent, richly documented expositions of Wertheimer in "Das Denken der Naturvölker," *Zeitschrift für Psychologie, 60* (1912), 321 ff.

90. H. C. v. d. Gabelentz, *Die melanesischen Sprachen,* p. 23; cf. Codrington, *The Melanesian Languages,* p. 241. Similar collective terms are found in the Melanesian languages of New Guinea, which for example use a separate undivided word to designate 4 bananas or 4 coconuts, 10 pigs, 10 long objects, etc. Cf. Ray, *Torres Straits Expedition, 3,* 475.

Not every number applies to every thing: it does not yet express abstract multiplicity as such, but expresses the mode, class and form of a concrete multiplicity. In the American Indian languages, for example, different groups of numerals are used to designate persons or things, animate or inanimate objects. Or a different group of numerals may be used to designate fishes or pelts, standing, lying or sitting objects. The Moanu Islanders have different sets of numbers from one to ten for coconuts or men, spirits and animals, trees, canoes and villages, houses, poles and plantations.[91] In the Tsimshian language of British Columbia there are special series of numerals for counting flat objects and animals, round objects and time intervals, men, boats, long objects and measurements;[92] in other, neighboring languages the differentiation of the various series of numerals goes even further and seems almost unlimited.[93] As we see, enumeration is by no means oriented toward "homogeneity." The tendency of language is rather to subordinate the quantitative difference to the generic difference expressed in its classifications and to modify the expression of quantitative difference accordingly. This tendency is evident even where language has progressed to the point of using universal numerals, but where each numeral is still followed by a specific *determinative* indicating the particular class to which the group belongs. Seen intuitively and concretely, there is obviously a great difference between the gathering of men into a "group" and the gathering of stones into a "heap," between a "row" of resting objects or a "swarm" of moving objects, etc. Language seeks to retain such classifications and shadings in the choice of its collective terms and in the regularity with which it combines such words with actual numerals. In the Malayo-Polynesian languages, for example, numerals are not directly attached to substantives, but instead to certain determinatives which are required to classify the group. The term for "five horses" is literally "horses, five tails," for "four stones" it is "stones, four round bodies" etc.[94] In the Mexican languages, the expression of number and of the enumerated object is likewise followed by a term of group classification, which differs for

91. Cf. P. Jos. Meyer in *Anthropos, 1*, 228 (quoted by Wertheimer, op. cit., p. 342).

92. Cf. J. W. Powell, *Introduction to the Study of Indian Languages* (2d ed., Washington, 1880), p. 25, and the compilation of different classes of numerals (numerals for flat objects, round objects, long objects, human beings, measurements) in Boas, "Tsimshian" (*Handbook, 1*, 396 ff.).

93. Cf. the examples collected by Levy-Bruhl from the linguistic and ethonological literature.

94. Cf. Müller, *Novara-Reise*, pp. 275, 303; Codrington, *The Melanesian Languages*, p. 148; H. C. v. d. Gabelentz, *Die melanesischen Sprachen*, pp. 23, 255.

example for round and cylindrical objects like eggs and beans, or for long rows of persons, things, walls, and furrows, etc.[95] The Japanese and Chinese have developed a particularly subtle system of "numeratives," differentiated according to the class of objects numbered. These languages, which lack the general grammatical distinction between singular and plural, are extremely strict in their insistence that a collective grouping be designated according to its specific character. While in the process of abstract enumeration the units must be emptied of all intrinsic content before they can be combined with one another, here this content subsists and determines the specific type of grouping into collective units, groups and multiplicities.[96] Here both thought and language are far more concerned with identifying and differentiating certain groups than with breaking down these groups themselves into units and particulars: they characterize a multiplicity by apprehending its general intuitive content and so distinguishing it from others, not by building it up logically and mathematically from its constitutive elements.

In the means by which language carries out the formal and universal distinction between singular and plural, we encounter the same basic approach. If we consider the idea of plural as implying the logical and mathematical category of "plurality," i.e., the category of a multiplicity constructed of distinct, similar units, we find that many languages have no plural at all. A great number of languages lack forms by which to designate the antithesis between singular and plural. The substantive in its basic form can serve equally well to designate a class embodying an indeterminate number of individuals, or to designate a single member of the class. It lies halfway between a singular and a plural signification and in a manner of speaking has not yet decided between the two. Only in special cases, where the distinction seems essential, it is indicated by special linguistic means, and often it is the singular rather than the plural signification that is so distinguished. Thus, for example, the Malayo-Polynesian languages, according to Fr. Müller, "have never risen to the concept of number as a category encompassing a multiplicity in a living unity," so that their substantives are neither truly concrete nor truly abstract, but are something between the two. "To the Malay, 'man' means neither a man *in concreto* nor man = mankind *in abstracto*, but designates men whom

---

95. For details, see Buschmann in his notes on Humboldt's *Kawi-Werk*, 2, 269 ff.

96. Cf. the system of Japanese and Chinese "numeratives" in Hoffmann, *Japanische Sprachlehre*, pp. 149 ff.

one has seen and knows. However, the word (ôran) corresponds more to our plural than to our singular, and the singular must be indicated by a word meaning 'one.' "[97] Here then we are not dealing with a bare conceptual unity which takes on a plural signification through a morphological change; instead, we have an undifferentiated multiple to which a plural signification can be given by the addition of certain nouns with a general collective sense, and a singular signification by the use of certain individualizing particles.[98] The same intuition of the singular-plural relationship is to be found in many of the Altaic languages, where one and the same word without grammatical differentiation can be used to express both singular and plural. This appellative can designate the individual, the whole genus, or an indeterminate number of individuals.[99] But even in those languages which have developed a clear formal distinction between singular and plural, there are phenomena which make it apparent that this strict distinction was preceded by a stage of relative indifference. Often a word with the outward form of a plural is treated grammatically as a singular and is conjugated with the singular form of the verb, because its fundamental signification is felt to be not so much a discreet plurality as a simple collective whole.[100] In ur-Indo-Germanic and Greek the neuter plural is linked with a singular verb because the ending -a of these nouns originally had no plural signification but went back to the feminine singular ending -a which was used for collective abstractions. Thus the forms in -a were originally neither plural nor singular, but simply collectives, which could be construed in either way as the need arose.[101]

97. Fr. Müller, *Novara-Reise*, pp. 274 ff.; cf. for the Australian languages, pp. 246 ff.; see also Fr. Müller, *Gundriss*, 2, Pt. 2, 114 ff.

98. Cf. Codrington, *The Melanesian Languages*, pp. 148 ff.; H. C. v. d. Gabelentz, *Die melanesischen Sprachen*, pp. 23, 255.

99. Cf. Böthlingk, *Über die Sprache der Jakuten*, pp. 340 ff.; H. Winkler, *Der Uralaltaische Sprachstamm*, p. 137; on the "plural formation" in the Altaic languages see also Grunzel, *Vergleichende Grammatik der altaischen Sprachen*, pp. 47 ff.

100. In Egyptian, according to Erman (*Ägyptische Grammatik*, pp. 108 ff.), many concepts that are purely plural in meaning are rendered by collective abstract nouns in the singular form, and the form of the verbal predicate is transposed accordingly. Similarly in the South Semitic languages, according to Brockelmann (*Grundriss*, 1, 437 ff.; cf. 2, 77 ff.), the boundaries between singular, collective and plural are still in constant flux, so that collectives can revert to the singular by a slight phonetic shift and then form a new plural. For the Indo-Germanic family see the examples from the Romance languages given by Meyer-Lübke, *Grammatik der romanischen Sprachen*, 2, 69 ff.; 2, 26 ff.

101. From the ur-Indo-Germanic period on, according to Brugmann, a noun was put in the singular if its content was conceived as unitary and no articulation of the unit was taken

On the other hand, we find that analogously to what has been observed in the process of counting, language does not abruptly juxtapose an abstract category of unity to an abstract of plurality, but finds all manner of gradations and transitions between them. The first pluralities that it distinguishes are not general but specific pluralities, with a distinctive qualitative character. Aside from the use of dual and trial, many languages employ a double plural; that is, a narrow form for two or a few objects, and another for many objects. This usage, which Dobrizhoffer found in the language of the Abipones,[102] has its exact counterpart in the Semitic languages, for example the Arabic.[102a] In his account of the plural forms in Arabic (which beside the dual has a limited plural for 3 to 9 and a multiple plural for 10 and over, or for an indeterminate number of objects), Humboldt remarks that the underlying conception, which in a sense situates the generic concept outside the category of number, so that both singular and plural are distinguished from it by inflection, must "undeniably be called a very philosophical one." [103] In truth, however, this generic concept does not seem to be conceived in its determinate generic character and thus *raised above* the category of number; on the contrary, the category of number does not yet seem to have entered into this form. The distinction which language expresses by singular and plural has not been taken up into the genus; indeed, it has not yet been sharply drawn; the quantitative opposition of unity and multiplicity has not yet been overcome by a qualitative unity which encompasses them both, because for the present this opposition has not yet been clearly determined. The unity of the genus signifies a distinct *one,* opposed to the no less distinct multiplicity of its members—but in the indeterminate collective signification, from which in many languages both singular and plural significations crystallize out, the decisive factor is precisely indistinctness. The multiplicity is regarded as a mere heap or mass, hence as a sensuous, not as a logical whole. Its universality is that of an impression, which has not yet been broken down into its separate elements and components, not that

---

into account; the plural on the other hand was used where several members of a class or several separate occurrences and actions were distinguished, or a concept was regarded as plural in character. Brugmann, *Kurze vergleichende Grammatik der indogermanischen Sprachen* (Strassburg, K. J. Trübner), p. 413; *Griechische Grammatik,* 3d ed., pp. 369 ff.

102. Dobrizhoffer, *Historia de Abiponibus,* 2, 166 ff. (quoted in Humboldt, "Über den Dualis," *Werke, 6,* No. 1, 10 ff.); Eng. trans., 2, 162 ff.

102a. Cf. Brockelmann, *Grundriss, 1,* 436 ff.

103. "Über den Dualis," p. 20.

of a concept above them all, encompassing the particular as something separated out and distinct.

But it is precisely through this fundamental factor of *separation* that the strict concept of *number* can arise from the mere notion of a group and multiplicity. So far we have seen two paths by which language approaches this concept, which characteristically it can apprehend only in a sensuous cloak. On the one hand, linguistic thought, even in those primitive counting methods oriented toward the parts of the human body, fixated the factor of "order in progression." If these methods of counting were to produce any result at all, they could not pass arbitrarily from one part of the body to another but had to observe some rule of progression. On the other hand, it was the impression of multiplicity as such, the consciousness of a still indeterminate whole which is in some way divided into "parts," that guided language in its formation of general collective terms. In both cases, the idea of number and its linguistic expression seem bound up with the fundamental forms of intuition, with the intuition of spatial and temporal reality. Epistemological analysis shows how the two forms must work together in order to produce the essential content of the concept of number. In apprehending collective "togetherness," number bases itself on the intuition of space, but it requires the intuition of time in order to form the characteristic counterpart of this specification, the concept of *distributive unity and particularity*. For the logical problem which number must solve consists not only in fulfilling these two requirements separately but in apprehending them as one. Every numerically defined multiplicity is at the same time conceived and apprehended as a unit, and every unit as a multiplicity. Now it is true that this correlative union of opposing factors recurs in every fundamental act of consciousness. The elements which enter into the synthesis of consciousness are not simply left to stand side by side, but are apprehended as the expression and product of one and the same fundamental act—synthesis is made to appear as analysis, analysis as synthesis. But necessary as is this interdetermination, one or the other of the two factors may assert its preponderance in the general synthesis, according to the specific character of the problem involved. In the exact mathematical concept of number a pure equilibrium seems to be achieved between the function of analysis and synthesis; here the requirements of unification into a whole and of absolute discreteness of elements are both ideally fulfilled. In the consciousness of time and space, however, one of these factors predominates. In space the favored factor is the coexistence and mutual involvement of elements; in time it is their succession and separateness. We cannot intuit or conceive a *particular* spatial form unless at the same time we represent the space as a *whole* "in" which it is contained: the particularity of the form is possible only as a limitation of all-encompassing "unitary" space. On the other hand, although the temporal moment is what it is because it appears as a factor in a sequence, this very sequence can be constituted only if every single moment excludes all others, if we represent a simple, indivisible "now," a pure punctual present, which is absolutely differentiated from the past and the future. The concrete idea of number, as expressed in language, makes use of both achievements, that of the spatial and that of the temporal consciousness, and through them develops two different factors of number. Through the differentiation of spatial objects, language arrives at its concept of collective multiplicity—through the differentiation of temporal acts, it arrives at its expression of particularity and separation. This twofold content of number seems to be clearly manifested in plural formation, which may be governed either by the intuition of complexes of things or by the rhythmically recurrent phases of a specific temporal process; in the one case it is oriented predominantly toward objective totalities consisting of multiple parts, in the other toward the repetition of events or actions linked together in an unbroken sequence.

And indeed, those languages which are predominantly *verbal* in structure have developed a characteristic, purely "distributive" conception of the plural, differing sharply from the collective conception. In these languages a sharp characterization of verbal acts seems to underlie the whole notion of plurality. The language of the Klamath Indians, for example, has developed no specific instrument for distinguishing between the designation of *particular* objects and the designation of a *multiplicity* of objects. Instead, it distinguishes accurately and logically between an event consisting only in a single temporal act and an event embracing several phases different in time, but similar in content. "To the observing mind of the primeval Klamath Indian," Gatschet writes, "the fact that sundry things were done repeatedly, at different times, or that the same thing was done severally by distinct persons, appeared much more important than the pure idea of *plurality*, as we have it in our language. This category of severalty impressed itself on his mind so forcibly that he rendered and symbolized it in a very appropriate manner by means of the *distributive reduplication* of the first syllable." In the Klamath, all expressions of the "plural" in our

sense are demonstrably of recent origin, whereas the idea of breaking down
an act into a plurality of similar processes is sharply designated by means
of reduplication which permeates the whole language down to its post-
positions and certain adverbial particles.[104] Hupa, a language of the Athapascan group, often uses the singular where we would use the plural,
namely when a plurality of individuals participate in an action but the
action itself appears as a unit. Even here, however, the distributive relation is always precisely designated by the use of a special prefix.[105] And
reduplication occurs in the same function in other language groups.[106]
Here again an intrinsically abstract concept has found its immediate sensuous expression in language. The simple phonetic repetition is both the
most primitive and the most effective means of designating the rhythmic
recurrence and the rhythmic articulation of an act, particularly of a human activity. Here perhaps, if anywhere, we can gain some insight into
the earliest motives of language formation and into the relationship between language and art. Attempts have been made to trace the beginnings
of poetry back to those first primitive *work songs* in which for the first
time the rhythm felt by man in his own physical movements was, as it
were, objectified. Bücher's compendious study of work and rhythm has
shown how these work songs are still to be met with all over the world,
and how similar they are to one another in their basic structure. Every form
of physical labor, particularly when performed by a group, occasions a
specific coordination of movements, which leads in turn to a rhythmic
organization and punctuation of work phases. This rhythm is manifested
to the consciousness in two ways: in pure motor sensation, in the alterna-
tion of muscular tension and relaxation, and on the other hand objectively,
in auditory perceptions, in the regularity of the sounds accompanying the
work. Consciousness of the activity and its nuances is bound up with these
sensuous differences. Grinding and rubbing, pushing and pulling, pressing
and trampling: each is distinguished by a rhythm and tone quality of
its own. In all the vast variety of work songs, in the songs of spinners and
weavers, threshers and oarsmen, millers and bakers, etc., we can still hear

104. Gatschet, *Klamath Language*, pp. 419, 464, 611.

105. Goddard, "Athapascan" (Hupa), in Boas, *Handbook*, *1*, 104; cf. Boas, "Kwakiutl"
(op. cit., *1*, 444): "The idea of plurality is not clearly developed. Reduplication of a noun
expresses rather the occurrence of an object here and there, or of different kinds of a particular
object, than plurality. It is therefore rather a distributive than a true plural. It seems that this
form is gradually assuming a purely plural significance."

106. Cf. the use of reduplication in designating the "distributive" plural in the Hamite
languages. See Meinhof, *Die Sprachen der Hamiten*, pp. 25, 171.

with a certain immediacy how a specific rhythmic sense, determined by the character of the task, can only subsist and enter into the work if it is at the same time objectified in sound.[107] And perhaps certain forms of reduplication in the verb, expressive of an act containing a number of rhythmically recurrent phases, grew out of an objectivization of this sort, originating in man's own activity. In any case, language could acquire consciousness of the pure forms of time and number only through association with certain contents, certain fundamental rhythmic experiences, in which the two forms seem to be given in immediate concretion and fusion. Here, it is a differentiation of acts rather than of things which gave rise to "distribution" as one of the basic factors of enumeration. This seems to be confirmed by the fact that many languages employ a plural verb not only where there is an actual plurality of subjects, but also where a *single* subject directs one and the same action toward different objects.[108] Where the intuition of plurality is oriented toward the pure form of the act itself, the number of individuals participating in an action is secondary, the essential question is whether the action is performed in one or several phases.

So far we have considered the part played by the basic forms of pure intuition, the forms of space and time, in the development of numbers and plurals. Yet perhaps we have not yet penetrated to the deepest and most fundamental root of the enumerative act. For our inquiry cannot be restricted to objectivity and to distinctions within the objective world

107. Cf. Bücher, *Arbeit und Rhythmus.*

108. This corresponds exactly to the reverse phenomenon which we have just (p. 240) observed in the Hupa language, where the singular of the verb is used even with a plurality of subjects if the action itself (such as the execution of a dance) is regarded as an indivisible unit; in most of the American Indian languages a transitive verb occurs in the plural when its direct *object* is plural, that is, when the action is directed toward several objects and is thus looked upon as split. In other languages as well, the use of the plural in the verb depends not so much on the plurality of the subject as of the object, or upon both at once. (Examples from the Kivai, a Papuan language, are given by Ray, *Torres Straits Expedition, 3,* 311 ff.; among the African languages, Nuba, for example, draws a distinction in the verb form according to whether the object of the action is singular or plural (Reinisch, *Die Nuba-Sprache,* pp. 56 ff., 69 ff.). Tagalog, which is described in detail by Humboldt in his *Kawi-Werk,* often attaches a certain plural prefix to the verb in order to indicate the plurality of the subject, but also to indicate that the action consists in different parts or is repeated. In this case the concept of plurality refers sometimes to the actors, sometimes to the action or its more or less frequent performance. Thus, for example, *mag-súlat* (from *sulat* "to write") has both the common plural meaning of "many write" and the frequentative meaning of "he writes much," or it can express an "habitual mood" ("it is his business to write"). Cf. Humboldt, *2,* 317, 376.

of space and time; it must also return to the fundamental oppositions arising from pure subjectivity. There are numerous indications that language drew its first numerical distinctions from this sphere—that the first consciousness of number arose not so much through perception of the material togetherness and apartness of objects or events as of the opposition between the "I" and the "thou." This sphere would seem to disclose a far subtler differentiation, a far greater sensitivity to the distinction between "one" and "many," than occurs in the field of mere objective perceptions. Many languages which have not developed a true plural form of the noun, disclose a plural form of the personal pronoun; [109] others possess two different plural signs, one of which is used exclusively for pronouns.[110] Often the plural of a noun is expressed only in the case of animate and rational beings, not in the case of inanimate objects.[111] In the Yakut, garments and parts of the body usually stand in the singular, even though two or several of them are present in *one* individual, but they are placed in the plural if they belong to several persons; [112] thus the distinction of number is here developed more sharply for the intuition of individuals than for the intuition of mere objects.

In the enumerations arising from this personal sphere we again encounter that same correlation between number and object enumerated, which we have discussed above. We have seen that the first numerical terms originated in specific, concrete enumerations and seem to retain their color. This characteristic coloration is most apparent where the number arises

109. For the American language cf., for example, Roland B. Dixon's account of Maidu (Boas, *Handbook, 1,* 683 ff.): "Ideas of number are unequally developed in Maidu. In nouns, the exact expression of number seems to have been felt as a minor need; whereas, in the case of pronominal forms, number is clearly and accurately expressed" (p. 708). Also in the Melanesian, as in the Polynesian and Indonesian languages, number is sharply differentiated in the pronoun; cf. Codrington, *The Melanesian Languages,* p. 110, and H. C. v. d. Gabelentz, *Die melanesischen Sprachen,* p. 37. Bakairi, which knows no difference between singular and dual and has no general designation of the plural, shows suggestions of a plural form in the first and second persons of the pronoun; cf. v. d. Steinen, *Die Bakaïri-Sprache,* pp. 324, 349 ff.

110. This is the case in Tibetan for example; cf. J. J. Schmidt, *Grammatik der tibetanischen Sprache* (Petersburg, 1839), pp. 63 ff.

111. Varied examples of this usage in Fr. Müller, *Grundriss, 2,* Pt. 1, 261, 314 ff.; *3,* Pt. 2, 50; for the Melanesian languages see v. d. Gabelentz, op. cit., p. 87. In Hupa only few nouns have a plural form: those which indicate a man's age or rank or a relation of kinship (Goddard, "Athapascan," in Boas, *Handbook, 1,* 104). In the Aleutian language there are two different expressions of plurality, one of which is used for animate beings, the other for inanimate objects; cf. Victor Henry, *Esquisse d'une grammaire raisonnée de la langue aléoute* (Paris, 1879), p. 13.

112. Böthlingk, *Über die Sprache der Jakuten,* p. 340.

from a differentiation not of things but of persons. For then number does not appear primarily as a universal logical principle or endless process; it is restricted from the outset to a specific sphere, whose limits are defined less by objective intuition than by pure subjective feeling. It is this feeling which differentiates "I" from "thou," and "thou" from "he"; but there is no immediate need to progress beyond this sharply defined triad, given in the differentiation of "three persons," to the intuition of a further multiplicity. Where such a multiplicity is conceived and designated in language, it lacks the "distinctness" of the personal spheres. Beyond "three" the realm of indefinite plurality, of mere undifferentiated collectivity, begins. And everywhere we find that the first enumerations are subject to this limitation. The languages of many primitive peoples show that the activity of differentiation growing out of the distinction between "I" and "thou," progresses from "one" to "two" and often accomplishes the significant step to "three," but that beyond this, the faculty of differentiation, of "discretion," which lies at the base of enumeration, seems paralyzed. Among the Bushmen the numbers, strictly speaking, extend only to two: the term for three means only "many" and is used, in conjunction with finger language, for all numbers up to ten.[113] Similarly, the aborigines of Victoria have developed no numerals beyond two. The Binandele language of New Guinea has only the numerals one, two and three, while numbers above three must be expressed by circumlocutions.[114] All these examples, to which many others might be added,[115] make it clear how closely the act of counting was originally bound up with the intuition of I, thou and he, from which it detaches itself only gradually. This seems to be the ultimate basis of the special role played by the number three in the language and thinking of all nations.[116] It has been said that among primitive peoples, each number has a kind of individual mystical physiognomy. This is par-

113. Cf. Fr. Müller, *Grundriss, 1*, Pt. 2, 26 ff.

114. Cf. Sayce, *Introduction to the Science of Language, 1*, 412.

115. Such examples, particularly from the Papuan languages, may be found in Ray, *Torres Straits Expedition, 3*, 46, 288, 331, 345, 373; see also Fr. Müller, "Die Papuasprachen," *Globus*, 72 (1897), 140. In Kivai the same word (*potoro*) that serves to designate the trial is used also for four: its meaning is probably "few," while all numbers over three are rendered by *sirio*, "many" (Ray, p. 306). For the Melanesian languages, see H. C. v. d. Gabelentz, p. 258. According to K. v. d. Steinen, there are clear indications that among the Bakairi two was the "limit of the old arithmetic," the term for multiplicity as such; he traces the word used for two back to a combination of words meaning literally "with thee" (*Die Bakaïri-Sprache*, pp. 352 ff).

116. Cf. H. K. Usener, "Dreizahl," *Rheinisches Museum für Philologie*, N. S., Vol. 58.

ticularly true of the numbers two and three. They seem to possess a specific spiritual tonality, which sets them apart from the uniform and homogeneous sequence of numbers. Even in those languages which possess a richly developed, "homogeneous" system of numbers, this special position of the numbers one and two, sometimes of three and four, is reflected in certain formal characteristics. In the Semitic, the words for one and two are adjectives, while the other numerals are abstract nouns assuming the opposite gender from that of the counted objects which stand in the genitive plural.[117] In ur-Indo-Germanic, as the Indo-Iranian, Baltic-Slavic and Greek languages all indicate, the numbers from one to four were inflected, while those from five to nineteen were rendered by uninflected adjectives, and those beyond nineteen by substantives commanding the genitive of the counted objects.[118] Such grammatical forms as the *dual,* persist much longer in personal pronouns than in other parts of speech. The dual, which otherwise disappeared from the whole declension, was preserved up to a relatively late period in the German first and second person pronouns; [119] likewise in the Slavic languages, the "objective" dual was lost much earlier than the "subjective" dual.[120] And in many languages, the etymology of the first numerals suggests a link with the personal pronouns: in Indo-Germanic, for example, the words for "thou" and "two" seem to disclose a common root.[121] In speaking of this relationship Scherer concludes that we stand here at a common linguistic source of psychology, grammar, and mathematics; that the dual root leads us back to the original dualism upon which rests the very possibility of speech and thought. [122] For according to Humboldt, language was made possible by address and response, by a tension which arises between I and

117. Cf. Brockelmann, *Grundriss, 1,* 484 ff.; *2,* 273 ff.

118. Cf. A. Meillet, *Introduction à l'étude comparative des langues indo-européennes* (1st ed., Paris, Hachette, 1903; 7th ed., 1934, pp. 409 ff.; German trans. by W. Printz from 2d French ed., Leipzig and Berlin, 1909, pp. 252 ff.); Brugmann, *Kurze vergleichende Grammatik,* pp. 369 ff.

119. The Westphalian and Austro-Bavarian dialects still retain vestiges of this use of the dual; cf. Jacob Grimm, *Deutsche Grammatik, 1,* 339 ff.

120. Miklosich, *Vergleichende Grammatik der slawischen Sprachen, 4,* 40; on the analogous phenomena in the Finno-Ugrian languages see József Szinnyei, *Finnisch-ugrische Sprachwissenschaft* (Leipzig, G. J. Göschen, 1910), p. 60.

121. On this question cf. Benfey, *Das indogermanische Thema des Zahlworts "Zwei" ist du* (Göttingen, 1876); Brugmann and Delbrück, in *Grundriss,* 2d ed., 2, Pt. 2, 8 ff., also assumes that the ur-Indo-Germanic *duwō "ultimately goes back to a personal intuition."

122. Scherer, *Zur Geschichte der deutschen Sprache,* pp. 308 ff., 355.

thou and which is resolved in the act of speech; so that this act appears to be the true and authentic "mediation between mind and mind."

On the basis of this speculative view Humboldt strove, in his treatise on the dual, to illuminate this form from within. Whereas most grammarians had hitherto regarded it as mere ballast, as a useless linguistic refinement, he traced it to a twofold source, subjective and objective, and an original signification which he found to be partly sensuous and partly intellectual. According to Humboldt, wherever the dual is employed predominantly as an expression of a purely objective intuition, language follows the first direction, i.e., takes duality as a sensuously tangible fact given in nature. This usage is found in almost all linguistic families. To the linguistic sense, things existing in pairs represent a special generic grouping. In the Bantu languages, for example, such natural pairs as the eyes, ears, shoulders, breasts, knees, feet, etc., form a special class, characterized by a special nominal prefix.[123] And there are also artificial pairs; language stresses, for example, the duality of certain implements. In most languages, however, this use of the dual for pure nominal concepts has steadily declined. In Semitic it belonged to the basic language but dwindled in the individual languages.[124] In Greek the dual had disappeared from certain dialects before the end of the prehistoric period; in Homer it was beginning to disintegrate. It survived relatively late only in the Attic dialect but was dying out by the fourth century B.C.[125] This phenomenon is not limited to any particular region or set of conditions and apparently expresses a general principle of linguistic logic.[126] The decline of the dual coincides with progress from the individual, concrete number to the abstract numerical series. As the idea of the *numerical series,* as a whole constructed according to a strictly unitary principle, gains ground, the particular number ceases to represent a specific content and becomes a mere member of the series, equivalent to other members. Heterogeneity began to

123. Meinhof, *Grammatik der Bantusprachen,* pp. 8 ff.

124. Cf. Brockelmann, *Kurzgefasste vergleichende Grammatik,* p. 222.

125. Brugmann, *Griechische Grammatik,* 3d ed., p. 371; Meillet, German ed., p. 6; cf. also Friedrich Müller, "Der Dual im indogermanischen und semitischen Sprachgebiete," *Sitzungsberichte der Kaiserlichen Akademie der Wissenschaften,* Philos.-hist. Classe, *35* (Vienna, 1860), 51 ff.

126. In Old Egyptian the use of the dual is still extensive, while in Coptic it has died out except for certain vestiges (see Erman, *Ägyptische Grammatik,* p. 106; Steindorf, *Koptische Grammatik,* pp. 69, 73.

make way for pure homogeneity. But understandably, this new approach gained acceptance far more slowly in the personal than in the material sphere: for in its whole origin and essence, the personal sphere is oriented toward heterogeneity. The "thou" is not similar to the "I," but confronts it as an opposite, as a not-I: here the "second" is not a mere repetition of the first, but is qualitatively "other." True, the "I" and the "thou" can fuse into the community of the "we"—but this form of union is quite different from a collectivization of things. As early a writer as Jacob Grimm stressed the difference between objective plural concepts and personal plural concepts; he pointed out that whereas the objective plural can be defined as a sum of similar elements, "men" for example as "man and man," the "we" can by no means be represented as a sum of this sort, since it must be construed not as "I and I," but rather as "I and thou" or "I and he." [127] The purely "distributive" factor in enumeration, the pure *differentiation* of units, is here more prominent than in that form of enumeration which starts from the intuition of time and temporal events.[128]

The same striving to preserve the specificity of the elements which enter into the "we" is revealed in the usage of the *trial* and of the *inclusive* and *exclusive* plural. These phenomena are closely related. The use of the dual and trial is particularly strict in the Melanesian languages which insist on the appropriate term in speaking of two or three persons; and in these languages the first person pronoun takes a different form depending on whether the speaker includes himself in the designation "we" or excludes himself from it.[129] The languages of the Australian aborigines also tend to interpolate dual and trial forms between the singular and plural; both dual and trial possess one form which includes the person addressed and another which excludes him. "We two" can mean either "thou and I" or "he and I": "we three" can signify either "I and thou and

127. Cf. Jacob Grimm, *Kleinere Schriften, 3,* 239 ff.

128. Cf. Fr. Müller, *Grundriss, 2,* Pt. 1, 76 ff. In *Die Sprachwissenschaft,* pp. 296 ff., G. v. d. Gabelentz remarks: "Grammatically speaking . . . family life embodies all the personal pronouns, singular, dual and plural; the family or clan has a sense of itself as a permanent unit, opposed to other families. 'We' stands in opposition to 'you' and 'them.' I believe that this is no mere playing with words. Where better could the personal pronoun be rooted than in the habits of a continuous family life? Sometimes it even seems as though languages contained memories of the relation between the perception of the woman and the perception of the 'thou.' Chinese designates both with the same word. . . . Likewise in the Thai languages the syllable *me* combines the significations of 'thou' and 'mother.' "

129. Cf. Codrington, *The Melanesian Languages,* pp. 111 ff.; Ray, *Torres Straits Expedition, 3,* 428, and elsewhere.

he" or "I and he and he," etc.[130] In some languages this distinction is expressed in the form of the plural—in the Delaware language, for example, the inclusive plural consists, according to Humboldt, in a combination of the pronouns "I" and "thou," while the exclusive form consists in a repetition of the pronoun "I." [131] The development of a homogeneous number series and a homogeneous intuition of number sets a limit to this strictly individualizing tendency. The distinct individual gives way to the genus which embraces all individuals alike, the qualifying differentiation of elements gives way to the uniformity of method and rule by which they are encompassed in a quantitative whole.

If we look back over the whole process by which language forms its numerical concepts and terms, we find that its separate factors can be derived *per antiphrasin* from the exact method of number formation prevailing in pure mathematics. We find that before the logical mathematical *concept* of number can become what it is, it must first be derived from its antithesis and opposite. The essential logical attributes of the mathematical series of numbers have been designated as its necessity and universality, its uniqueness, its infinity and the absolute equivalence of its members.[132] None of these characteristics applies to that first method of enumeration which finds its expression in language. Here there is no necessary and universal principle which makes it possible to encompass all numerical representations at *one* glance and to master them by a unitary rule. Here there is no unique number series; instead, as we have seen, each new class of enumerable objects requires new instruments of enumeration. Nor can there be any question of an endless series of numbers: it is neither necessary nor possible to carry the intuitive and perceptual combination of objects any farther than groups with a very definite intuitive group character.[133] Furthermore, the enumerated object does not enter into the act of enumeration as a unit divested of all qualitative attributes, but preserves

130. Cf. Matthews, "Aboriginal Languages of Victoria," *J. and Proc. of the Roy. Soc. of N. S. Wales*, *36* (1902), 72, and "Languages of Some Native Tribes of Queensland," etc., ibid., pp. 155 ff., 162. The personal pronouns also have more than one form in the Munda and Nicobarese languages (cf. P. W. Schmidt, *Die Mon-Khmer Völker*, pp. 50 ff.). For the American Indian languages see the different examples of "inclusive" and "exclusive" in Boas, *Handbook*, pp. 573 ff., 761, 815; also v. d. Steinen, *Die Bakāiri-Sprache*, pp. 349 ff.

131. Humboldt, *Kawi-Werk*, 2, 39.

132. Cf. G. F. Lipps, "Untersuchungen über die Grundlagen der Mathematik," in Wilhelm Wundt, *Philosophische Studien* (20 vols. Leipzig, 1883–1903), Vols. *9–11, 14*.

133. Cf. the apt remarks of Wertheimer, op. cit., *Zeitschrift für Psychologie*, Vol. 60, particularly pp. 365 ff.

its specific material and qualitative character. An indication of this is that forms denoting degrees of qualitative concepts develop very gradually. If, for example, we consider the comparison of adjectives, the forms of positive, comparative and superlative developed in our civilized languages, we find that they all contain a universal concept, a specific generic characteristic, which only varies in size in the process of comparison. But in most of these languages we can still discern, side by side with this purely quantitative differentiation, another approach, in which the quantitative difference is itself perceived as a substantial, generic difference. The suppletives occurring in the comparison of adjectives both in the Semitic and Indo-Germanic languages bear witness to this approach. In the Indo-Germanic languages for example, certain qualitative concepts—such as good and bad, large and many, little and few—are formed not from a single basic root but from entirely different roots (as for example our "good" and "better," Latin *bonus, melior, optimus,* Greek ἀγαθός, ἀμείνων, ἄριστος, βελτίων and βέλτιστος, κρείττων and κράτιστος). The explanation usually advanced for this phenomenon is that an older "individualizing" trend has not been entirely submerged by the later "grouping" trend—that in these cases the original "qualitative language formation" has resisted the growing tendency toward "quantitative formation."[134] In place of the abstraction of a uniformly conceived and uniformly designated attribute, differentiated only in degree, we have here a basic intuition in which each "degree" of an attribute retains its own unique character, and which does not regard it as a mere "more" or "less"; but as specific and distinct. This view appears still more clearly in languages that have not developed a specific form of adjective comparison. In the vast majority of languages the forms that we call "comparative" and "superlative" are totally lacking. Here degrees can be distinguished only indirectly: verbal terms such as "exceed," "surpass," etc.,[135] may be employed, or the two terms of comparison may appear side by side in simple parataxis.[136] Or else adverbial particles may indicate that a thing is large or beautiful, etc., in comparison with

134. Osthoff, *Vom Suppletivwesen der indogermanischen Sprachen* (Heidelberg, 1899), pp. 49 ff.

135. Examples particularly from the African languages in Meinhof, *Grammatik der Bantusprachen,* p. 84; Westermann, *Grammatik der Ewe-Sprache,* p. 102 (Eng. trans. by Bickford-Smith, p. 140), and *Die Gola-Sprache,* pp. 39, 47; Roehl, *Grammatik der Schambalasprache,* p. 25.

136. See examples in Roehl, p. 25; Codrington, *The Melanesian Languages,* p. 274; Gatschet, *Klamath Language,* p. 520.

another thing.[137] Many of these particles have originally a spatial sense, so that the qualitative gradation seems to be based on local relations of high and low, above and below.[138] Here again linguistic thought makes use of a spatial intuition, where abstract, logical thought seems to call for a pure concept of relation. And again the circle of our inquiry closes. Again it becomes evident that concepts of space, time and number are the essential framework of objective intuition as it develops in language. But they can fulfill this function only because their general structure situates them in an ideal middle region—because, precisely by holding fast to the form of sensuous expression, they progressively imbue the sensuous with intellectual content and mould it into a symbol of spiritual life.

4. Language and the Sphere of "Inner Intuition." Phases of the I-Concept

I. FORMATION OF SUBJECTIVE CONSCIOUSNESS IN LINGUISTIC EXPRESSION. So far our analysis of language has essentially been directed toward the categories in which it constructs the objective world of intuition. But it is already evident that this methodological limit has not been strictly observed. In our exposition of the "objective" categories we have at every step been led into the subjective sphere; we have found that every new specification which language gives to the world of objects is also reflected in the specification of the subjective world. For we are dealing with correlative spheres of intuition, which determine each other's limits. Every new configuration of the objective sphere, whether spatial, temporal or

137. See F. W. H. Migeod, *The Mende Language* (London, 1908), p. 65, etc. Of the Semitic languages only the Arabic has developed a specific form of adjective comparison, a so-called "elative"; according to Brockelmann (*Grundriss, 1*, 372; *2*, 210 ff.) this is a very late, specifically Arabic development.

138. In the Nuba language (cf. Reinisch, *Die Nuba-Sprache*, p. 31) the comparative is suggested by a postposition which literally means "over"; in Fiji the same function is performed by an adverb meaning "upwards" (cf. H. C. v. d. Gabelentz, *Die melanesischen Sprachen*, pp. 60 ff.). The comparative suffixes of the Indo-Germanic -ero, -tero are also derived, according to Brugmann (*Kurze vergleichende Grammatik*, pp. 321 ff.), from adverbs of local signification.

numerical, has produced a new picture of subjective reality and disclosed new traits in this purely "inner" world.

But language also has its own independent means of opening up and giving form to this other, "subjective" existence: and they are no less firmly rooted and no less fundamental than the form in which it apprehends and represents the world of things. Even today, it is true, the opinion is often expressed that the terms with which language reflects personal reality and its relations are merely derived from those applying to the objective world. Attempts at systematic classification of the parts of speech often proceed from the assumption that the *pronoun* is no independent part of speech with a spiritual content of its own, but merely a substitute for the noun, the substantive, that it does not embody one of the autonomous ideas of language formation but merely stands for something else.[139] But as early a writer as Humboldt raised decisive arguments against this "narrowly grammatical view." He pointed out that the pronoun cannot possibly be the latest part of speech: for the first element in the act of speech is the personality of the speaker himself, who stands in constant contact with nature and in speaking must inevitably express the opposition between his I and nature. "But in the I, the thou is automatically given, and through a new opposition the third person arises, which, now that language has gone beyond the circle of those who feel and speak, is extended to dead things." [140] On the basis of this speculative view, empirical linguists have often attempted to demonstrate that the personal pronoun is, as it were, the "bedrock" of language formation, the most ancient and obscure, but also the firmest and most enduring component of languages.[141] But although Humboldt stresses in this connection that the original feeling of the I cannot be an invented, general, discursive concept, we must bear in mind on the other hand that this original feeling cannot be sought exclusively in the explicit *designation* of the I as the first person pronoun. The philosophy of language would indeed reduce itself to the narrow, logical-grammatical view which it combats, if it strove to measure the form and configuration

---

139. This conception of the pronoun as a mere *idée suppléante* is put forward for example by Raoul de la Grasserie, *Du verbe comme générateur des autres parties du discours* (Paris, 1914). The name "pronoun" or ἀντωνυμία coined by the ancient grammarians goes back to this conception; cf. for example Apollonius, *De syntaxi*, Bk. 2, ch. 5.

140. Humboldt, "Einleitung zum Kawi-Werk," *Werke*, 7, No. 1, 103 ff.; cf. "Über den Dualis," *Werke*, 6, 26 ff., and "Über die Verwandtschaft der Ortsadverbien mit dem Pronomen," *Werke*, 6, No. 1, 304 ff.

141. Jacob Grimm, *Deutsche Grammatik*, 1, 355 ff.; W. Scherer, *Zur Geschichte der deutschen Sprache*, p. 215.

of the *I-consciousness* solely by the development of the pronoun. In the psychological analysis of children's language, the mistake has often been made of identifying the earliest phonetic expression of I with the earliest stage of the I-feeling. Here it is overlooked that the psychological content and its linguistic expression never fully coincide and above all that *unity* of content need not be reflected in *simplicity* of expression. Language has many different means of expressing a specific fundamental intuition, and we must consider them as a whole in order to see clearly the direction to which they point. The formation of the I-concept is not bound up exclusively with the pronoun, but proceeds equally through other linguistic spheres, through the medium of the noun, the verb, etc. It is particularly in the verb that the finest distinctions and shadings of the I-feeling can be expressed, since it is in the verb that the objective representation of a process is most characteristically permeated with the subjective representation of an action, and since in this sense verbs, as the Chinese grammarians put it, are truly "living words" in distinction to nouns which are "dead words." [142]

At first, it is true, the expression of the I and the self seems to require the support of the nominal sphere, the sphere of substantial, objective intuition, from which it liberates itself only with great difficulty. In the most diverse languages, we find terms for I which are derived from objective terms. In particular, language shows that at first the concrete feeling of self is entirely bound up with the concrete intuition of one's own body and limbs. We find here the same orientation toward physical existence and particularly toward the human body as in the expression of spatial, temporal and numerical relations. This system of designating the I is especially apparent in the Altaic languages. All the branches of this family show a tendency to designate whatever we express through personal pronouns, by nouns provided with case endings or possessive suffixes. The words for "I" or "me" are replaced by terms signifying "my being," "my essence," or by such "drastically material" terms as "my body" or "my bosom." Even a purely spatial term, one for example whose basic significance might be rendered approximately as "center," can be used in this sense.[143] Similarly, in Hebrew the reflexive pronoun is rendered not only by words such as

142. Cf. G. v. d. Gabelentz, *Chinesische Grammatik* (Leipzig, T. O. Weigel, 1881), pp. 112 ff.

143. Cf. H. Winkler, *Der uralaltaische Sprachstamm*, pp. 59 ff., 160 ff., Hoffmann, *Japanische Sprachlehre*, pp. 91 ff., and J. J. Schmidt, *Grammatik der mongolischen Sprache* (Petersburg, 1831), pp. 44 ff.

"soul" or "person," but also by "face," "flesh" or "heart" [144]—while similarly the Latin *persona* originally meant the actor's face or mask and was long used in German to indicate the outward appearance, figure and stature of an individual.[145] In Coptic, "self" is rendered by the noun "body," to which possessive suffixes are attached.[146] Likewise in the Indonesian languages, the reflexive object is designated by a word which can mean "person," "spirit" or "body." [147] Finally this usage extends even to the Indo-Germanic languages; in Vedic and classical Sanskrit, for example, the self and the I are rendered sometimes by the word for soul (*ātmàn*) and sometimes by the word for body (*tanu*).[148] All this makes it plain that where the intuition of the self, the soul, the person, first appears in language, it clings to the body—just as in mythical intuition man's soul and self are at first conceived as a mere repetition, as a "double" of the body. In many languages, nouns and pronouns long remain formally undifferentiated, inflected in the same patterns and assimilated to one another in number, case and gender.[149]

If, however, we inquire not so much into the form in which language clothes the perception of the I, as into the intellectual content of this perception, we find that it can be sharply defined within the sphere of purely

144. On the general method by which the Semitic languages express the reflexive pronoun, see Brockelmann, *Grundriss*, 2, 228 and 327; in most cases the reflexive must be indicated by the word for soul or its synonyms (man, head, being).

145. Cf. Grimm, *Deutsches Wörterbuch*, 7, cols. 1561–62.

146. Steindorff, *Koptische Grammatik*, p. 88; similarly in Egyptian, cf. Erman, *Ägyptische Grammatik*, p. 85.

147. Cf. Brandstetter, *Indonesisch und Indogermanisch im Satzbau* (Lucerne, 1914), p. 18.

148. Wm. Dwight Whitney, *A Sanskrit Grammar* (London, 1879), p. 179; B. Delbrück, *Vergleicheude Syntax, 1,* 477.

149. Cf. Wundt, *Die Sprache, Völkerpsychologie,* 2d ed., *2,* 47 ff. and the examples here cited from Fr. Müller's *Grundriss*. Those substantival and adjectival circumlocutions for the personal pronouns which have arisen out of considerations of etiquette and ceremonial are not to be considered in the same light as the phenomena here discussed. According to Humboldt (*Werke, 6*, No. 1, 307 ff. and *Kawi-Werk, 2,* 335), they belong to a "state of half civilization." Terms of exaltation (e.g., commander, magnificence) are used for the second person. The Japanese language has gone farthest in this direction. Here the personal pronoun has been entirely submerged by such polite circumlocutions, which are precisely graduated according to the rank of the speaker and of the person addressed. "The differentiation of the three grammatical persons (I, thou, he)," says Hoffmann (*Japanische Sprachlehre*, pp. 75 ff.), "has remained foreign to the Japanese language. All persons, that of the speaker as well as the person to whom one speaks, are considered as perceptual *content,* that is according to our idiom, in the *third* person and it is for etiquette to decide, on the basis of the adjectives employed, which person is meant by which word. Etiquette alone distinguishes between I and not-I, abasing the one and exalting the other."

nominal or verbal expression. In almost all languages which divide nouns into specific classes, a personal class and an object class are clearly distinguished. And here we are not dealing with a simple biological distinction between the animate and inanimate, which as such would belong to the intuition of *nature*, but with often surprising subtleties and shadings in the representation of personal existence. In the Bantu languages a special class, identified by a particular prefix, designates man as an independent, active personality, while another class embraces animate but not personal beings. Man is included in the latter class when he appears as not acting independently, but as the instrument and representative of another, e.g., as his messenger, emissary, or agent. Here, then, language distinguishes types and degrees of personality according to the function it performs and according to the dependent or independent form of *will* manifested in it.[150] The germ of this basic intuition can also be found in those languages which distinguish the designations of personal beings from those of mere objects by preceding them with a special "personal article." In the Melanesian languages such an article regularly precedes the names of individuals and tribes; it is used also with inanimate objects such as trees or boats, ships or weapons, if they are considered not as mere representatives of their genus but as individuals, and provided with a name of their own. Certain languages have developed two different personal articles for different classes of animate beings, based evidently on a kind of value gradation within the concept of personality.[151] A feeling for such purely subjective differences is also disclosed by certain of the Australian aboriginal languages which select one form of the nominative to indicate that a subject merely *is* and another to designate the subject as *active* in an independent sense.[152] Similar distinctions can be indicated in the verb; a special prefix for ex-

---

150. Cf. Meinhof, *Grammatik der Bantusprachen*, pp. 6 ff.

151. Codrington, *The Melanesian Languages*, pp. 108 ff., and Brandstetter, *Der Artikel des Indonesischen*, pp. 36, 46. Among the American Indian languages Hupa, for example, possesses a special third person pronoun used for the adult male members of the tribe, another for children, old people, members of other tribes and animals; see Goddard, "Athapascan," in Boas, *Handbook, 1,* 117.

152. Here the simple nominative serving solely to designate a person or object is distinguished from the *nominativus agentis,* which is used where a transitive verb is connected with the subject. "If, for example, one sees a person in the distance and asks: Who is that?—the answer will be *ḳore* (a man); but if one wishes to say, the man has killed the kangaroo, one uses another form, the subjective nominative, which must always be employed where the noun is represented as acting." See Fr. Müller, *Novara-Reise,* p. 247; cf. Matthews, "Aboriginal Languages of Victoria," *J. and Proc. of the Roy. Soc. of N. S. Wales, 36,* 78, 86, 94.

ample, may indicate whether the occurrence in question is a simple "natural" event, whether it represents the intervention of an *active* subject or is performed by *several* such subjects acting in common.[153] These distinctions are not outwardly *pronominal,* yet it is evident that in them the pure *concept* of personal existence and action is clearly apprehended and developed in a variety of gradations.

The extraordinary wealth of these gradations is particularly evident in the abundance of means by which language indicates so-called "generic distinctions" in verbs. From the standpoint of sharp logical analysis, only a single clear distinction would seem at first glance to be possible: that between independent action and mere being acted upon, between active and passive. Thus Aristotle strove to raise the grammatical distinction which we express by the opposition between "active" and "passive" to the level of a universal logical and metaphysical category. But it is by no means correct to maintain that in thus placing central emphasis on the fundamental opposition between acting and being acted upon, between ποιεῖν and πάσχειν, Aristotle followed tendencies which were given and in a sense imposed upon him by the Greek language. Language in itself would have pointed in a different direction: for precisely in the Greek, the "passive" is not sharply distinguished from the other voices of the verb either in form or meaning. The Greek passive developed only gradually, in part from the active and in part from the middle voice.[154] When we fully consider other linguistic families, it becomes apparent that the simple opposition of action and being acted upon plays no exclusive role in the development of verbal expression, but is constantly crossed by a number of other antitheses. Even where languages have clearly developed this opposition, where a sharp distinction is made between "active" and "passive" forms, this distinction is only one among many: it belongs to a totality of conceptual gradations that are verbally expressed. In other languages this opposition may be totally lacking, so that formally at least, there is no spe-

153. Cf. Codrington, *The Melanesian Languages,* pp. 183 ff. One Indonesian idiom, the Buginese, has two different "passive prefixes" which it attaches to the verb. One expresses the "unintentional," i.e., an event which occurs "by itself," without the intervention of an active subject. Cf. Brandstetter, *Sprachvergleichende Charakteristik eines indonesischen Idioms* (Lucerne, 1911), pp. 37 ff. According to Reinisch (*Die Nuba-Sprache,* pp. 63 ff.), the Nuba language draws a sharp distinction between the passive and the inchoative form of the verb: the former is used when a state is induced by the active intervention of a subject, the second when it is brought about by mere natural conditions, through a normal course of events.

154. Cf. Brugmann, *Griechische Grammatik,* 3d ed., pp. 458 ff.

cialized passive use of the verb. Significations which we are accustomed to express in passive terms are rendered by active verb forms, particularly the third person plural of the active verb.[155] In the Malay languages, according to Humboldt, the "passive" is formed by transposition of the verb into a nominal form: there is no true passive because the verb itself is not conceived as active, but has rather a nominal character. Essentially, the designation of an occurrence implies in these languages neither an agent nor an object acted upon: the verb merely takes note of the occurrence, without explicitly connecting it with the energy of the subject or giving any formal indication of its relation to the object affected.[156]

But this deficient development of the abstract opposition of active and passive does not arise from any deficiency in the concrete intuition of action and its nuances: this intuition is often astonishingly varied in the very languages which lack a formal distinction between active and passive. Not only are the individual "genera" of the verb often sharply defined in these languages, but they can overlap in a great variety of ways and combine to produce expressions of astonishing complexity. First of all we have those forms which designate a *temporal character* in an action, but which, as we have seen, are less concerned with the expression of relative *time* than with the type of action. A sharp distinction is made between "perfective" and "imperfective," "momentary" and "cursive," unique or iterative action: between action completed at the time of speaking and action still in process of development; between action limited to a specific moment or extending over a more protracted time span; between action effected all at once or in several stages. Such distinctions can be expressed by specific genera of the verb in addition to the above-mentioned modal forms.[157] A simple state an be designated as such by the use of a "stative,"

155. Examples from the Melanesian languages in Codrington, pp. 191 ff.; from the African languages in Westermann, *Die Sudansprachen*, p. 70; Migeod, *The Mende Language*, p. 82. The missing passive is often replaced by impersonal locutions or by active forms embodying a passive nuance. "He is struck," for example, can be rendered by locutions such as "he receives or suffers striking" or by such a very material formulation as "he eats blows." (Examples in Fr. Müller, *Novara-Reise*, p. 98.) By means of an auxiliary verb whose basic meaning is "obtain, acquire," the Japanese language forms verbs which indicate acquisition of an action coming from outside and in this sense can be designated as passive verbs. (Hoffmann, *Japanische Sprachlehre*, p. 242.) Similarly in Chinese, the "passive" is frequently formed by means of such auxiliary verbs as "see, find, receive" (e.g., "see hate" for "to be hated"). Cf. G. v. d. Gabelentz, *Chinesische Grammatik*, pp. 113, 428.

156. Humboldt, *Kawi-Werk*, 2, 80, 85; cf. the parallels from Australian languages in Fr. Müller, *Novara-Reise*, pp. 254 ff. See also Codrington, p. 192.

157. Cf. above pp. 224 ff.

a gradual inception by an "inchoative," a concluded action by a "cessative" or "conclusive." If the action is to be characterized as protracted and regular, hence as habitual or customary, the "habitual" form is used.[158] Other languages have developed the differentiation of momentary and frequentative verbs to a high degree.[159] And in addition to these distinctions which essentially concern the objective character of the action, the verb form can express the inner attitude of the I toward the action. This attitude can be either theoretical or practical, it can be a product of pure volition or of judgment. The action can be characterized as desired or demanded, or, where judgment is implied, as assertoric or problematic. It is in this direction that the true "modal" distinctions, like the older "modes of action," develop: the subjunctive which has a "volitive," "deliberative" and "prospective" significance; the optative, which is used sometimes in the sense of a wish, sometimes to express a prescription or a mere possibility.[160] The volitive form is capable of expressing further gradations extending from wish to command, and these may be reflected, for example, in the distinction between a "precative" and an "imperative" mood.[161] Besides imperative, implorative, desiderative and obligative moods, indicating that an action should be performed, many American Indian languages have purely theoretical moods which the grammarians call "dubitative" or "quotative," indicating that an action is doubtful or reported on the basis of someone else's testimony.[162] Often a special suffix attached to the verb makes it clear whether the subject himself has seen or heard an occurrence or whether he knows of it, not through immediate sense perception, but through supposition and inference; and sometimes knowledge of an event acquired in a dream is distinguished in the same way from knowledge acquired in a waking state.[163]

158. For this usage of the "stative," "inchoative" and "habitual" see the examples in L. Reinisch, *Die Nuba-Sprache*, pp. 53 ff., 58 ff., and A. Hanoteau, *Grammaire kabyle* (Alger, 1858), pp. 122 ff.

159. Particularly the Finno-Ugrian languages, see Szinnyei, *Finnisch-ugrische Sprachwissenschaft*, pp. 120 ff. Hungarian has eight different frequentative suffixes; cf. S. Simonyi, *Die ungarische Sprache* (Strassburg, 1907), pp. 284 ff.

160. As in Indo-Germanic, cf. Brugmann, *Kurze vergleichende Grammatik*, pp. 578 ff.

161. Such a distinction occurs, for example, in Mongolian; cf. J. J. Schmidt, *Grammatik der mongolischen Sprache*, p. 74. On the Sanskrit "precative" cf. Albert Thumb, *Handbuch des Sanskrit* (Heidelberg, 1905), pp. 385 ff.

162. Cf. Powell, *The Evolution of Language* (Smithsonian Institution, Washington, *Annual Report*, No. 1, p. 12.

163. Examples in Goddard, "Athapascan," Swanton, "Haida," and Boas, "Kwakiutl," in Boas, *Handbook, 1*, 105, 124, 247 ff., 443.

In these instances the I expresses an attitude of willing or demanding, doubting or questioning toward objective reality. But this attitude is most sharply manifested when the I acts upon the object. Many languages which are relatively indifferent toward the differentiation of active and passive, distinguish with the utmost precision between degrees of such action and its greater or lesser mediacy. A simple phonetic instrument (such as doubling of the middle radical in the Semitic languages) can serve to derive from the simple root of a verb a second root which is primarily intensive but also causative, and a third having a specific causative function. From causatives of the first degree may be formed causatives of the second and third degree which give an originally intransitive verb a doubly or triply transitive signification.[164] Such linguistic phenomena clearly reflect the increasing complexity of the intuition of personal action: subject and object of an action are no longer simply kept apart; instead, more and more middle links are interpolated which, even when they are of a personal nature, serve as it were to convey the action from its origin in a willing I and transpose it into the sphere of objective reality.[165] This intuition of several subjects collaborating in an action, may be expressed differently depending on whether the mere *fact* of collaboration is indicated or whether attention is given to the *form* of the collaboration. In the first case, language uses the "cooperative form" of the verb, or forms a "social stem," indicating that one person participates in some way in the action or state of another.[166] Certain languages employ special collective infixes to indicate that an action is not undertaken by an individual but by a group.[167] Where there is reflection on the form of collaboration the essential consideration is whether the collaboration is directed only outward or whether it is directed inward, i.e., whether a plurality of subjects confronts a simple material ob-

164. Cf. Aug. Müller, *Türkische Grammatik* (Berlin and New York, 1889), pp. 71 ff.; for the Semitic languages see Brockelmann, *Grundriss, 1,* 504 ff. According to Dillmann (*Grammatik der äthiopischen Sprache,* pp. 116 ff. [Eng. trans., 2d ed., pp. 141 ff.]) Ethiopic contains, in addition to the basic root, an "intensive" and an "influential root"; from all three, causative roots can be derived by the addition of the same morphological element, without altering their peculiarities.

165. Thus for example the Tagalog language makes use of two different prefixes in forming causative verbs: one expresses the mere production of a thing, the simple action of the subject, while the other indicates that another subject is caused to act, so that we now have two active subjects. Cf. Humboldt, *Kawi-Werk, 2,* 143.

166. Cf. the examples from the Bedauye language in L. Reinisch, *Bedauye, 2,* 130 ff. A cooperative form of the verb occurs also in Yakut; cf. Böthlingk, *Über die Sprache der Jakuten,* pp. 364 ff.

167. E.g., the language of the Taoripi; see Ray, *Torres Straits Expedition, 3,* 340.

ject, or whether in their action the individuals stand to one another in a reciprocal subject-object relationship. From the latter intuition arises the form of expression which language creates for *reciprocal* action. Even primitive languages sometimes distinguish sharply as to whether subjects direct their action toward an outward object or toward one another.[168] And here we would seem to be on our way to another significant step. In reciprocal action the agent and the thing acted upon coincide in a certain sense: both belong to the personal sphere, and it depends only on the point of view whether we consider them as subject or object. The relation becomes still closer when a plurality of subjects is replaced by a single subject, so that the starting point and goal of an action are first separated and then rejoined into *one* content. This is the character of reflexive action, in which the I acts not upon another thing or person but upon himself—in which he directs his action back on himself. In many languages this reflexive form replaces the missing passive.[169] This reference and turning back of the action upon the I, and the active subjective consciousness it discloses, are most purely manifested in the Greek use of the *middle* form. This form has with good reason been called an essential and distinguishing feature of the Greek language, the trait which characterizes it as the truly "philosophical" language.[170] The Sanskrit grammarians have aptly called the active form of the verb, "a word for another" and the middle form "a word for oneself."[171] Actually, the fundamental significance of the middle is that it situates the process within the sphere of the subject and stresses the participation of the subject in it. "In a simple active," says Jacob Grimm,

> it remains essentially doubtful whether an intransitive or a transitive concept is dominant, e.g. "I see" can signify either "I see with my eyes" or "I see something"; κλαίω implies either inward weeping or weeping

168. E.g., the Bungandity language of South Australia, described by Matthews in *J. and Proc. of the Roy. Soc. of N. S. Wales*, 37 (1903), 69.

169. Cf. for the Semitic languages, the Ethiopic (Dillmann, pp. 115, 123; Eng. trans., 2d ed., pp. 140 f., 151 ff.) and Syriac (Nöldeke, *Kurzgefasste Syrische Grammatik* [Leipzig, Weigel, 1880], pp. 95 ff.; Eng. trans., *Compendious Syriac Grammar* [London, 1904], pp. 105 ff.); according to Aug. Müller, *Türkische Grammatik*, p. 76, the reflexive is also often used for the passive in Turkish.

170. Cf. J. Stenzel, "Über den Einfluss der griechischen Sprache auf die philosophische Begriffsbildung," *Neue Jahrbücher für das Klassische Altertum* (1921), pp. 152 ff.

171. "The Middle as Âtmanepadam," in Pânini, *I*, III, 72–74; the first European grammarian to characterize the middle as a special *genus verbi* was Dionysius Thrax; cf. Benfey, *Geschichte der Sprachwissenschaft*, pp. 73 and 144.

for another. The middle removes this doubt and refers the meaning clearly to the subject of the sentence, e.g., κλαίομαι (I weep for myself). . . . The true middle is made to designate a living action in the soul or body of the speaker, so that all languages by a miraculous agreement include in it concepts such as rejoice, grieve, to be astonished, to fear, hope, dwell, rest, speak, clothe, wash, etc.[172]

If we now look back over the rich differentiations of verbal genera and consider that most of these genera can be combined into new and complex forms—e.g., the passive and causative into a causative passive, the causative and reflexive into a reflexive causative or a reciprocal causative, etc.[173]—we recognize that the power demonstrated by language in such formations lies in not regarding the opposition between subjective and objective as a rigid, abstract opposition between two mutually exclusive spheres, but in conceiving it as dynamically mediated in the most diverse ways. Language does not represent the two spheres in themselves but reveals their reciprocal determination—it creates as it were a middle realm in which the forms of substance and the forms of action are referred to one another and fused into a spiritual unity of expression.

2. PERSONAL AND POSSESSIVE EXPRESSION. When we turn from the implicit formation of the I-concept in nominal and verbal expression to its explicit linguistic formation in the gradual development of the true pronouns, it becomes clear, as Humboldt stressed, that, although the feeling of the I must be regarded as an original and irreducible component of all language formation, the entrance of the pronoun into actual language was attended by great difficulties. For, Humboldt pointed out, the essence of the I is that it is a subject, while both in thought and speech every concept must become an object in relation to the actually thinking subject.[174] This contradiction can only be resolved if the same relation which we have observed within the spheres of nominal and verbal expression, is repeated on a higher level: Pronominal expression can arrive at a sharp designation of the I only by placing itself in opposition to the objective world and at

172. *Deutsche Grammatik*, *1*, 598 ff.

173. Aside from the Semitic languages, examples can be found in Yakut (Böthlingk, p. 291), in Turkish (Aug. Müller, pp. 71 ff.), in Nuba (Reinisch, *Bedauye*, pp. 62 ff.), etc.

174. Humboldt, *Über die Verwandtschaft der Ortsadverbien mit dem Pronomen*, *Werke*, *6*, No. 1, 306 ff.

the same time passing through it. Even where language has arrived at a determinate idea of the I, it must at first lend it an objective form; it must, as it were, find its designation for the I through its designation of objective things.

This presupposition of Humboldt is confirmed by the manner in which language expresses personal relations, not at first by using true personal pronouns, but by means of possessive pronouns. For the idea of possession which these pronouns represent occupies a peculiar middle position between objectivity and subjectivity. What is possessed is a thing or object: in becoming a content of possession, it is made known as a mere object. And yet by being identified as a possession, this thing acquires a new character, it moves from the natural to the personal-spiritual sphere. Here we have, as it were, a first animation, a transformation of material form into I-form. On the other hand, however, the self does not apprehend itself in a free, original act of spiritual and volitional spontaneity, but sees itself, one might say, in the image of the object which it acquires as "its own." A psychological light is thrown on this mediation of purely "personal" expression through "possessive" expression by the speech of children, in which the I seems to be designated much earlier by possessive than by personal pronouns. However, these observations are not entirely reliable and are subject to varying interpretations.[175] More conclusive are certain phenomena in the general history of language, which show that the sharp formation of the I-concept in language is preceded by a state of *indifference,* in which the expression of "I" and "mine," "thou" and "thine," etc., are not yet clearly differentiated. The distinction between the two, Humboldt remarks, is felt, but not with the formal sharpness and determinacy which are necessary before it can pass into linguistic expression.[176] Most of the American Indian languages, as well as the Ural-Altaic languages, form the conjugations of the verb by adding a possessive affix to the indefinite infinitive form—so that the term for "I go" literally means "my going" and the terms for "I build, thou buildest, he builds" disclose exactly the same structure as those for "my house, thy house, his house."[177] There is no

175. Cf. Clara and William Stern, *Die Kindersprache,* 2d ed., pp. 41 and 245 ff.

176. Humboldt, "Einleitung zum Kawi-Werk," *Werke,* 7, No. 1, 231. K. v. d. Steinen also points out that the "possessive and personal pronoun are still identical" in the Bakairi language. One and the same word (*ura*) means not only "I" but also "mine," "that is mine," "that belongs to me." Another means "thou" and "thine," a third "he" and "his" (*Die Bakaïri-Sprache,* pp. 348 ff., 380).

177. H. Winkler, *Der uralaltaische Sprachstamm,* pp. 76 ff., 171; examples from other

doubt that a peculiar intuition of the relation between "I" and "reality" underlies this peculiarity of expression. Wundt offers a psychological explanation of this persistence of the nominal form in transitive verbal concepts: since the object of the transitive verb is always immediately given to the consciousness, it demands to be expressed before anything else; hence, he believes, the nominal concept can stand for the whole sentence expressing the action.[178] But this is not so much an explanation as a roundabout description of the process in question. The designation of the pure act and the designation of its objective aim and result present two different views of action. In the first case the expression of action refers back to subjectivity as its origin and source; in the second, it concentrates on the product of action, which it restores, as it were, to the sphere of the I by means of a pronoun indicating possession. The relation between I and objective content is present in both cases, but it operates in two different directions, in one case from center to periphery, in the other form periphery to center.

This relation between I and not-I, expressed in the possessive pronoun and hence mediated by the idea of possession, is especially close when the not-I is not a random object in the outside world but belongs to a sphere in which the "inward" and the "outward" seem to touch and flow immediately into one another. Even speculative philosophers have designated the *human body* as the reality in which this interchange occurs most patently. According to Schopenhauer, the I and the body are not two objectively recognized different states connected by a bond of causality; they do not stand to one another in a relation of cause and effect but are one and the same thing given in totally different modalities. The action of the body is nothing other than an objectified act of the will—i.e., an act that has entered into the world of intuition; the body is nothing other than the *objectivity of the will itself*.[179] From this point of view, it becomes understandable that there should be an interpenetration of objective and subjective expression in the terms which language creates for the human body and its parts: that an expression of personal relation should often fuse into an inseparable whole with a purely objective term. This characteristic is particularly apparent in the languages of primitive peoples. In most of the American Indian languages, a part of the body can never

---

languages in Fr. Müller, *Grundriss*, e.g., *1*, Pt. 2, 12, 116 ff., 142, 153; 2, Pt. 1, 188; *3*, Pt. 2, 278, etc.

178. Wundt, *Die Sprache, Völkerpsychologie*, 2d ed., 2, 143.

179. A. Schopenhauer, *Die Welt als Wille und Vorstellung*, ed. Grisebach, *1*, 151 ff.; 2, 289 ff.

be designated by a general term, but must always be more closely specified by means of a possessive pronoun: there is no abstract term for hand or arm, but only a term for a hand or arm belonging to a particular man.[180] K. v. d. Steinen tells us that in seeking to ascertain the names for the parts of the body in Bakairi, it was necessary to distinguish carefully whether the part in question belonged to one's own body, to the body of the person questioned, or to a third party, since in each case the answer would be different. "Tongue," for example can only be rendered in the forms: my tongue, thy tongue, his tongue, or the tongues of all those here present.[181] The same phenomenon is reported by Humboldt from the Mexican, by Boethlingk from the Yakut language.[182] In the Melanesian languages, a different term is used for parts of the body in general and for parts of the body belonging to a specific individual: in the first case, a generalizing suffix must be added to the usual, individualizing term.[183] This fusion of a nominal term with a possessive pronoun is not limited to parts of the human body but extends to other contents, in so far as they are conceived as standing in close relationship with the I and in a sense to form a part of its spiritual-natural substance. Often terms of blood relationship, "father" and "mother," etc. appear only in conjunction with the possessive pronoun.[184] Here language does not look upon objective reality as a single homogeneous mass, simply juxtaposed to the world of the I, but sees different strata of this reality: the relationship between object and subject is not universal and abstract; on the contrary, we can distinguish different degrees of objectivity, varying according to relative "distance" from the I.

And from this concretion of the subject-object relationship another consequence follows. The fundamental characteristic of the "pure I," in contrast to all objects, is absolute *unity*. The I, conceived as a pure form of consciousness, is not susceptible of inner differentiations: for such differentiations belong to the world of objective contents. Consequently, wherever the I is taken as an expression of the nonobjective in the strict sense, it

180. Cf. Buschmann, "Der athapaskische Sprachstamm," *Abhandlungen der Berliner Akademie der Wissenschaften* (1854), pp. 165, 231; Powell, *Introduction to the Study of Indian Languages*, 2d ed., p. 18; Goddard, "Athapascan," in Boas, *Handbook, 1*, 103.

181. K. v. d. Steinen, *Unter den Naturvölkern Zentral-Brasiliens*, 2d ed., p. 22.

182. Cf. Böthlingk, *Über die Sprache der Jakuten*, p. 357; even in Hungarian, according to Simonyi, p. 260, designations of kinship and parts of the body are relatively seldom used without possessive personal suffixes.

183. Codrington, pp. 140 ff.

184. Cf. Reinisch, *Die Nuba-Sprache*, p. 45; for the American Indian languages see Boas, *Handbook*, e.g., *1*, 103.

must be conceived as "pure identity with itself." In his treatise "On the I as a Principle of Philosophy," Schelling drew this inference with extreme sharpness. If the I is not identical with itself, if its original form is not the form of pure identity, he points out, the strict limit which divides it from all objective reality and which makes it into something unmistakably independent and specific, is immediately blurred. Hence we must think of the I in this original form of pure identity or not at all.[185] But *language* cannot pass directly to this intuition of the pure, "transcendental" I and its unity. For since in language the personal sphere only gradually grows out of the possessive, since the intuition of the person adheres to the intuition of objective possession, the diversity inherent in the relationship of mere possession must react upon the expression of the I. Actually my arm, which is organically bound up with the whole of my body, belongs to me in quite a different way than my weapon or my implement—my parents, my children, are connected with me in a totally different, more natural and more immediate way than my horse or dog—and even in the sphere of pure objective possessions, there is a discernible difference between mobile and immobile possessions. The house in which a man lives "belongs" to him in another and firmer sense than the coat he wears. At first, language conforms to all these differences: instead of a unitary and universal expression of the relationship of possession, it will seek to develop as many different expressions as there are distinct classes of *concrete* possession. Here we find the same phenomenon as in the genesis and gradual development of *numerals*. Just as the different objects and groups of objects originally have different "numbers"—so they have a different "mine" and "thine." Consequently, the diverse "numeral" substantives which certain languages use in enumerating different objects have a parallel in the diverse "possessive substantives." The Melanesian and many Polynesian languages designate the relationship of possession by augmenting the term for the possessed object with a possessive suffix which changes according to the class to which it belongs. Originally, all these diverse expressions of the relationship of possession were nouns, as is formally shown by the fact that prepositions can precede them. Among these nouns there are gradations distinguishing different kinds of possession or appurtenance. One possessive noun of this sort, for example, is added to designations of kinship, to parts of the human body, to parts of a thing, another to things that

185. F. W. J. v. Schelling, "Vom Ich als Prinzip der Philosophie," *Werke*, ed. O. Weiss (Leipzig, 1907) *1*, Par. 7, 177.

one possesses or to implements one uses—one applies to everything one eats, another to everything one drinks.[186] Often a different term is used for a possession coming from outside and for an object owing its existence to the personal activity of the possessor.[187] Most of the American Indian languages draw a similar distinction between the two fundamental types of possession: natural, untransferable possession and artificial, transferrable possession.[188] A diversity in the expression of the possessive relationship may also arise from purely numerical considerations, a different possessive pronoun being selected according to whether there are two or more possessors, or whether there are one, two or more possessed objects. In the Aleutian language, for example, these factors and their combinations give rise to nine different personal pronouns.[189] From all this we see that the homogeneous expression of possession, like the homogeneous expression of number, was a relatively late product, which had to be detached from the intuition of heterogeneity. Just as number achieved its character of "uniformity" by transforming itself progressively from an expression of objects to an expression of pure relation, so gradually the simplicity and uniformity of the I-relation gained primacy over the diversity of the contents which can enter into this relation. Language appears to be on its way to this purely formal designation of the possessive relation and hence to a mediate intuition of the formal unity of the I, wherever it expresses possession by the genitive rather than by possessive pronouns. For although the genitive is rooted in concrete intuitions, particularly of a spatial character, it develops little by little into a purely "grammatical" case, expressing "possession as such" and restricted to no special form of possession. Perhaps we may find a transition between these two intuitions in the instances where the genitive bears a particular possessive character and a special possessive suffix is required for the completion of the genitive relation.[190]

186. Cf. Ray, "The Melanesian Possessive," *American Anthropologist*, 21, 349 ff.

187. Cf. Codrington, *The Melanesian Languages*, pp. 129 ff.

188. Such different possessive suffixes for transferable and nontransferable possession occur, for example, in the Haidan and the Tsimshian languages, where a further distinction is made between the transferable possession of animate creatures (my dog) and inanimate things (my house), and in the languages of the Sioux Indians; cf. Boas, *Handbook, 1*, 258, 393, 946 ff.

189. Cf. Victor Henry, *Langue aléoute*, p. 22. A similar condition prevails in the Eskimo language; cf. Thalbitzer, in Boas, *Handbook 1*, 1021 ff. Szinnyei (p. 115) remarks that in the Finno-Ugrian languages there were originally two paradigms with possessive suffixes: one for singular, one for plural possession, but that in most of the individual languages this distinction has been obscured, being best preserved in the Vogul.

190. As in Turkish, where the phrase "the father's house" is rendered as "the father's *his*

Language moves towards expression of the purely formal unity of the I by another road when, instead of characterizing an activity by its objective aim and result, it goes back to the origin of the action, the active subject. This is the direction followed by all those languages which regard the verb as a pure expression of action and designate the person by the personal pronoun. The I, thou, he, detaches itself far more sharply from the objective sphere than the mere mine, thine, his. The subject of the action can no longer appear as a mere thing among things, as a content among contents, but is the living energetic nucleus from which the action begins and from which it takes its direction. Attempts have been made to distinguish types of language formation according to whether they designate verbal occurrences essentially from the standpoint of sensibility or from the standpoint of action. In the first case, the expression of action becomes a mere "it seems to me"—while conversely, in the second case, mere appearance is interpreted as action.[191] But where the expression of activity is thus intensified, the expression of the I also takes on a new form. The *dynamic* expression of the I-percept comes far closer than a nominal, objective expression to apprehending it as a pure formal unity. And now indeed, the I is transformed more and more clearly into an expression of pure relation. If not only every action but every expression of passivity or even of a mere condition is attached to the I by the personal form of verbal expression, the I itself ultimately becomes this ideal center. It is no content of perception or intuition but, as Kant says, it is solely that "in reference to which representations have synthetic unity." In this sense, the *representation* "I" is "the poorest of all," because it seems emptied of all concrete content, but this absence of content implies an entirely new function and signification. For this signification, it is true, language possesses no adequate expression; for, even in its highest degree of spirituality, it must refer to the sphere of sensory intuition and hence cannot attain to this "pure intellectual representation" of the I, this I of "transcendental apperception." But nevertheless it can, mediately at least, prepare the way for the I, by developing more and more subtly and sharply the opposition between the objective reality of things and subjective, personal reality, and by defining the relation between the two in different ways and with diverse instruments.

---

house." Cf. Aug. Müller, *Türkische Grammatik*, p. 64. A similar construction occurs in the Finno-Ugrian languages; cf. H. Winkler, *Das Uralaltaische und seine Gruppen*, pp. 7 ff.

191. Cf. F. N. Finck, *Die Haupttypen des Sprachbaus*, pp. 13 ff.

3. THE NOMINAL AND THE VERBAL TYPE OF LINGUISTIC EXPRESSION.
The science and philosophy of language have long concerned themselves
with the controversy as to whether the original words of language were of a
verbal or *nominal* nature, whether they designated things or activities.
The opinions were sharply divided; arguments bearing on the history of
language and considerations of a general speculative nature were adduced
on both sides. It seemed for a time that the controversy had died down,
since the concept around which it turned had itself become problematic.
Modern linguists have gradually abandoned the attempt to surprise the
secret of the genesis of language by explorations of primeval times. They
have ceased to endow the concept of the "linguistic root" with empirical,
historical existence, and have come to regard it as a mere product of grammatical analysis—as indeed Humboldt with his usual critical circumspec-
tion had done before them. The supposed "original forms" of language
have paled to mere logical abstractions. As long as linguists believed in an
actual "root period" of language, they could attempt to reduce linguistic
forms as a whole to a "limited number of matrices or types"—and combining this view with the belief that all speech had its origin in the group
performance of human activities, they proceeded to seek the traces of this
activity in the fundamental linguistic form of these types. It was in this
light that Max Müller, for example, following the lead of Ludwig Noiré,
undertook to reduce the roots of Sanskrit to a limited number of original
linguistic concepts, to the terms for the simplest human activities, for braid-
ing and weaving, sewing and binding, cutting and dividing, digging and
thrusting, breaking and beating.[192] Attempts of this sort seemed to have
lost their meaning, however, once the concept of the root had come to be
taken in a formal rather than a material sense, once it had come to be regarded less as the factual element of language formation than as a methodological element of linguistic *science*. And even those who did not go so far
as this total methodological dissolution of the root concept, who felt justified in assuming that in the Indo-Germanic, for example, the roots had
real existence in a time preceding inflection—now seemed enjoined from
asserting anything with regard to their actual form.[193] Nevertheless, there
are signs of a revival of interest in the nature and structure of the original

192. Cf. Ludwig Noiré, *Der Ursprung der Sprache*, pp. 311 ff., 341 ff., and Max Müller,
Das Denken im Lichte der Sprache (Leipzig, 1888), pp. 371 ff., 571 ff.
193. This is the standpoint for example of B. Delbrück in *Grundfragen der Sprachforschung*,
pp. 113 ff.

roots, even among empirical linguists. The thesis most frequently encountered is that these roots were verbal in character and structure. In seeking to revive this old thesis which was early put forward by Pânini, a French linguist, de la Grasserie, expressly invokes metaphysical considerations as well as observations drawn from the history of language. Language, he says, must have started with the designation of verbal concepts and thence progressed gradually to the expression of objective concepts, because only activities and changes are perceived by the senses as phenomena, while the thing that lies at the base of these changes and activities can only be apprehended mediately as their vehicle. Like thought, language must pass from the known to the unknown, from what is perceived by the senses to what is merely thought, from the "phenomenon" to the "noumenon"; the designation of the verb and of verbal attributes must therefore have preceded the designations of substance, the linguistic "substantives." [194]

But precisely this μετάβασις εἰς ἄλλο γένος, this surprising turn to metaphysics, reveals the methodological weakness in the formulation of the problem. The entire demonstration is based on an unmistakable *quaternio terminorum:* the concept of substance which provides the middle term of the syllogism is used in two different significations, once in a metaphysical, once in an empirical sense. The major premise speaks of substance as the metaphysical subject of changes and attributes, as the "thing in itself," which lies "behind" all qualities and accidents—the conclusion speaks of the nominal concepts of language, which, since they serve to express objects, can take them only as "phenomenal objects." Substance in the first sense is the expression of an absolute essence, while in the second sense it can only be the expression of a relative, empirical permanence. But if the problem is taken in this latter sense, the inference drawn, in so far as it is based on *epistemological* grounds, loses all cogency. For epistemology does not teach us that the idea of the variable attribute or state is necessarily "prior" to the idea of the "thing" as a relatively permanent unity: it rather shows that the concept of the thing and the concept of the attribute or state are equally justified and equally necessary conditions in the construction of the world of experience. They are not distinguished from one another as expressions of given realities, according to the order which these realities assume, either intrinsically or in reference to our cognition—but as forms of thought, as categories which determine one another. In *this* sense the criterion of permanence, the criterion of the "thing" is given neither before

194. Cf. Raoul de la Grasserie, *Du verbe comme générateur des autres parties du discours.*

nor after the criterion of change but only with it as its correlative. And this line of reasoning operates also conversely: it disproves not only the alleged primacy of verbs and verbal concepts, but also the psychological arguments which have been adduced to demonstrate the primacy of purely objective intuition and mere nominal concepts. "It is impossible to suppose," remarks Wundt, for example, "that man ever thought solely in verbal concepts; for psychological reasons, we might far more readily believe that he thought only in material concepts; and indeed, there are distinct vestiges of such a state, not only in the speech of children but also in numerous extant languages which have preserved a more original level of conceptual development." [195] However, the notion that man once thought solely in nominal concepts involves the same *fundamental* fallacy as the opposite thesis according temporal and objective priority to verbal concepts. Here we are confronted with one of those problems which cannot be solved by a simple either-or, but only by a basic, critical *reformulation* of the question itself. The dilemma which has long divided students of language into two camps is ultimately a dilemma of method. If one accepts the *reproduction theory,* if one assumes that the purpose of language consists solely in the outward designation of certain distinctions which are *given* in the perceptual world —then it is meaningful to ask whether it first emphasized things or activities, states or attributes. Essentially, however, this way of putting the question merely embodies the old fallacy of hypostatizing the fundamental categories of thought and language. A distinction which first occurs "in" the spirit, i.e., through the totality of its functions, is looked upon as substantially present and preceding the whole of these functions. The problem takes on a new meaning if we reflect that "things" and "states," "attributes" and "activities" are not given contents of consciousness, but modalities and directions of its formation. Then it becomes apparent that none of them is immediately perceived, and expressed by language according to this perception; what takes place is rather that an undifferentiated diversity of sensory impressions is *defined* in accordance with one or another form of thought and language. It is this fixation *into* an object or activity, not the mere naming of the object or activity, that is expressed in the spiritual operation of language as in the logical operation of cognition. The question then is not whether the act of designation first seizes upon things or activities as self-contained distinct forms of reality, but whether it is situated

195. Wundt, *Die Sprache, Völkerpsychologie,* 2d ed., *1,* 594.

in one or another linguistic and logical *category*—whether, as it were, it is performed *sub specie nominis* or *sub specie verbi*.

We may assume that a simple a priori answer to *this* question will not be possible. If language is no longer regarded as a distinct reproduction of a distinct given reality, but as a vehicle of that great process in which the I "comes to grips" with the world, in which the limits of the two are clearly defined, it is evident that the problem is susceptible of many diverse solutions. For the medium of communication between I and world is not finished and determinate from the outset but comes into being and gains efficacy only by giving form to itself. Hence we cannot speak of a system, a temporal or logical progression of linguistic categories, which all linguistic development must always follow. As in epistemological inquiry, each particular category which we single out and place in relief against the others, can only be interpreted and judged as a single *factor* which may develop very different concrete configurations according to the relations into which it enters with other factors. It is from the interpenetration of these factors and their varying relations with one another that the "form" of language arises, which, however, should be regarded as a form not of being but of movement, not as static but as dynamic. Accordingly there are no absolute oppositions but only relative oppositions—oppositions of meaning and of *direction*. The emphasis may fall now on one, now on another factor, the dynamic accents may be distributed in any number of ways among attributes, states, activities, and only in this oscillating movement do we find the special character of all linguistic form as creative form. The more sharply we seek to apprehend this process as it operates in the particular languages, the more evident it becomes that the parts of speech which our grammatical analysis seeks to differentiate, the substantive, adjective, pronoun, verb, are not present from the start, acting upon one another like rigid substantial units, but that they seem, as it were, to produce and delimit one another. The designation does not issue from the finished object; on the contrary, it is through the development of the sign and the consequent definition of the contents of consciousness that our world takes on progressively clearer outlines as a totality of "objects" and "attributes," of "changes" and "activities," of "persons" and "things," of local and temporal relations.

If then language represents a process of differentiation, it may be presumed to have grown out of a relatively undifferentiated state. The history

of language confirms this assumption, disclosing a phase when the parts
of speech which we distinguish in the highly developed languages, were
separated from each other neither in form nor content. At this phase, one
and the same word can fulfill very different grammatical functions, can
serve as a preposition or an independent noun, as a verb or as a substantive,
according to the particular conditions. Especially the *indifference* of *noun*
and *verb* is the rule which determines the structure of most languages. It
has sometimes been said that though all language resolves into the categories of the noun and the verb, very few languages have a verb in our
sense. The Indo-Germanic and Semitic languages seem to be almost alone
in their sharp distinction between the two classes, and even here we still
find fluid boundaries between the nominal and the verbal sentence forms.[196]
In the Malay languages, Humboldt tells us the boundary between nominal
and verbal expression is so fluid that the verb seems to be lacking. He also
points out that the Burmese language is totally lacking in formal designations for the verbal function and that those who speak it seem to have no
feeling for the principle of the verb.[197] Progress in comparative linguistics
has shown what Humboldt apparently regarded as an anomaly to be a
general and widespread phenomenon. In place of sharply distinguished
nouns and verbs, we encounter a seemingly amorphous form.[198] The formal distinction between expressions of things and expressions of activities
emerges only gradually. "Conjugation" and "declension" often merge.
Wherever the type of "possessive conjugation" is observed, we find a complete parallelism between nominal and verbal expression.[199] Similar relations are to be found between the designations of activities and of attributes:
one and the same system of inflection can apply both to verbs and adjectives.[200] Even complex phrases, even whole sentences are sometimes "con-

196. Cf. Nöldeke, *Kurzgefasste Syrische Grammatik*, p. 215 (Eng. trans., p. 245): "The
nominal sentence, i.e., a sentence having a substantive, adjective, or adverb as its predicate, is
not too sharply distinguished from the verbal sentence in the Syriac. The participle, which
very frequently serves as a predicate, which is on its way to becoming a pure verbal form
but does not conceal its nominal origin . . . suggests a transition from the nominal to the
verbal sentence. . . . And the nominal and verbal sentence do not reveal a great difference
of inner structure in Syriac."

197. Humboldt, "Einleitung zum Kawi-Werk," 7, No. 1, 222, 280 ff., 305; cf. *Kawi-Werk*,
2, 81, 129 ff., 287

198. For examples see Fr. Müller, *Grundriss*: from the Hottentot, *1*, Pt. 2, 12 ff.; from the
Mandingan languages, *1*, Pt. 2, 142; from the Samoyed, *2*, Pt. 2, 174; from the Yenisei-
Ostyak, *2*, Pt. 1, 115.

199. See above, p. 261.

200. For varied examples of this "adjectival conjugation," see de la Grasserie, op. cit., 32 ff.

jugated" in this way.[201] Such phenomena should not be regarded as indications of the formlessness of a language, but rather as evidence of a characteristic "growth towards form." For this indeterminacy, this deficient formation and differentiation of linguistic categories, conceals a factor of plasticity and essential formative power. The undifferentiated word contains within it all the potentialities of differentiation and leaves each particular language free, as it were, to choose whatever potentialities it pleases.

Any attempt to establish a general schema of this development would seem futile, for the source of its concrete richness is precisely that each language follows a *different* method in building up its system of categories. Nevertheless, without doing violence to this concrete abundance of expressive forms, we can group them according to certain basic types. Certain languages and groups of languages have developed the nominal type in full sharpness and purity, their whole structure seems to be dominated by the intuition of objects, while in others both grammar and syntax are determined by the verb. The verbal group, moreover, comprises two different forms, according to whether the verb is taken as an expression of a mere *occurrence* or of pure *activity,* according to whether it immerses itself in the objective event or whether it gives central emphasis to the active subject and its energy. The nominal type is most sharply developed in the languages of the Altaic family. Here the entire sentence structure is such that one objective term simply follows another and is linked with it attributively: and yet this simple principle of articulation is implemented so rigorously and universally that it can provide clear and self-contained expression for the most complex relations. "I do not hesitate," writes H.

In Malay every word without exception can be transformed into a verb by a suffix; conversely one can turn any verb into a noun simply by preceding it with the definite article (Humboldt, *Kawi-Werk*, 2, 81, 348 ff.). In Coptic the infinitive form of the verb even has the gender of substantive nouns: the infinitive is a noun and can take a masculine or feminine form. In accordance with its nominal character, moreover, it has originally no direct object; this signification is expressed by a genitive which immediately follows the infinitive as it would a substantive (cf. Steindorff, *Koptische Grammatik*, pp. 91 ff.). In the Yenisei-Ostyak as in the Dravidian languages, verb forms can take case suffixes and are thus "declined"—while in some languages the noun can be provided with certain indications of tense and are thus "conjugated" (cf. Fr. Müller, *Grundriss*, 2, Pt. 1, 115, 180 ff.; 3, Pt. 1, 198). In the language of Annatom—according to G. v. d. Gabelentz, *Die Sprachwissenschaft*, pp. 160 ff.—not the verb but the personal pronoun is conjugated. The pronoun opens the sentence and indicates whether we are dealing with the first, second or third person, singular, dual, trial or plural, and whether the action is present, past, future, volitive, etc.

201. E.g., in Aleutian cf. V. Henry, *Langue aléoute*, pp. 60 ff.

Winkler of this principle, which he illustrates by a discussion of the Japanese verb,

> to call it a most wonderful structure. In the most succinct form, it expresses an inexhaustible variety of subtle and minute shadings: what we in our language express by numerous circumlocutions, by dependent clauses of all sorts, relative as well as conjuctional, is clearly rendered by a single term or by a single substantive noun governing a verbal noun; a verbal noun of this sort can clearly express what in our formulation requires a main clause and two or three subsidiary clauses, and moreover each of the three or four links can encompass the sublest and most diverse distinctions of tense, of active or passive, causative, continuative, in short, the most manifold modifications of action. . . . And all this is largely accomplished without recourse to most of the formal elements with which we are so familiar and which strike us as indispensable. Thus the Japanese is in our sense a formless language par excellence; by this I do not mean to disparage this language but merely to indicate how vastly its structure diverges from that of our languages.[202]

The essence of this divergence is that while the feeling for the conceptual shadings of action is by no means lacking, it can only be expressed in so far as the expression of action is enmeshed, as it were, with the expression of the object and enters into it as a specification. The existence of the thing forms the center of designation and all expression of attributes, relations and activities remains dependent on it. Thus this language manifests a "substantial" point of view in the strictest sense. In the Japanese verb we frequently find a pure statement of existence where we would expect to find a predicative statement. Instead of expressing a *relation* between subject and predicate, it stresses the *presence* or nonpresence, existence or nonexistence of the subject or predicate. And this first statement of being or nonbeing is the point of departure for all further specifications of "whatness," of acting and being acted upon, etc.[203] This is most strikingly shown by the negative locution in which even non-being seems to be taken substantially. The negation of an action is expressed by a positive statement

202. H. Winkler, *Der uralaltaische Sprachstamm*, pp. 166 ff.

203. A sentence such as "it is snowing" is consequently rendered in Japanese as "snow's falling (is)." "The day has ended, it has grown dark" runs "the day's having-grown-dark (is)." Cf. Hoffmann, *Japanische Sprachlehre*, pp. 66 ff.

of its nonbeing: there is no "not coming" in our sense, but rather a non-being or nonpresence of coming. This nonbeing itself is expressed as "the being of the not." And like the *relation* of negation, other expressions of relation are transformed into substantial expressions. The Yakut expresses the relation of possession by asserting the existence or nonexistence of the possessed object: a locution such as "my house existing" or "my house not existing" states that I possess or do not possess a house.[204] Likewise the numerical terms are often so constructed that the property of number seems to possess an independent objective content: instead of many men or all men, one says "man of manyness" or "man of allness"; instead of five men, "man of fiveness," etc.[205] The modal and temporal properties of the verbal noun are expressed in similar ways. A substantive such as "imminence," linked attributively to the verbal noun, indicates that the action referred to is regarded as future, hence that the verb is to be taken in a future sense [206]—a substantive such as "demanding" serves to form the desiderative form of the verb, etc. Other modal shadings such as the conditional or the concessive are indicated in accordance with the same principle.[207] Here language expresses an infinite variety of conceptual forms and combinations through the simple juxtaposition of independent substantive terms.

We encounter a very different fundamental approach where language, still preserving this original indifference of noun and verb, accentuates the opposite aspect of the indifferent form. In the cases just considered, all linguistic expression takes the *object* as its point of departure. But there are other languages which just as definitely and significantly start from the designation of the occurrence. Here the verb, as pure expression of occurrence, is manifestly the true center of language: while in the nominal idioms all relations, even those of occurrence and action, are transposed into objective relations, here, conversely even these are transposed into

---

204. Cf. Winkler, pp. 199 ff.; Böthlingk, *Über die Sprache der Jakuten*, p. 348.

205. Winkler, pp. 152, 157 ff.

206. Cf. in Yakut (Böthlingk, pp. 299 ff.): My imminent cutting = the object subjected to my future cuting, but also "I will cut," etc. Cf. tense formation in the Japanese verb, where the forms which serve to express future or past, completion or duration, are all combinations of a dependent verbal noun, designating the *content* of the action, with a governing verbal noun indicating its *temporal* character. Thus "seeing's striving," "willing," "becoming" (for "will see"); "seeing's going away" (for "to have seen"), etc. Cf. Winkler, pp. 176 ff. and Hoffmann, *Japanische Sprachlehre*, pp. 214, 227.

207. For more details see Winkler, 125 ff., 208 ff., and *Uralaltaische Völker und Sprachen*, pp. 90 ff.

relations of occurrence. In the first case one might say that the form of
dynamic change is drawn into the form of static substance; in the second,
substance is apprehended only in relation to change. But this form of
change is not yet permeated with the pure I-form and hence, despite its
dynamism, still presents a predominantly objective, impersonal aspect.
In this respect we are still in the sphere of things, but its center has shifted.
The emphasis is no longer on the existence but on the change. We have
seen that in the nominal languages the substantive, as expression of the
object, was the dominant structural factor; here we may expect the verb,
as expression of change, to be the dynamic center. While nominal expression tended to transpose even the most complex relations into the substantival form, here language will strive to encompass and, as it were,
catch all these relations in the verbal form. This seems to be the general
approach of most American Indian languages. There have been attempts
at a psychological explanation of it based on the structure of the Indian
mind.[208] But whatever we may think of this explanation, these languages
show a unique *method* of language formation. The general lines of this
method were clearly delineated by Humboldt in his account of "incorporation" in the Mexican language. The relations which other languages express by the analytical articulation of the sentence are here expressed syn-
thetically in a single complex "word-sentence." The core of the word-
sentence is the expression of verbal action, to which however any number
of modifiers are affixed. The governing and the governed parts of the verb,
particularly the designations for its more or less immediate object, are incorporated into the verbal term and are required to complement it. "The
sentence," Humboldt remarks, "is conceived as formally completed in the
verb and is only specified more closely through a kind of apposition. The
Mexican verb cannot be conceived without these complementary, subsidiary specifications. When there is no specific object, a special indefinite
pronoun, with different forms for persons and things, is combined with the
verb: ni-tla-qua, I something eat, ni-te-tla-maca, I someone something
give. . . ." The incorporative method thus forces the entire content of a
statement into a single verb, or where the statement is too complex and this
is impossible, it sends out "pointers, as it were," from the verbal center of
the sentence, "to indicate the directions in which the particular parts are
to be sought in relation to the sentence." Even where the verb does not
encompass the entire *content* of the statement, it thus contains the gen-

208. Cf. the remarks of G. v. d. Gabelentz, *Die Sprachwissenschaft*, pp. 402 ff.

eral *schema* of the sentence structure: here a sentence is not constructed, not gradually built up out of its heterogeneous elements, but is stamped into a unit and given all at once. Language first produces a connected whole which is formally complete and self-sufficient: it expressly designates what is not yet individually defined as an undefined something by means of a pronoun, and then goes on to fill in the particulars of this undefined residuum.[209]

Later investigations of the American Indian languages have modified Humboldt's general picture of the incorporation process, in certain respects; they show that this method can take very different forms in different languages with regard to the type, degree and scope of the incorporation [210] —but his general characterization of the unique way of thinking which underlies it, remains essentially valid. To employ a mathematical image, we might compare this method of language formation to the setting up of a formula which designates the universal quantitative relations of magnitude but leaves the particular magnitudes unspecified. The formula merely renders in a unitary, comprehensive expression the universal forms of connection that obtains between certain sets of magnitudes: but before it can be applied to a specific case, the unspecified magnitudes, x, y, z must be replaced by specific magnitudes. Similarly in the verbal word-sentence, the form of the statement is fully outlined and anticipated at the outset; to complete it, the indefinite pronouns incorporated in the word-sentence must merely be more closely defined by terms added later. The verb as designation of an occurrence strives to concentrate within itself the living whole of the meaning expressed in the sentence; but the farther it advances in this direction, the more it is in danger of being submerged in the flood of new matter which it is called upon to master. Around the verbal core of the statement there forms so dense a mesh of modifiers, indicating the manner of the action, its local or temporal circumstances, its more or less distant object, that it becomes difficult to detach the content of the statement itself from this involvement and apprehend its independent meaning content. The expression of action never seems generic, but is always individually determined, characterized by special particles with which it is

209. Cf. Humboldt, "Einleitung zum Kawi-Werk," *Werke*, 7, No. 1, 144 ff.
210. Cf. in particular the investigations of Lucien Adam on "Polysynthesism" in the Nahuatl, Quechua, Quiche, and Mayan languages, in his *Études sur six langues américaines* (Paris, 1878). See also Brinton, "On Polysynthesis and Incorporation as Characteristics of American Languages," *Transactions of the American Philosophical Society of Philadelphia, 23* (1885), and Boas, *Handbook, 1,* 573, 646 ff. (Chinook), 1002 ff. (Eskimo), etc.

inseparably bound up.[211] Although an action or occurrence is represented as a concrete intuitive *whole* by means of all these particles, the unity of an occurrence and particularly of the subject of an action is not sharply set forth.[212] The full light of language seems to strike only the content of the occurrence itself—not the I which actively participates in it. In most of the American Indian languages, for example, the inflection of the verb is not governed by the subject but by the object of the action. The transitive verb takes its number not from the subject but from its direct object: it must stand in the plural when it represents an action directed toward a plurality of objects. Thus the grammatical object of the sentence becomes its logical subject, governing the verb.[213] The construction of the sentence and of the language as a whole takes the verb as its point of departure, but the verb remains in the sphere of objective intuition. The essential factor in this linguistic approach is the beginning and the course of the event, not the energy of the subject, manifested in an action.

This basic intuition changes only in those languages which have progressed to a purely personal configuration of verbal action, in which conjugation does not basically consist in the combination of the verbal noun with possessive suffixes but in a synthetic bond between the verb and the personal pronoun. What distinguishes this synthesis from the method of the so-called "polysynthetic" languages is that it is based on a preceding analysis. This synthesis is no mere fusion of opposites—on the contrary, it presupposes the sharp differentiation of these opposites. With the development of personal pronouns the sphere of subjective reality has become distinct from the objective sphere—and yet in the inflection of the verb, the

211. Cf. the characteristic remarks of K. v. d. Steinen on the Bakairi language: *Unter den Naturvölkern Zentral-Brasiliens*, 2d ed., pp. 78 ff.; *Die Bakaïri-Sprache*, pp. ix ff.

212. Gatschet (pp. 572 ff.) points out that the verb in Klamath expresses a verbal act or state only in the impersonal and indefinite form—comparable to our infinitive. In a construction such as "thou-to-break-stick," the verbal term only designates breaking as such without reference to its subject. Similarly, the Mayan languages possess no transitive active verbs in our sense: they have only nouns and absolute verbs designating a state, attribute or activity, which are construed as predicates of a personal pronoun or of a third person acting as subject, but can take no direct object. The words which serve to represent a transitive action are radical or derived nouns which as such are combined with the possessive prefix. In Mayan, sentences such as "thou hast killed my father," "thou hast written the book" are rendered as "thy killed one is my father," "thy written thing is the book." (Cf. Ed. Seler, *Das Konjugations-system der Maya-Sprachen* pp. 9, 17 ff.) In the verbal expression of the Malay such "impersonal" locutions are also frequent, e.g., "my seeing (was) the star" for "I saw the star," etc., cf. Humboldt, *Kawi-Werk*, 2, 80, 350 ff., 397.

213. Cf. Gatschet, p. 434 and particularly Seler.

terms for subjective reality join with the terms for objective occurrence to form a new unity. Wherever we find the essential and specific nature of the verb expressed in this junction, we must infer that for its completion the verb must enter into a synthesis with the terms for personal reality. "For the actual being which is characterized in the grammatical representation of the verb," says Humboldt, "cannot easily be expressed by itself, but can only be manifested as a being with a certain modality, a specific *time* and *person;* the expression of this character is inextricably woven into the root, so demonstrating that the root can only be conceived with these attributes and must in a sense be permuted into them. Its (the verb's) nature lies precisely in this mobility, this inability to be fixated except in the specific case." [214] But neither the temporal nor personal specification of the verb, neither its temporal nor its personal fixation is part of its original substance; both represent a goal that is attained only relatively late in the development of language. We have already followed the process of temporal specification; [215] as to the relation of the verb to the I, we can gain an idea of the gradual changes that took place by considering the way in which certain languages distinguish between "transitive" and "intransitive" verbal expression. In various Semitic languages, for example, the intransitive or semi-passive verb, which expresses not a pure action but a state or a being-acted-upon, is distinguished by a specific vowel pronunciation. In Ethiopic, according to Dillmann, this differentiation of intransitive verbs by pronunciation has remained in full force: all verbs designating attributes, physical or spiritual qualities, passions or unfree activities, are pronounced differently from those designating a free and independent activity.[216] This phonetic symbolism is indicative of that fundamental spiritual process which becomes more and more evident as language develops. The I grasps itself through its counterpart in verbal action, and only as this latter becomes more elaborated and sharply defined, does the I truly find itself and understand its unique position.

214. Humboldt, *Kawi-Werk,* 2, 79 ff.
215. Cf. above, pp. 218–219.
216. Dillmann, *Grammatik der äthiopischen Sprache,* pp. 116 ff.

Chapter 4

Language as Expression of Conceptual Thought. Concept and Class Formation in Language

1. The Formation of Qualifying Concepts

THE PROBLEM of concept formation marks the point of closest contact between logic and the philosophy of language; at this point they seem to fuse into an inseparable unit. For all logical analysis of concepts seems eventually to lead to the study of words and names. The resulting nominalism concentrates the two problems into one: the content of the concept merges with the content and function of the word. Truth itself then becomes a linguistic rather than a logical term: *veritas in dicto, non in re consistit*. It is an agreement which is to be found neither in things nor in ideas, but has reference solely to combinations of signs and particularly of phonetic signs. An absolutely "pure," speechless thought would not know the opposition between true and false, which arises only in and through speech. Thus the question of the significance and origin of the concept inevitably leads back to the question of the origin of the word: inquiry into the genesis of word significations and word classes becomes the only means of elucidating the immanent meaning of the concept and its function in the development of knowledge.[1]

Closer investigation, to be sure, shows this nominalistic solution to the problem of the concept to be a pseudo-solution, since it forms a vicious circle. For on the one hand language is expected to supply the ultimate, in a sense, the only "explanation" of concept formation, while on the other hand, it requires the support of this function at every step in its own development. And this vicious circle confronts us in every part of the theory. Traditional logic tells us that the concept arises "through abstraction": it instructs us to form a concept by comparing similar things or percepts and

1. Cf. above, p. 137 ff.

abstracting their "common characteristics." That the contents of comparison *have* specific "characteristics," that they possess qualitative properties according to which we can divide them into classes, genera, species, is usually taken as a self-evident premise, requiring no special mention. And yet this seemingly self-evident premise embodies one of the most difficult problems of concept formation. First of all, the old question arises as to whether the "characteristics" according to which we divide things into classes, are given us *prior* to language formation or whether they are supplied only *by* language formation. "In the theory of abstraction," Sigwart rightly remarks,

it is forgotten that before a represented object can be resolved into its particular characteristics, judgments are required whose predicates must be general ideas (as concepts are ordinarily called); and that *these* concepts must ultimately be gained by some means other than abstraction, since it is they which make this process of abstraction possible. The advocates of this theory also forget that abstraction presupposes some definition of the sphere of objects to be compared, and they tacitly posit a motive for selecting this particular grouping and for seeking its common characteristics. Ultimately this motive, if it is not absolutely arbitrary, can only be that these objects have been recognized as similar a priori, because they all have a specific content in common, i.e., that there is already present a general idea by means of which these objects are distinguished from the totality of objects. The whole theory that concepts are formed by comparison and abstraction has meaning only if, as it often the case, the problem is to indicate the common factor in things which general *linguistic usage* actually designates by the same word, and thus to elucidate the true signification of the word. If one is asked to describe the concept of the animal, of gas, of theft, one might be tempted to seek the common characteristics of all the things which are called animals, of all the bodies which are called gases, of all the actions which are called thefts. Whether this is successful; whether this means of concept formation is practicable, is another question; it might be plausible, if we could assume that there is no doubt as to what should be called animal, gas, theft—i.e., if we already have the concept we are seeking. Thus any attempt to form a concept by abstraction is tantamount to looking for the spectacles which are on your nose, with the help of these same spectacles.[2]

Indeed, the theory of abstraction solves the question of *conceptual form* only by referring it, consciously or tacitly, to the *form of language*. And with this the problem is not so much solved as relegated to another field. The process of abstraction can be carried out only with respect to such contents as have already been in some way defined and designated, which have been classified in language and thought. But how, we must now ask, do we arrive at this classification itself? What are the conditions of that first *primary formation* which is effected in language and which provides the foundation for all the subsequent and more complex syntheses of logical thought? How does language succeed in escaping from that Heraclitean river of change, in which no content recurs truly identical—how does language place itself, as it were, in opposition to this flux, and abstract determinate forms from it? Here lies the true secret of "predication" as a problem both of logic and of language. The beginning of thought and speech is not this: we do not simply seize on and name certain distinctions that are somewhere present in feeling or intuition; on the contrary, on our own initiative we draw certain dividing lines, effect certain separations and connections, by virtue of which distinct individual configurations emerge from the uniform flux of consciousness. In the usual logical view, the concept is born only when the signification of the word is sharply delineated and unambiguously fixed through certain intellectual operations, particularly through "definition" according to *genus proximum* and *differentia specifia*. But to penetrate to the ultimate source of the concept, our thinking must go back to a deeper stratum, must seek those factors of synthesis and analysis, which are at work in the process of word formation itself, and which are decisive for the ordering of all our representations according to specific linguistic classifications.

For the *primary* function of concept formation is not, as most logicians have assumed under the pressure of a centuries-old tradition, to raise our representations to ever greater universality; on the contrary, it is to make them increasingly determinate. In so far as "universality" is expected of the concept, it is not an end in itself but only a means of attaining to the true purpose of the concept, which is precision. Before any contents can be compared with one another and ordered into classes according to the degree of their similarity, they themselves must be defined as contents. But for this a logical act of *postulation* and *differentiation* is required, which will provide certain intervals in the continuous flow of consciousness, which in a sense will halt the restless coming and going of sense impressions and create certain stopping places. Hence the original and decisive achievement of the concept is not to compare representations and group them according to genera and species, but rather to form impressions into representations. Among modern logicians Lotze has expressed this relationship most clearly, although in his interpretation of it he has not entirely freed himself from the fetters of the logical tradition. His theory of the concept starts from the idea that the most basic operation of thought cannot consist in the combination of two given representations, but that we must take a further step backward. In order that representations may be combined into the form of *thought,* they themselves must undergo a process of formation which makes them into logical elements. We tend to pass over this first operation of thought, because it has already been performed in the formation of our traditional language and consequently seems to be a self-evident premise, and no longer to be the achievement of one's own thinking. But in truth, says Lotze, the creation of words, if we disregard mere formless interjections and expressions of excitement, implies the fundamental form of thought, the form of *objectivization.* Language cannot yet aim to institute connections of the manifold, which come under a universal rule, but it must first perform the preliminary task of giving to each particular impression an intrinsic signification. This type of objectivization has as yet nothing to do with attributing an entirely independent reality to the content—it is concerned solely with fixing the content *for* knowledge and characterizing it for consciousness as something identical with itself and recurrent amid the flux of impressions. "Thus through the logical objectivization effected in the creation of the names, the named content is not moved into an outward reality; the common world in which others are expected to find the content to which we refer, is in general only the world of the thinkable; here the first suggestion of an existence of its own, and an inner necessity identical for all thinking beings and independent of them, is imputed to this world."

And now this first fixation of whatever qualities can be apprehended in thought and speech is augmented by further specifications, through which they enter into certain *relations* with one another, through which they are articulated into orders and series. The particular quality not only possesses in itself an identical "whatness," an enduring character of its own, but through it it is related to others—and this relation is not arbitrary, but discloses a characteristic objective form. Yet, although we recognize this form as such, we cannot juxtapose it to the particular contents as something independent and separable; we can only find it in them and through them. If, after having fixed and named several contents as such, we group them into the form of a series, we seem, in so doing, to have postulated a *common* characteristic which is specified in the particular members of the series, which is manifested in all of them, yet in each one with a specific difference. This *first universal* is however, as Lotze stresses, essentially different from the current generic concepts of logic.

We communicate the general concept of an animal or of a geometric figure to others by prescribing a precise series of logical operations of synthesis, analysis or relation to be performed upon a number of particular representations assumed to be known; at the end of this logical operation the content which we wished to communicate will be present in his consciousness. But we cannot in this way explain wherein consists the generic blue which included our representation of light blue or dark blue, or the generic *color* which formed part of our representation of red and yellow. . . . The common factor in red and yellow, by virtue of which they are both colors, cannot be detached from what makes red red and yellow yellow; that is to say, this common factor cannot be detached and made into the content of a third representation of the same kind and order as the other two. Our sensation communicates only a particular color shade, a particular pitch, volume and quality of tone. . . . Anyone who wishes to apprehend the universal in color or tone will inevitably come up against the fact that what he has in mind is the intuition of a specific color or sound accompanied by the reflection that every other tone or color has an equal right to serve as an intuitive example of the universal which is itself not subject to intuition; or else, his memory must present many colors and tones successively, while again he reflects that what he is seeking is not these particulars but that which is common to them and which cannot be intuited in itself. . . . In truth, words such as "color" and "tone" are only indications of logical problems which cannot be solved in the form of a self-contained representation. Through them we instruct our consciousness to represent and compare the particular, perceptible tones and colors, and in this comparison to apprehend the common factor which, as our sensation tells us, is contained in them but which no effort of thought can truly detach from that wherein they are different to make them into the content of an equally intuitive new representation.[3]

3. H. Lotze, *Logik* (2d ed., Leipzig, 1880), pp. 14 ff., 29 ff. Eng. trans., by B. Bosanquet (Oxford, Clarendon Press, 1884), pp. 22–24.

We have here reported Lotze's theory of the "first universal" at length, because, correctly understood and interpreted, it may provide the key to an understanding of the original form of linguistic concept formation. As Lotze's remarks clearly show, the logical tradition finds itself in a strange dilemma in regard to this problem. Traditional logicians are convinced that the concept must be oriented purely towards universality and that its ultimate achievement must be to provide universal representations; but then it develops that this essentially uniform striving for universality cannot everywhere be fulfilled in the same way. Consequently, we must distinguish two forms of universal: in one, the universal is given only implicitly, as it were, in the form of a relation disclosed by the particular contents, while in the other it emerges also explicitly after the manner of an independent intuitive representation. But from here only one step is required to reverse our viewpoint: to look upon the enduring relation as the true content and logical foundation of the concept, and to regard the "universal representation" as a psychological accident which is not always desirable or attainable. Lotze did not take this step; instead of drawing a sharp distinction in principle between definition by stipulation, in which the concept makes the claim, and the postulate to universality, he transformed the primary definitions to which the concept leads back into primary universals, so that instead of the two characteristic works of the concept there are only two forms of the universal, a "first" and a "second" universal. But from his own presentation it follows that these two types have little more than the name in common and are very distinct in their logical *structure*. For the relation of subsumption, which traditional logic regards as the constitutive relation through which the universal is connected with the particular, the genus with the species and individuals, is not applicable to the concepts which Lotze designates as the "first universal." Blue and yellow are not particulars subordinated to the genus "color in general"; on the contrary, color "as such" is contained nowhere else but in them and in the totality of other possible color gradations, and is thinkable only as this aggregate in its graduated order. Thus universal logic points to a distinction which also runs through the whole formation of linguistic concepts. Before language can proceed to the generalizing and subsuming form of the concept, it requires another, purely *qualifying* type of concept formation. Here a thing is not named from the standpoint of the genus to which it belongs, but on the basis of some particular *property* which is apprehended in a total intuitive content. The work of the spirit does not consist in subordinating the content to another content, but in distinguishing it as a concrete, undifferentiated whole by stressing a specific, characteristic factor in it and focusing attention on this factor. The possibility of "giving a name" rests on this concentration of the mind's eye: the new imprint of thinking upon the content is the necessary condition for its designation in language.

For the aggregate of these questions the philosophy of language has created a special concept, which however is so ambiguous and discordant in its usage that instead of offering a definite solution it seems to present one of its most difficult and controversial problems. Since Humboldt, the term "inner form" has been used to designate the specific law according to which each language, as set off from others, effects its concept formation. By inner form Humboldt meant the enduring, uniform factor in the endeavor of the spirit to raise the articulated sound to the level of an expression of ideas; he set out to apprehend this factor as fully as possible in its context and to expound it systematically. But even in Humboldt this definition is not unequivocal: for sometimes this form is said to express itself in the laws of linguistic *combination*, and sometimes in the formation of *roots*. Thus, as has sometimes justifiably been argued against Humboldt, it is taken now in a morphological, now in a semiotic sense; on the one hand it applies to the interrelation of certain grammatical categories, e.g., the noun and the verb; on the other hand it goes back to the origin of word significations.[4] If, however, we survey Humboldt's definition of concepts as a *whole*, it is unmistakable that for him the latter standpoint was predominant. That each particular language has a specific inner form meant for him primarily that in the choice of its designations it never simply expressed the objects perceived in themselves, but that this choice was eminently determined by a whole spiritual attitude, by the orientation of man's subjective view of objects. For the word is not a copy of the object as such, but reflects the soul's image of the object.[5] In this sense, the words of different languages can never be synonyms—their meaning, strictly speaking, can never be encompassed in a simple definition which merely lists the objective characteristics of the object designated. There is always a specific mode of *signification* which expresses itself in the syntheses and coordinations underlying the formation of linguistic concepts. If the moon in Greek

4. Humboldt, "Einleitung zum Kawi-Werk," *Werke*, 7, No. 1, 47 ff.; cf. the remarks of B. Delbrück, *Vergleichende Syntax, 1*, 42.

5. Cf. "Einleitung zum Kawi-Werk," *Werke*, 7, No. 1, 59 ff., 89 ff., 190 ff., etc.; see pp. 158 ff., above.

is called the "measurer" (μήν), in Latin the "glittering" (*luna, luc-na*), we have here one and the same sensory intuition assigned to very different notions of meaning and made determinate by them. It no longer seems possible to give a general account of the way in which this specifying of intuition is effected in the different languages, precisely because we have to do with a highly complex cultural process, which varies with each special case. The only road that seems to lie open for us is to place ourselves in the midst of the immediate intuition of the particular languages, striving not to describe their method in an abstract formula, but to feel it immediately in the particular phenomena.[6] Yet, although philosophical analysis can never claim to grasp completely the special subjectivity that expresses itself in the different languages, still the universal subjectivity of language remains within the scope of its problems. For while languages differ in their perspectives of the world, there is a perspective of language itself, which distinguishes it from the other cultural forms. This perspective offers certain points of contact with those of scientific cognition, art and myth, but it also defines itself over against them.

What primarily distinguishes linguistic concept formation from strictly logical concept formation is that it never rests solely on the static representation and comparison of contents but that in it the sheer form of reflection is always infused with specific *dynamic* factors; that its essential impulsions are not taken solely from the world of being but are always drawn at the same time from the world of action. All linguistic concepts remain in the zone between action and reflection. Here there is no mere classification and ordering of intuitions according to specific objective characteristics; even where there is such classification, an active interest in the world and its constitution expresses itself. Herder said that originally language, like nature, was for man a pantheon of animated, active beings. And indeed, it is the reflection not of an objective environment, but of man's own life and action that essentially determines the linguistic view of the world, as it does the primitive mythical image of nature. Man's will and action are directed toward *one* point, his consciousness strains and concentrates on it, and so he becomes ripe, as it were, for the process of linguistic designation. In the stream of consciousness which seemed to flow along uniformly, waves arise with their crests and troughs: particular, dynamically stressed

6. A highly interesting and instructive attempt to carry out this task was performed by James Byrne on the basis of an extraordinary wealth of empirical material. See *General Principles of the Structure of Language* (2 vols. London, 1885).

contents take form and others group around them. And now the ground is prepared for those *coordinations* which make it possible to single out linguistic-logical "characteristics" and to collect these into distinct, characteristic groups; the foundation is provided upon which language can build its edifice of qualifying concepts.

This general trend of language formation has been disclosed in the transition from mere sensuous sounds of excitement to the *cry*. The cry, e.g., of fear or pain, may remain entirely within the sphere of the mere interjection; and yet it already means more than that, in so far as it is not the mere reflex following instantly upon a sense impression, but is rather the expression of a definite and conscious intent. For now consciousness no longer stands in the sign of mere reproduction, but enters the sphere of anticipation: it no longer clings to what is given and present, but reaches out to represent futurity. Accordingly, the sound no longer merely *accompanies* a present state of feeling and excitement, but itself acts as a *factor* intervening in a process. The changes in this process are not merely designated, but in the strictest sense "provoked." When the sound thus acts as an *organ of the will,* it has once and for all gone beyond the stage of mere "imitation." Among children, we can observe how, in the period preceding actual language formation, the infantile outburst gradually becomes a cry. When the cry becomes differentiated, when particular sounds, though not yet articulated, come to be used for different emotions and different kinds of desire, the sound is guided as it were towards specific contents and thus the way is paved for its first "objectivization." The language of mankind developed in essentially the same way if we accredit the theory advanced by Lazarus Geiger and Ludwig Noiré that the original sounds originated not in the objective intuition of substance but in the subjective intuition of action. According to this theory it became possible for the phonetic sign to represent the objective world only as this world itself gradually took form from man's work and activity. For Noiré it was above all the *social* form of action which made possible the social function of language as a means of mutual understanding. If the phonetic sign had merely expressed an individual representation produced in the individual consciousness, it would have remained imprisoned in the individual consciousness, without power to pass beyond it. There would have been no bridge between the perceptual and phonetic worlds of one man and another. But since language arises not in isolated but in *communal* action, it possesses from the very start a truly common, "universal" sense. Language as a *sensorum commune* could only grow out of the sympathy of activity.

It was from communal activity directed toward a common purpose, it was from the primeval labor of our ancestors that language and rational life sprang forth. . . . In its beginnings, the linguistic sound accompanied communal activity as an expression of an enhanced feeling of community. . . . A common representation and designation of other things, of sun and moon, tree and animal, man and child, pain and joy, food and drink, was absolutely impossible; this alone—common activity, not individual activity—was the solid, unchanging ground upon which common understanding could rise. . . . Things enter into the scope of human vision, i.e., they become things only in so far as they *undergo* human activity, and it is then that they obtain their designations, their names.[7]

The empirical demonstration by which Noiré strove to justify this speculative thesis has to be sure been discredited: what he says concerning the original form of linguistic roots and words remains as hypothetical and doubtful as the whole notion of an original "root period" in language. But even if we give up hope of penetrating to the ultimate metaphysical secret of linguistic origins from this standpoint, a study of the *empirical* form of the different languages shows how deeply rooted they are in the sphere of action and activity. This relationship is particularly evident in the languages of primitive peoples [8]—and the advanced languages reveal it more and more clearly as we pass beyond the sphere of general concepts and consider the development of "occupational languages" in the various fields of human activity. Usener pointed out that these languages contain a common structural factor which is characteristic for the trend of linguistic as well as mythico-religious concept formation. "Special names" like "special gods" are gradually superseded only as man progresses from special to more general activities, as his action becomes more universal and with it his consciousness of that action: only the extension of his activity, as Usener writes, enables man to rise to truly universal linguistic and religious concepts.[9]

The content of these concepts and the principle which determines their

7. Cf. Lazarus Geiger, *Ursprung und Entwicklung der menschlichen Sprache und Vernunft* (2 vols. Frankfurt a. M.), pp. 1868 ff.; Ludwig Noiré, *Der Ursprung der Sprache* especially pp. 323 ff.; idem, *Logos-Ursprung und Wesen der Begriffe,* especially pp. 296 ff.

8. Cf. C. Meinhof's essay, "Über die Einwirkung der Beschäftigung auf die Sprache bei den Bantustämmen Afrikas," *Globus,* 75 (1899), 361 ff.

9. H. Usener, *Götternamen: Versuch einer Lehre von der religiösen Begriffsbildung* (Bonn, 1896), especially pp. 317 ff.

structure become fully intelligible only if beside their abstract *logical* meaning we consider their *teleological* meaning. The words of language are not reflections of stable concretions in nature and in the perceptual world, they rather indicate directions which the process of determination may follow. Here consciousness does not passively confront the aggregate of sensory impressions, it permeates them and fills them with its own inner life. Only what in some way touches on man's inner activity, what seems "significant" for it, obtains the linguistic stamp of signification. It has been said of concepts in general that the principle of their formation is a principle of *selection* rather than "abstraction"—and this eminently applies to the formation of linguistic concepts. What happens here is not that existing distinctions, given to consciousness by sensation or perception, are simply stabilized and provided with a certain phonetic sign as a kind of trademark, but rather that dividing lines are drawn within the consciousness as a whole. The determinants and dominants of linguistic expression arise through the determination which the action itself undergoes. The light does not simply pass from objects into the sphere of the spirit, but spreads progressively from the center of the action itself,[10] and thus makes the world of immediate sensation into a world illumined from within, formed both in intuition and language. In this process, language formation shows its kinship with mythical thought and representation, and yet distinguishes itself by a characteristic, independent tendency of its own. Like myth, language starts from the basic experience and basic form of personal activity; however, it does not, like mythology, weave the world in infinite variations around this one central point, but gives it a new form in which it confronts the mere subjectivity of sensation and feeling. In language, the process of animation and the process of definition constantly merge to form a spiritual unity.[11] And it is through this twofold movement, from

10. We cite an example of this process from H. K. Brugsch, *Religion und Mythologie der alten Ägypter* (Leipzig, J. C. Hinrichs, 1888), p. 53: "In ancient Egyptian the word *ḳod* designates successively the most diverse concepts: to make pots, to be a potter, to form, create, build, work, draw, navigate, travel, sleep; and substantively: likeness, image, metaphor, similarity, circle, ring. The original representation, "to turn around, to turn in a circle," underlies all these and similar derivatives. The turning of the potter's wheel evoked the representation of the potter's formative activity, out of which grew the significations "form, create, build, work."

11. This twofold process is perhaps best followed by an examination of the form which the linguistic expression of activity, the *verb*, assumes in the inflected languages. Here two entirely different functions unite and permeate one another, for the verb is the clearest expression of the power of objectivization on the one hand and of the power of personification

the inside out and back again, through this ebb and flow of the spirit, that inner and outer reality take form and definition.

So far, to be sure, we have only set up an abstract schema of linguistic concept formation; we have outlined its framework, as it were, without entering into the details of the picture. To gain closer understanding of the process, we must follow the manner in which language progresses from a purely "qualificative" to a "generalizing" view, from the sensuous and concrete to the generic and universal. If we compare the concepts of our advanced languages with those of primitive languages, the contrast in basic approach is immediately evident. The languages of primitive peoples designate every thing, every process and activity, with the most intuitive concretion; they strive to express as plainly as possible all the distinguishing attributes of a thing, all the concrete details of an occurrence, every modification and shading of an action. In this respect they possess a richness which our advanced languages cannot even begin to approach. As we have seen, *spatial* specifications and relations are expressed with the most meticulous care.[12] Yet this verbal expression particularizes not only spatially, but from countless other points of view. Every modifying circumstance of an action, whether applying to its subject or object, its aim or the instrument with which it is performed, immediately affects the choice of term. In certain North American languages, the activity of washing is designated by thirteen different verbs, according to whether it applies to the washing of the hands or face, of bowls, garments, meat, etc.[13] According to Trumbull, no American Indian language has an equivalent for our general term "to eat"; instead, they have any number of verbs, one of which for example is used in connection with animal, another with vegetable nutriment, one indicating the meal of an individual, another a

on the other. The first factor was already noted by Humboldt, who regarded the verb as the immediate linguistic expression of the spiritual "act of synthetic postulation." "By one and the same synthetic act, it joins the predicate with the subject in being, but in this fashion: being, which with an energetic predicate passes into an activity, is attributed to the subject, so that what was thought of as merely linkable in thought becomes an existing thing or an occurrence in reality. It is not merely that we think of the striking lightning, it is the lightning itself that strikes. . . . The thought, if one may express oneself in such sensuous terms, leaves its inner dwelling place with the help of the verb and passes into reality." ("Einleitung zum Kawi-Werk," *Werke*, 7, No. 1, 214.) On the other hand Hermann Paul, for example, points out that the linguistic form of the verb as such embodies an element of animation of nature, akin to the mythical animation of the universe: that "a certain degree of personification of the subject" is implicit in the very use of the verb (*Prinzipien der Sprachgeschichte*, 3d ed., p. 89).

12. See above, p. 198 ff.

13. Sayce, *Introduction to the Science of Language*, *1*, 120.

meal eaten in common, etc. In the case of *striking,* a different verb is used for striking with the fist or the flat of the hand, with a rod or with a whip; *breaking* is variously designated according to the type of breaking and the instrument used.[14] And the same almost unlimited differentiation applies to things as well as activities. Here again, before language can create specific class designations and "generic concepts," it concentrates on the designation of "varieties." The aborigines of Tasmania had no word to express the concept tree, but a special name for every variety of the acacia, the blue rubber tree, etc.[15] K. v. d. Steinen reports that the Bakairi had different names for every variety of parrot and palm tree, but no equivalent for the general concepts of parrot and palm.[16] The same phenomenon occurs in otherwise highly developed languages. The Arabic language, for example, is so rich in terms for animal and plant varieties that it has been cited as an example of how language study can advance our knowledge of natural history and physiology. In a monograph on the subject, Hammer listed no less than 5,744 names for camel in Arabic, varying according to sex, age, and individual characteristics. There are special terms for the male and female, for the foal and the adult, and for the subtlest gradations within these classes. The foal that has not yet grown its side teeth, the foal that is beginning to walk, a camel between the age of one and ten, each has its own special name. Other distinctions have to do with mating, pregnancy, foaling, and still others with physical peculiarities: for example, there are special names for a camel with big or with little ears, with a cut ear or a hanging ear lobe, with a large jawbone or a sagging chin, etc.[17]

Here, apparently, we are not dealing with an accidental luxuriation of some isolated linguistic impulse, but rather with an original tendency of linguistic concept formation, which often leaves discernible vestiges in languages that have in general passed beyond it. Those phenomena which since the time of Hermann Osthoff have been called suppletives are usually

14. J. Hammond Trumbull, "On the Best Method of Studying the North American Languages," *Transactions of the American Philological Association, 1869–70* (Hartford, 1871), pp. 55–79; cf. Powell, *Introduction to the Study of Indian Languages,* 2d ed., p. 61. For details, see the examples from the Algonquin and Sioux languages in Boas, *Handbook, 1,* 807 ff., 902 ff., etc.

15. Cf. Sayce, *2, 5.*

16. K. v. d. Steinen, *Unter den Naturvölkern Zentral-Brasiliens,* 2d ed., p. 84.

17. Cf. Hammer-Purgstall, "Das Kamel," *Denkschriften der Kaiserlichen Akademie der Wissenschaften zu Wien,* Philos.-hist. Classe, Vols. 6 and 7 (1855 ff.).

interpreted in this light. Often, particularly in the Indo-Germanic languages, words which combine into a system of inflection, e.g., the cases of a substantive, the tenses of a verb, the degrees of adjectives, are not formed from one, but from two or more stems. Side by side with the "regular" conjugation of verbs and comparison of adjectives, we find cases such as fero, tuli, latum, φέρω, οἴσω, ἤνεγκον, which at first sight seem to be mere arbitrary "exceptions" to the principle of designating the different forms of the same concept by words built from the same root. Osthoff discovered the law governing these exceptions, by tracing them back to an older stratum of language formation, in which an "individualizing" trend still outweighed the "grouping" tendency. He believed that the closer the concepts and significations stabilized in the language lay to men's natural range of perceptions, to their immediate activities and interests, the longer the "individualizing" view would predominate. "Just as man's physical eye differentiates most sharply what is closest to him in space, his spiritual eye, whose mirror is language, will most sharply differentiate and individualize those things of the perceptual world which stand closest to his feeling and thoughts, which most intensely grip his soul and excite his psychic interest, whether as an individual or a people." And indeed, from this point of view it seems significant that precisely those concepts for which the languages of primitive peoples have the most diverse designations, are also those for which, in the Indo-Germanic languages, suppletives are most richly developed and endure the longest. Among verbs, it is first those of motion, "to go," "to come," "to run" and then those of eating, striking, seeing, speaking, etc. in which we find the most varied particularization. Curtius has shown that ur-Indo-Germanic, for example, differentiated the *varieties* of "going" before it arrived at the general *concept* of going. He demonstrated that such varieties as peering, spying, looking, watching, etc., must have been designated earlier than seeing as such, and the same for the other sensory activities, hearing, feeling, etc. And such verbs as the post-Homeric αἰσθάνεσθαι, *sentire,* designating sense perception in general, developed last of all.[18] Since other families of languages, such as the Semitic, disclose phenomena quite analogous to the Indo-Germanic suppletives, we must conclude that word formation here reflects a general trend in the development of linguistic concepts. True,

18. Curtius, *Grundzüge der griechischen Etymologie,* 5th ed., pp. 98 ff.; on the whole subject see Osthoff, *Vom Suppletivwesen der indogermanischen Sprachen,* Akademische Rede (Heidelberg, 1899).

we cannot speak of an original "individualizing" tendency in language: for every *appellation* of a particular intuition, however concretely formulated, goes beyond the purely individual view of that intuition and stands, as it were, in opposition to it. Nevertheless, different degrees of universality can be expressed in linguistic concepts. If we conceive of the whole intuitive world as a uniform plane, from which certain individual figures are singled out and differentiated from their surroundings by the act of appellation, this process of specification at first affects only a particular, narrowly limited portion of the plane. Nevertheless, since all these individual areas are adjacent to one another, the whole plane can gradually be apprehended in this way and covered by an even denser network of appellations. Yet fine as the meshes of this net may be, it still presents gaps. For each word has only its own relatively limited radius of action, beyond which its force does not extend. Language still lacks the means of combining several different spheres of signification into a new linguistic whole designated by a unitary form. The power of configuration and differentiation inherent in each single word begins to operate, but soon exhausts itself, and then a new sphere of intuition must be opened up by a new and independent impulsion. The summation of all these different impulses, each of which operates alone and independently, can form collective, but not truly generic unities. The totality of linguistic expression here attained is only an aggregate but not an articulated system; the power of articulation has exhausted itself in the individual appellation and is not adequate to the formation of comprehensive units.

But language takes a further step towards generic universality when, instead of contenting itself with creating specific designations for specific intuitions, it proceeds to combine these designations, in such a way as to imprint the objective *kinship* of contents on their linguistic form. This endeavor to create a stricter relation between sound and signification by coordinating specific series of conceptual signification with specific phonetic series, characterizes the progress from purely qualifying concepts to classifying concept formation. This occurs in its simplest form where language characterizes groups of different words as a unit by marking them with a common suffix or prefix. It complements the special signification of each word as such by adding a new determining element, which discloses its relation to other words. Such a group, held together by a classificatory suffix is to be found, for example, in the indo-Germanic titles of family relationship: in the names for father and mother, brother, sister, and daughter. The common ending *-tar* (*ter*) which appears in them (*pitár, mātár, bhrátar, svásar, duhitár,* πατήρ, μήτηρ, φράτωρ, θυγάτηρ, etc.) joins these names into a self-contained series and thus marks them as expressions of one and the same "concept"—which however does not exist as an independent, detachable unit *outside* of the series, but whose signification lies precisely in this function of encompassing the individual links of the series. It would be a mistake, however, if for this reason we were not to accept the operation here performed by language as a *logical* operation in the strict sense. For the logical theory of concepts clearly demonstrates that the "serial concept" is not posterior to the "generic concept" in force and significance, but is an integral part of the generic concept.[19] If we bear this in mind, the principle which operates in these linguistic phenomena stands out in all its significance and fruitfulness. And we shall not do full justice to the spiritual content of this principle if we suppose that the psychological law of association by similarity provides an explanation for those forms. The accidental course of associations, different from case to case and individual to individual, can no more explain the foundation and origin of linguistic than of purely logical concepts. "From the psychological point of view," Wundt remarks,

the only possible way of conceiving the process by which the terms of kinship were formed in the Indo-Germanic languages is to presume that from one term to another there extended an association of the two ideas and of the feelings accompanying them, and that this association brought about an assimilation of those phonetic elements of the word, which did not serve to express the special content of the idea. Thus such a determining phonetic sign, common to a whole class of ideas, can have arisen only through successive associative assimilation and not through the simultaneous formation of inclusive conceptual signs. And consequently the concept of an affinity of objects did not precede the formation of these linguistic determinants but developed simultaneously with them. For it is evidently the expression of affinity immediately presenting itself in the transition from one object to another that constitutes the *concept* of affinity, so that this concept rests rather upon certain similarly colored attendant feelings than on actual comparison.[20]

19. Cf. my book, *Substance and Function*, especially chs. 1 and 4.
20. Wundt, *Völkerpsychologie*, 2d ed., 2, 15 ff.

Contrary to this it must be said, however, that whatever may have been the original psychological *motive* in forming a specific group of names, the grouping itself constitutes an independent logical act with a specific logical form. A determination which remained exclusively in the sphere of feeling, could not by itself create a new objective specification. For some sort of associations of feeling can exist between any, even the most heterogeneous contents of consciousness; so that, consequently, such associations cannot lead to that kind of "homogeneity" which is established or at least postulated in the logical and linguistic concept. Feeling can join anything with anything; hence it provides no adequate explanation for the grouping of *specific* contents into *specific* unities. For this we rather require a logical basis of comparison, and such a basis is discernible in linguistic series even where it is expressed only in the form of a classifying suffix and not as an independent substantive.[21] When language expresses the existence of a generic relationship between contents, it serves as a vehicle of intellectual progress, regardless of whether or not it states *wherein* this relationship consists. Here again it anticipates a function which can be truly fulfilled only by scientific cognition: in a sense it foreshadows the logical concept. The logical concept not only asserts a coordination and affinity of contents, but inquires into the "why" of this coordination, striving to apprehend its law and "foundation." Here analysis of the relations between concepts ultimately leads back to their "genetic definition": to the statement of a *principle* out of which they can grow, from which they can be derived as its varieties. Language can rise to this task neither in its qualifying, nor its "classifying," nor its strictly "generic" concepts. But it prepares the way by creating a first schema of coordination. This schema may encompass little of the objective kinship of the contents, yet it seems to stabilize the subjective aspect of the concept, to embody the significance of the concept as *question*. And indeed, historically speaking, the problem of the concept was discovered when men learned not to accept the *linguistic* expression of concepts as definitive, but to interpret them as *logical questions*. This was the origin of the Socratic expression of the concept, the τί ἔστι: the Socratic induction consisted in starting from the provisional and presumptive unity of the word form and thence "leading" to the specific

---

21. There is no doubt that many of these "classifying suffixes," like other suffixes, go back to concrete substantives (cf. Chapter 5), though in the Indo-Germanic languages etymological proof of this relationship seems largely impossible; cf. Brugmann and Delbrück, *Grundriss*, 2d ed., 2, Pt. 2, 184, 582 ff., etc.

and definitive form of the logical concept.[22] In this sense, we may say that precisely in the subjectivity which inevitably adheres to them, the co-ordinations and classifications of language contain a certain *ideality,* a tendency towards the objective unity of the "idea."

2. Basic Trends in Linguistic Class Formation

The task of describing the various types of concept and class formation which operate in the particular languages, and of disclosing their ultimate spiritual factors, lies beyond the scope and methodological means of the philosophy of language. It can be undertaken only by general linguistics and the special linguistic sciences. The processes at work are so interwoven and obscure that they can be elucidated only by the closest and most sensitive immersion in the details of the particular languages. For the type of class formation is an essential factor in that "inner form" which makes one language different from another. Yet, although this rich and varied spiritual formation cannot be captured once and for all in any finished, abstract schema, a comparison of the particular phenomena nevertheless points to certain general considerations on the basis of which language arrives at its classifications and coordinations. We may attempt to arrange these by taking as our guiding principle the constant progress from the "concrete" to the "abstract" which determines the general development of language: yet we must bear in mind that we have to do not with a temporal, but with a methodological stratification and that in a given historical configuration the strata which we shall attempt to differentiate may exist side by side or may be intermingled in a variety of ways.

We seem to find ourselves at the lowest step of the cultural scale where the comparison and coordination of objects are based solely on some similarity in the sensory impression which they evoke. The languages of primitive peoples offer a variety of examples of this type of grouping. The most diverse contents may be grouped into a "class," provided they reveal some analogy in their sensuous form. The Melanesian and American Indian languages reveal a tendency to employ special prefixes for round or long objects. In accordance with this tendency, the terms for sun and

22. See above, pp. 123 ff.

moon, for example, are grouped with those for human ear, for fishes of a particular shape, for canoes, etc.; while another group is composed of long objects such as nose and tongue.[23]

To an entirely different level would seem to belong those class distinctions which are based not on a mere similarity in the content of things perceived, but on some relation between them; here objects are differentiated according to their size, number, and position. The Bantu languages, for example, use a special prefix to designate particularly large objects, while other prefixes serve as diminutives; objects which regularly occur as elements in a collective multiplicity, as "one of many," are distinguished from such "things doubly present" as the eyes, ears, and hands.[24] As for position and situation, many American Indian languages determine the class of a word according to whether the object it designates is thought of as standing, sitting, or lying.[25] Side by side with this classification of objects according to direct, intuitively grasped characteristics, we find a noteworthy *intermediary* principle: here things as a whole are coordinated with parts of the human body and, through this relationship with one part or another, assigned to different linguistic groups. Here we discern a theme already encountered in the linguistic building of spatial intuition and the formation of certain primary spatial terms, namely that the human body and the differentiation of its parts serves as one of the first and necessary pillars of linguistic orientation.[26] In certain languages the differentiation of the parts of the body serves as a general schema for the articulation of the world as a whole: each particular thing designated by language is first linked with a part of the body, the mouth, the legs, the head, the heart, etc., and according to this basic relation assigned to a specific class or "genus." [27] Such

23. Codrington, *The Melanesian Languages*, pp. 146 ff. Among the American Indian languages, Haida, for example, divides all nouns into groups distinguished by sensuous characters; e.g., long, thin, round, flat, angular, thread-shaped objects, each form a separate group. Cf. Swanton, "Haida," in Boas, *Handbook, 1*, 216, 227 ff.

24. See the account of the class prefixes in Meinhof, *Grammatik der Bantusprachen*, pp. 8 ff., 16 ff.

25. Cf. Powell, *Introduction to the Study of Indian Languages*, 2d ed., p. 48. In the Ponca language, which distinguishes between animate and inanimate objects, special prefixes serve to indicate a resting member of the first class, a moving member, a single animate being that is standing, one that is sitting, etc. Cf. Boas and Swanton, "Siouan," in Boas, *Handbook, 1*, 940.

26. See above, pp. 206 ff.

27. Particularly characteristic of this process is the highly remarkable classification system of the South Andaman languages, described in detail by E. H. Man, *On the Aboriginal Inhabitants of the Andaman Islands, with Report of Researches into the Language of the South Andaman Islands by A. J. Ellis* (London, 1883). A supplement to this has been given by M. J.

classifications make it very clear that the first conceptual differentiations of language are still thoroughly bound up with a material substrate, that the relation between the members of a class can only be *thought* if it is *embodied* in an image. Yet the most richly and subtly developed systems of classification, such as that of the Bantu languages, seem to have acquired a general view extending far beyond this first sphere of mere sensuous differentiation. Here language already reveals the power to apprehend the entirety of being—in so far as it is a spatial entity—as a complex of *relations* and to let it grow, as it were, out of those relations. When in the precisely graduated system of "locative" prefixes employed in the Bantu languages there is a sharp definition of the varying distance of objects from the speaker and also the diverse spatial relations prevailing among objects, their "interpenetration," "juxtaposition," "separation," then the immediate form of spatial intuition begins, as it were, to assume a *systematic* structure. Language seems to construct space as a manifold determined in different ways, to form it, by various distinctions of situation and direction, into a self-enclosed, yet differentiated unity.[28] Such classifications seem already to disclose a drive and an energy for *organization* which, even where the object itself remains entirely within the sphere of sensuous intuition, surpasses it in *principle* and points to new and characteristic "syntheses of the manifold."

True, it lies in the very nature of language that each of these syntheses is not governed exclusively by theoretical but by imaginative factors as well, and that consequently much of linguistic "concept formation" seems to be the product less of logical comparison and combination than of the linguistic *fantasy*. The form of grouping is never determined solely by the objective "similarity" of the particular contents, but also by the subjective imagination. In so far as we can gain insight into them, the factors which guide language in its classifications seem closely related to primitive mythical concepts and classifications.[29] Here again language, as a general cul-

---

Portman, *Notes on the Languages of the South Andaman Group of Tribes* (Calcutta, 1898). In this system human beings form a special class which is distinguished from other nouns; next, the particular parts of the body and terms of kinship are divided into groups which are sharply differentiated. Each group, for example, has its own set of possessive pronouns, its own special terms for mine, thine, his, etc. The parts of the body and the kinship groups are related by various coordinations and "identities." (Cf. Man, pp. 51 ff., and Portman, pp. 37 ff.)

28. Cf. the account of the system of "locative prefixes" in Meinhof, *Grammatik der Bantusprachen*, pp. 19 ff.

29. Cf. my essay *Die Begriffsform in mythischen Denken, Studien der Bibliothek Warburg*, Vol. *1*.

tural form, stands on the borderline between myth and logos and also represents an intermediary between the theoretical and aesthetic approach to the world. That most familiar form of linguistic classification, the division of nouns into three genders, masculine, feminine, and neuter, must have originated largely in such half-mythical, half-aesthetic factors, as certain of its manifestations still indicate. Students of language who combined profound artistic intuition with rigorous grammatical analysis have believed that the system of genders offered an opportunity to study the principle of linguistic concept formation at its very source. Jacob Grimm derived the difference of gender in the Germanic languages from a transference of natural gender in the earliest period of language. He imputed a "natural origin" not only to the masculine and feminine but to the neuter as well, whose source he sought in the "concept of the *foetus* or *proles* of living creatures." He attempted to show that the masculine designates the earlier, larger, more solid, more resistant, the active, mobile, generative, while the feminine designates the later, smaller, softer, quieter, the suffering and receptive, and the neuter indicates whatever is engendered, what is worked upon, the material, general, collective, undeveloped. Here, to be sure, modern linguistics has followed him only in small part. In the case of the Indo-Germanic languages, Grimm's aesthetic theory was countered by Brugmann who attributed the extending of the sexual distinctions to all nouns not to any general trends of the linguistic imagination but to certain formal and in a sense accidental analogies. In his more sober theory, language, in developing and fixing this distinction, was not guided by an animistic intuition, but rather by essentially meaningless similarities of phonetic form: thus, for example, from the circumstance that certain "natural feminines"—i.e., designations for female beings—ended in -a (-η), all nouns having this ending came gradually to be assigned to the feminine gender by a process of pure association.[30] Compromise theories have attributed the development of grammatical gender partly to intuitive and partly to formal factors and attempted to draw dividing lines between the two.[31] But the basic problem here involved could be grasped in its full meaning and scope only when linguistic studies were extended beyond the Indo-Germanic and Semitic families and it became evident that the distinction of gender in these languages is merely a special case, a vestige perhaps of

30. Brugmann, "Das grammatische Geschlecht in den indogermanischen Sprachen," in Techmer's *Zeitschrift für Allgemeine Sprachwissenschaft, 4,* 100 ff.; cf. also *Kurze vergleichende Grammatik,* pp. 361 ff.

31. Cf. for example, Wilmans, *Deutsche Grammatik, 3,* 725 ff.

far richer and far more sharply elaborated classifications. When we consider those which we find most particularly in the Bantu languages, we cannot but conclude that the distinction of "sex" occupies only a relatively small place among all those means which language employs to express "generic" classifications and that consequently it represents only a particular trend in linguistic imagination and not a universal *principle*. Indeed, a large number of languages do not classify nouns according to natural gender or any analogy based on it. In these languages the masculine and feminine gender are not distinguished at all in inanimate beings and in the case of animals they are expressed either by special words or by the addition of a word designating sex to the general name of the species. Similarly in the human sphere, an addition of this sort will transform a general term such as child or servant into son or daughter, manservant or maidservant, etc.[32]

Humboldt, who like Jacob Grimm finds the source of linguistic classifications in a basic function of the linguistic "imaginative faculty," consequently interprets this faculty in a broader sense by starting not from the distinction of natural gender but from the general distinction between the animate and inanimate. Here he bases his argument essentially on his observations in the American Indian languages, most of which designate the difference in natural gender either not at all, or only occasionally and incompletely, but reveal the keenest sense of the contrast between animate and inanimate objects. The whole structure of the Algonquin language is governed by this contrast. A special suffix (-*a*) designates an object combining the attributes of life and independent motion; another (-*i*) designates objects lacking in these attributes. Every verb or noun must fall into one or the other of these classes: but the classification is not determined solely by empirical *observation;* mythical imagination and the mythical animation of nature also play a crucial part in it. In these languages, for example, a great number of plants, among them such all-important varieties as corn and tobacco, are assigned to the class of animate objects.[33]

32. This method is most typical of the Finno-Ugrian and Altaic languages, none of which has designations of gender in the Indo-Germanic sense, but it is also widespread in other groups. For the Altaic languages, see Böthlingk, *Über die Sprache der Jakuten*, p. 343, and J. J. Schmidt, *Grammatik der mongolischen Sprache*, pp. 22 ff.; for other languages see H. C. v. d. Gabelentz, *Die Melanesischen Sprachen*, p. 88; Westermann, *Die Sudansprachen*, pp. 39 ff.; Matthews, "Languages of Some Native Tribes of Queensland," *J. and Proc. of the Roy. Soc. of N. S. Wales, 36* (1902), 148, 168.

33. On the classification of the Algonquin languages, see W. Jones, "Algonquin" (Fox), in Boas, *Handbook, 1,* 760 ff.

In another context, the heavenly bodies are placed in the same class with men and animals, and Humboldt regards this as the clearest verification of his theory that these peoples think of them as beings which move with an energy of their own, which are endowed with personality and probably guide human destinies from above.[34] If this reasoning is sound, it means that in devising such classifications language is still intimately bound up with mythical thinking, but is already beginning to rise above the first primitive stratum of this thinking. For this stratum is still dominated by a form of "pan-animism" which embraces and permeates the whole world and everything in it. But in the linguistic distinction between persons and things there gradually emerges from the general sphere of the "animate" a distinctly personal existence endowed with a peculiar significance and value of its own. In the Dravidian languages, for example, all nouns fall into two classes, one of which comprises the "reasoning," the other the "unreasoning"—to the first belong men, gods and demigods, to the second inanimate objects and animals.[35] The dividing line that is here drawn through the world as a whole follows a principle essentially different from the simple, almost undifferentiated mythical animation of the universe. The Bantu languages also distinguish sharply between man as an independently acting personality and every sort of animated but not personal being. They use a special prefix for ghosts, which they regard not as independent personalities but as what animates or as something that "befalls" a man, and accordingly the same prefix is used for such *natural forces* as diseases, smoke, fire, streams, the moon.[36] Thus the conception of a personal, spiritual existence and activity in the restricted sense has created a linguistic expression of its own, by which it distinguishes itself from the merely animistic view of life and the soul, which regards the soul as a universal but utterly undifferentiated mythical power

Here again the distinction of special classes of persons and things as well as the subsumption of particular objects under them does not follow "objective" criteria; the conceptual structure of reality represented in language is still permeated with purely subjective distinctions which can only be apprehended by immediate feeling. This classification is never determined by mere acts of perception or judgment but always at the same time by acts of the emotion and will, by inner attitudes. Therefore a

---

34. Humboldt, "Einleitung zum Kawi-Werk," *Werke,* 7, No. 1, 172 ff.

35. Fr. Müller, *Grundriss, 3,* Pt. 1, 173; *Novara-Reise,* p. 83.

36. For examples, see Meinhof, *Grammatik der Bantusprechen,* pp. 6 ff.

speaker may frequently place a thing which normally belongs to the object class in the personal class, in order to stress its value and importance.[37] Even in the languages which, in the form known to us, have divided nouns according to natural gender, sometimes reveal, by the manner in which they employ this distinction, that it goes back to an older differentiation of persons and things, which was also felt to be a value judgment.[38] Strange as such phenomena may seem at first glance, they merely disclose the basic principle of all linguistic concept formation. Language never simply follows the lead of impressions and perceptions, but confronts them with an independent action: it distinguishes, chooses and directs, and through this action creates certain centers of objective intuition. And because the world of sensory impressions is thus permeated with the inner measures of judgment, the theoretical nuances of signification and the affective nuances of value tend at first to shade off continuously into each other. However, language reveals its inner logic in that the distinctions which it creates do not immediately vanish but reveal a certain tendency to endure; in that they possess a peculiar logical consistency and necessity, by virtue of which they not only maintain themselves, but spread from particular spheres of language formation over the whole. Through the rules of *congruence* which govern the grammatical structure of language and which are most clearly developed in the prefix and class languages, the conceptual distinctions applied to the noun spread to the other parts of speech. In Bantu every numeral, adjective, or pronoun which

37. In the Gola language of Liberia (according to Westermann, *Die Gola-Sprache*, p. 27) a noun which ordinarily takes another prefix, takes the *o-* prefix of the human and animal class if it is to be stressed as particularly large, outstanding, valuable. These qualities place it in the class of living creatures: "Side by side with *kesie*, oil palm, they say *osie*, thus characterizing this palm as one of the most important trees; *kekul*, tree, but *okul*, a particularly large, beautiful tree; *ebu*, field, but *obuo*, the beautiful, luxuriantly growing field. Trees or other objects which speak in fairytales are also put into this o-class." In the Algonquin languages, small animals are often assigned to the class of "inanimate" objects, while particularly important plants are assigned to the "animate" class. See above, p. 299, and Boas, *Handbook*, *1*, p. 36.

38. Characteristic examples of this are cited by Meinhof and Reinisch from the Bedauye language, where for example, *ša'*, the cow, as main support of the whole economy, is masculine, while *ša'*, the meat, is feminine, because it is less important (see Meinhof, *Die Sprachen der Hamiten*, p. 139). Likewise in the Semitic languages, according to Brockelmann, *Grundriss*, *1*, 404 ff., the division of nouns between the masculine and feminine genders probably had originally nothing to do with natural sex, but was rather based on a differentiation of rank and value, vestiges of which are still discernible in the use of the feminine as a pejorative and diminutive. Cf. Brockelmann, *Grundriss*, *2*, 418 ff. and *Kurzgefasste vergleichende Grammatik*, pp. 198 ff.

enters into an attributive or predicative relation with a substantive must assume the characteristic class prefix of that word. Similarly, the verb is allied with its subject and object by a special prefix.[39] Thus, the principle of classification, once arrived at, not only governs the formation of nouns, but thence spreads to the whole syntactical structure of the language, becoming the actual expression of its organization, its spiritual "articulation." Here the work of the *linguistic imagination* seems throughout to be closely bound up with a specific methodology of linguistic thinking. Once again language, with all its involvement in the sensuous, imaginative world, reveals a tendency towards the logical and universal, through which it progressively liberates itself and attains to a purer and more independent spirituality of form.

39. Cf. the account of the *syntax* of the Bantu languages in Meinhof, op. cit., pp. 83 ff. A similar phenomenon prevails in most of the American Indian languages; cf. Powell, *Introduction to the Study of Indian Languages,* 2d ed., pp. 48 ff.

Chapter 5

Language and the Expression of the Forms of Pure Relation. The Sphere of Judgment and the Concepts of Relation

FOR EPISTEMOLOGICAL inquiry an unbroken path leads from sensation to intuition, from intuition to conceptual thought, and thence to logical judgment. Yet in following this path, the epistemologist is aware that sharply as its phases must be distinguished in reflection, they must never be regarded as independent data of consciousness, existing separately from one another. On the contrary, every more complex factor here includes the simpler ones, and every "later" one the "earlier," while conversely the latter contains within it the seeds of the former. All those components which constitute the concept of knowledge are related to one another and to the unitary aim of knowledge, the "object": consequently a rigorous analysis can discover in each one of them a reference to all the others. The function of simple sensation and perception is not merely "connected" with the basic functions of intellection, judgment and inference; it is itself such a basic function, containing implicitly what in these functions achieves a conscious and independent form. And in language we may expect to find the same indissoluble correlation of the spiritual instruments with which it constructs its world; we may expect each of its factors to contain the universality and specific *totality* of language as a whole. This expectation is confirmed when we note that the true and original element of all language formation is not the simple word but the sentence. This is another of the fundamental insights which Humboldt contributed to the philosophy of language. "We cannot possibly conceive of language," he wrote, "as beginning with the designation of objects by words and thence proceeding to their organization. In reality, discourse is not composed from words which preceded it, on the contrary, words issued from the whole of discourse." [1] This conclusion, which Humboldt drew from the speculative concept underlying his whole philosophy of language—from the concept of "synthesis" as the source of all thought and speech [2]—has been fully confirmed by empirical, psychological analysis, which also regards the "primacy of the sentence over the word" as one of its first and most secure findings. [3] The same conclusion follows from the history of language, which at every point seems to teach that the separating out of particular words from the sentence as a whole and the delimitation of the parts of speech from one another were only gradually accomplished and were almost totally lacking in early and primitive languages. [4] Here again language shows itself to be an organism in which, as the old Aristotelian definition put it, the whole is prior to its parts. Language begins with a complex total expression which only gradually breaks down into its elements, into relatively independent subsidiary units. As far back as we can trace it, language confronts us as a formed whole. None of its utterances can be understood as a mere juxtaposition of separate words; in each and every one, we find provisions which serve purely to express the *relation* between the particular elements, and which articulate and graduate this relation in a variety of ways.

This principle seems indeed to be belied when we consider the structure of the so-called "isolating languages," which have often been cited as proof of the possibility and actual existence of absolutely "formless" languages. For here the above-described relation between sentence and word does not seem to be confirmed. On the contrary, the word seems to possess that independence, that genuine "substantiality" by virtue of which it "is" in itself and must be so conceived. The separate words simply stand side by side in the sentence as material vehicles of signification, and their gram-

1. "Einleitung zum Kawi-Werk," *Werke*, 7, No. 1, 72 ff.; cf. especially p. 143.

2. Cf. above, p. 161.

3. This primacy is asserted by Wundt and particularly by Ottmar Dittrich, *Grundzüge der Sprachpsychologie*, Vol. 1 (1903), and *Die Probleme der Sprachpsychologie* (1913).

4. Cf. the remarks of Sayce in *Introduction to the Science of Language*, 1, 111 ff. and B. Delbrück, *Vergleichende Syntax*, 3, 5. In the so-called "polysynthetic" languages no sharp distinction can be drawn between the individual word and the whole of the sentence; cf. particularly the accounts of the American Indian languages in Boas, *Handbook*, 1, 27 ff., 762 ff., 1002 ff., etc. H. Winkler tells us that the Altaic languages have likewise been deficient in the development of word units, that in general the word becomes a word in these languages only in its membership in the sentence. (*Das Uralaltaische und seine Gruppen*, pp. 9, 43, etc.) And even in inflected languages we often find vestiges of an archaic state in which the boundaries between sentence and word were quite fluid; cf. for the Semitic languages the remarks in Brockelmann, *Grundriss*, 2, 1 ff.

matical relation is not made explicit in any wáv. In Chinese, which is the principal example of this type of isolating language, one and the same word may serve as a substantive, adjective, adverb or verb, without incurring any change indicative of its grammatical category. There is nothing in the form of a word to indicate whether a substantive is used in this or that number or case, or a verb in this or that genus, tense, or mood. Philosophers of language long believed that this characteristic of the Chinese language offered an insight into that original period of language formation in which all human speech consisted in series of simple, monosyllabic "roots": but this belief was increasingly discredited by historical research which showed that the strict isolation prevailing in modern Chinese was by no means an original state, but a derivative result. The assumption that the words in Chinese had never undergone a transformation and that this language had never possessed any kind of morphology becomes untenable, as G. v. d. Gabelentz pointed out, as soon as Chinese is compared to those languages which are most closely related to it. Then it becomes apparent that Chinese still contains numerous vestiges of an older agglutinative and even inflectional form. In this respect the development of Chinese has often been compared to that of modern English, where a transformation from an inflected to a relatively uninflected state seems to have gone on before our very eyes.[5] Even more significant than such historical changes is the circumstance that where pure isolation has been achieved, this by no means signifies a triumph of "formlessness"; it means rather that form has imprinted itself here with great force and clarity on a seemingly resistant material. For the isolation of words from one another is far from negating the content and ideal meaning of the sentence form, since the logical and grammatical relations between the particular words are clearly expressed in the *word order*, without recourse to phonetic changes in the words themselves. This instrument of word order, which the Chinese language has developed to the highest consistency and sharpness, might indeed, from a purely logical point of view, be regarded as the only truly adequate means of expressing grammatical relations. For it would seem possible to designate them more clearly and specifically *as* relations pure and simple, possessing no perceptual base of their own, through the pure *relation* of words expressed in their order, than by special words and affixes. In this sense Humboldt, who in general regarded the inflected languages as the expression

5. G. v. d. Gabelentz, *Die Sprachwissenschaft*, pp. 252 ff.; *Chinesische Grammatik*, pp. 90 ff.; cf. also B. Delbrück, *Grundfragen der Sprachforschung*, pp. 118 ff.

of the perfect, "absolutely lawful" form of language, said that the essential advantage of Chinese lay in the consistency with which it carried out the principle of inflectionlessness. Precisely the seeming absence of all grammar, he declared, had sharpened the people's sense of the formal element in discourse—the less outward grammar the Chinese language possesses, the more inner grammar inheres in it.[6] So strict indeed is this inner structure that Chinese syntax has been said to consist essentially in the logical development of a few basic laws, from which all special applications can be derived by pure logical deduction.[7] If we compare this finely articulated language with isolating languages of a primitive type—such as the Ewe language of Africa [8]—it becomes discernible that the most diverse formal gradations and constrasts are possible within a single "linguistic type." One of the flaws in Schleicher's attempt to characterize different languages on the basis of the connection between signification and relation within them, and accordingly to construct a progressive dialectical series in which the isolating, agglutinative and inflected languages stand to one another as thesis, antithesis, and synthesis,[9] was that it distorted its principle of classification by failing to consider the very different forms which this connection between "relation" and "signification" can assume *within* one and the same type. Moreover, the rigid demarcation between inflected and agglutinative language has gradually broken down in the light of empirical research.[10] Here again that relation between "essence" and "form," which is expressed in the old Scholastic dictum *forma dat esse rei,* is confirmed also for language. Epistemology cannot analyze the substance and form of knowledge into independent contents which are only outwardly connected with one another; the two factors can only be thought and defined in relation to one another; and likewise in language, pure, naked substance is a mere abstraction—a methodological concept to which no immediate "reality," no empirical fact corresponds.

Even in the inflected languages, in which the antithesis between expression of substantial signification and expression of formal relation is most clearly marked, we find that the balance between the two is rather unstable.

6. Humboldt, "Einleitung zum Kawi-Werk," *Werke,* 7, No. 1, pp. 271 ff., 304 ff.

7. G. v. d. Gabelentz, *Chinesische Grammatik,* p. 19.

8. Cf. Westermann, *Grammatik der Ewe-Sprache,* pp. 4 ff., 30 ff. (Eng. trans., by Bickford-Smith, pp. 4 ff.)

9. Schleicher, *Sprachvergleichende Untersuchungen, 1,* 6 ff.; 2, pp. 5 ff.; cf. above, pp. 164 ff.

10. See as early a writer as Böthlingk, *Über die Sprache der Jakuten* (1851), p. xxiv, cf. below, p. 309, n. 15.

For clearly as the categorial concepts are in most cases distinguished from the substantive concepts, there is nevertheless a constant flux between the two spheres, since substantive concepts serve as a basis for the expression of relations. This becomes most evident when we consider the etymological origins of the *suffixes* used in the inflected languages to express quality, attribute, type, character, etc. The history of language shows that a great number of these suffixes originated in words of material signification, which gradually cast off this initial character and became transformed into terms of general relation.[11] And it was this use of suffixes which prepared the way for the designation of pure concepts of relation. What first served as a special thing-indication developed into the expression of categorial determination, e.g., of an attributive concept as such.[12] But though this transition bears so to speak a negative sign from a psychological standpoint, a positive act of language formation is inherent in this very negation. At first sight, to be sure, suffix formation might seem to be essentially characterized by the fact that the original substantial signification of the word from which the suffixes derive, is progressively thrust into the background and ultimately forgotten altogether. This forgetfulness sometimes goes

11. In German, for example, this is borne out by the development of the suffixes *-heit*, *-schaft*, *-tum*, *-bar*, *-lich*, *-sam*, *-haft*. The suffix *-lich*, which is one of the principal instruments of adjective formation, goes back directly to the substantive *lîka* (= body): "The type of a word such as *weiblich*," writes H. Paul in *Principien der Sprachgeschichte*, 3d ed., p. 322, "goes back to an old bahuvrihi composite, ur-Germanic *wibolîkis*, literally 'woman's form,' then metaphorically, 'having woman's form.' Between a composite of this sort and the simplex Middle High German *lich*, New High German *Leiche*, there is so great a discrepancy, first of signification, then of phonetic form, that all connection is annulled. From the material signification of the simplex 'form,' 'outward appearance,' the more abstract 'quality' had developed." In the case of the suffix *-heit*, the substantive from which it originated was still in use as an independent word in the Gothic, Old High German, Old Saxon and Old Norse languages. Its basic signification seems to have been of person or rank and dignity, but the general signification of quality or manner (Gothic *haidus*) seems to have developed at an early date; transformed into a suffix it served to designate any abstract attribute (cf. Grimm, *Deutsches Wörterbuch*, 4, No. 2, col. 919 ff.). The Romance languages formed their adverbs of manner on the basis of a different basic intuition but in accordance with the same tendency and principle. They did not, to be sure, employ a concept of bodily substance or form, but the term for spirit, which gradually assumed the character of a suffix of relation, was originally taken in a concrete sense (*fièrement = fera mente*, etc.).

12. In Sanskrit, for example, the suffix *-maya* originally goes back to a substantive (*maya* = substance, material) and was first used, accordingly, to form adjectives designating the substance of a thing—only later, as the noun became transformed into a suffix, the general signification of attribute and "quality" developed from the special concept of material property (*mrn-maya*, made of clay, but *maha-maya* "built on delusion," etc. Cf. Brugmann and Delbrück, *Grundriss*, 2d ed., 2, Pt. 2, 13, and Thumb, *Handbuch des Sanskrit*, p. 441.

so far that new suffixes may arise, which owe their origin to no concrete intuition but to what one might call a misguided impulsion of linguistic analogy formation. In German, for example, the suffix -*keit*, goes back to a linguistic "misunderstanding" of this sort: in words such as *ewic-heit*, the final *c* of the stem blended with the initial *h* of the suffix, so as to form a new suffix which was propagated by analogy.[13] From a purely formal and grammatical point of view, such processes are regarded as "aberrations" of the linguistic sense; actually they are far more, they represent *progress* to a new formal view, a development from substantial expression to the expression of pure relation. The psychological obscuring of the former becomes a logical instrument and vehicle for the progressive development of the latter.

Of course, in exploring this progress we must not stop at the level of mere *word formation*. The law and basic tendency of the advance are rather to be apprehended in the relations of sentence formation, for if the sentence is the true vehicle of linguistic "meaning," it is only through an investigation of the sentence that the logical shadings of this meaning can be made clear. By its very form every sentence, even the so-called simple sentence, embodies the possibility of such an inner articulation. But the articulation itself can be effected in very different degrees and phases. Synthesis may outweigh analysis—or conversely, analytical power may attain a relatively high development while synthetic power lags behind. The dynamic interaction and tension between the two forces yields what we call the "form" of each particular language. In the so-called "polysynthetic" languages the combinatory impulse seems very much predominant, expressing itself above all in the striving to represent the functional unity of linguistic meaning materially and outwardly in a highly complex but self-contained *phonetic configuration*. The whole of the meaning is pressed into a single word-sentence where it appears, as it were, encased in a rigid shell. But this unity of linguistic expression is not yet a true unity of thought, since it can only be achieved at the expense of the logical *universality* of this expression. The more modifiers the word-sentence acquires by incorporation of whole words and particles, the better it serves for the designation of a particular concrete situation, which it seeks exhaustively to detail but which it cannot connect with other similar situa-

13. The documentation is compiled in Grimm, *Deutsches Wörterbuch*, Vol. 5, cols. 500 ff. (s. v. "*keit*"). Similar processes of suffix formation by "misunderstanding" are found in other linguistic families; for example, cf. Simonyi, *Die ungarische Sprache*, pp. 276 ff.

tions to form a comprehensive general context.[14] In the inflected languages, on the other hand, we find an entirely different relation between the two fundamental powers of analysis and synthesis. Here the word itself contains a kind of inner tension which it also resolves and overcomes. The word is built up of two distinct, yet inseparably linked and related factors. One component which serves solely for the objective designation of the concept confronts another whose sole function it is to place the word in a specific category of thought, to characterize it as a "substantive," "adjective," "verb," as a "subject" or direct or indirect object. Here the index of relation, by means of which the particular word is linked with the sentence as a whole, is no longer attached to the word from without, but fuses with it and becomes one of its constitutive elements.[15] The differentiation of the word and its integration with the sentence form correlative methods which join in a strictly unitary operation. Humboldt and the older philosophers of language looked upon this circumstance as a proof that the true inflected languages represent the summit of all language formation and that in them, and only in them, the "absolutely lawful form" of language expressed itself in ideal perfection. But even if we show a certain skepticism and reserve toward such absolute evaluations, there is no doubt that the inflected languages provide a highly important and effective organ for the development of purely *relational thought*. The more this relational thinking progresses, the more distinctly it must mould the articulation of language to its purpose—while on the other hand this very articulation reacts decisively on the form of thought.

And the same progress towards sharper articulation, the same development from the unity of a mere aggregate to the unity of a systematic "form" is evident when we advance from the relation of word to sentence to the

14. Cf. above, pp. 289 ff., on "concept formation" in the American Indian languages, and pp. 273 ff.

15. In his account of the Yakut language (1851), Böthlingk already stressed that this process itself admits of very different degrees and levels, and that in this respect there is no sharp and absolute dividing line between the inflected languages and the so-called agglutinative languages. He points out that although the Indo-Germanic languages in general create a far more intimate bond between "substance" and "form" than the so-called agglutinative languages, certain of the Ural-Altaic languages, particularly Finnish and Yakut, are far from attaching the two as superficially as is often assumed. Here too, on the contrary, we find a constant development toward "formation," and entirely different phases of this development are manifested in different languages, e.g., Mongolian, Turkish-Tatar and Finnish. (Böthlingk, *Über die Sprache der Jakuten*, Intro., p. xxiv; cf. especially H. Winkler, *Das Uralaltaische und seine Gruppen*, pp. 44 ff., on the "Morphology" of the Ural-Altaic languages.)

relation between sentences. In the earliest stages of language formation which we can examine from a psychological point of view, simple *parataxis* is the basic rule of sentence structure. The language of children is everywhere governed by this principle.[16] One word follows another in mere coordination, and where several sentences occur, they disclose a loose connection, for the most part without coordinating conjunctions. The clauses may be strung together, but they are not yet inwardly linked and "interlocked," since there is as yet no linguistic instrument by which to designate and sharply differentiate their subordination and superordination. The Greek grammarians and rhetoricians saw the touchstone of style in the development of the period, in which clauses do not run along in an indeterminate sequence, but support one another like the stones of an arch.[17] And indeed, this style is the ultimate and highest product of language. It is lacking in the languages of primitive peoples,[18] and seems to have been acquired only gradually in the highly developed languages. At this early stage a complex logical relation of causal or teleological type— a relation of cause and effect, of condition and conditioned, end and means, etc., must be expressed by simple coordination. Often an absolute construction comparable to the Latin ablative absolute or the Greek genitive absolute serves to indicate highly complex relations of "since" and "after," of "because" and "therefore," of "although" and "consequently." The separate ideas that constitute discourse here lie as it were on a single linguistic plane: there is still no differentiation of perspective between foreground and background in speech itself.[19] Language reveals its power of differentiation and

---

16. Cf. Clara and William Stern, *Die Kindersprache*, pp. 182 ff.

17. Demetrius, *De elocutione*, pars. 11–13 (quoted in Humboldt, *Werke*, 7, 223).

18. Examples of the prevalence of parataxis in the languages of primitive peoples can be drawn from the accounts of most African languages and American Indian languages. For the former see Steinthal, *Die Mande-Neger-Sprachen*, pp. 120 ff., 247 ff.; and Roehl, *Grammatik der Schambalasprache*, p. 27; for the latter see Gatschet, *Klamath Language*, pp. 656 ff. In Ewe, according to Westermann, *Grammatik der Ewe-Sprache*, p. 106 (Eng. trans., by Bickford-Smith, p. 147), all dependent clauses are concluded with the article *lá* if they precede the main clause; they are thus regarded as nouns and not really as clauses. In the Nuba language, subordinate clauses are treated as nouns and take the same case endings (Reinisch, *Die Nuba-Sprache*, p. 142).

19. The most characteristic examples of this seem to occur in the Finno-Ugrian and Altaic languages. H. Winkler tells us that the basic sentence structure of these languages leaves no room for subordinate clauses of any sort: the whole sentence is an adnominal, self-enclosed wordlike complex, or merely represents the gapless linking of a subject-like part with a predicate-like part. In both cases, everything that we consider secondary, such as temporal, spatial, causative or conditional specifications, is placed between the two essential parts of the

articulation in the coordination of the parts of the sentence; but it does not yet succeed in raising this purely static relation to a dynamic relation of reciprocal logical dependency, and expressing it explicitly as such. In place of precisely graduated subordinate clauses, a simple gerundial construction may serve, without departing from the law of coordination, to express the most diverse specifications and modifications of action, encompassing them in a stable, but characteristically rigid construction.[20]

This form of thought and speech finds a negative but no less characteristic expression in the absence of those classes of words which, as the grammarians' term for them suggests, must be regarded as one of the basic instruments of relational thought and its linguistic expression. The relative pronoun appears to be a late development and, if we consider language as a whole, rather rare. Before language arrives at this formation, the relations which we express by relative clauses must be rendered by more or less complex circumlocutions, various types of which Humboldt illustrated by examples from the American Indian languages, particularly the Peruvian and Mexican.[21] The Melanesian languages also use a simple coordination of statements in place of subordination by relative sentences and

---

sentence or word-sentence. "This is no fiction but is almost unmistakably the true nature of the sentence in most of the Ural-Altaic languages, for example, in Mongolian, Tungusic, Turkish and Japanese . . . this strangely developed idiom [Tungusic] seems to have no place for anything that suggests relative connection. In the Votyak language our Indo-Germanic dependent conjunctional clause regularly takes the form of an interpolated phrase after the manner of the Indo-Germanic genitive, ablative or accusative absolute." (Winkler, *Der uralaltaische Sprachstamm*, pp. 85 ff., 107 ff.). Similarly in Chinese, according to G. v. d. Gabelentz (*Chinesische Grammatik*, pp. 168 ff.), whole sentences are often simply strung together in such a way that one can gather only from the context whether the relation between them is temporal, causal, relative, or concessive.

20. Striking examples of such sentence structure are cited, for example, in J. J. Schmidt, *Grammatik der mongolischen Sprache* (especially pp. 62 ff. and 124 ff.). A sentence such as "After I had obtained the horse from my elder brother and given it to my younger brother, the latter took it, mounted it while I went into the house to get a rope, and rode away without saying a word to anyone," runs in Mongolian, literally translated: "I obtaining the horse from my elder brother, having given it to my younger brother, the latter taking it from me, (while) I went into the house to get a rope, the younger brother, without saying a word to anyone, mounting it, rode away." (Here, as Winkler points out, p. 112, the word "while" in the translation has woven a conjunctional relation into the sentence, whereas the text itself contains no conjunction.) Other characteristic examples of sentence construction by means of gerunds, supines and participle-like forms are cited from the Tibetan by J. J. Schmidt, *Tibetanische Grammatik*, p. 197.

21. See "Einleitung zum Kawi-Werk," *Werke*, 7, No. 1, 253 ff. The Klamath language also uses a participial or verbal expression where we use interpolated relative clauses. See Gatschet, *Klamath Language*, p. 657.

relative pronouns.[22] H. Winkler points out that fundamentally the Ural-Altaic family has no room for independent subordinate units and that accordingly none of its members originally had relative conjunctions, or at most had feeble suggestions of them. Where such conjunctions were later used, they were usually if not always derived from pure interrogatives. Particularly the Western, Finno-Ugrian group of the Ural-Altaic languages have developed such relative pronouns derived from interrogatives, but here Indo-Germanic influence may have played a part.[23] In other languages independent relative clauses are formed by special particles, but are felt to be substantive nouns and consequently preceded by the definite article, or used as the subject or object of a sentence, as a genitive, after a preposition etc.[24] All these phenomena seem to show how language takes up the pure category of relation hesitantly, as it were, and learns to apprehend it only deviously, through other categories, particularly those of substance and attribute.[25] And this is true even of those languages which in their general structure have subsequently developed the true "style" of discourse, the art of hypotactic articulation, to its highest refinement. Even the Indo-Germanic languages, which thanks to their astonishing faculty of differentiating the expression of relation have been called the true languages of philosophical idealism, developed this faculty only gradually.[26] A comparison, for example, between Greek and Sanskrit shows that the different members of this group represent entirely different stages with regard to the power and freedom of relational thought and expression. In the "ur-period" the independent clause seems to have predominated

22. Examples in H. C. v. d. Gabelentz, *Die melanesischen Sprachen, 1*, 202 ff., 232 ff.; 2, 28; Codrington, *The Melanesian Languages*, p. 136.

23. Winkler, *Der Uralaltaische Sprachstamm*, pp. 86 ff., 98 ff., 110 ff.; cf. also Simonyi, *Die ungarische Sprache*, pp. 257, 423.

24. Cf. Steindorff, *Koptische Grammatik*, pp. 227 ff.; similarly in the Semitic languages the "substantivization of asyndetic relative sentences" is frequent; see Brockelmann, *Grundriss, 2*, 561 ff.

25. Thus, for example, Japanese (according to Hoffmann, *Japanische Sprachlehre*, p. 99) possesses no relative clauses but must transform them into adjectival clauses; similarly in Mongolian, cf. J. J. Schmidt, *Grammatik der mongolischen Sprache*, pp. 47 ff., 127 ff.

26. "Les langues de cette famille semblent créées pour l'abstraction et la métaphysique. Elles ont une souplesse merveilleuse pour exprimer les relations les plus intimes des choses par les flexions de leurs noms, par les temps et les modes si variés de leurs verbes, par leurs mots composés, par la délicatesse de leurs particules. Possédant seules l'admirable secret de la période, elles savent relier dans un tout les membres divers de la phrase. . . . Tout devient pour elles abstraction et catégories. Elles sont les langues de l'idéalisme." E. Renan, *De l'origine du langage*, 8th ed., p. 194.

over the subordinate clause, the paratactic over the hypotactic connection. Although this ur-language possessed relative clauses, it lacked, according to the evidence of comparative linguistics, a sharply delimited set of conjunctions by which to express cause, consequence, coordination, opposition, etc.[27] In Sanskrit, conjunctions are almost totally lacking as a distinct class of words: what other languages, particularly Latin and Greek, express by subordinating conjunctions is here rendered by the almost unlimited use of nominal composition and the amplification of the main clause by participles and gerunds.[28] But in Greek itself, the progress from the paratactic structure of the Homeric language to the hypotactic structure of Attic prose occurred only gradually.[29] All this indicates that what Humboldt called the act of autonomous, synthetic postulation in language, and found embodied (apart from the verb) chiefly in the use of conjunctions and relative pronouns, was one of the latest accomplishments of language formation, to which it attained through a variety of intermediary phases.

This is particularly true of that linguistic form which is fundamentally set apart from all substantial expression, serving solely as an expression of synthesis *as such,* of pure combination. Only in the use of the *copula* does the logical synthesis effected in judgment achieve its adequate linguistic designation. In its analysis of the pure function of judgment, the *Critique of Pure Reason* pointed to this relationship. For Kant, judgment meant the "unity of action," by which the predicate is referred to the subject and linked with it to form a whole meaning, to form the unity of an objectively subsisting and objectively constituted relationship. And it is this intellectual unity of action which finds its linguistic representation and counterpart in the use of the copula. "But if I investigate more closely the relation of given cognitions in every judgment"—he writes in the section on the transcendental deduction of the concepts of the pure understanding—"and

27. "Relative clauses," writes A. Meillet in his *Introduction à l'étude comparative des langues indo-européennes* (German trans., p. 231; French 7th ed., p. 377), "are the only subordinate clauses which may properly be regarded as Indo-Germanic. The other types, particularly conditional clauses, have a different form in every Indo-Germanic dialect." This relation is interpreted somewhat differently by Brugmann, who explains the lack of agreement by the theory that although conjunctional particles existed in the "ur-period," they were not yet extensively used and had not yet been fixed as expressions for particular individual relations (*Kurze vergleichende Grammatik,* p. 653).

28. Examples in Whitney, *Sanskrit Grammar,* p. 369, and Thumb, *Handbuch des Sanskrit,* pp. 434, 475 ff.

29. Cf. Brugmann, *Griechische Grammatik,* 3d ed., pp. 555 ff.

distinguish it, as belonging to the understanding, from the relation which is produced according to the laws of the reproductive imagination (which has only subjective validity), I find that a judgment is nothing other than the mode of bringing given cognitions under the *objective* unity of apperception. This is plain from our use of the term of relation *is* in judgments, in order to distinguish the objective unity of given representations from the subjective unity. For this term indicates the relation of these representations to the original apperception, and also their *necessary* unity." If I say "bodies are heavy," this means that corporeity and heaviness are joined in the object and not merely that they always coexist in subjective perception.[30] Thus even for Kant, the pure logician, the objective *meaning* of judgment was intimately related to the linguistic form of predicative statement. It is clear, however, that language could only gradually attain to the abstraction of that pure being which is expressed in the copula. For language, which in its beginnings is entirely bound up with the intuition of substantial objective *existence,* the expression of "being" as a pure transcendental form of relation can only be a late product arrived at through a variety of mediations. A great many languages are utterly lacking in a copula in our logical-grammatical sense and have no need of one. A unitary and universal expression of what is designated in our "term of relation *is*" is not only lacking in the languages of primitive peoples—as in most of the African languages, the languages of the American Indians, etc.—but is not to be found in other, highly developed languages. Even where the predicative relation is differentiated from the purely attributive relation, the former does not necessarily have a special linguistic designation. In the Ural-Altaic languages, for example, the subject is almost always linked with the predicate by simple juxtaposition, so that "the city big" means "the city is big," "I man" means "I am a man," etc.[31] In other languages we often encounter locutions which at first sight seem to correspond to our use of the copula, but which in truth are far from possessing its universality of function. Here, as closer analysis reveals, the "is" of the copula is not a universal term, serving to express relation *as such,* but possesses a special and concrete, usually local or temporal, secondary signification. Instead of a purely relational "being" we have a term which designates existence in this or that place, a being-here or being-there, or else an existence in this

---

30. *Kritik der reinen Vernunft,* 2d ed., pp. 141 ff. (Everyman ed., p. 99).

31. Cf. H. Winkler, *Der uralaltaische Sprachstamm,* pp. 68 ff.; for the Finno-Ugrian languages see, e.g., Simonyi, *Die ungarische Sprache.*

or that moment. Thus the apparent copula is differentiated according to the diverse spatial situation of the subject or other intuitive modifications in its existence, so that one "copula" is used when the subject in question is standing, another when he is sitting or lying, one when he is awake and another when he is asleep, etc.[32] Formal "being" and the formal meaning of relation are replaced by more or less materially conceived terms which still bear the coloration of a particular sensuously given reality.[33]

And even where language has progressed to the point of encompassing all these specifications of existence in a universal expression of "being," there remains an appreciable difference between even the most comprehensive expression of mere *existence* and "to be" as an expression of purely predicative "synthesis." Here the development of language reflects a problem which extends far beyond its sphere and which has played a crucial part in the history of logical and philosophical thought. In this point more clearly than in any other we see how this thought has developed *with* language but at the same time *in opposition to* it. From the Eleatic philosophers down, we can follow the great struggle carried on by philosophical idealism with language and with the ambivalence of its concept of being. The precise task that Parmenides set himself was to resolve the controversy

32. Examples of this occur particularly in the American Indian languages: the Algonquin languages for example lack a universal verb of "being," but possess a great number of words designating being in this or that place, at this or that time, or in this or that special condition. In the Klamath language the verb (*gi*) which is used to express copulative "being" is actually a demonstrative particle signifying being here or being there. (Cf. Gatschet, *Klamath Language*, pp. 430 ff., 674 ff., and Trumbull, *Transactions of the American Philological Association, 1869–70.*) The Indian languages of the Maya family also use certain demonstrative particles for predicative statement; when combined with tense signs, these particles very much resemble true substantive verbs. Yet none of them is equivalent to the universal and purely relational term "to be": some express the nominal concept "given, postulated, present," while others indicate situation in a certain place or happening at a certain time. (Cf. Seler, *Das Konjugationssystem der Maya-Sprachen*, pp. 8 and 14.) A similar differentiation occurs in the Melanesian languages and many of the African languages. "A true substantive verb," writes H. C. v. d. Gabelentz for example, "is lacking in Fiji; sometimes it is rendered by *yaco*, 'to happen,' 'to become,' *tu*, 'to be there' or 'present,' *tiko* 'to be there,' or 'to endure,' etc., and there always remains a secondary signification corresponding to the true concept of these verbs." (*Die melanesischen Sprachen*, p. 40; cf. p. 106.) For the African languages cf. the various terms for the substantive verb cited by Migeod (*The Mende Language*, pp. 75 ff.) from the Mandingan and by Westermann (*Grammatik der Ewe-Sprache*, p. 75; Eng. trans. by Bickford-Smith, pp. 92 f.) from the Ewe.

33. In Nicobarese, for example, being as a mere copula is not expressed: the "substantive verb" always has the sense of "to exist," "to be present," particularly "to exist in a particular place." See Roepstorff *A Dictionary of the Nancowry Dialect of the Nicobarese Language* (Calcutta, 1884), p. xvii, xxiv ff.

over true being by means of pure reason. But is this true being of the Eleatic philosophers grounded purely in logical judgment, does it correspond solely to the ἔστι of the copula as the basic form of every valid statement—or does it retain some vestige of another, more concrete, original signification, which makes it comparable to the intuition of a "well-rounded sphere." Parmenides undertook to free himself from the fetters both of language and of the common, sensuous world view. ". . . all things that mortals have established, believing in their truth," he declared, "are just a name: Becoming and Perishing, Being and Not-Being, and Change of position, and alteration of bright colour." [34] And yet, in the expression of his supreme principle, he too succumbed to the power of speech and the diversity of its concept of being. In the basic Eleatic formula, in the sentence ἔστι τὸ εἶναι the verbal and substantival, the predicative and absolute signification of "being" merge with one another. Even Plato arrived at a sharper distinction only after long intellectual struggles which are most clearly reflected in his *Parmenides*. In the *Sophists,* which concludes this struggle, the logical nature of the pure concepts of relation is clearly developed and their specific "being" defined for the first time in the history of philosophy. On the strength of this newly acquired insight, Plato was able to argue that though all earlier philosophers had sought the principle of being, what they had discovered and had taken as their foundation was not the true and radical *source* of being but only certain of its varieties, specific forms of *what is*. Yet even this pregnant formulation did not resolve the opposition concealed in the concept of being, but only defined it precisely for the first time. This opposition runs through the entire history of medieval thought. The question of how to delimit "essence" and "existence," the two basic modalities of being, and of how to unite them despite this delimitation, became the central problem of medieval philosophy. It became most acute in connection with the ontological proof of the existence of God, which lay at the very heart of medieval theology and metaphysics. But even the modern, critical form of idealism, which renounced the "proud name of ontology" and more modestly called itself an "analytic of the pure understanding," found itself involved again and again in the ambivalence of the concept of being. Even after Kant's critique of the ontological proof, Fichte found it necessary to point explicitly to the difference between predicative and absolute being. In his *Foundations of General Scientific*

34. Parmenides, Fragments 7, 8, in Diels, *Die Fragmente der Vorsokratiker.* Eng. trans. by K. Freeman, in *Ancilla to the Pre-Socratic Philosophers,* p. 44.

Theory he postulated the proposition A *is* A as the first, absolute principle of all philosophy, and added that this proposition, in which the "is" has the sole signification of a logical copula, says nothing whatsoever regarding the existence or nonexistence of A. "Being" postulated without a predicate, he went on, expresses something entirely different from "being" with a predicate: the proposition "A *is* A" asserts only that if A is, then A is; but it does not so much as raise the question of whether A truly is or not.[35]

If even philosophical thought engaged in a constant struggle to distinguish the two concepts of being—it is understandable that in linguistic thinking the two should have been intimately linked from the outset and that the pure meaning of the copula could only very gradually be disengaged from this involvement. The use of one and the same word to designate existence and the predicative relation is a widespread phenomenon, not limited to any particular languages. To consider only the Indo-Germanic languages, we find that the various terms by which they designate predicative "being" all go back to an original signification of "existence": either in a very general sense as mere presence, or in a special and concrete sense as living and breathing, growing and becoming, enduring and dwelling. "The copula," says Brugmann,

> was originally a verb of intuitive signification (the original signification of *es-mi* 'I am' is unknown, but the oldest demonstrable one is 'I exist') and the substantive or adjective stood in apposition to the subject which was closely connected with the predicative verb (the earth is a ball = the earth exists as a ball). The so-called degeneration of the verb into a copula occurred when the emphasis shifted to the predicate noun, so that the perceptual content of the verb lost its importance and vanished. The verb thus became a mere form . . . In the ur-Indo-Germanic period *es-* "to be" assuredly functioned as a copula, and probably forms of *bheu-* "to grow, to become," which at that time entered into a suppletive relation with *es-*.[36]

The use of the two roots seems to have developed as follows: *es* (*as*) appears to have been taken as an expression of continued, unchanging existence, and accordingly used for the durative forms of the present stem, while the root *bheu*, as expression of becoming, was eminently used for such tenses as the aorist and the perfect, designating an incipient or completed action

35. Cf. J. G. Fichte, "Grundlage der gesamten Wissenschaftslehre," *Werke, 1,* 92 ff.
36. Brugmann, *Kurze vergleichende Grammatik,* p. 627.

(cf. ἔ-φ⁵-ν, πέ-φῦ-κα, fui).³⁷ The underlying sensuous signification of the latter root is still apparent in words such as φύω I engender, φύομαι I grow. In Germanic, the root *bheu* entered into the formation of the present stem (*ich bin, du bist*, etc.), and the auxiliary root *ues* (Gothic *wisan*, I was, etc.) with the original signification of "dwelling" and "enduring" (OHG *weren*) also came into use. Still different was the development in the Romance languages, where the copula is linked with the intuitive signification of standing.³⁸ And just as the expression of being is here based on the percept of local stability and rest, the expression of becoming is based on the perception of motion: the intuition of becoming is developed from that of turning.³⁹ And the general signification of becoming can also develop from the concrete signification of coming and going.⁴⁰ All this shows that even those languages in which the sense for the logical singularity of the copula is sharply developed, *designate* it not very differently from others which are totally lacking in that sense, or which at least have not developed a comprehensive and universal expression of the substantive verb. Here again, the spiritual form of relational expression can be represented only in a certain material cloak, which however comes ultimately to be so permeated with the relational meaning that it no longer appears as a mere barrier, but as the sensuous vehicle of a purely ideal signification.

In the universal term of relation, the copula, we thus find confirmed the same fundamental tendency of language that we have followed in the linguistic configuration of the special terms of relation. Here again we find the same reciprocal determination of the sensuous by the spiritual and the spiritual by the sensuous as in the linguistic representation of the relations of space, time, number, and the I. One is tempted to interpret the involvement of the two factors in language in a sensationalist sense, and Locke, on the basis of such an interpretation, claimed language as one of the main supports for his basic empiricist view of knowledge.⁴¹ But even in refer-

37. Curtius, *Grundzüge der griechischen Etymologie*, 5th ed., p. 304, 375.

38. Cf. Italian *stato*, French *été* (from Lat. *stare*) as participles of *essere* and *être*. According to Osthoff, *Vom Suppletivwesen der indogermanischen Sprachen*, p. 15, this auxiliary use of *sta* "to stand" was also known to Old Celtic.

39. Thus Gothic *wairþan* (*werden*, to become) is etymologically linked with Latin *vertere*, and likewise the Greek πέλω goes back to a root which in Sanskrit means "to move, wander around, travel." Cf. Brugmann, *Kurze vergleichende Grammatatik*, p. 628 and Delbrück, *Vergleichende Syntax*, *3*, 12 ff.

40. Cf. in the modern languages *diventare, divenire, devenir*, English, to become; cf. also Humboldt, "Einleitung zum Kawi-Werk," *Werke*, 7, 218 ff.

41. See above, pp. 133 ff.

ence to linguistic thinking, we must counter such interpretations by pointing to the sharp distinction which Kant, in his critique of "empirical knowledge," made between "beginning with" and "arising from." Even though sensuous and spiritual elements seem to have been inextricably intertwined in the origin of language, this *correlation,* precisely because it is a correlation, does not argue a relation of *one-sided* dependency between the two. For intellectual expression could not have developed through and out of sensuous expression if it had not originally been contained in it; if, as Herder said, sensuous designation did not already embrace a basic act of "reflection." The maxim πάντα θεῖα καὶ ἀνθρώπινα πάντα is perhaps nowhere so clearly confirmed as by the study of signification and form in the highly developed languages: the characteristic meaning of language is not contained in the opposition between the two extremes of the sensuous and the intellectual, because in all its achievements and in every particular phase of its progress, language shows itself to be *at once* a sensuous and an intellectual form of expression.

General Index

Index of Proper Names